CROSSINGS
Early Mediterranean Contacts with India

CROSSINGS

Early Mediterranean Contacts with India

Edited by
F. DE ROMANIS
A. TCHERNIA

CENTRE DE SCIENCES HUMAINES
NEW DELHI

ITALIAN EMBASSY CULTURAL CENTRE
NEW DELHI

MANOHAR
2005

Centre de Sciences Humaines
Italian Embassy Cultural Centre

First published 1997
Reprinted 2005

ISBN 81-7304-194-6 (Hb)
ISBN 81-7304-658-1 (Pb)

Published by
Ajay Kumar Jain for
Manohar Publishers & Distributors
4753/23 Ansari Road, Daryaganj
New Delhi 110 002

Typeset by
A J Software Publishing Co. Pvt. Ltd.
New Delhi 110 005

Printed at
Lordson Publishers Pvt. Ltd.
Delhi 110 007

Distributed in South Asia by
FOUNDATION BOOKS
4381/4, Ansari Road
Daryaganj, New Delhi 110 002
and its branches at Mumbai, Hyderabad,
Bangalore, Chennai, Kolkata

Contents

Preface

Over the last fifteen years Italian and French scholars have published various studies of contacts between India and Rome, including the ancient sources related to the subject. But the place of publication and the languages in which they were written have until now hindered the diffusion of these studies among many potential readers, in particular Indian scholars and other English-speaking students. The aim of this book is to make them more accessible. We, the editors, are convinced that a more thorough dialogue between scholars east and west of the Indian Ocean will greatly advance the progress of historical research in this field. Although the opinions and approaches of the authors differ in certain respects, the seven articles are on the whole coherent, and, when complemented by M.-F. Boussac and J.-F. Salles, *Athens, Aden, Arikamedu* (Manohar, 1995), provide a reliable panorama of modern research which has developed within this sphere in Latin countries.

We are grateful to the Centre de Sciences Humaines (Cultural Section of the French Embassy, New Delhi), formerly directed by Olivier Guillaume, and now by Bruno Dorin, and to the Italian Cultural Centre in New Delhi, directed by Carlo Coen, both of whom have welcomed the project, financed the translation and taken part in its publication. We also express our thanks to the editors of journals in which the articles first appeared for permission to translate and reprint the texts. Finally, we warmly thank Professor Romila Thapar who has kindly agreed to write, from her own broad perspective, an introduction which provides a general framework for the articles and opens up new vistas, and Dr. C.R. Whittaker who has greatly improved the English translation.

F. De R., A.T.

References to Original Publications*

Chr. Robin, *L'Arabie du Sud et la date du* Périple de la Mer Erythrée (*nouvelles données*), in *Journal Asiatique*, 279, 1991, 1-2, pp. 1-30.

G. Fussman, *Le Périple et l'histoire politique de l'Inde*, in *Journal Asiatique*, 279, 1991, 1-2, pp. 31-8.

Santo Mazzarino, *Sul nome del vento hipalus ("ippalo") in Plinio*, in *Helikon*, 22-27, 1982-87, pp. VII-XIV.

F. De Romanis, *Roma e i* Nótia *dell'India, ricerche sui rapporti tra Roma e l'India dravidica dal 30 a.C. all'età Flavia*, in *Helikon*, 22-27, 1982-7, pp. 63-164.

F. De Romanis, *Romanukharaṭṭha e Taprobane: sui rapporti Roma-Ceylon nel I sec. d.C.*, in *Helikon*, 28, 1988, pp. 5-58.

F. De Romanis, *Ancora a proposito di* A.E. *1954, n. 121a*, in *Helikon*, 29-30, 1989-90, pp. 369-71.

A. Tchernia, *Le dromadaire des* Peticii *et le commerce oriental*, in *Mélanges de l'Ecole Française de Rome (Antiquité)*, 104, 1992, 1, pp. 293-301.

A. Tchernia, *Moussons et monnaies: les voies du commerce entre le monde gréco-romain et l'Inde*, in *Annales HSS*, 1995, 5, pp. 991-1009.

*Chr. Robin's and A. Tchernia's articles have been slightly abridged, and those by F. De Romanis' slightly modified.

Early Mediterranean Contacts with India: An Overview

ROMILA THAPAR

At the turn of the eighteenth century, references to maritime trade with India in Greek and Latin texts began to be noticed and collated. A hundred years later these texts were among the sources used for the reconstruction of Indian history. In the early twentieth century, the history of the trade between the Roman empire and India was narrated in monographs essentially using these sources. Inevitably therefore the orientation at the time was 'Classicist'. There was simultaneously a recognition of more recent European activities in Asia culminating in the creation of colonial empires, the imprint of which did not by-pass the visualisation of this much earlier trade. Subsequently, when what was viewed as the first Roman intervention in Indian trade established through archaeology, it happened to be at Arikamedu in the environs of Pondicherry, and perhaps this underlined the subconscious association with European maritime trading centres of recent times. To compare the Roman trade with India, or what is sometimes referred to as the Indo-Roman trade, with European colonialism is however inept, since the Roman trade, although it intervened in many circuits and networks of exchange and dominated some, did not disrupt these or replace them. If anything the pattern was one of using and intensifying the existing networks; nor was there a change from private entrepreneurs to state-supported trading companies; or for that matter the acquisition of territory, the imposition of political authority and the re-ordering of Indian economies, as happened in the colonies of our times. The assessment of the Roman maritime trade with India is changing owing to the more focused analysis of trade in both the economy of the Roman empire as well as in regions of the Indian subcontinent involved in this commerce. It should also be recognised that irrespective of its role in India, it was a major activity in the trading networks of Egypt and Rome, the evaluation of which has been the source of much debate.

Looking westwards, India has had long associations and close connections with ancient West Asia and with the Hellenistic kingdoms. Attested first in the third millennium BC when the cities of the Indus civilisation traded with the Gulf and Mesopotamia, these connections continued through the centuries, extending their reach to ports of the Arabian peninsula. The more spectacular maritime trade was occasional, but in its interstices there was a steady small-scale contact, often coastal, which involved transporting essential supplies quite apart from luxury items. These would be ships which, to use the felicitous phrase of Braudel, tramped from port to port and were travelling bazaars, largely covering the more confined circuits (Braudel 1972). Such a low profile trade continues to the present. Within the arc of the Arabian Sea, bounded by its coasts, there was unabated historical activity.

This collection of papers is addressed to some of these historical activities, but within the more limited compass of what has been called the Roman trade with India. The papers were originally published in French and Italian and have now been translated into English so as to make them accessible to a wider readership. Concerned with questions of seminal importance, they carry the discussion further, some into themes already controversial and some into investigating new ideas.

Trading links between the Red Sea and India may be viewed as passing through distinct phases. The earliest of these dates to pre-Roman times and is recorded in the Ptolemaic appointment of an officer, the *epistrategos* or 'officer superintendent' of the Erythraean and Indian Sea, signalling an interest in exploring links. It is thought (Scullard 1947) that this interest may have been prompted by the wish to obtain elephants from South Asia, believed to be virtually invincible on the battle-field! This eastward interest may have had precursors in the third century BC when a royal edict of the Mauryan king Aśoka, mentions Ptolemy Philadelphus. The ports of Barygaza and Sopara on the west coast of India became important, although Seleucid activity in the Gulf may have made the primary contribution to this. That the coasts of the Arabian Sea were in maritime contact, quite apart from the Ptolemies and the Seleucids, is likely but may not be recorded. The earliest use of scripts in India, as documented in the edicts of Aśoka, were inscriptions engraved in *kharoṣṭhī* in the north-west, which had been contiguous with the Achaemenid empire, and *brāhmī* elsewhere. *Brāhmī* has some similarities with the Semitic scripts (Dani 1963) and may have evolved from the literate communities of traders involved in a maritime trade between India and West Asia. Subsequently, in early Imperial Roman times, judging by the artefactual remains found in India and the statements in various Greek and Latin texts, there appears to have been a spurt in the trade between the Red Sea and India (concentrating on the western Deccan and south India) from the late first century BC to the mid-first century AD. A later phase dates to the second century AD when the east coast of India becomes more prominent.

The most daunting aspect of what has been called the Roman maritime trade with India is that, if it is to be seen as a whole and not examined piece-meal, it requires a control over a vast span of diverse literature and of archaeological sources. Greek and Latin texts are no longer the sole evidence for there is material in Tamil literature, in Prākrit inscriptions, and increasingly in larger volume from numismatics and archaeology. This range of sources was known to earlier scholars but nevertheless it was difficult to project an overall view. Such a view remains distant. But at least the fragments can now be better juxtaposed. This is ably demonstrated in the paper by Federico De Romanis, 'Romanukharaṭṭha and Taprobane: Relations between Rome and Sri Lanka in the First Century AD'. It is something of a *tour de force* in examining the chronology and the content of these relations and points up the complexities as well as the advantages of using texts from sources in different languages. Arguing that the dating of one inscription on the Coptos-Berenice road cannot be based on the Romano-Alexandrian calendar he uses the old Egyptian time reckoning to date this inscription to 5 July AD 6. He then examines the narrative of a freedman of Annius Plocamus claiming to have visited Taprobane (Sri Lanka) as recorded by Pliny. The discussion introduces comments from texts in Pāli, Tamil and Sanskrit, apart from Greek and Latin.

In the context of Indian history the Indo-Roman maritime trade has a specific meaning. It refers to the Roman demand, in particular for pepper, pearls, semi-precious stones and textiles, all imported from South Asia and most of which were exchanged for high value coins. The qualifier of 'Roman' refers narrowly to the eventual destination of the items as well as broadly to the Mediterranean participation in the trade being part of the activities of those included within the Roman empire. This trajectory of the trade does not reduce the importance of the Indian counterparts, who saw it essentially as exchange and trade with the 'Yavanas'. The initiative more likely was taken largely by merchants based in Egypt and the eastern Mediterranean, specifically Alexandria, although this did not preclude those from other parts of the Mediterranean world from joining in. Indian interests ranged from merchants established in trading ports to suppliers of cargo, either acting for merchants or functioning independently. The Roman state does not appear to have participated directly in this trade but it was not averse to collecting substantial taxes on the cargo. It also considered the enterprise important enough to protect the routes from the Red Sea ports to Alexandria with forts, garrisons and military camps and to establish watering places along the routes. These facilities were doubly useful since the routes also gave access to profitable mining activities in the region. Inscriptions along the route record the coming and going of merchants and one, dating to 2 BC, refers specifically to the person having recently returned from India. Kingdoms of the Indian subcontinent may well have drawn a revenue from the trade, but here again there is little evidence of direct state-controlled participation. Where cargoes were acquired from independent agents, sometimes functioning in areas of indistinct state-formation, there of course the question of state participation does not arise.

Detailed discussion of this trade is to be found in Greek and Latin texts and the more important among them are: Strabo's *Geography*; the *Periplus Maris Erythraei*, a manual for traders containing information on itineraries, harbours, navigation, and cargoes, all relating to the ports of the Arabian Sea and their hinterlands; Pliny's *Natural History*; and to a lesser extent, dating to the second century AD but possibly with later additions, the *Geography* of Ptolemy. The writing of a Geography or a *Periplus* was familiar to Greek categories of knowledge and the two differed in that the *Periplus* was intended as a technical guide.

The author of the above-mentioned *Periplus* is unknown. Gathering information from diverse sources, the attempt seems to have been to collapse the many circuits of trade of the Arabian Sea into one long itinerary. The date of the text has been the subject of much discussion, although there is a preference generally for the first century AD. Gerard Fussman, in his paper entitled, 'The *Periplus* and the Political History of India', argues for a date of about AD 40 on the basis of his reading of the evidence from Indian chronology. Fussman's argument also draws on his reading of the Vikrama era of 58/57 BC having been founded by Azes I. Generally it is the *Periplus* which is said to date events in western India but Fussman reverses the procedure. The date suggested by him would suit the time bracket for the trade. It would also not be contradicted by the discussion in the paper of Christian Robin, 'The date of the *Periplus of the Erythraean Sea* in the Light of South Arabian Evidence'. Robin, basing his arguments on the possible identification of south Arabian rulers, is of the view that the date has to be located in the first century AD and he finds the attempts to place it later unacceptable. The evidence discussed by Robin would not contradict a first century AD date. Most scholars working on southern Arabia date the *Periplus* to between AD 40-70, although, as Robin adds, the evidence is too imprecise to permit the fixing of an incontrovertible date.

In contrast to the *Periplus* and arising from a different perspective are Pliny's comments on this trade. In his assessment of the economics of the trade he condemns it as an agency of the financial drain which he perceives afflicting the Roman economy. He discusses the nature of the exchange, refers to the items of the trade and to the Roman financial involvement. From these statements, attempts have been made to deduce its affect on the Roman economy and the ways in which it relates to contemporary problems. Prior to Pliny, Tiberius had expressed his moral indignation at the costliness of Roman luxuries which were provided in large part by this trade. Pliny echoes this sentiment but tries to strengthen the argument by attempting to calculate the financial loss.

Pliny and the *Periplus* are therefore very different in nature, origin and purpose. Pliny continues the earlier Classical interest in Indian phenomena but also introduces the specific role of the eastern trade. The *Periplus,* by its very function, is informative but far from polemical on the Indian trade and barely concerned with its affect on the Roman economy. Pliny's complaint has resulted in some discussion on the role, if any, of the eastern trade in the decline of the Roman empire (Miller 1969, Bernardi 1970, Veyne 1979). This has relevance to the debate on the economy of empires as projected in the models proposed by Karl Polanyi and by Emmanuel Wallerstein, which could be the starting point of an analysis of the economic aspects of the trade which is now long overdue. André Tchernia in his paper, 'Winds and Coins: From the Supposed Discovery of the Monsoon to the *Denarii* of Tiberius', reconsiders the debate on Pliny's complaint and points out that it cannot be dismissed but that it has to be seen together with the statement of Tiberius and reflects a serious Roman concern with the problem. Further, that from the perspective of the economy, the patterns of trade and exchange varied at different times and therefore there could be no continuing drain.

Incidental references to India and the Indian trade are scattered in other Greek and Latin texts and inscriptions, from the late first century BC to the third century AD, and these have been compiled by various scholars (e.g. Schmitthenner 1979). Ptolemy's *Geography* is essentially a compendium of existing information in the tradition of Greek Geographies, with fuller descriptions of the eastern coast of India and the Ganges delta than in the *Periplus,* which would be in keeping with its later date. The brief inscriptions on the road from the Red Sea ports to Alexandria, associated with those recently returned from India, such as the inscription of *C. Numidius Eros* in 2 BC and that of the slave of *Annius Plocamus* in AD 6, tie in with the expansion of the trade. If the slave of Annius Plocamus can be identified with his freedman mentioned by Pliny, it would provide evidence for links with Sri Lanka as well.

Neither the Tamil nor the Prākrit sources contain the same

detailed descriptions as found in the Greek texts, which is one reason why the latter have come to dominate our view of this trade. Nevertheless the Tamil and Prākrit sources provide a perspective on some new aspects of these activities. Tamil sources refer incidentally to the Yavanas who have been identified with those who came with the Roman trade from Egypt and the eastern Mediterranean. Originally the term Yavana, which is derived from the Prākrit *yona* and the Old Persian *yauna*, referred to the Greeks, but came gradually to refer to those from lands to the west of India, although the Hellenistic associations continued during this period. A distinction therefore has to be made between the Yavanas of the north-west and those from the Red Sea. The Indo-Greeks were Yavanas but so were the astronomers of Alexandria. The separation has to be made in the context of their activities, their artefacts and their proclaimed identities. In some cases, such as in the Tamil texts, references to Yavanas coming in their ships bringing gold and taking back pepper are unambiguously referring to those from the Red Sea. There are two categories of Tamil texts from south India which refer to the Yavanas. The earlier is the *Caṅkam* literature, a collection of poems dealing largely with love and war and which have been described as Tamil heroic poetry (Kailasapathy 1968). The date of the composition and later compilation of these poems has been controversial but a period just prior to the Christian era and continuing for a couple of centuries would be acceptable to most. The texts described as the Tamil epics, of which the *Cilappatikaram* has passing references to the Yavanas, date to the early centuries of the Christian era but are later than the *Caṅkam* anthologies. The poetry is more sophisticated, the context is often urban and they assume the existence of kingdoms. There is an echo of Jaina ethics. Tamil-Brāhmī inscriptions which coincide with the Tamil texts have little to say directly on the Yavanas although they do refer to professions such as that of the lapidary which were prominent in the trade. Votive inscriptions in Prākrit from the western Deccan are more specific and record donations by Yavanas, suggesting the presence of traders from the eastern Mediterranean and directing attention to events in the western Deccan.

Such attention is endorsed by data from numismatics and archaeology. The presence, though sporadic, of coins of the Roman Republic may suggest an earlier start to the trade although more likely, these earlier coins could have been circulating even at a later period in southern India when the trade had considerably increased (MacDowall 1990). Their occurrence generally together with early Imperial coins would tend to support this view. High value early Imperial coins, the *aurei* and *Denarii* of Augustus and Tiberius in particular, occur in hoards found in south India and coincide with the period of Roman demands for oriental luxuries and with complaints about the paucity of such coins in the empire. It has been argued that the hoarding of these coins actually began after the mid-first century AD, probably between AD 70-96, although the coins were of an earlier period and were specially selected for their high metal content (MacDowall 1991). Others however maintain that the hoards were contemporary with the availability of the coins and prior to the debasement introduced by Nero. The debasement, it is thought, may have led to the rejection of the later silver *Denarii*. Some coins are defaced with chisel cuts, the purpose of which remains unclear.

In the early second century AD the number of hoards increase, as do the numbers of *aurei* in Kerala and Andhra Pradesh, with many imitations (Berghaus 1991). In the latter half of the second century the hoards decline but soon after *aurei* occur in hoards in Andhra Pradesh. Some of these coins are double pierced. After a long break there is a recurrence of chisel cuts, both on Roman issues and, interestingly, on imitations. The imitations could be of a later period. The *aurei* decline in number in the third century. The late third century sees the arrival of Roman bronze coins which are even more common in the fourth century in southern Tamilnadu. Late Roman and Byzantine *solidi* of the fifth and sixth centuries occur in Karnataka and Tamilnadu. These changes were occasioned in part by the gradual moving of commercial interests from Rome to Constantinople and by the expanding trade with Sri Lanka and possibly through the tapping of the Indian trade with South-East Asia. There are therefore many shifts in the import of Roman coins and these need to be examined in the context of where they occur in India and their function in the local society and economy. In the Indian context the sheer numbers of Roman Imperial coins has suggested that the Roman input overwhelmed the trade, even if the number is small compared to the hoards along the Roman frontier in Europe. But such a reading has to be considered in juxtaposition with the Indian evidence from which a different picture seems to emerge.

The seeming uniformity of functioning within the regulations of the Imperial Roman system makes a more emphatic imprint than that of the variety of states and polities with diverse economic systems in India. But this imprint may be deceptive in as much as the varied Indian systems exploited the trade to their own advantage. A historical sketch of the context to this trade in India goes back to the third century BC when the Mauryan empire claimed virtually the entire subcontinent, barring the extreme south. But by the early second century it had fragmented into successor states, each eventually establishing the required administrative and economic infrastructure of a monarchy. The core areas of the erstwhile empire retained some similarities but the peripheral areas trod their own path to political change. The Mauryas received embassies from the Hellenistic kingdoms of west Asia and the Mediterranean, and requested from them sweet wine, figs and a sophist. The Mauryan emperor Aśoka makes special mention by name of contemporary rulers in these kingdoms. Possibly the importance of the port of Sopara in Mauryan times may have had something to do with attempts at contacts across the Arabian Sea (Thapar 1987). Although its political control over the peninsula appears to have been loose, nevertheless the Mauryan empire extended its reach fairly far south in exploiting local resources, such as gold and semi-precious stones, and setting up networks and exchange connections with and among the local megalithic settlements. Reaching out into various networks enabled the drawing of revenue from the resources which they controlled. This was the task of Mauryan administration and possibly its attempts were confined to collecting resources rather than restructuring the economic patterns of the peninsula (Thapar 1961, 1988a). Mauryan political control and economic interests opened up subcontinental India as well as overland routes to the Hellenistic kingdoms and possibly some maritime connections between western India and the Gulf and the opposite coasts of the Arabian Sea. Aśoka's endorsement of Buddhism coincided with the growth of a mercantile community which came to be associated with the patronage of Buddhism.

North-western India had seen a succession of dynasties from the second century BC with Indo-Greek, Saka/Scythian and Parthian rulers. The best known of the Indo-Greeks was Menander who had claimed territory in the western Ganges valley. These were dynasties with varying Hellenistic associations and connections. Eventually the north-west was brought under the control of the Kuṣāṇas coming from Central Asia in the first century AD The Indo-Greeks and Kuṣāṇas directed the attention of north India to Central Asia and Iran. Indian artefacts and imitations of these or stylistic similarities are noticeable in these areas and suggest links with northern and central India. In western India the dominant power was that of the Kṣatrapas who were often in conflict with the dynasty to the south of them, the Sātavāhanas, based in the Deccan. The political history of the east coast and the eastern Deccan remains a little unclear at this time. Asoka campaigned in Kalinga in the third century BC A lengthy inscription of Khāravela of Kalinga in about the first century BC mentions his conflict with the Sātavāhanas and the peoples of the south. The exploits of Khāravela suggest that the east coast of India formed a maritime network, probably dating back to the Mauryan period. The fertile Krishna valley in the eastern Deccan, in modern Andhra Pradesh, which was the location of Roman coin hoards, may have earlier been the route along the east coast to the Kolar gold-fields in addition to the Mauryan movement southwards from the western Deccan. In the extreme south of the peninsula, three powerful peoples are frequently referred to in the Tamil *Caṅkam* literature: these were the Cēras on the west coast in present day Kerala and the Colas and Pāṇḍyas further east in present day Tamilnadu. These were chiefships or at best incipient kingdoms and therefore different from the monarchies of northern and western India (Gurukkal 1995). In such a situation the transition from chiefships to kingships would have been close in time to the Roman trade, and their involvement with the trade therefore takes on dimensions other than just the economic. For this area, trade with the West was its first major exposure to an external trade from a distant place.

The last half of this century has seen in South Asia an increase in the discovery of artefacts, some Roman or from the eastern Mediterranean and some Indian imitations of these. Archaeological data complement the texts, but also suggest other patterns of analysis. Excavations at sites such as Arikamedu, Alagankulam, Kodumanal, Karur, Ter, Bhokardan, to name a few, not only register such artefacts but also bring into purview both local circuits of exchange as well as the possible relationship of existing populations to the new traders. Recent excavations at Arikamedu have suggested that the Yavana presence be dated to the first century BC although the megalithic occupation of the site goes further back in time (Begley 1993). Alagankulam is located opposite the Sri Lankan coast and was possibly in contact with Mantota on the island, some graffiti from this site being read as Sinhala Prākrit (Mahadevan, 1996). The occurrence of Black and Red Ware and other early pottery prior to rouletted ware and amphorae sherds again suggests an earlier settlement (Nagaswamy 1991). The megalithic connections between coastal Tamilnadu and Sri Lanka are well-established (Seneveratne 1984). The demand for pearls in the Roman trade are likely to have made these links more firm.

The presence of the Yavanas does not connote the kind of Roman townships familiar from the Mediterranean world and Europe. In India they are generally pre-existing settlements where, as in Arikamedu, some Yavana traders established a base to facilitate both the manufacture and acquisition of items required in the trade, whereas others were centres of exchange which were doubtless visited by Yavana traders, as they were by local traders, agents and suppliers, involved in this and other trade. Not all Roman artefacts have been found in stratified excavations, for many are stray finds. Indian imitations, such as those of rouletted ware or of some Roman bronzes, or the frequency of clay bullae indicate the more fashionable and popular objects and this would doubtless have enhanced the value of the original. A detailed study of the imitations of Roman artefacts, which MacDowall has referred to as 'sub-Roman', could clarify, to some degree, the nature of the contact. The more significant among the Roman artefacts, apart from coins, are amphorae sherds, *terra sigillata* and a variety of bronze objects. These are either absent or occur sporadically in north India but are available in larger numbers in the peninsula. Most are of Mediterranean provenance and are therefore beginning to attract the attention of archaeologists working on Roman artefacts of the 'Classical world' (Begley and De Puma 1991). Some Roman objects were obviously fashionable among Indians. How did the taste for these come to develop in India? Were they brought by Indian traders making frequent visits to the ports of the Red Sea, for which there is limited evidence, or were they brought by Yavana traders visiting India? How influential the presence of the Yavanas may have been in setting these fashions can only be gauged by the context of the objects and this varies greatly.

That the travel of traders was not uni-directional and that there was a small presence of Indians in Egypt is suggested by earlier discussions of such a presence (Schmitthenner 1979), as well as the more recent discovery of Tamil-Brāhmī graffiti on typically Indian megalithic Black and Red Ware pot-sherds of the first century AD excavated in the manufacturing sector at Quseir-al-Qadim, on the Red Sea. One sherd has an incomplete inscription reading, *...atan*, which could have been the name *Catan*, well-attested in Tamil-Brāhmī cave inscriptions and in *Caṅkam* literature. A reading of a graffito on an Arikamedu sherd is also said to refer to a *Catan* (Wheeler 1946). A cave inscription from near Coimbatore refers to a *Cattan* who traded in gem-stones—perhaps beryl—and made a substantial donation to the local monks. An ostracon from Quseir carries what has been read as a Prākrit inscription mentioning three persons, with seemingly Prākrit names—Halaka, Vinhudatta and Nakada—suggesting a home base in the Deccan, as well as a list of provisions. The language and script, according to one reading, show a southern influence (Salomon 1991). It is interesting that this almost incidental epigraphic evidence again underlines the links between the Deccan, south India and the Red Sea.

Initial studies of the Roman maritime trade with India were largely concerned with listing and identifying items together with their geographical source, providing descriptions of ports and hinterlands and attempting to establish claims to cultural influence (Rawlinson 1916, Charlesworth 1924, Warmington 1928). Reading from the Greek and Latin texts, some historians assumed that commercially advanced traders from the Roman empire were able to swamp what were believed to be the more primitive Indian markets. This was prior to the evidence from archaeology on the earlier and extensive trade between India and West Asia and within the Indian subcontinent. The notion of cultural influence was much in the air, further encouraged by views such as those of Tarn (1938) arguing for a substantial Greek imprint in northern India. Wheeler, having excavated at Arikamedu and aware of the potential of the new data which was starting to emerge from archaeology, sought nevertheless to incorporate the trade more closely with the Roman empire (Wheeler 1946). This was not only a reflection of current imperial perceptions but also of the limits to archaeological interpretation at the time. Miller's study of the spice trade, pursued the identification of plants, but nevertheless introduced further questions relating to the wider activities of trade and was to that extent a departure from earlier works. Recent publications have taken up specific aspects of the data both in terms of the fresh editing of texts (Casson 1989) and the analyses of numismatic and archaeological finds (Raschke 1978, Turner 1989, Begley and De Puma 1991). The input from a variety of new sources as well as our improved understanding of trade and exchange generally in South Asia, has required a re-ordering of the historiography of this trade and a reconsideration of its varied patterns in relation to other categories of trade and exchange (Thapar 1992a).

Given the geographical reach of Roman maritime trade and the fluctuations in volumes and profits over time, it would be unrealistic to treat it as a uniformly active trade for all places in the Indian subcontinent and over the early centuries AD. There were smaller, localised circuits with a relatively more evenly balanced continuity. These the Roman trade entered when it could use a particular circuit to advantage. There were some with which its concerns were marginal. Thus, by and large, in the earlier period of the trade the intention appears to have been to move swiftly from the Red Sea ports to the west coast of India and more specifically to Malabar and its hinterland.

Routes clinging to the Arabian peninsula and the Gulf were largely left to local initiative or the political authority of the land-based powers of the region. The Roman interest in Barygaza was more to derive profits from this terminus than to intervene in any major way in the trade of northern India. Such an intervention would probably not have met with success given that the area was already known to be commercially active. Clearly the requirements and the nature of exchange at Muziris were different. A detailed analysis of local circuits in peninsular India would provide a better understanding of the nature of the intervention of the Roman trade in this area and the differences between the Deccan and south India. For temporary periods, at least, one could assume that it led to intensifying production and exchange, but even the pattern of this process would not have been identical throughout the peninsula. There is also a differentiation in the categories of trade; for example, a down-the-line coastal trade in food items and essential supplies is very different in nature and intent from a luxury trade and particularly one using mid-ocean routes. The economic base of local circuits drew on the availability of resources, the carriers of resources and their varying techno-logies, the navigational use of energy in the case of boats and ships and the existence of a range of markets. Trade which may have begun as coastal, using smaller, existing circuits, could have changed to long-distance mid-ocean routes if there was a demand for bulk supplies of non-perishables and quicker service. Generalisations about the nature of trade would therefore vary from period to period and be determined by the value of the items involved.

Mechanisms of exchange range over a broad spectrum from the barter of goods to complex market transactions. These were not exclusive and could co-exist in the same region. Barter and gift exchange are often most effective when there is a social back-up from an extended family or a clan, but a simplified form can also occur as part of market transactions at some levels. The latter is generally associated with formal trade involving merchants, guilds and possibly even state administration, and is essentially concerned with the sale and purchase of commodities. The sifting of these forms becomes an exercise in analysing what the sources reveal about the conditions of exchange. Given their evidently multiple dimensions, an item had multiple functions as did the exchange of the items.

Circuits of trade were in part dependent on the technology of navigation. The maritime trade along the Gulf was significant during the Seleucid period (Salles 1987, Potts 1990) but at the turn of the Christian era had been over-shadowed by the Red Sea route, perhaps because of the extensive use of monsoon winds by ships directed at the ports of south India, apart from the impetus of the Alexandrian trade. Much has been written about the so-called 'discovery' of the monsoon winds by a Greek navigator, Hippalus, a theory which has been doubted by many. André Tchernia's paper, 'Winds and Coins: From the Supposed Discovery of the Monsoon to the *Denarii* of Tiberius', questions this 'discovery' and examines the related references to navigation and the use of winds for mid-ocean crossings. He also supports the argument from the essay of Santo Mazzarino, 'On the name of the Hipalus wind (*Hippalus*) in Pliny', arguing for the reading *hypalus* as the name of a wind and not a navigator, a reading which should now put this controversy to rest. There is a discrepancy in the spelling of the name which Mazzarino explains and which may initially have caused confusion. (Not that using the monsoon winds simplified navigation, for the direction of travel had to be carefully oriented and co-ordinated with the movement and velocity of the monsoon and dates for sailing adjusted according to the location of the ports.) Tchernia points out that the north-south orientation of the Indian peninsula which can be assumed from the *Periplus* made it feasible to attempt a mid-ocean crossing without the fear of going completely off course. Curiously Ptolemy seems unaware of this orientation. Possibly this reflects the difference between the more imaginary construction permitted in ancient geographies and the reliance on the experience of navigators in the *Periplus*.

If the monsoon wind was already known and used prior to *c.* 25 BC, then it may well be asked what motivated the Roman trade with India. Unlike the Ptolemies, the Romans were not searching for elephants. Were they already familiar with aromatics and spices, perhaps brought by Indian and Arab traders in smaller quantities to the south Arabian ports and trans-shipped to the Red Sea? The entry of Roman interests in this trade appears to have increased the volume and frequency. The conquest of Egypt would have alerted the local Roman administration to the revenue which the trade could provide, as indeed it alerted traders to the vision of profits. The answer would lie both in the administrative change to empire and in the growth of varied Indian economies.

Earlier works on this trade tended to treat South Asia as a uniform region. However, it is important to recognise the diversity in political and economic forms which prevailed in the different parts of India involved with this trade, a diversity which becomes apparent even from a critical reading of the *Periplus,* apart from the dissimilarities evident from Indian sources. The nature of negotiations required with those who supplied cargo would have varied considerably, as also the perceptions of this trade among Indians. The distribution of items does not support a uniformity in trading patterns. A comparison, for example, of rouletted ware and amphora sherds points to the former being concentrated in the Krishna valley and the latter around the Gulf of Cambay. But in coastal Tamilnadu the two occur together. Similarly the distribution of coins and amphora sherds do not overlap noticeably. If some ceramic remains are indications of the presence of Yavanas, such as amphorae bringing olive oil and garum which were unlikely to have been intended for Indian use, they are found more commonly in coastal Tamilnadu. The distribution of amphorae sherds is geographically wide and includes northern India, but the areas of heavier concentration are specific.

The items in demand from India were not found uniformly everywhere and this too resulted in variations in the patterns of trade. The Roman markets required plants and spices, precious stones and pearls, ivory, textiles and timber. Aromatic plants were available in many places, but pepper was restricted to the far south. Chalcedonies had a wider distribution but beryls were more easily obtainable in the Coimbatore region and pearls were largely from Sri Lanka. Textiles were produced in many parts of the subcontinent, but Chinese silk, for example, was easier reached in the northern markets although not altogether absent in the southern ports. Teak and sandalwood grew along the western coast but ebony had its habitat in south

India. Some trade focused on products from local resources but in other cases the cargo came from distant places. Barygaza was special in that it combined both categories, whereas the ports of south India were, in the main, exporting items derived from local resources. Bulk items, such as pepper and to a lesser degree spices, were exported in their natural state, as also were pearls. Pepper ripens just after the monsoon and a few days of sunning dries it and turns it black, after which it can be stored. This coincided with the arrival of ships from the Red Sea at the tail end of the South-West monsoon when it had abated, and their return a few months later, sailing with the North-Eastern monsoon. Pepper had the useful quality of being inexpensive where it was produced but was exported for a high price. Pepper and spices required horticultural cultivation and the demand would have led to an increase in pepper vines and spice plants, especially as these were items which continued in demand long after the export of other goods had declined. This was not however a labour intensive cultivation. The processing of timber would have required a labour input. Some luxury goods were based on artisanal production, such as the cutting of gemstones and the weaving and dying of textiles. The production would be specialised but relatively limited. Specialisation would have taken the form of either family labour or working in a guild. Such activities were already familiar to the Indian scene. The Roman demand increased the volume but did not require a major re-orientation of the local economies.

The demand from the Indian markets was for lead, tin, coral, glass, wine and in some areas, specie. The function of Roman gold and silver coins present something of a problem. In northern and western India Roman coins occur largely as strays. In western India, at Barygaza, they could be exchanged profitably for local currency according to the *Periplus*. As a contrast to this, there are substantial coin hoards in the south, in the Coimbatore area and along the Kaveri valley, and some later in the eastern Deccan, especially in the Krishna valley. The extensive hinterland of Barygaza, bringing in and sending out a large range of cargo, had a very different economic network compared to what are often regarded as the chiefships of the Cēras, Coḷas and Pāṇḍyas in south India, where the hoarding of Roman coins may have been a significant aspect of local concerns. Northern and western India had long been familiar with punch-marked coins to be succeeded by Indo-Greek issues and the coins of the Kṣatrapas and the Kuṣāṇas. In western India coins of the Sātavāhana dynasty were in circulation but there were also those of lesser authority. The western Deccan was familiar with monetary systems and royal investments in guilds were often in the form of money. In the southern regions the Mauryas had probably introduced punch-marked coins although there seems to have been less familiarity with other issues. This makes it difficult to accept, as some scholars do, the statement of Pausanias in the second century AD that all exchange in India is by barter and coins are meaningless to Indians.

A more fundamental question relates to why so many coins were hoarded in specific areas. It has been said that they were treated as bullion or used in jewellery and ornaments as also was the case with some local coins. Other uses can also be suggested. Were they hoarded as protection money for the safe passage of goods, if goods were being transported overland from the west coast to the east or from ports to hinterland? Were they used as capital by local suppliers for further transactions? The pooling of capital facilitates a variety of commercial activities. If the participants in such a pool are kin-related and inter-dependent, as some of the suppliers could well have been, then the observance of reciprocal obligations creates it own sanctions for the use of such capital. The hoarding of coins could be used to back up credit arrangements. This would not exclude the existence of market systems in certain places, such as the ports, but would also not have been alien to prestation economies in the hinterland. Were the hoards accumulated by the suppliers of pepper and beryl, possibly the local chiefs, and thus the coins functioned as prestige goods to endorse political hierarchies in negotiating alliances? Coins make useful prestige tokens, since they have durability and homogeneity. Were the hoards seen as status symbols and used as part of the gift-exchange among chiefs? Gift-exchange would imply a competition for socio-political status and a reinforcing of alliances. Where clay bullae occur in association with hoards, they could perhaps have symbolised token return gifts. The coins therefore could have played a dual role: as high value currency in the trading markets but as prestige items in the hinterlands of the markets. Subsistence wealth would be converted into prestige wealth, necessary to both political and marital alliances.

The area of the beryl mines and its vicinity is also the location of some coin hoards and of megalithic sites. The peoples of these areas were not unknown to the Mauryas, since Aśoka in his edicts refers to the Cēras and Satiyaputras, as well as to the Pāṇḍyas and Coḷas, as his neighbours. But interestingly he does not give them the title of *rājās* as he does in the case of the Hellenistic kings. These were peoples in the peripheral areas of the empire who had their own networks of exchange and were occasionally hinged to the larger networks of the Mauryas (Thapar 1988a). They were not isolated settlements, but were part of a system in which competition and status was significant. The defacement of some high-value coins found in the hoards has been interpreted as a mechanism to ensure that their circulation would be limited to Indian circuits or more specifically to those of the Roman trade. But if they were used largely as high-value currency, as has been suggested, then the majority of such coins should occur at the site of markets or at least urban centres, which does not seem to be the case. A further question relates to the degree to which the availability of such hoards assisted in the transition from chiefships to emergent kingship.

Where the imported coins are used as high-value currency, there presumably a more sophisticated trade should be registered with a greater incidence of formal trade based on monetised commodity exchange and involving markets; although the simpler forms of barter and gift-exchange as an additional activity need not be absent. If the coins first went into circulation at ports such as Muziris, they would have been tested by valuers. But the coins are used variously further inland, where valuers may not have been readily available. Yet these could well have been the traditional collection points for raw materials and centres for the manufacture of items for trade.

The appropriateness of referring to this trade as the Roman trade has been questioned although the arguments for doing so are in turn subject to question (Ray 1994). Various assertions have been made: that there was a simultaneity with other relationships of exchange and circuits of trade and that by speaking of it as the Roman trade, the Indian component in the trade is under-emphasised; that the Roman and eastern Mediterranean component of this trade did not play a dominant role in the South Asian trade for it was merely a more visible pattern among the many, its visibility deriving from the extensive mention of it in Greek and Latin texts; that references to Yavanas in Indian sources do not necessarily refer to those coming from the Red Sea and could quite often be those of north-western India or coming from the Gulf to western India. And finally, that the decline in Roman trade was responsible for the urban decline in the Indian subcontinent subsequent to the fourth century AD, is unacceptable. Such views are largely a reaction to the assessment of earlier scholars, that the thrust of the trade came from the West and appropriated the East, which was perceived as something of a foretaste, as it were, of colonial times when Asia was drawn into the network of the commercial activities of Europe and was subordinated to European capitalism. Such an analogy is of course, for historical reasons, untenable, as has been discussed earlier.

Minimising the importance of the Roman trade altogether, is to misjudge the evidence. It was one among a number of trading patterns, but in assessing the role of these it has to be conceded that, in some areas of the subcontinent and for specified periods, the Roman trade played an economically significant role, drawing into its orbit various local circuits. It would not be accurate to subsume all trading activities in India of the period from the first century BC to the fourth century AD within Roman trade, but this does not justify understanding the role of the Roman trade where and when it is central. Insistence on emphasising indigenous networks does not require discounting the importance of external trade. To link a general decline in urbanism in India—which is in any case controversial, to a decline in Indo-Roman trade, can hardly be taken as a causal factor. Admitting that the Roman trade was influential in limited regions does not support its being a causal factor in either urban growth or decline on a generalised scale for the subcontinent. In some parts of the peninsula urban growth is recorded subsequent to the decline of the Roman trade.

Perhaps the obvious has to be restated and a definition of

the Indo-Roman trade requires a reiteration of basic facts. The Roman part of it is so-called because the areas most closely involved in the trade, such as Egypt and the eastern Mediterranean, were a part of the Roman empire. The trade was conducted largely by the merchants of Egypt and the eastern Mediterranean but this did not preclude merchants from other parts of the Mediterranean. The destination of much of the merchandise was Rome, however much other places may have had intermediary roles. The trade was not controlled by the Roman state but the state was not averse to deriving an income from it by creaming off taxes on the profits. Some aspects of the trade involved the functioning of the Roman administrative system, as in Egypt. If there was any overwhelming influence, it would seem to have been within the Roman empire in the fiscal relations between Rome and Egypt. The application of the term, Roman trade, in the Indian context is for limited periods, with the Indian circuits affected by the trade shifting over time. As and when it was a substantial trade, as is suggested by Roman artefacts in India and in textual sources, it was a long-distance, maritime, overarching, trade since it included more than one local circuit in the network of its activities and touched on others.

More relevant to the understanding of the Roman trade would be an attempt to analyse the economic facets and underpinnings of the trade with reference to the societies involved both in India and the Roman empire. Not all changes in the patterns of the trade were concerned solely with navigational and technical matters. The shift from one area to another or a heavier concentration in some, such as the focus moving from Barygaza to Muziris, was frequently occasioned by the availability of, and demand for, particular items. Such shifts could also have triggered off the establishing of a new local circuit. Thus the port of Muziris attracted merchants from western India, doubtless drawn by the growth in trade handled by the southern port. The trade cannot be viewed as conforming to a single economic pattern. The patterns of exchange and the relationships varied within India, with Egypt and in Rome. The economic dimensions of these links have not so far been seriously pursued. This makes the contribution of Federico De Romanis, 'Rome and the *Nótia* of India', all the more valuable, since it is not only an exploration of the relations between Rome and southern India from 30 BC to the Flavian period, but as part of this exploration he enters into the ramifications of the commerce of varied economies. The discussion which he introduces should go a long way towards pointing up the need for an input from economic history into a subject which in the past has been treated more as a compendium of information from a range of source materials.

On the Roman side the trade was in the hands of the Greek and Jewish merchants of Egypt, and of the Palmyrene and Levantine merchants from the Hellenistic world. This would be logical given that the concentration of this trade was in Alexandria, Coptos and ports along the Red Sea. However, more direct Roman interests and investments were not only possible but even likely. André Tchernia's paper, 'The Dromedary of the Peticii and Trade with the East', is a creative reconstruction of the possibility of an established family of traders residing in Italy but extending their enterprise to trade and transportation in the Red Sea and beyond. The linking of the evidence from inscriptions suggests four generations of a family trading in wine and one among these seems to be associated with the eastern trade. Wine was an established export to India, even if on a small scale. The same merchants would import pepper and pearls and this process would have required personal supervision. Possibly they had counterparts or even partners in Rome. The financial outlay on such enterprises could have come from the investments of wealthy Romans, although investments closer to Alexandria are equally likely. An echo of such activities comes from what has been called the Archive of Nicanor among the Coptos ostraca. This provides information on a family running a business in transportation between Coptos and the ports of Myos Hormos and Berenice and possibly trading with India, during the earlier half of the first century AD. The agents include slaves and freedmen, and mention is also made of a woman, who was actively involved in this trade. The link between high officials of considerable wealth and the trade with India is re-iterated in this record (Fuks 1951).

There is perhaps a clearer identity of the traders than of the crews of the ships carrying the trade. An initial utilisation of local ships from southern Arabia already trading with western India for essential supplies and navigating with the monsoon winds is possible. A small trade in consumables may have preceded the Roman trade, since there are no artefacts as witness to a connection. With the increased potential of the trade it is likely that there was a greater use of Roman shipping. Strabo refers to the double campaign of Augustus against Ethiopia and Arabia which included the building of a navy to protect the Red Sea ports. He does not mention where the shipyards were located but presumably they were on the Red Sea coast with the possibility of obtaining timber from the forests reaching into Lebanon. Some of these ships may have been adapted to commercial use and to a technology appropriate to utilising monsoon winds, and these may have been included in the fleet of a hundred and twenty ships which Strabo mentions as going to the east to trade. The figure could be exaggerated but it remains indicative of a perception of the enhancement of the trade, also reflected in other sources. If indeed such a large fleet sailed each year and if, according to Pliny, ships were armed with archers as a protection against piracy (the existence of which is attested in Tamil and other sources as well), then the ships are unlikely to have been a random collection of local vessels, and the *sagittarii*/archers would have been mercenaries employed by the merchants or the ship captains. That by the second century AD ships captains were observing regulations prevailing in Egypt regarding cargo and trade, is evident from the Muziris contract. The same document mentions the name of the ship as the Hermapollon, clearly a Greek name (Casson 1989). The *Periplus* makes it a point to describe the local vessels when referring to the coasts of the Arabian Sea and the east coast network of the Indian peninsula and Sri Lanka but is silent regarding the ships used in the Red Sea trade with India. Would this be because it is assumed that the bulk of the shipping going out from the Red Sea is Roman? Such ships would have been used for specific trade, ports and cargoes, as is suggested by the remarks of Strabo and in the Muziris contract. Had there been an extensive use of local shipping, then the *Periplus* would surely have made some comment on preferences and on negotiations. This should not however be seen as precluding the use of a variety of other vessels for various other categories of exchange and transportation within the parameters of the Arabian Sea.

That there were possibly traders or ships crews who spent some time in India is suggested by a few votive inscriptions by Yavanas in the western Deccan, inscribed in the locally used language, Prākrit. These occur in major rock-cut Buddhist monasteries, known to have functioned as points along the more frequented trade routes (Kosambi 1956, Heitzman 1984). It is likely that most were originally from Egypt and the eastern Mediterranean for, if they were the local clients of such traders, or even Indians trading with Egypt, it is unlikely that they would call themselves Yavanas. (Judging by the evidence of the Quseir ostracon in Prākrit, those that traded in Egypt retained their Indian names.) A couple of persons among them state that they have come from Gata, generally identified with Trigarta in north India but which I have argued elsewhere, could be a Prākritisation of Coptos (Thapar 1992a). In one inscription the donor identifies himself as a northerner from Dattamitri and makes a special point of this. The Yavanas mention the name of the place from where they come and these are places generally associated with the Deccan, the most frequently mentioned being Dhenukākaṭa, which in another inscription is specifically described as a *vaniya-gāma*, a community of traders. There is a concentration of donors from Dhenukākaṭa at the important monastery of Karle in the western Deccan. That most of these were not north-Indian Yavanas, who came into India in the wake of the Indo-Greeks, Śakas/ Scythians and Parthians, is indicated not only by their associating themselves with places in the Deccan rather than northern India but also because the provenance of most of the Roman objects found in the Deccan is the Mediterranean and not the Hellenistic sources from the north-west of the subcontinent. Ceramics from the Mediterranean or bronzes made in Campania are more likely to have come via the frequently used Red Sea route than to have tangled with Parthian hostility.

The degree of Indianisation of the Yavanas resident in India is striking, for their names are recognisably and perhaps even a little self-consciously, Buddhist—Dhammadeva, Dhammarakhita, Yasavadhana, Culayakha, Sihadhaya—almost suggesting that they were recent converts to Buddhism! There are no descriptions of their profession which is unusual in such votive inscriptions and the assumption is that they were all traders (Kosambi 1955). But in any case they were wealthy enough to finance the donation of pillars, cisterns, caves. The Yavana from Dattamitri was evidently very wealthy, as he donates a cave to contain a votive *stupa* and hall of worship and cisterns, and associates his father and his son with the donation. He uses a term, *dhammātmana,* referring to his closeness to Buddhism which one scholar interprets as meaning a recent conversion (Senart 1981). These votive inscriptions are part of a larger body of such donations which articulated the centrality of a community patronage to the Buddhist *saṅgha.* Included also are donations from members of various families and of guilds of artisans and merchants. Some of the donors were women from the families of traders, artisans and small-scale land-owners, as well as nuns (Thapar 1992b).

In the context of the western Deccan, the conversion to Buddhism of Yavanas was doubtless at one level a matter of religious persuasion, but at another level it could provide an enabling factor to gain entry into the community of traders and artisans. Patronage to Buddhist places of worship by the Yavanas, was to a partial extent a replacing of kinship networks of production and distribution by a network of a community identified by religious practice. In as much as this was a step away from kinship networks, it was a more impersonal system in the Deccan, although not completely so. Kinship networks help control competition in buying and selling. Identifying with a community would retain some of that control but with a freer play. But possibly from the perspective of the socio-political function of such a conversion there was an even more important association: that of the nexus between the ruling family, the Buddhist *saṅgha*/Order and the *śreṇīs*/guilds of artisans and traders. At the same site of Nasik, where the wealthy Yavana makes an impressive donation, there is an inscription of about the same period recording money donations made by a member of the royal family to guilds of weavers, the interest from which was to go towards providing robes for the Buddhist monks and their sundry expenses. This triangular nexus was not a rarity and would have been useful even to Yavana traders. References to *yavana-rājās* suggest that some Yavanas living in India were regarded as people of status (Pingree 1978).

Wheeler referred to Arikamedu as an Indo-Roman trading station. Earlier scholars hint at Roman colonies through which the artefacts came and ideas were diffused. But colonies require the direct appropriation of resources, labour and land, and are intended as permanent settlements, none of which would apply to those Yavanas who came to India as part of the maritime trade. Settlements register a range of variations. Some are temporary to the point of coming into existence only for the period that the traders and the crew are present and would therefore hardly find reference in Indian sources. Others, more permanent, could be located in a separate part of a town to supervise production or to make contact with local agents. The settlement believed to be the production centre for overseas commerce at Arikamedu begins as a separate sector to the north but gradually expands to include the pre-existing settlement to the south. Such an expansion should not be seen as the Yavanas taking over the settlement but as the expanding interface between the new arrivals and those already there. The differentiation was not restricted to that between the local people and the visiting foreigners, for within both categories there could be degrees of 'otherness'. One wonders whether this otherness was expressed in multi-lingualism, where, at a place such as Arikamedu, the graffiti attests literacy in Tamil and Sinhala Prākrit, written in *brāhmī,* and one may assume the use of some Greek (Begley 1993, Mahadevan 1973). This underlines the wider connections of the place. Such multi-lingualism would have become more regular in the later period when the *Cilappatikaram* refers to Yavana houses in the port of Kāveripaṭṭinam.

A tantalising question relates to the finding of small quantities of *terra sigillata* tableware at Arikamedu (and it is thought at other sites nearby), as also Egyptian glass bowls, wine containers from the eastern Mediterranean, Spanish jars for garum and olive oil and other containers from southern France (Begley 1993). The combination of items is a pointer to where they came from. Who used these objects? the visiting Yavanas or the local elite? or both, where the former might have set the fashion for the latter? Megalithic burials in the vicinity reveal an appreciation of sophisticated gold jewellery (Casal 1949) for which there were both makers and users. This would point to goldsmiths and lapidaries working in the area, and, not surprisingly, it was a craft centre for cameos of onyx, gemstones, shell bangles and ornamental objects. The nature of these settlements is historically significant not just to the maritime trade but to the debate on the nature of urbanisation in south India. The establishing of trading centres would have accelerated the functions of urbanism in the existing settlements, some of which would normally evolve into towns, but perhaps at a slower pace. But did the centres also indirectly create the pre-conditions for urbanisation at other sites involved with the supply of resources? These towns may in turn have been linked to the process of state-formation among the Cēras, Coḷas and Pāṇḍyas.

The Indian perception of the Yavanas was again not uniform (Thapar 1988a). The Brahmanical reaction to the Yavanas could be severe and hostile, as in the *Yuga Purāṇa.* But at the same time there was considerable respect for and borrowing from the Hellenistic theories of astronomy and astrology, some of which came from centres such as Alexandria, a case in point being the *Yavanajātaka* based on a Greek original from Alexandria and probably written in western India (Pingree 1978). Part of the brahmanical hostility may have been due to the patronage which the Indo-Greek and Śaka rulers extended to the Buddhists whom the *brāhmaṇas* saw as heretics. The Buddhists were not just appreciative of the patronage to the *saṅgha* but also appear to have been curious about Yavana society, commenting on its dual order of master and slave. Ideologically Buddhism was more sympathetic to the function and status of traders than were the Brahmanical normative texts. A different perspective again emerges from the Tamil *Caṅkam* poems. Here the Yavanas are aliens although some of their cargoes such as wine and gold are welcomed. However, the later Tamil texts express admiration for the Yavana homes in Kāveripaṭṭinam and the Yavana soldiers guarding the gates of the town of Madurai, where they were employed by the local ruler. The Yavanas seem to be living as a segregated group, unlike the impression given in their votive inscriptions in the western Deccan which point to a greater integration with Indian society. Wheeler (1955) points out that the building of the Graeco-Bactrian city of Sirkap at Taxila in northern India coincides with the more active period of the Roman maritime trade, but the two situations show divergent manifestations in the pattern of living and the diffusion of ideas.

The discussion on Roman trade has been dominated by the evidence of the coins and, although these provide precise information, there are other categories of evidence which provide a wider perspective. The initial and occasional discovery of a Roman or 'sub-Roman' object has now been gradually extended to larger numbers and varieties of such objects, some from stratified excavations, although overall the numbers are not excessive. Excavations provide not only the discovery of objects but also their localisation and contextualisation, both of which are crucial to the reconstruction of the trade. The combining of research from literary sources with archaeology and an attempt to interpret the numismatic evidence in terms of social and economic history can take us much further in assessing the significance of the trade than the more limited investigation of each of these sources individually. Excavations are of course not restricted to just the digging up of artefacts. Even more instructive at this point would be the horizontal excavation of ports known to have been used at the time, such as Sopara, and the search for others mentioned in the trade, such as Muziris. Equally important would be the technological study of the items sought from India. This would involve examining the ecological locations and the gathering and distribution of domesticated pepper, of the mining of chalcedonies and beryls and their manufacture into items, and of varieties of textiles.

The changing patterns of this trade would also provide insights into its nature. There appears to have been a shift in the locus of the trade in the second century, with a concentration on the east coast which had become an area of commercial activity, as is indirectly attested by votive inscriptions and the rich embellishment of the Buddhist *stūpa* at Amarāvatī and the wharf at Dharanikoṭā (Sarma 1985). The direction of the major maritime trade was now turning towards South-East Asia. Yavana trading interests would have made a bid to intervene but were likely to have been stymied by the initiative taken by Indian traders. In his *Geography* which shows a familiarity with the east coast, Ptolemy claims that he has used the information provided by merchants and others who have resided in the area. This could be closer to the time of the *Cilapattikaram* references to Yavanas resident at Kāveripaṭṭinam. The Yavana presence in the eastern Deccan may have been both a following up of trade routes from the western Deccan as well as a movement along the east coast. The mention of what are taken to be embassies from South Asian rulers to the Roman emperors, begins in the time of Augustus but references in Latin sources increase after the first century AD. Curiously, Indian sources seem uninterested in these and make no mention of them, in spite of Aśoka in the third century BC registering communication with five Hellenistic kings. The embassies, it would seem, were not concerned with political alliances but could have been facilitating trade.

And finally there remains the as yet unanswered question as to why the Roman input into this trade seems to decline after the second century AD, as the Indian evidence shows. Much of the answer would lie in the historical changes which took place in those regions of India most closely connected with the trade, and some with changes in west Asia and the eastern Mediterranean. Was there for example a greater participation of Indian traders, who may have gradually edged out the earlier traders in supplying pepper and textiles to Alexandria? Or, the Indian involvement in the trade with Central Asia and South-East Asia may have led to the tapping of new resources and products different from the earlier ones, and the supply of these to Central and South-East Asia would have diverted attention from the Roman trade. Did the fashion for Yavana items decline and therefore these do not appear in later excavations? The hoarding of coins would become unnecessary with changes in patterns of exchange and the function of the hoard as a social agency would also have become redundant. The decline of the Red Sea as a major artery would have had to do with the transfer to other routes, particularly with the increasing importance of Byzantium. Historical changes in West Asia are pertinent to this possibility.

Roman objects in India became a passing fancy and even

wine was not in permanent demand. Only the import of coral persisted, perhaps because it was believed to be a talisman. But in Europe the Roman trade had created an insatiable demand for pepper and spices, which flowed unfailingly westward, whilst textiles found their way into the markets of Byzantium. Empires came and went, but the demand for pepper was permanent. And, whether it was the Venetians or later the Portuguese, control over the pepper trade via Alexandria is seen as fundamental to a commercial economy in the Mediterranean (Lane 1973, Bautier 1971). This in turn required a flow of bullion to the east (Clay 1984, Braudel 1972). There is a persistent anxiety in European writings which echoes Pliny, and insists that these luxuries from the east are devastating the economy.

The Date of the *Periplus of the Erythraean Sea* in the Light of South Arabian Evidence

CHRISTIAN ROBIN

THE MANUSCRIPTS OF THE *PERIPLUS OF THE ERYTHRAEAN SEA*

The Periplus of the Erythraean Sea is a small work in *koine* Greek of the post-classical period. The Codex Palatinus Gr. 398, preserved in Heidelberg, is the only manuscript on which it is possible to base a reconstruction of its text. In this, the *Periplus* occupies 15 leaves (fol. 40-54) or 30 pages. The best edition of the text, remarkable for its meticulousness and prudence, was published by Hjalmar Frisk[1] in 1927 and has been reproduced as it is in the book of Lionel Casson (1989).

Hjalmar Frisk distinguished two different handwritings in the manuscript of Heidelberg. He attributed the first to a scribe who supposedly copied the text and wrote the copious notes in the margin and then introduced the numerous corrections, either immediately or during a subsequent revision. But 'it is difficult to know whether by these additions the copyist was correcting the faulty reading of the model or simply faults resulting from his negligence' (Frisk 1927, p. 27). He attributed another series of corrections to a second more recent scribe. These appeared to him to be mainly judicious, never suggesting by their tenor that a better exemplar of the text was used.

In the editor's view, while the earlier scribe definitely gave proof of good judgement, his predecessors were not endowed with the same qualities. As a result, in the course of transmission, 'the text became considerably distorted and is now in a rather vitiated state' (*ibid.*, p. 33). Hjalmar Frisk felt that the original *Periplus* was probably a document of everyday use in cursive writing, which is liable to all types of erroneous interpretations and, furthermore, contained abbreviations which have been incorrectly expanded.

A second manuscript of the *Periplus* is preserved at the British Museum in London under the classification number Add. mss 19391, but it does not help in the establishment and reconstruction of the text, as it was copied from the manuscript of Heidelberg before the inclusion of the corrections made by the second scribe.

We do not know the name, origin or profession of the author of the *Periplus*. However, it is clear that he was not very cultivated. While his language is coherent and more or less correct, his style and grammar are mediocre. He also displays very little knowledge of history and literature except of the most popular kind and nothing seems to interest him beyond his own speciality—maritime commerce. In brief, his horizon appears to be rather limited. He is primarily a professional who has collected a series of technical notes useful in his area of work.

In fact, the variety of information collected in the *Periplus* would have been handy for any Roman merchant who wished to undertake a commercial expedition towards the Indian Ocean. It indicates itineraries, distances, the principal anchorage points, the facilities available on land and the merchandise which was being actively traded. And since the political situation in these regions was also important for the merchant, the work mentions the names of the principal sovereigns in the coastal regions.

A unique document in its genre, it is clear that the *Periplus* is of immense interest for the economic history of the ancient Orient. But in order that the profusion of facts contained in it may be exploited, it is necessary to date the text and its possible sources with precision. This is where the problem arises. The *Periplus* was certainly written during the Empire but, curiously, though it mentions several rulers of Petra (now in south Jordan), Ethiopia, South Arabia and India, its date remains disputed.

THE HYPOTHESES REGARDING THE DATE OF THE *PERIPLUS OF THE ERYTHRAEAN SEA*

An Austrian scholar has amused himself by preparing a list of the diverse hypotheses propounded by ingenious scholars with regard to the date of the *Periplus*.[2] However, if we overlook the details on which they differ, we may narrow down the periods when the *Periplus* was supposedly written to two: the first century AD and the first half of the third century. The gap is not negligible, spanning a period of about 150 to 200 years.

For a long time, the mention of a king of Petra, capital of Nabataea, was regarded as the decisive argument in favour of a date earlier than AD 106. In this year, Nabataea was annexed to the Roman Empire by the emperor Trajan (Rodinson 1975, p. 212, which may be supplemented with Bowersock 1983). A. M. Boyer's work on Indian chronology and particularly his article in the *Journal asiatique* published in 1897 seemed to confirm this hypothesis which quickly came to be generally accepted.

However, in 1961, going against the general tide of opinion, Jacqueline Pirenne used her immense scholarly resources to revise this date radically. In an article in volume 249 of the *Journal asiatique*[3] she claimed that none of the arguments in favour of the first century as the date of the *Periplus* were incontestable, especially when well established evidence provided compelling proof for a later date. Her conviction was based on the examination of evidence relating to South Arabia. Persuaded correctly that the text should be treated in its entirety, she went on to give her opinion on the most controversial and the most difficult problems of Indian chronology claiming that she would substantiate this further with proofs and numismatic reclassifications which other activities had prevented her from completing until her death in 1990. Her conclusion was that the *Periplus* had been written around 225-30.

Pirenne almost immediately received the enthusiastic support of Franz Altheim and Ruth Stiehl, two German historians who, like her, were engaged in addressing themselves to the most controversial issues. The strength of her conviction progressively led most of the specialists on South Arabia, be it historians or archaeologists, to accept her position.[4] However, her thesis did not find support among the totality of researchers and there were many who continued to date the *Periplus* from early Empire.[5] Dissent was also encountered among the specialists of South Arabia[6] but, in the face of repeated affirmation that the evidence relating to South Arabia in the *Periplus* dated from the third century, their weakened certitude prompted them to adopt a middle path whereby the *Periplus* was seen as a composite work.[7]

Without going into the details, it may be useful to reiterate the principal arguments on which the dating of the *Periplus* is based.

There are firstly the names of the kings. The *Periplus* mentions a certain Malichas, King of the Nabataeans (?) (Greek *anabataiôs* corrected in *Nabataiôn* <*anabasis*>) at Petra (paragraph 19). It is generally agreed that the presence of a king at Petra, capital of the Nabataean kingdom is out of question after AD 106, the date of its annexation by Rome. By way of greater precision, there are two kings of Nabataea whose names would be transcribed as Malichas in Greek but only the second among these two, whose reign extends from AD 40 to 70 (Bowersock, 1983, particularly pp. 59 and 71), belongs to the Imperial age and hence can be retained for consideration. The *Periplus* could thus date from this period. According to the supposition of certain authors, Malichas may be a derivation of the common noun *malik* (king) in Arabic, used as a proper noun. In this eventuality, also, the *Periplus* may be regarded as being contemporaneous with the kingdom of Nabataea, that is, prior to 106. The mention of Malichas is a strong chronological argument and one of the most difficult to refute.

Despite this and even though there is no supportive evidence for it in any source whatsoever—coins, inscriptions or literary texts—those in favour of a later date uphold that Malichas could have ruled at Petra in the third century. It appears very unlikely. As Maxime Rodinson has remarked 'It is difficult to conceive that, at the beginning of the third century, a (chief of a small tribe) had seized power in the large majestic city of Petra, the second city of the province of Arabia which had been elevated to the rank of a colony under Elagabalus (218-22) and where there was a regular succession of governors nominated in Rome' (1975, p. 216).

The problems posed by the Indian kings mentioned in the *Periplus* are still more difficult, whether it be with regard to their identity, the extent of their kingdoms or their date. However, one of them, Manbanos, has been identified as Nahapana, satrap of Iranian origin known through the Indian literary tradition, inscriptions and coins, after this was established by A.M. Boyer in his article published in 1897. The mention of Nahapana who, according to Boyer, acceded to the throne in AD 78, would situate the facts relating to India in the *Periplus* after this date.

In 1961, Pirenne had taken care to emphasize that this hypothesis posed difficulties. During the course of his voyage, the author of the *Periplus* had noted the names of two personalities who were not exactly contemporary: a Nabataean king, Malichas whose reign terminates in AD 70 and an Indian king, Manbanos, who seizes power in AD 78; in sum a difference of eight years. In general, the supporters of a later date for the *Periplus* had little difficulty in showing that the thesis of A.M. Boyer rested on several hypotheses which could not be easily proved but they were unable to offer a convincing chronological table of Indian kings in which Nahapana would date from about AD 225.

Finally, very recently, the identification of Manbanos with Nahapana has been questioned (Fussman *infra*, pp. 66-71).

A second method of dating employed by numerous scholars consisted of analysing the political situation in the regions where upheavals had taken place between the first and the third century. Kalyan in south India, the lower valley of the Indus and Oman were studied from this perspective but for a long time nothing decisive emerged from these studies. However, in the past fifteen years, epigraphic and numismatic discoveries in north-west India have led to the view that the information about this region in the *Periplus* corresponds only with the period from AD 30 to 50 (Fussman *ibid.*).

One last approach appears to be promising at first view. The geographical knowledge of ancient people about the Erythraean Sea (now known as the Red Sea, the Persian gulf and the Sea of Oman), was still rather vague even up to the beginning of the Roman Empire. Considerable progress was made in this regard in the first few centuries of the Christian era as illustrated by three works: Pliny's *Natural History*, Ptolemy's *Geography* and the *Periplus of the Erythraean Sea*.

Unusual for the ancient period, the date of Pliny's *Natural History* is precisely known. Dedicated to Titus in 77, this work was still not published on 25 August 79 when Pliny died while aiding the inhabitants of Stabiae (south of Pompeii), who were menaced by the eruption of the Vesuvius. A gigantic work of compilation which bears testimony to the innumerable fields which interested the author, this *Natural History* reflects the works which, though not necessarily recent, were in circulation in cultivated milieux during the third quarter of the first century AD.

The *Geography* of Ptolemy was composed around the middle of the second century, though it is possible that it was touched up by later scholars. The famous geographer and astronomer had assembled all the information relating to the toponyms and the peoples of the known world. The *Natural History* of Pliny and the *Geography* of Ptolemy are two chronological aids which, though not as precise as might be desired, can help in dating the *Periplus*.

Many arguments are worthy of attention. The first relates to the orientation of the coast of East Africa. The author of the *Periplus* knew that it slanted towards the west whereas Ptolemy believed that this coast turned eastwards, bordering an unknown continent and finally rejoined Asia. With regard to the Indian coastline below the Indus region, the *Periplus* was aware that it curved towards the south whereas Ptolemy was ignorant of this. It should also be remarked that while Ptolemy distinguished between the Seres and the Sines whom he regarded as two different peoples, the *Periplus* knew that they were one. The name of Ceylon, also, varying as it does according to the sources, furnishes arguments of a similar sort.

We may conclude that on many important points the *Periplus* appears to be better informed than Ptolemy, though this is not always the case. The problem is to ascertain whether this gap in geographical knowledge necessarily implies that the *Periplus* is a later work than Ptolemy's *Geography*. It is clear that the author of the *Periplus* and Ptolemy belonged to two different worlds. The first sailed between Egypt and India; his literary and scientific knowledge was perfunctory but he had direct experience of the world about which he spoke. The second was a scholar whose scientific knowledge was based on documents which represented a long tradition of erudition but who had never visited the regions about which he wrote. It is not inconceivable that certain facts with which sailors and merchants were already familiar had not, even after a few decades, succeeded in gaining admission in scholarly circles, especially because some of them directly challenged certain theories which were in vogue during the period.

Several other arguments have been given for proposing different dates for the *Periplus*, each emphasizing one fact to the detriment of the others. The impressive list of these divergent dates has already been signalled earlier.

Basically, there are three principal opinions which hold sway at present. Most researchers date the *Periplus* to the reign of Malichas, King of Nabataea between AD 40 to 70. Most of the specialists of South Arabia, including some of the important ones, consider that the evidence relating to South Arabia in the *Periplus* is consistent with the political situation that prevailed there in the first quarter of the third century. Finally, there is an intermediate position which regards the *Periplus* as a composite work in which technical notes from different works and different periods were assembled.

This last hypothesis is a compromise which is proposed only in view of the difficulty in arriving at a unanimously acceptable date. It is all the more unsatisfactory as the contents and the language of the *Periplus* appear to be homogeneous.

It is thus the specialists of South Arabia who are the principal opponents of a wide, if not general acceptance of the earlier date. Our aim in this paper is to examine if their opinion is well founded in the light of the studies which firmly establish the chronology of South Arabia from the first to the third century AD.[8]

SOUTH ARABIA IN THE *PERIPLUS OF THE ERYTHRAEAN SEA*

South Arabia clearly occupies an important place in the *Periplus*. The ships which sailed from Egypt towards India inevitably halted in many of its ports, if only to replenish their stock of food and water. The author of the *Periplus*, who knew these ports well, has described them in great detail. However, in this veritable mine of information relating to maritime commerce, only those facts which refer to the prevailing political situation are useful in establishing the date of the text. Several references are made to the kingdom of the Homerites (=Himyar^{um}[9]) and to Mapharitis (=Ma^{c}âfir^{um}).

16. *Two runs beyond this island* [Menuthias, to-day Pemba or Zanzibar] *comes the very last port of trade on the coast of Azania, called Rhapta ['sewn']…. The region is under the rule of the governor of Mapharitis, since by some ancient right it is subject to the kingdom of Arabia as first constituted….*

22. *A three-day journey inland from Mouza lies Sauê, the city of the province, called Mapharitis, that surrounds it. The governor, Cholaibos, has his residence there.*

23. *Nine days further inland is [S]aphar, the metropolis, residence of Charibaêl, legitimate king of the two nations, the Homerite and the one, lying next to it, called the Sabaeans; he is a friend of the emperors, thanks to continuous embassies and gifts.*

25. *About a 300-stade sail past this port* [Mouza], … *is Okêlis, an Arab village on the coast that belongs to the same province; it is not so much a port of trade as a harbor, watering station, and the first place to put in for those sailing on.*

26. *Beyond Okêlis,… about 1200 stades distant is Eudaimôn Arabia, a village on the coast belonging to the same kingdom, Charibaêl's…. And now, not long before our time, Caesar sacked it.*

Other statements refer to the kingdom of Hadramawt:

27. *Immediately after Eudaimôn Arabia come a long coast and bay, populated by the villages of Nomads and Ichtyhophagoi, that stretch for 2000 stades or more, at which point, beyond the projecting headland, is another port of trade on the coast, Kanê, belonging to the kingdom of Eleazos, the frankincense bearing land; near it are two barren islands, one called Orneôn ['of the birds'] and the other Troullas, 120 stades offshore from Kanê. Above it inland lies the metropolis of Saubatha, which is also the residence of the king….*

(Translation based on Casson 1989, pp. 61 and foll.[10])

From the observations recorded in the *Periplus*, we learn that there were four major ports in South Arabia: Mouza,[11] Okêlis,[12] Eudaimôn Arabia[13] and Kanê[14] (to locate these

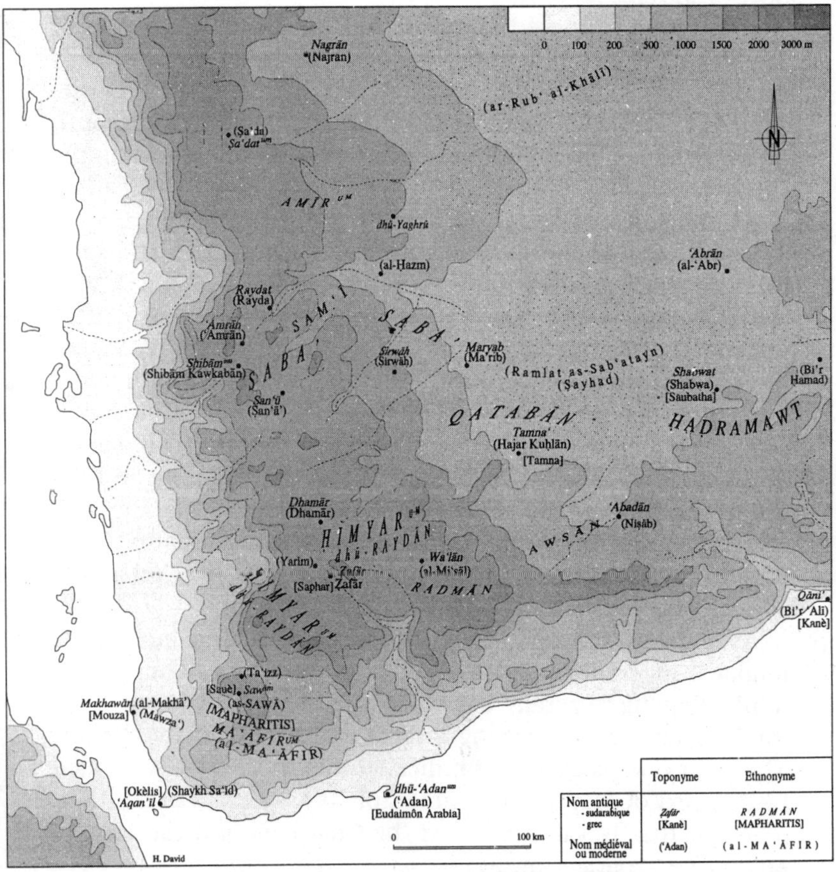

Map 1: Yemen in the first century AD

toponyms, see Map 1). These ports were located in one principality and two kingdoms.

The first country mentioned in the *Periplus* is Mapharitis which is under the feudal lord Cholaibos and whose capital Sauê is situated inland, at a distance of three days from the port of Mouza.

It was long supposed that Sauê was located in the region of Ta^{c}izz and it was not until 1987 that its location was firmly established when ^{c}Abd al-Ghanî ash-Shar^{c}abî, a Yemenite student, discovered the ruins of an important town 22 km south of Ta^{c}izz where he found an inscription[15] commemorating the construction of a temple 'under the town of Saw^{âm}' by 'Kulayb Yuha'min son of (Yashm)ur Yuhahmid dhû-Ma^{c}âfir^{um}'.[16]

The name of the ancient city Saw^{âm} survives in the local toponymy today as as-Sawâ, with the addition of the Arabic article *al-* and the disappearance of the South Arabian ending *-m*, but it refers not to this site but to the surrounding region. This correspondence is proof that the stone on which the inscription was engraved was from the same spot. The location of Saw^{âm} is thus established beyond doubt and its identification as the Sauê of the *Periplus* is unquestionable. The one and the other were dependent on the lord of Mapharitis/Ma^{c}âfir^{um}.

The interest of the inscription of as-Sawâ resides also in the identity of the noble who had written the text, Kulayb Yuha'min, who appears to be the Cholaibos of the *Periplus*.[17]

As a matter of fact, Cholaibos was not a king but only a feudal lord, implying a situation of dependence. There is no doubt that his suzerain was Charibaêl. This is deduced from the information concerning Rhapta and Azania in the *Periplus* where, in one passage, it is indicated that this region was ruled by the lord of Mapharitis (paragraph 16), whereas in another, it is said that it was controlled 'by Charibaêl and the lord of Mapharitis' (paragraph 31).

The principality of Cholaibos included Sauê, most probably Mouza (because it is suggested that in this port gifts should be offered 'to the king and the lord' (paragraph 21), Okêlis ('which is dependent on the same lord', paragraph 25) and the African possessions Rhapta and Azania which are mentioned in paragraph 16.

Besides this principality, the *Periplus* mentions two other kingdoms in South Arabia. The first was governed by 'Charibaêl, legitimate king of the two nations, the Homerite and the one, lying next to it, called the Sabaeans'; its capital was [S]aphar. It is not difficult to recognize the South Arabian anthroponym Karib'îl and a paraphrased version of the title 'King of Saba' and dhû-Raydân'. In fact, in South Arabian inscriptions, Himyar^{um} and dhû-Raydân are names which are often interchangeable: dhû-Raydân is a general term which designates all the tribes under the occupants of the palace of Raydân in Zafâr, whereas Himyar^{um} was the main constituent of these tribes. As for [S]aphar, the capital of Charibaêl, it is a corrupted form of Zafâr, capital of the Himyar^{um} tribe.

The kingdom of Charibaêl included [S]aphar and the port named Eudaimôn Arabia and, in a dependent position, Mapharitis and its African possessions.

The second kingdom, the land of incense, was the kingdom of Eleazos. Its metropolis, Saubatha, where the king resided, was situated in the interior of the country. These two proper names are easily identifiable as Ilî^{c}azz and Shabwat[18] in South Arabian. The land of incense, that is Hadramawt, included Saubatha and Kanê and extended deep into the east (paragraph 29-30 and 32-3). It also exercised its tutelage on the island of Dioskouridês (today Suqutra).

One last point needs to be emphasized. It is clear from the several cross-references within the text that the information concerning South Arabia is not merely a compilation of facts but the unified account of a single person. Thus, with regard to the tutelage exercised by Hadramawt over Dioskouridês, the work states: 'The island is subject to the aforementioned king of the frankincense-bearing land—just as Azania is to Charibaêl and the governor of Mapharitis—'(paragraph 31), that is Eleazos, who has just been mentioned above. Besides, this passage also confirms that Charibaêl, Eleazos and Cholaibos were contemporaries.

THE POLITICAL SITUATION IN SOUTH ARABIA FROM THE FIRST TO THE THIRD CENTURY AD

As we have seen, the best reasoned theses lead to two possible dates for the *Periplus*: around the middle of the first century AD on the one hand and the first half of the third century, on the other. We propose to examine, one by one, all that we know about Yemen during these two periods in order to determine which of the two corresponds best with the facts contained in the *Periplus*. But, before this, it might be useful to review briefly the principal actors on the scene in the first few centuries of the Christian era.

Yemen is a land of high mountains where communication is relatively difficult and where each massif and each valley lived in a state of autarky. Since the earliest times, a fortress perched on a highland had sufficed for resisting attempted hegemonies by enterprising neighbours or foreign powers. Political dispersion was a constant feature here, reinforced by the tribal nature of social organisation.

The earliest states emerged in the valleys flanking the desert. Three of these which successively enjoyed some degree of hegemony during the centuries preceding the Christian era deserve to be mentioned: Saba', Qatabân and Hadramawt. They exercised control over the lower inland valleys as well as the mountain chain and the coastal plain.

Around the second century BC the balance of power broke down. Arab nomads, who were no doubt already present in all the foothills bordering the desert, seized control of Jawf, one of the principal valleys. The Qatabânite territories in the highlands seceded to form a new entity called Himyar^{um} or dhû-Raydân. It is quite possible that the Roman attack against Maryab,[19] the capital of Saba', in 25 BC profoundly weakened this kingdom.

Be that as it may, in the first century AD the political landscape presented new traits: the first state whose rulers were entitled 'Kings of Saba' and dhû-Raydân' and which consisted of a union of the old kingdom of Saba' and the Qatabânite tribes of the highlands (Himyar^{um}) dominated the whole of western Yemen. It had two capitals (Maryab and Zafâr), with the notable innovation of having one of them, Zafâr, situated in the highlands. Deprived of part of its territories, Qatabân had to be satisfied with a modest role. Only Hadramawt remained capable of contending for hegemony over the whole of South Arabia.

Without elaborating on the details of the history of Yemen it will suffice to indicate that the kingdom of Saba' and dhû-Raydân broke up into two violently opposed states around the beginning of the second century AD after the reign of 'Amdân Bayân Yuhaqbid, forming the new Saba' (capital Maryab) and Himyar^{um} (capital Zafâr). This separation was contested by both the sides with the sovereign of each continuing to call himself 'King of Saba' and dhû-Raydân' (see chronological table, fig. 1).

It is easy to imagine how the utilisation of the same title made it extremely difficult to identify these two states. The problem was further complicated by the sporadic reappearance of the title 'King of Saba' assumed by viceroys or Sabaean usurpers. And finally, the unequal distribution of epigraphic sources, which are abundant on the Sabaean side but meagre on the Himyar^{um}, also contributed to errors of perspective.

It is only recently, in the 1980s, that a satisfactory ordering of these events was made possible by the discovery of a whole series of Himyarite documents, of which some were dated.[20] Earlier studies should be reviewed in their light.

The most important result of the wars between Saba', Himyar^{um} and Hadramawt in the second century was the annexation of the remaining Qatabânite territories by the last mentioned.

Subsequently, Himyar^{um} was to face a serious menace when, at the very beginning of the third century, the Abyssinians attacked Arabia. Allied initially with Saba', their troops posted themselves in the whole of western Yemen from dhû-^{c}Adan^{um} to Nagrân.[21] Thrice the Himyarite capital, Zafâr, was threatened, if not occupied. These wars once again opposed four protagonists, Saba', Himyar^{um}, Hadramawt and the Abyssinians. They ended in 270 with the complete victory of Himyar^{um} which succeeded in driving the Abyssinians away from the peninsula and successively annexing Saba' and Hadramawt.[22]

THE IDENTIFICATION OF THE SOUTH ARABIAN KINGS MENTIONED IN THE *PERIPLUS OF THE ERYTHRAEAN SEA*

For numerous specialists of South Arabian studies, the *Periplus*—or rather the information in the *Periplus* concerning South Arabia—dates from approximately AD 225. This date was upheld by Marcel-Toussaint Reinaud[23] in the nineteenth century but its present vogue was initiated by Pirenne. It would therefore be useful to recapitulate the evidence on which her conviction was founded.

To begin with, Pirenne identified the Charibaêl mentioned in the *Periplus* with Karib'îl Watâr Yuhan^{c}im, King of Saba' and dhû-Raydân, a ruler of whom little was known at the time but for his coins. Basing herself on stylistic arguments and paleographic classifications, Pirenne dated these coins from the beginning of the third century.[24] We are aware today that the king Karib'îl Watâr Yuhan^{c}im had ruled around the middle of the first century.

The second argument of Pirenne was the absence of any reference to Qatabân in the *Periplus.* According to her, this implied that the *Periplus* was written after the disappearance of this kingdom (dated today between AD 160 and 210[25]). It should however be remembered that after the foundation of the kingdom of Saba' and dhû-Raydân, Qatabân was left with no port and, as mentioned earlier, since the *Periplus* was interested only in maritime commerce, it had no reason to mention a small continental kingdom. This weakens her argument considerably.

Finally, Pirenne attempted to establish her thesis on the basis of a comparison between Pliny and the *Periplus* arguing that, since the knowledge of the former regarding the coast of Arabia was much less, he was necessarily anterior to the latter. We have already pointed out the fragility of this reasoning.

The strongest argument in Pirenne's demonstration was the date of Karib'îl Watâr Yuhan^{c}im which has been proved now as erroneous. The very basis of her thesis thus stands demolished. But this is not sufficient reason for rejecting it. It is also necessary to be convinced that this thesis is incompatible with the latest evidence.

In the third century, there are South Arabian rulers whose name corresponds to Charibaêl and Eleazos (see chronological table, fig. 1). With regard to Charibaêl, the only ruler with whom he could be identified is Karib'îl Ayfa^{c}, King of Himyar^{um} entitled 'King of Saba' and dhû-Raydân'. The one precise indicator available for situating his reign is an inscription dating from 179 of the Radmânite era (AD 253-4, with the possibility of an error of some years since the beginning of the Radmânite era is not known precisely[26]). In this year a baron (*qayl*) of the sovereign commemorated the victorious end of a battle between Saba' and Himyar^{um}.

It appears that in 179 Radm. Karib'îl Ayfa^c had just recently acceded to the throne—not more than ten years earlier.[27] His reign extended up to a date falling between 179 and 198 Radm. (AD 272-3), not too close to 179 because an inscription mentions many important wars conducted by Karib'îl after this date.

The second king mentioned in the *Periplus* is Eleazos, an exact transcription of the South Arabian name Ilî^{c}azz. Only one ruler of Hadramawt bore this name in the third century, Ilî^{c}azz Yalut, son of ^{c}Ammîdhakhar. On the basis of several Radmânite inscriptions dating between 144 and 148 (AD 218-19 and AD 222-3) which mention him, it is possible to say that Ilî^{c}azz Yalut had already acceded to the throne in 144 Radm. From other sources we also know that Ilî^{c}azz was the contemporary of the Himyarite king Tha'rân Ya^{c}ûb Yuhan^{c}im who, it should be noted, was anterior to Karib'îl Ayfa^c, with two reigns intervening between them.[28] The reign of Ilî^{c}azz finally ended when he was captured by the Sabaean king Sha^{c}r^{um} Awtar, approximately between AD 229 and 240.[29]

It is almost certain that Karib'îl Ayfa^c, 'King of Saba' and dhû-Raydân was not a contemporary of Ilî^{c}azz Yalut, son of ^{c}Ammîdhakhar, King of Hadramawt. Hence these two kings cannot be the Charibaêl and the Eleazos of the *Periplus*, both of whom ruled during the same period.

The occupation of western Yemen by the Abyssinians from about AD 200 to 270 constitutes an even stronger argument against the later date suggested for the *Periplus*.

The earliest mention of an Abyssinian military presence in Arabia dates to the reign of ^{c}Alhân (Nahfân). The exact dates of ^{c}Alhân's reign are not known. All we know is that his son Sha^{c}r^{um} Awtar already succeeded him in AD 222-3. The date of the arrival of the Abyssinians would thus be situated in the two decades preceding 220. The last military operations conducted by the Abyssinian troops in Arabia date from the sixties or the seventies.[30]

During this period western Yemen was divided into two states: Saba' in the north and Himyar^{um} in the south. Two phases marked the relations between the Abyssinians and Saba', eginning with an alliance between them up to the time when Saba' defeated Hadramawt and captured its king, Ilî^{c}azz Yalut, around AD 229-40, followed by a period of continuous wars.

The relations between the Abyssinians and Himyar^{um} followed a different course. They were initially hostile because the first Abyssinian conquests in Arabia were probably made to the detriment of Himyar^{um}. During the reign of Li^{c}azz^{um} Yuhanîf Yuhasdiq, the Abyssinians, led by Baygat, the son of the Negus, even occupied the Himyarite capital (Ja 631/21).

On the contrary, the successor of Li^{c}azz^{um}, Shammir Yuhahmid, was an ally of the Abyssinians and we have every reason to believe that he had been placed on the throne by the invaders. When Shammir Yuhahmid ceded to Karib'îl Ayfa^{c}, who is one of the possible candidates for identification with Charibaêl, hostilities between the Abyssinians and the Himyarites had resumed. The region of Zafâr was occupied for seven months (MAFRAY-al-Mi^{c}sâl 3[31]).

The conflict continued under the next king during whose reign two Abyssinian co-regents invaded Himyar^{um} and two more battles took place close to the Himyarite capital (MAFRAY-al-Mi^{c}sâl 5[32]).

Let us assume now that the Himyarite king Karib'îl Ayfa^{c} is the Charibaêl of the *Periplus.* During the reign of this Karib'îl, the conflict is acute between the Abyssinians on the one hand and the Himyarites and the Sabaeans, on the other. The Abyssinians are present in the whole of western Yemen from Nagrân to Saw^{âm} passing through Zafâr, an indication that they are in occupation of the whole coast including the ports.

The Ma^{c}âfir^{um} tribe which is under Himyar^{um}, according to the *Periplus,* is mentioned three times in the inscriptions of the third century, under three different reigns, of Li^{c}azz^{um} Yuhanîf Yuhasdiq (Ja 631/33), of Karib'îl Ayfa^{c} (MAFRAY-al-Mi^{c}sâl 3/9[33]) and of Yâsir^{um} Yuhan^{c}im (MAFRAY-al-Mi^{c}sâl 5/10[34]). Each time it is the ally of the Abyssinians during their attacks against the Himyarite capital. It is to be noted that one of these attacks took place during the reign of Karib'îl Ayfa^{c}.

The capital of Ma^{c}âfir^{um}, Saw^{âm}, is also mentioned in the South Arabian inscriptions of this period. The Abyssinians received a Sabaean mission here and a Himyarito-Abyssinian mission was sent from here to the Sabaean kings (Ja 585/5 and foll.; CIH 314+954/13-18). There is every reason to think that Saw^{âm} was the residence of the Abyssinian princes who were warring in Yemen at this time.[35]

The political situation in west Yemen in the third century is thus fairly clear. A substantial part, if not the totality of the western side of the Yemenite mountain range was occupied by the Abyssinians. All the ports were certainly under their control. A variety of evidence also indicates that they settled Africans in Arabia.[36] Finally they also had a Yemenite ally, the tribe of Ma^{c}âfir^{um}—whose capital was the centre of Abyssinian power in Arabia—which was firmly on their side, participating in all the operations against the capital of Himyar^{um}.

The *Periplus* projects a very different picture. Himyar^{um} exercises a tutelage on the Ma^{c}âfir^{um} tribe. Together these two have possessions in Africa towards the Tanzania of today. The Arabian ports are controlled either by Ma^{c}âfir^{um} (Mouza and Okêlis) or by Himyar^{um} (Eudaimôn Arabia). Abyssinia, which is not mentioned by name in the *Periplus* but which is easily recognisable by the mention of its capital, Aksum, is a vast country whose king does not exercise any influence on the Arabian coast of the Red Sea.

Such divergent information leads to the conclusion that it is not the Yemen of the third century which is described in the *Periplus*. I have not referred to the Abyssinian—or more precisely the Adoulis—ruler Zôskalês whose name is mentioned in the *Periplus* but does not figure in the South Arabian inscriptions of the third century which, nevertheless, mention the names of four kings and two princes of Abyssinia. But this argument is not decisive, as the name by which a sovereign is commonly known and which a traveller is likely to record is not necessarily the one which is found in official documents such as inscriptions. Besides, it is not certain that we know the names of all the Abyssinian kings from the third century.

It now remains to be seen whether the facts recorded in the *Periplus* conform with what we know about Yemen in the first century AD.

During this period, Himyar^{um} and Saba' were united under the same crown. This conforms well with the definition of the kingdom of Charibaêl as given in the *Periplus* which describes him as 'legitimate king of the two nations, the Homerite and the one, lying next to it, called the Sabaeans'. But this argument is not conclusive.

There are two kings in the first century named Karib'îl: Karib'îl Watâr Yuhanᶜim, son of Dhamarᶜalî Bayân and his grandson Karib'îl Bayân (see chronological table, fig. 1). We do not possess any inscription with a date prior to the middle of the second century AD but we know the exact order in which the rulers succeeded each other and thus we are in a position to situate Karib'îl Watâr Yuhanᶜim around 40-50 and Karib'îl Bayân around 80-90, with the margin of error not exceeding 10-20 years (see chronological table, fig. 1).[37] It is difficult to identify the Charibaêl of *Periplus* (whose date would be prior to 70, if we go by the dating of Malichas, and to 50, if we base ourselves on the political situation in north-west India) with Karib'îl Bayân but there is nothing that runs counter to his being Karib'îl Watâr Yuhanᶜim, grand father of Karib'îl Bayân.

Around this period, a king named Ilîᶜazz Yalut had ruled in Hadramawt. His complete identity is Ilîᶜazz Yalut son of Yadaᶜ'îl (Pirenne-Khawr Rûrî 1 and 2, Hamilton 8). Pirenne dates him from the first century BC on the basis of her paleographic classifications[38] but Alfred F.L. Beeston prefers a later date because of certain linguistic traits.[39] It must be admitted that South Arabian evidence does not permit us to date him more precisely.[40]

Thus, though it is possible, it is not perfectly established that Ilîᶜazz Yalut (son of Yadaᶜ'îl) was the contemporary of the Karib'îl mentioned in the *Periplus* (Karib'îl Watâr Yuhanᶜim I, King of Saba' and dhû-Raydân, son of Dhamarᶜalî Bayân).

The *Periplus* also mentions the name of the lord of Mapharitis, Cholaibos. The term 'lord' corresponds to the Greek *tyrannos*, which is probably the translation of *qayl* in South Arabian. Only a very insignificant number of inscriptions are available up to now from Mapharitis. Among these, the only one of some importance is Sharᶜabî-as-Sawâ 1, to which we have already referred and whose author's name is Kulayb (Yuha'min) which exactly corresponds to Cholaibos in Greek. Kulayb is the lord of Maᶜâfir^{um} (or Mapharitis) and the writing in his inscription is reminiscent of that of the inscriptions of Ilîᶜazz of Hadramawt. This would situate him around the first century AD (compare with the inscriptions from the end of the first century BC or the first century AD[41]).

Does the Yemen of the first century correspond to its description in the *Periplus*? Its inscriptions mention three personalities who seem to correspond to Cholaibos (lord of Mapharitis), Charibaêl (king of the Homerites and the Sabaeans) and Eleazos (king of the land of incense), but only one of these three kings is dated with any precision. Besides, epigraphic sources have not yet thrown up evidence confirming the existence of Himyarite or Ma^{c}âfirite colonies in East Africa.

We may thus conclude by stating that evidence concerning South Arabia overrules the third century AD as the possible date of *Periplus*, contrary to the supposition of Pirenne. It also rules out the second century because there is no evidence either of a Karib'îl or an Ilî^{c}azz on the throne of Himyar^{um} and Hadramawt during this period. It does not, on the contrary, run counter to a date in the first century AD but is too imprecise to permit the establishment of this date incontestably.

REFERENCE OF THE INSCRIPTIONS

CIH: *Corpus inscriptionum semiticarum*, Pars quarta, *Inscriptiones himyariticas et sabaeas continens.*

Hamilton 8: W.L. Brown and A.F.L. Beeston, *Sculptures and Inscriptions from Shabwa*, in *Journal of the Royal Asiatic Society*, 1954, pp. 55-6 and pl. XVIII, 2.

Ja 585, 631 and 643: Albert Jamme, *Sabaean Inscriptions from Mahram Bilqîs (Mârib)*, with foreword by Wendell Phillips (Publications of the American Foundation for the Study of Man, III), Baltimore (The Johns Hopkins Press), 1962.

Ja 923: A. Jamme, *The Al-^{c}Uqlah Texts* (South Arab Documentation III), Washington, D.C. (The Catholic University of America Press), 1963, p. 40 and pl. I B.

Pirenne-Khawr Rûrî 1 and 2: J. Pirenne, *The Incense Port of Moscha*, op.cit. n. 38, pp. 82-5 and pl. 1 (p. 83) and 2 A (p. 87).

RES: *Répertoire d'épigraphie sémitique.*

Shar^{c}abî-as-Sawâ 1: Ch. Robin, *Kulayb Yuha'min*, op.cit. n. 45.

AD	Ḥaḍramawt *(kings)*	Saba' and dhū-Raydān/Ḥimyar^{um} *(kings)*	Radmān; Ma'āfir^{um} *(qayls)*
	(Abīyaśa')	(Sumhu'alī Dharīḥ)	
	Yashhur'īl Yuhar'ish	*Dhamar'alī Watār Y.*	
	(Yada''īl)	(Dhamar'alī Bayān)	
50 *c.*	Ilī'azz Yaluṭ (= Éléazos)	*Karib'īl Watār Yuhan'im I* (= Charibaêl)	Kulayb Yuha'min (M) (= Cholaibos)
74			[beginning of radm. era]
80 *c.*		*Dhamar'alī Dharīḥ*	
85-90 *c.*	Yada''īl	*Karib'īl Bayān* (Yuhaqīm) *Nasha'karib Yuha'min	
100 *c.*		*'Amdān Bayān Yuhaqbiḍ* (Wadd'īl)	

[Saba']	[Ḥimyar^{um}]
Ilīsharaḥ Yaḥḍub I	*Yāsir^{um} Yuhaṣdiq* (Shammir) (La'izz)
Watār^{um} Yuha'min	

? Rabbîshams^{um} Nimrān?

Sa'dshams^{um} Asra'
Marthad^{um} Yuhaḥmid

AD			Radmān; Ma'āfir^{um}
146-7			Wahab'īl Yaḥūz (R)

Fig. 1: Chronological table of Hadramite, Sabaean and Himyarite kings from the first to third century AD (as well as of some nobles of the Radmân and Ma^{c}âfir^{um} tribes).

AD	Ḥaḍramawt	[Saba']	[Ḥimyar^{um}]	Radmān
			Dhamar'alī Yuhabirr	
		*Wahab'īl Yaḥūz		
		*Anmār^{um} Yuha'min		
			Tha'ran Ya'ub Yuhan'im	
		*Karib'īl Watār Y. II *Yarīm Ayman		
	Yada''īl Yada'ab Ghaylān ('Ammīdhakhar)	*'Alhān Nahfān		
218-23	Ilī'azz Yaluṭ	*Sha'r^{um} Awtar*		Nāṣir^{um} Yuhaḥmid (R)
		Laḥay'athat Yarkham	*Li'azz^{um} Yuhanif Y.*	
		*Fāri'^{um} Yanhub	*Shammir Yuhaḥmid*	
		Ilīsharaḥ Yaḥḍub II *Ya'zil Bayān*		
253	Yada''īl Bayān Ilīriyām Yadūm		*Karib'īl Ayfa'*	
		Nasha'karib Yuha'min Y.		
272-3			*Yāsir^{um} Yuhan'im*	
			Shammir Yuhar'ish	

Sabaean and Himyarite kings:
— in italics, kings bearing the title 'King of Saba' and of dhû-Raydân'
— with an asterix, kings bearing the title 'King of Saba',
— in brackets, members of the royal family.

Qayls:
— of Ma^{c}âfir^{um}: M
— of Radmân: R.

NOTES

1. For an exhaustive bibliography of older editions, refer to this work.
2. Walter Raunig, *Die Versuche einer Datierung des Periplus maris Erythraei*, in *Mitteilungen der Anthropologischen Gesellschaft in Wien*, C, 1970, pp. 231-42.
3. Jacqueline Pirenne, *Un problème-clef pour la chronologie de l'Orient: la date du 'Périple de la mer Erythrée'*, in *Journal asiatique*, 1961, 249, pp. 441-59 (communication présentée lors de l'Assemblée générale du 15 juin 1961: see ibid., p. 596).
4. See for example Jacques Ryckmans, *L'apparition du cheval en Arabie ancienne*, in *Jaarbericht van het Vooraziatisch-egyptisch Genootschap 'Ex Oriente Lux'*, 17, 1963 (published in 1964), p. 212; Hermann von Wissmann, *Die Geschichte des Sabäerreichs und der Feldzug des Aelius Gallus*, in *Aufstieg und Niedergang der römischen Welt*, herausgegeben von Hildegard Temporini und Wolfgang Haase, II/9/1, 1976, pp. 308-544, tabl. 22 between pp. 448 and 449; Jean-François Breton, *Shabwa, capitale antique du Hadramawt*, in *Journal asiatique*, 275, 1987, p. 13, etc.
5. See for example *L'Arabie préislamique et son environnement historique et culturel*, Actes du colloque de Strasbourg, 24-7 June 1987, Edited by T. Fahd (Université des Sciences humaines de Strasbourg, Travaux du Centre de recherche sur le Proche-Orient et la Grèce antiques, 10), Leiden (Brill), 1989, index under the term 'Erythrée (Mer)'.
6. Yuzo Shitomi, *On the Date of Composition of the Periplus Maris Erythraei. A Study of the South Arabian Epigraphic Evidence*, in *The Memoirs of the Toyo Bunko*, 34, 1976, pp. 15-45.
7. See Rodinson 1976, p. 218; L.P. Kirwan, *A Pre-Islamic Settlement from al-Yaman on the Tanzanian Coast, in L'Arabie préislamique et son environnement historique et culturel*, op. cit., p. 431; other references in Casson 1989, p. 7, n. 12.
8. See in particular, Christian Robin, *Les inscriptions d'al-Mi*[c]*sâl et la chronologie de l'Arabie méridionale au III*[e] *siècle de l'ère chrétienne*, in *Académie des Inscriptions et Belles-Lettres, Comptes rendus*, 1981, pp. 315-39; Ch. Robin et Muhammad [c]Abd al-Qâdir Bâfaqîh, *Deux nouvelles inscriptions de Radmân datant du II*[e] *siècle de l'ère chrétienne*, in *Raydân*, 4, 1981, pp. 67-90; M. Bâfaqîh, *L'unification du Yémen antique, La lutte entre Saba', Himyar et le Hadramawt du I*[er] *au III*[e] *siècle de l'ère chrétienne* (Bibliothèque de Raydân, 1), Paris (Geuthner), 1990, XII + 469 pp.; Ch. Robin, *Guerre et épidémie dans les royaumes d'Arabie du sud, d'après une inscription datée (IIe siècle de l'ère chrétienne)*, in *Académie des Inscriptions et*

Belles-Lettres, Comptes rendus, 1992, pp. 215-34.

9. *Hmyr^m* in epigraphic South Arabian, the conventional name of the four languages of South Arabia in ancient times, which are related to Arabic and classical Ethiopian. The script has its own alphabet which only notes consonants (29 in number), like many other Semitic scripts. The hypothetical vowels of the South Arabian languages are based on South Arabian words preserved in Arabic, Greek, Latin, Syriac or Ethiopian.
10. Also see J. Pirenne, *Le royaume Sud-Arabe de Qatabân et sa Datation d'après l'archéologie et les Sources Classiques jusqu'au Périple de la Mer Erythrée* (Bibliothèque du Muséon, 48), Louvain (Publications universitaires—Institut orientaliste), 1961, pp. 168 and foll.
11. Makhawân in South Arabian, al-Makhâ in Arabic (Moka written in different ways in the European languages). The Greek Mouza is the transposition of a South Arabian toponym from which we have the Arabic Mawza^c, now the name of the fertile (upriver) valley of al-Makhâ and of its capital.
12. Now Shaykh Sa^cîd; the South Arabian name is perhaps ^cAqan'îl.
13. In South Arabian, dhû-^cAdan^um, now ^cAdan (or Aden).
14. Qânî' in South Arabian, now Bi'r ^cAlî.
15. ^cAbd al-Ghanî ash-Shar^cabî, *Madînat as-Sawâ.* Dirâsa ta'rîkhiyya athariyya, magister of the University of San^câ', 245 pp. typed; Ch. Robin, *Kulayb Yuha'min est-il le Cholaibos du* Périple de la mer Erythrée?, in *Raydân,* 6, 1994, pp. 91-9 and pl. 47 (p. 191).
16. In South Arabian inscriptions, the term dhû-Ma^câfir^um denotes lineage which implies that Kulayb is a lord (probably with the title *qayl*) from the Ma^câfir^um tribe (= Mapharitis).
17. Ch. Robin, *L'Arabie du sud et la date du Périple,* op. cit., pp. 12 and 24-5; *Kulayb Yuha'min,* op. cit.
18. Capital of Hadramawt, now Shabwa.
19. Now Ma'rib.
20. See the works mentioned in n. 8.
21. Now Najrân in Saudi Arabia, very close to the Yemenite frontier.
22. Ch. Robin, *Les inscriptions d'al-Mi^csâl,* op. cit.; *La première intervention abyssine en Arabie méridionale (de 200 à 270 de l'ère chrétienne environ),* in *Proceedings of the Eighth International Conference of Ethiopian Studies,* University of Addis Ababa, 1984, vol. 2, edited by Taddese Beyene, Addis Ababa (Institute of Ethiopian Studies), 1989, pp. 147-62.
23. Marcel-Toussaint Reinaud, *Mémoire sur le commencement et la fin du royaume de la Mésène et de la Kharacène, d'après les témoignages grecs, latins, arabes, persans, indiens et chinois,* in *Journal asiatique,* Cinquième série, tome XVIII, July-December 1861, pp. 161-262 (on the Periplus of the Erythraean Sea, see pp. 225 and foll.).

24. J. Pirenne, *Un problème-clef*, op. cit., p. 450; *Le Royaume Sud-Arabe de Qatabân*, op. cit., pp. 64-5, and fig. VI.
25. Ch. Robin, *Les inscriptions d'al-Mi^{c}sâl*, op. cit., pp. 335-6.
26. The beginning of the Radmânite era is 184 years later than the Himyarite era. An inscription gives the Himyarite equivalent of a Radmânite date (Ch. Robin, *Les inscriptions d'al-Mi^{c}sâl*, op. cit., pp. 323 and foll.; *La première intervention abyssine*, op. cit., p. 148 and nn. 15 and 32). As for the beginning of the Himyarite era, it is possible to establish it approximately on the basis of events such as the persecution of Himyarite Christians and the Himyarito-Abyssinian war which are mentioned in local inscriptions and Oriental (Syriac and Ethiopian) and Byzantine sources. It is either 110 or, with a lesser likelihood, 115 BC.
27. Two other Himyarite kings, Li^{c}azz^{um} Yuhanîf Yuhasdiq and Shammir Yuhahmid ('Shammir dhû-Raydân' in Sabaean inscriptions) must be accommodated between 148 and 179 Radm.
28. During a ceremony in al-^{c}Uqla, near Shabwa, probably on the occasion of his accession, Ilî^{c}azz is accompanied by the ambassadors of the Himyarite King Tha'rân Ya^{c}ûb Yuhan^{c}im (RES 4909 = Ja 923/1). Thus he was already ruling when Himyar^{um} was governed by a king whose reign is anterior to Karib'îl's reign with two successors between them—Li^{c}azz^{um} Yuhanîf Yuhasdiq and Shammir Yuhahmid (see chronological table, fig. 1).
29. See Ir 13 (in J. Ryckmans, *Himyaritica* 3, in *Le Muséon*, LXXXVII, 1974, pp. 247-56). The capture of Ilî^{c}azz Yalut by Sha^{c}r^{um} Awtar takes place well before 179 Radm. The following events are recorded on the Sabaean side between his capture and 179:
    1. The reign of Lahay^{c}athat Yarkham;
    2. The co-regency of Fâri^{cum} Yanhub and his sons Ilîsharah Yahdub and Ya'zil Bayân;
    3. The beginning of the co-regency of Ilîsharah and Ya'zil (with all the wars between these two kings and the Himyarite king, Shammir Yuhahmid). On the Himyarite side there are two reigns (Li^{c}azz^{um} Yuhanîf Yuhasdiq and Shammir Yuhahmid). The capture of Ilî^{c}azz may thus be situated around 155-65 Radm. (around AD 229-40).
30. Ch. Robin, *La première intervention abyssine*, op.cit.
31. Text cited in Ch. Robin, ibid., p. 151.
32. Ibid.
33. See Ch. Robin, *Les inscriptions d'al-Mi^{c}sâl*, op. cit., p. 326.
34. Text cited in Ch. Robin, *La première intervention abyssine*, op. cit., p. 151.

35. Ibid., pp. 153 and 154.
36. Ibid., p. 154.
37. See also Ch. Robin, *ʿAmdân Bayyin Yuhaqbid,* in *Etudes sud-arabes, Recueil offert à Jacques Ryckmans* (Publications de l'Institut orientaliste de Louvain, 39), Louvain-la-Neuve (Université catholique de Louvain, Institut orientaliste), 1991, pp. 167-205. To be more precise, these dates are based:
    1. on the succession of the kings of Saba' and dhû-Raydân as well on that of the qayls of Radmân-and-Khawlân, which provide a relative chronology.
    2. on the number of generations, a number which is approximate because of the adoptions and the breaks in the genealogy.
    3. on two absolute dates. The earliest, 72 Radm. = AD 146-7 is given by the dated inscription MAFRAY-Sâriᶜ 6 (Ch. Robin and M. Bâfaqîh, *Deux nouvelles inscriptions of Radmân,* op. cit.). The second is based on conjecture: the beginning of the Radmânite era (AD 74) apparently corresponds with the establishment of the principality 'Radmân-and-Khawlân'.
38. J. Pirenne, *The Incense Port of Moscha (Khor Rori) in Dhofar,* in *The Journal of Oman Studies,* 1, 1975, p. 91.
39. A.F.L. Beeston, *The Settlement at Khor Rori,* in *The Journal of Oman Studies,* 2, 1976, p. 39.
40. Another indication, the name of the father of Ilîᶜazz, does not yield better results. If his father, named Yadaᶜ'îl, could be identified with the king who fought Karib'îl Bayân (Ja 643), it would permit us to date Ilîᶜazz after 80-90. However, not only are we unaware of all the Hadramite kings of this period, we also do not know in which order they succeeded each other. Finally, the name Yadaᶜ'îl is extremely common (see chronological table, fig. 2). This hypothesis should not be taken into account until we have more reliable proof.
41. For example in H. von Wissmann, *Die Geschichte des Sabäerreichs,* op. cit., tabl. 23 and 24, pp. 445 and 447.

The *Periplus* and the Political History of India

GERARD FUSSMAN

Christian Robin ends his article on a dissatisfied note: 'Evidence concerning South Arabia does not run counter to a date [of the *Periplus of the Erythraean Sea*] in the first century AD, but is too imprecise to permit the establishment of this date incontestably.' I am of the opinion that the date actually suggested by Indian chronology is about AD 40. However, my views are based on a very recent discovery (1980) and I can well understand Christian Robin's desire not to enter into an old debate, elements of which in any case are today outdated and which requires knowledge of difficult numismatic sequences and a comparison of Sanskrit and Middle Indian inscriptions. Under these circumstances, I think it was judicious to avoid choosing between conflicting theories, although this means not accepting unreservedly Lionel Casson's assertion, backed by recent references, that the political situation in north-west India, as described in the *Periplus*, should be dated between AD 20 and 50.[1] But before discussing the conclusions drawn from recent discoveries, it would perhaps be in order to briefly outline, for those who do not specialize in India, the nature and outcome of work carried out before 1980.

Reference to most of these texts, often accompanied by a useful commentary, can be found in Raschke (1978). Apart from some recent exceptions,[2] the general trend has been not to rely on Indian chronology for fixing the date of the *Periplus*. For the chronology of ancient India has been entirely reconstructed from external synchronisms of which the *Periplus* offers several examples and which no historian working on

India can afford to ignore. Accordingly, it is the generally accepted date of the *Periplus* which is used to ascertain the political chronology of India and not the other way round.

The arguments given are, by force of circumstance, extremely weak. For want of conclusive evidence, one has no choice but to consider any hypothesis as verified or acceptable if all or most of the otherwise known facts fit in with it. Now this has never been the case: every new combatant to enter the fray has promptly demolished the conclusions of his predecessors and suggested new hypotheses which necessarily have become subject to the same kind of criticism. What then are the arguments for dating the *Periplus* after AD 78? We can divide them into two categories. The passage most frequently referred to is *Periplus* 41, 1-3: 'Immediately after the gulf of Barakê is the gulf of Barygaza and the coast of the region of Ariakê, the beginning both of Manbanos's realm and of all of India.'[3] The main line of thinking consists in identifying Manbanos with an Indian sovereign of the region, Nahapâna, and equating year 1 of the era used by this sovereign with the Śaka era (AD 78) still used today; this era is sometimes considered to be an independent era, which may or may not have been founded by Nahapâna and is earlier than year 1 of Kaniṣka,[4] sometimes thought to be identical to the Kaniṣka era. But the synchronisms used in such demonstrations (Nasik inscriptions) are highly debatable; Manfred Raschke went as far as writing: 'The attribution of the Nasik inscriptions of Nahapâna to the Śaka era is thus mathematically impossible and the entire period of his reign must be placed in the first century of our era.'[5]

Moreover, there is nothing to justify the assertion that Greek Manbanos is a faithful transcription of the Indian Nahapâna, even if appearances are in favour of such an identification, as first suggested by that excellent epigraphist, Abbé A.M. Boyer. Boyer has pointed out that Manbanos (which he read as Nambanos) transcribed Nahapâna, just as the Greek *Dakhinabádēs* transcribes the Sanskrit *dakṣiṇāpatha* or the Greek *Maïs* the Sanskrit *mahī*.[6] The differences arise from the fact that Greek transcriptions provide us with forms in which consonant clusters taken from Sanskrit are simplified (*kṣ* > *kh*), intervocalic voiceless occlusives are voiced (*p* > *b*; *th* > *d*) and aspirated sounds either disappear or are not noted. As for the 'superfluous' nasalization of long vowels (*Nahapāna* > *Naabāna* > *Nābāna* > *Nambanos*), this is such a characteristic feature of Indian languages that it is often not written down. All this is true and can be stated in the following way today: the Indian names mentioned in the *Periplus of the Erythraean Sea* are not transcriptions of Sanskrit terms, which are far too archaic for that period, but rather of words belonging to a later stage of linguistic development, namely the Middle Indian period when Sanskrit consonant clusters were simplified, intervocalic voiceless occlusives were voiced and the old voiced occlusives were more often than not dropped.[7] Now unlike *dakṣiṇāpatha* or *mahī*, Nahapâna is not a Sanskrit form. It is a Middle Indian form—whose etymology is not known—as we can see from the monetary legends *raño kṣaharatasa nahapānasa* for the Sanskrit *rajñāḥ ... sya*, and could even be a name of non-Indian origin.[8] The name was thus actually pronounced as Nahapâna and it is this form or a form close to it (*Nāpāna, *Nāmpāna) which we ought to find in the *Periplus*, provided of course the king in question was really Nahapâna. Thus we cannot speak of any philological equation between Manbanos and Nahapâna.[9] In any case Raschke is quite right to emphasize that 'If one chooses to identify the two names, then the *Periplus* provides a date for Nahapâna/Manbanos, not the reverse.'[10]

The second line of argument, more recent, is to combine *Periplus* 38 and *Periplus* 47, to which I will refer later on, and to see in it a description of north-west India before its conquest by the Kushans, that is to say before the reign or the end of the reign of Wima Kadphises.[11] The relative chronology obtained in this way, which eventually came to be considered a firm chronology, depended until 1980 on the opinion one held about the date of Kaniṣka, Wima Kadphises' successor. MacDowall and Wilson opted for and still stand by a date that puts year 1 of Kaniṣka about AD 100-120, thereby making it possible (though not obligatory) to fix the date of *Periplus* after AD 78. But, in my opinion, it is just as plausible to say that year 1 of Kaniṣka corresponds to AD 78 (Fussman 1980, 36-42; Fussman 1987, 338), which implies that the *Periplus* describes the situation found several years before this date. I do none the less accept that the equating of year 1 of Kaniṣka with AD 78 has yet to be proved formally. We would thus do well to discard this argument, something we can now afford to do (*infra*). Whatever the case, one thing is certain: all the Indian evidence goes completely against dating the *Periplus* at around 225-30.[12] That is why the date suggested by Madame Pirenne has not, to use Ch. Robin's phrase, 'gradually met with the approval of most Indologists, historians or archaeologists'.

Let us now turn to the positive evidence. *Periplus* 38, 1-3 tells us: 'The metropolis of Skythia (Sind)... is Minnagar. The throne is in the hands of Parthians, who are constantly chasing each other off it.' *Periplus* 47, 3-6 adds that, 'Inland behind Barygaza there are numerous peoples: the Aratrioi, Arachusioi, Gandaraioi, and the peoples of Proklais, in whose area Bukephalos Alexandreia is located. And beyond these there is a very warlike people, the Bactrians, under a king....'[13] These data, already used by MacDowall-Wilson (1970), portray a North India deeply divided between Aratrioi (in Punjab?), Arachosioi (Kandahar region), Gandaraioi (Peshawar region and perhaps that of Taxila/Islamabad), inhabitants of Proklais—which despite all the etymologies proffered, can only be the lower course of the Jhelam since Bukephalos Alexandreia is located there and the Sind, under quickly succeeding Parthian sovereigns. In the north, we find the Bactrians, united under a king; their bellicose reputation indicates that they were considered a threat to north-west India. It is easy for the modern historian to interpret these data. The Bactrians, who were certainly not Greek and who had yet to conquer Arachosia and Gandhara (the status of the Kabul and Jalalabad regions is unclear) were necessarily, in this context, the Kushans from Bactria, united for the first time under the king known as Sôter Megas/Kujula Kadphises, if both refer to the same person, or under Kujula Kadphises, if Sôter Megas is thought to be later than Kujula Kadphises.[14] Scythia, that is Sind, or, to be more accurate, the right bank of the Sind close to Iran and Arachosia, was ruled by the petty Parthian kings. All this is in agreement with the evidence provided by numismatic sequences and finds according to which so many rulers—the last Indo-Greek kings, Indo-Scythians of the Azes lineage, Indo-Parthians, the most famous and powerful of whom was Gondophernes, Kṣatrapa Śakas, like Rajuvala and Śoḍāsa, local chiefs of Indian or Iranian origin—fought over Gandhara and the Punjab before the conquest and unification of these territories by the Bactrian Kushans. The discovery of the Apraca inscriptions in 1978-80[15] established that the 58/57 BC Vikrama era was founded by Azes I (or was the continuation of his ruling years). Interestingly this enabled us to ascertain the entire chronology of north-west India without having to refer to the various theories on the date of Kaniṣka. Consulting the table I published in 1980[16]—on which there is more or less general agreement today—is sufficient to show that between AD 20 and 50, Taxila was ruled by Jihoṇika/Zeionises, then alternatively or successively by the Kushan Kujula Kadphises, the Parthian Gondophernes, by Sasa, by Abdagases and finally by Wima Kadphises. This is without mentioning all the minor rulers who left no trace behind or whose trace has yet to be identified or without excluding the fluctuating fortunes which could preclude the possibility of Taxila having been *continuously* in the hands of Gondophernes between AD 20-46. The Kushan conquest of north India, begun in AD 20-30 by Kujula Kadphises, ended around AD 50: Wima's coinage was used from Sind to Mathura, but had not reached coastal Bengal.

Thus the political situation of north India, as described in the *Periplus*, reflects the conditions prevalent between AD 30 and 50. Even if we allow for the fact that the author of the *Periplus* did not go up the Indus and his knowledge was acquired by hearsay, meaning several years later, it seems unlikely that he could have gathered his information after AD 50. This is the *terminus ante quem*, give or take a few years, for the date of the composition of his text.

NOTES

1. Casson 1989, 189.
2. MacDowall 1964; Sircar 1966.
3. Casson 1989, 77.
4. Ancient examples summarized in Sudhakar Chattopadhyaya, *The Śakas in India*, Santiniketan, 1955, p. 41. Chattopadhyaya himself places year 1 of Nahapâna at about AD 71 (p. 47). More recently MacDowall-Wilson 1970, pp. 238-40, considers that the *Periplus* was written between AD 98-106. B.N. Mukherjee, *The Kushāṇas and the Deccan, I, Kanishka I and the Deccan*, Calcutta, 1968, pp. 101-9 and 123-7, acknowledges the identification of

Nahapâna with Manbanos, but puts the beginning of his rule between AD 48-50. Sircar 1966 is one of the few authors to reject such an identification.

5. Raschke 1978, p. 754 n. 475. It is true that Raschke adopts for the *Periplus* a date around AD 70 (pp. 663-9), using it as an argument on occasions.
6. Boyer 1897, p. 131.
7. Bloch 1911. On these problems of transcriptions, see also G. Fussman, *Gāndhārī écrite, gāndhārī parlée*, in *Dialectes dans les littératures indo-aryennes*, edited by Colette Caillat, Publications de l'Institut de Civilisation Indienne du Collège de France, fasc. 55, Paris, pp. 433-501.
8. Bloch 1911, 4/41, quoting F.W. Thomas, *Sakastana, Where dwelt the Śakas named by Darius and Herodotus*, in *JRAS*, pp. 181-220 (211), who goes further, suggesting an Iranian origin which to my mind seems just as dubious.
9. Bloch 1911, 4/41 followed by Raschke 1978, p. 755 n. 477.
10. Raschke 1978, p. 632.
11. MacDowall, Wilson 1970. The details of the article call for serious reservations. The insertion of the name Heraos and the word 'Kushan' in the text of the *Periplus* implies a correction both philologically and historically impossible (Fussman 1974, p. 48 n. 1). Moreover it is in contradiction with the identification suggested in the same article (pp. 230-1) of *kaltis* in *Periplus* 63 with the gold coins introduced by Wima Kadphises. Even this identification is improbable as the *Periplus* implies that this is a coinage specific to the Ganges delta, where in any case Wima never ruled. I do not quite know how to interpret the extremely technical *Periplus* 49, 23-4: 'In this port of trade there is a market for: ... Roman money, gold and silver, which commands an exchange at some profit against local currency.' Unlike that which constitutes the basis of MacDowall-Wilson's reasoning (pp. 234-6), it cannot be a question of manipulating exchange rates as there were no coins of indigenous gold in this region. Perhaps what is meant is that there was simply a great demand for this precious metal of foreign origin and that the state bought it there at a price higher than anywhere else.
12. MacDowall 1964; Sircar 1966.
13. Casson, pp. 75 and 81.
14. For this tricky question, see Fussman 1974, pp. 47-8.
15. A.D.H. Bivar, *The Azes Era and the Indravarma Casket*, in *South Asian Archaeology 1979*, Berlin, 1981, pp. 369-76; and Fussman, 1980, both independent works.
16. Fussman 1980, p. 43.

On the Name of the *Hipalus* (*Hippalus*) Wind in Pliny

SANTO MAZZARINO

The evidence we possess about the routes which had begun to be opened up between Arabia and India during the Hellenistic and Roman periods includes not least the well-known passage of Pliny (*N.H.* VI, 100, p. 472, 15-18 M. = p. 53, 11-13 A.).[1] In this passage Pliny mentions what he claims to have been the first (in chronological order) of the various sea routes connecting Arabia to India: *ab Syagro Arabiae promunturio* it led to Patale(-a). On the reading of this passage there is now general agreement among scholars: *postea ab Syagro Arabiae promunturio Patalen fauonio, quem hip<p>alum ibi uocant, peti certissimum uidebatur*[*] (after which the *aestimatio* of the distance from *Syagrum promunturium* to Patale, calculated as 1332 miles, is given). However, it seems to me that this current reading should be subjected to discussion and revision as regards *hip<p>alum*. The manuscript tradition presupposes an original reading *hipalum* or, more probably, *hypalum*: and this reading *hypalum*, without the double *-p-*, is in my view to be preferred.

To illustrate this point (the original reading *hypalum* or *hipalum* as implied by the Plinian manuscript tradition in VI, 100), a particular circumstance should be considered: none of the variant readings in the manuscript tradition (for which the reader is referred to the apparatus criticus in the editions by Detlefsen, Mayhoff and André) retains the double *-p-* (*pp*), found in the common reading *hip<p>alum*. This absence is not without significance. In fact, in nouns connected with ἵππος (or which may be assimilated to ἵππος in the linguistic consciousness), the Plinian manuscript tradition (either as a whole, or in part) generally retains the double *-p-* (*pp*). I quote the following examples, where *-pp-* is in fact retained: in some cases we find other kinds of corruption, but never involving the double *-p-* (haplography of *-p-* in one or more of the codices, in contrast to others, is indicated; page-numbers refer to M.; the codices' siglae are also adopted from M. Double *-p-* will be highlighted in Roman type).

*Hi*pp*onax* et sim.: XXXVI, 12, p. 310, 8 and 5;

*Hi*pp*ocrates*: XVIII, 75, p. 163, 9; XX, 230, p. 367, 20; XXII, 34, p. 450, 15; XXII, 136, p. 482, 19 and p. 482, 20 (-21);

*Hi*pp*ys*: XXXV, 141, p. 281, 14 (*-pp-* is retained in *hyppus* of **B**, and in *hyppis* of **d**; in the r., haplography of *p*, with corruption in *hypis*; *iphis*, v.);

*Hi*pp*archum*: XXXV, 200, p. 305, 14 (thus the excellent **B**, as well as v.; in the r., corruption which substitutes, as regards *-pp-*, double *-p-* with double *-l-*);

*hi*pp*os*, *hi*pp*uros*, - *hi*pp*ocampos*: XXXII, 149, p.100, 13 (*hippus* and *hyppus*, partially corrupt forms for *hippos*, however retain *-pp-*);

*hi*pp*ocampi* et sim.: XXXII, 58, p. 68, 17; XXXII, 67, p. 71, 16 (but **V** has a corrupt form with haplography); XXXII, 83, p. 77, 17; XXXII, 93, p. 81, 2; XXXII, 109, p. 86, 7; XXXII, 113, p. 87, 17; XXXII, 139, p. 96, 13; XXXVI, 26, p. 315, 8 (but **V** and **R** have haplography); for XXXII, 149, see *supra*;

*hi*pp*opotamius* et sim.: VI, 173, p. 501, 21-22; VIII, 95, p. 110, 13 (*-pp-* in all codices *siglis notati* with the exception of **a**); XI, 160, p. 334, 9 (again with the exception of **a**); XXVIII, 121, p. 316, 11 (with the exception of **x**);

*hi*pp*olapathum* et sim.: XX, 231, p. 368, 14; XX, 232, p. 369,1;

*hi*pp*omarathum* et sim.: XX, 255, p. 376, 8-9 and p. 376, 11; XX, 258, p. 377, 12 and p. 378, 1; XXI, 54, p. 398, 10;

*hi*pp*ophaes*: XXI, 91, p. 410, 15; XXII, 29, p. 449, 1 (on p. 449, 5, among the four codices siglis notati, three have corrupt forms yet retain *-pp-*; in one, **R**, the word is completely deformed, reduced to *hae*).

The examples I have cited seem, therefore, to confirm that, despite all the different corrupt forms and variants, the manuscript tradition of Pliny tends for the most part to retain the double letter in nouns beginning with *Hipp-* (*hipp-*). As I mentioned earlier, this does not occur in the case of the noun in VI, 100 indicating the name given to the West wind (*fauonius*) in the region of the *Syagrum promunturium*[2], such a name being invariably spelt in the manuscripts with a single *-p-*. Once again readers are referred to the apparatus criticus (in M., cfr. also p. 525, 8-9): particularly worthy of note are *hipalum* **E**^{s} and **g**; *hypilum* **Fa**; *ipilum* **R**; *pypylum* **D** (where the first *p* derives from a misreading of an original *h*, most possible in the course of transcription); *hypalum* r.; *hipalum* v.a.H. It goes without saying that the interchange between *y* and *i* is quite common in the manuscripts: thus *hipalum* in **E**^{s} and **g** may simply be considered as *hypalum* written from dictation, or at any rate misunderstood, since *y* could have been heard as *ü*, and written down as *i* by an inadvertent listener or copyist. As for the second *i*, found in **FaR** (*y* in **D**) , it is a corruption deriving from assimilation with the first vowel.

The absence of double *-p-* in the manuscript tradition of this passage must in itself lead us to have strong doubts about the standard reading *hip<p>alum*. How is the total absence within the tradition of any trace of double *-p-* in the reading *hypalum*, which has however left evident traces in the above-cited examples of nouns beginning with *hipp-*, to be explained?

Moreover, while the manuscript tradition of this passage by itself gives no support to the emendation *Hip<p>alum*, all the evidence suggests instead that we should retain *hypalum*, which is not only in the r. but is obviously implied by *hipalum* in **E**^{s} and **g**. We say 'all the evidence' because it is precisely the reading *hypalum* which is best suited to name a wind which - to borrow an expression used by Pliny himself (II, 128) in describing a totally different wind - *ex imo mari spirat* [**]. (So that the ship - to adopt in this case an expression of Joseph Conrad, which takes us back to voyages directed according to the monsoon - seems to be emerging from the steady and constant breeze of the monsoon). In the case of Pl. *N.H.* VI, 100, the West monsoon wind, which moves towards N/E from Syagrus to Patale, could indeed have been considered a "non-apogeus" wind, just as the other monsoon, blowing from N/E to S/W, was considered to be apogeus, i.e. blowing from the land, as the historians of Alexander the Great had rightly remarked

(Nearchus FGrHist 133 F 18; Aristob. FGrHist 139 F 35. Cf. Strabo 692_{17}: ἀπογαίας δὲ μηδεμιᾶς πνοῆς ἐκδεξαμένης***). In short, the monsoon wind which blew on the route from Syagrus to Patale could be defined as ἄνεμος (or πνοή or αὖρα) ὕφαλος, "(under-) sea wind"; and the pronunciation of ὕφαλος must in origin have sounded like *hupalos* or *hüpalos* (proparoxytone), on account of the normal interchange between *ph* and *p* (in other words, of the rendering of -φ- with -p-)[3].

My reading *hypalum* in Pl. *N.H.* VI, 100 raises a problem in the interpretation of Pliny. If we are to read *hypalum* in Pl. *N.H.* VI, 100, how then should we read the name of the same wind in VI, 104, p. 474, 8 M. = p. 55, 11 A.? In this passage the main variants are: *hipallo* **E**^{s}; *yppalo* **a**; *hypa-* vel *hipa-* v.a.H. The current reading is *hippalo*; and this is the reading which I also believe should be adopted. The fact that *-pp-* is retained in the Vienna codex **a** is to a certain extent in itself a guarantee that in VI, 104 the name of the wind was indicated by the noun *hippalus*, with double *-p-*: as we have seen through the examples given above, the tradition (either all, or, as in this case, in part) retains the double *-p-* in other nouns which may be connected with *hipp-*. In short, the reading *hippalo* in Pl. *N.H.* VI, 104 is supported by the manuscript tradition (albeit only in part), just as the very different reading *hypalum* is supported in Pl. *N.H.* VI, 100; and it would be a mistake to read *hypalo* instead of *hippalo* in VI, 104. Similarly, in *N.H.* VI, 100, it is a mistake to read *hip<p>alum* instead of *hypalum.* In both cases Pliny accurately transcribed the name he had obtained from his sources: in the first case it referred to a date almost four centuries before his time, whereas in the second case it was a contemporary reference. That is to say, in VI, 100 Pliny wrote *hypalum,* just as he read it in Nearchus or Onesicritus, or else in Iuba, who derived from them: these sources were referring, in this regard, to the early Hellenistic period; in VI, 104, by contrast, Pliny wrote *hippalo* in a context obtained from an entirely new, personal source of information, as he himself says in VI, 105 (*quae omnia gentium portuumue aut oppidorum nomina apud neminem priorum reperiuntur, quo apparet mutari locorum status* ****); and naturally Pliny's fidelity to his sources would apply to such new information as well, not excluding even such an almost negligible detail as the difference between the name given to the south-western monsoon during the early Hellenistic age and the one in use during the Roman period: *hyphalum* and *hippalo*, respectively.

We need to insist upon *apud neminem priorum reperiuntur*. We must also abandon the old, conventional and superficial misunderstandings of how Pliny worked.

Pliny was a scholar who based his work on written sources (*auctores*) - but also on direct information. The fact that the information from which VI, 104-105 is drawn is entirely new, is already evident from the toponym *Oceli* in VI, 104, which immediately precedes the reference to the *hippalus* wind: indeed, this toponym *Oceli* confirms that Pliny in such cases transcribes faithfully (which, from his point of view, means exactly) the different bits of information he has variously acquired without trying to reconcile them. In fact, the harbour which he calls *Ocelis* in VI, 104 is the very same as that which he calls *Acila* in VI, 151, and which he will subsequently call *Ocilia* in XII, 88 (in an extremely interesting passage, upon which attention should be focused: *hi recto cursu per sinus inpellunt, atque a promunturii ambitu argestae deferunt in portum Gebbanitarum qui uocatur Ocilia. Quam ob rem illi maxime id petunt, produntque uix quinto anno reuerti negotiatores et multos interire* *****).

The notion of an "under-sea" wind, *hyphalos*, attributed to the monsoon a characteristic which can be illustrated through yet another expression used by Pliny, this great mariner who was also a great scientist: describing the sea's relationship with the winds he says: *intra se esse uentos fatetur* (XVIII, 359)****** . (That Pliny was commander of the Roman fleet is too often forgotten.)

Such a combined scientist and admiral could not have failed to understand the nature and the development, variously characterized in its various stages, of the maritime relationship between India and the West. (Also in its economic repercussions: cf. De Romanis' remarks on *lucroque India admota est*[4].) Pliny was perhaps unaware of (or, more probably, did not believe) the tradition adopted by the *PME*, according to which a seafarer called *Hippalos* had discovered the monsoon. This tradition, which had no doubt originated among Egyptian sailors (who must have known that the name Hippalos appeared,

e. g., in the Ptolemaic prosopography, and were spontaneously led to link it with the history of trade between India and the West), was already doubted, rightly so, by several modern scholars; and must certainly be rejected. If Hippalos the "discoverer" of the monsoon really were an historical figure, it would be difficult to understand how Posidonius could have regarded Eudoxus of Cyzicus as the person who, following the directions of an unnamed Indian, had traced and pointed out the "monsoonal" route to India. Posidonius' account of Eudoxus of Cyzicus (FGrHist 87 F 28 = F 49 E.-K. = F 13 Th. Cf. Strabo 98-102) shows, in other words, that he was unacquainted with the tradition of Hippalos the "discoverer" of the monsoon, or alternatively that he knew of it but denied its historicity. In either case we have an extremely important argument for repudiating the historicity of the account about Hippalos in the *PME*[5].

Posidonius, moreover, was extremely interested in the etymology and the explanation of the names (προσηγορίαι) of the winds - as the Stoá had generally been long before him. The etymological derivation of the Greek name for the south-westerly monsoon wind from the name of a κυβερνήτης Hippalos could not fail to draw his attention; the fact that he mentions Eudoxus, and not Hippalos is conclusive evidence that such a derivation is at the very least questionable, and indeed must be rejected.

To sum up: the original προσηγορία of the south-westerly monsoon wind as indicated by Plin. *N.H.* VI, 100, was ὕπαλος (scil. αὔρα, or πνοή or ἄνεμος), "(under-)sea wind": it was retained by Pliny in that passage and understood by him exactly as a scholar and an admiral of genius would.

NOTES

1. Hereafter M. refers to the edition by Mayhoff (1906). In the edition by Detlefsen (1904) the passage is on p. 150, ll. 20-21. The most recent edition (1980) is the one by J. André (-J. Filliozat), hereafter cited as A.: here the passage in question is on p. 53, ll. 11-13.

"Later on it seemed safest to head for Patale from the Arabian promontory of Syagrus, profiting by the West wind (*fauonius*), which in that place they call *hi<p>palus*".

2. *Ibi* in VI, 100, p. 472, 17 M. = p. 53, 12 A. obviously refers to *Syagro* (*Siagro* codd.), rather than to *Patalen.*
   ** "Blows in from the sea's depths".
   *** "As no wind from the land turned up".
3. Cf. e. g. E. Schwyzer, *Griechische Grammatik*, I, München 1934, p. 204. The interchange is well known in the case of Latin renderings in which normally, before the last century of the Republic, Greek aspirates used to be transcribed as unvoiced stops. Yet it was also possible in the Near- and Middle East area (cf. e.g., Schwyzer, p. 154). In the case we are concerned with, we may think of ὕπαλος as a Greek term circulating in its Hadramût pronunciation (more precisely in the pronunciation of the *Syagrum promunturium*, if, as I have already mentioned above, n. 2, Pliny's *ibi* refers to *Syagrum promunturium*). Anyway, even if *ibi* were to refer to Patale, the rendering of -f- with -p- creates no difficulties.
   **** "And all these names of peoples, harbours or towns are found in none of the earlier authors, which shows that places change their status".
   ***** "They (the East Winds, *euri*) drive (the rafts on which the Trogodytae carry the precious 'cinnamon') straight across the gulfs, then the South-West Winds (*argestae*) push them back from the promontory's curve into the harbour of the Gebbanitae, which is called Ocilia. For this reason they (the Gebbanitae) most eagerly seek after it ('cinnamon') and relate that its merchants may not be back for as long as four years and that many of them meet their death (on the journey)".
   ****** "It (the sea) reveals that winds lie within itself".
4. Cf. F. De Romanis, *Rome and the* Nótia *of India*, included in the present volume, pp. 80-160. The information that my former pupil has deduced from Tamil texts on Roman trade relations with India are also important.
5. In fact, if the first hypothesis is correct (that Posidonius had no information about a κυβερνήτης Hippalos as "discoverer" of the monsoon), it follows that the tradition about Hippalos as the "discoverer" of the monsoonal route is either later than Posidonius, or otherwise gained currency after Posidonius. If the second hypothesis is correct (that Posidonius was acquainted with the tradition about Hippalos as the "discoverer" of the monsoon, but denied the historicity of such a tradition), then we must attach the greatest importance to Posidonius' denial. He wrote, in fact, around the second decade of the first century BC, approximately one generation after the Indian adventure of

of Eudoxus of Cyzicus - and possessed all the data needed to establish whether there had been, prior to Eudoxus, a discovery of the monsoonal route by a κυβερνήτης Hippalos. The first hypothesis, as I have already mentioned, is to be preferred. In the account of Eudoxus by Posidonius there may be an element of fiction (the ἀπίθανον alluded to by Strabo), but as far as Eudoxus' journey to India is concerned, it is undoubtedly true.

Rome and the *Nótia* of India: Relations between Rome and Southern India from 30 BC to the Flavian Period

FEDERICO DE ROMANIS

Peregrinandum est in historias et litteras orbis
(Tert. *Apol.* 19, 7)

INTRODUCTION

The aim of this paper is to investigate trade relations between the Roman empire and the southern region of the Indian subcontinent during the Julio-Claudian and Flavian periods.

Applying the method introduced by S. Mazzarino in his *Fra Oriente e Occidente* in 1947 to another field of research, the question will be tackled through the reading and interpretation of an imaginary bilingual inscription, showing on one side the Greek and Latin sources, and on the other the Indian ones (Tamil, Prakrit and Sanskrit).

The sources we will consider will thus comprise, on the one hand, the classical geographical literature of the early imperial period (Strabo, *Periplus Maris Erythraei,*[1] Pliny and Ptolemy) and the relevant Greek and Latin inscriptions, and, on the other, the ancient Tamil literary monuments (the *Tolkāppiyam*, the two 'superanthologies' of the *Caṅkam Ilakkiyam* (*Eṭṭuttokai* and *Pattuppāṭṭu*), the *Cilappatikaram*, the *Maṇimēkalai*), the Buddhist chronicles of Ceylon (*Dīpavaṁsa* and *Mahāvaṁsa*) together with inscriptions in Tamil and Prakrit.

Unfortunately our imaginary 'inscription' is not without lacunae and interpretational difficulties. But it does succeed in providing the historian, who is often hampered by even greater limitations, with a valuable framework of reference.

Passages containing Tamil poetry will be transcribed according to the system adopted by K.V. Zvelebil, *Tamil Literature*, Wiesbaden 1974, which is as follows:

a	= அ		ō	= ஓ		p	= ப்
ā	= ஆ		au	= ஔ		m	= ம்
i	= இ		k	= க்		y	= ய்
ī	= ஈ		ṅ	= ங்		r	= ர்
u	= உ		c	= ச்		l	= ல்
ū	= ஊ		ñ	= ஞ்		v	= வ்
e	= எ		ṭ	= ட்		ḻ	= ழ்
ē	= ஏ		ṇ	= ண்		ḷ	= ள்
ai	= ஐ		t	= த்		ṟ	= ற்
o	= ஒ		n	= ந்		ṉ	= ன்

In the quotations of classical Greek and Latin texts the apparatus has been added only where it appeared necessary or appropriate to do so.

When quoting Tamil or Prakrit inscriptions the criteria adopted are those of the editors cited from time to time.

THE AUGUSTAN AGE AND TRADE RELATIONS BETWEEN INDIA AND THE GRAECO-ROMAN WORLD

In the preface to his fundamental study *The Commerce between Roman Empire and India*, E.H. Warmington wrote that he willingly risked 'the imputation that in this book on one aspect of ancient commerce, *I* have given a description of which the beginning and the end are absent'.[2]

Further research has shed light on the Ptolemaic[3] and the even earlier Achaemenid precedents[4] to seaborne trade with India. So such an imputation could hardly be incurred by scholars today; the hypotheses of those who believed that it was only under Augustus, or worse still, under Claudius, that a supposedly 'full discovery' of the monsoon took place, are being increasingly discredited.[5]

Nevertheless, if we return to a 'Roman' approach to the issue, in other words if we again consider the Augustan age to be a fundamental stage in the history of commercial exchanges between India and the West, such an approach is then justified not because this period was marked by new discoveries in terms of how the monsoon could be exploited, but simply because the new state which had come about as a result of the battle of Actium was able to seize and exploit in an unprecedented manner the commercial opportunities offered by the monsoonal routes to India. The far-reaching consequences this had on the customs, social relations, and economy of the Roman world during the Julio-Claudian period made the ancients themselves conscious of the importance of the end of Actian War for the development of trade between India and the Roman empire.

It will be sufficient here to quote the testimony of Fenestella and Tacitus.

Romae in promiscuum ac frequentem usum uenisse (sc. *margaritas) Alexandria in dicionem redacta, primum autem coepisse circa Sullana tempora minutas et uiles Fenestella tradit, manifesto errore, cum Aelius Stilo* (=GRF Ael. Stil. F 43) *circa Iugurthinum bellum unionum nomen inponi cum maxime grandibus margaritis prodat.* [Plin. *N.H.* IX, 123 (=HRR II Fenest. F. 14)]

Fenestella records that they [se. pearls] came into common use at Rome after the reduction of Alexandria under our sway, but that small and cheap pearls first came in about the period of Sulla—which is clearly a mistake, as Aelius Stilo states that the distinctive name (*unio*) was given to large pearls just at the time of the wars of Jugurtha.

[...] *luxusque mensae a fine Actiaci belli ad ea arma, quis Seruius Galba rerum adeptus est per annos centum profusis sumptibus exerciti paulatim exoleuere.* (Tac. *Ann.* II, 55)

[...] and spendthrift table luxuries, after being practised with prodigality throughout the century between the close of the Actian War and the struggle which placed Servius Galba on the throne, went gradually out of vogue.

In the reflection of these two ancient Roman historians, the end of the war against Cleopatra's Egypt marked the beginning of a revolution in customs in Rome. This was identified by Fenestella[6] in a more widespread use of pearls, and by Tacitus in the *luxus mensae* : two aspects inseparably linked, as we shall see, to the seaborne trade with India.

It is worth briefly considering the connection established between the end of the Actian War and the change in Roman customs. Following the conquest of Egypt, an enormous quantity of precious metal reached Rome,[7] and this undoubtedly encouraged the pursuit of a more luxurious life-style. Moreover, this new-found taste for luxury led in turn to the rapid discovery of merchandise imported from India.[8] This was further proof—if such were needed—that Ptolemaic Egypt was engaged in regular trade relations with India at the time of the Roman conquest.

What continuity and progress there was in trade with India between Late Ptolemaic and Early Roman periods is clearly shown by the two passages by Strabo quoted below: (Strab. II, 5, 12)

ὅτε γοῦν Γάλλος ἐπῆρχε τῆς Αἰγύπτου συνόντες αὐτῷ καὶ συναναβάντες μέχρι Συήνης καὶ τῶν Αἰθιοπικῶν ὅρων ἱστοροῦμεν ὅτι καὶ ἑκατὸν καὶ εἴκοσι νῆες πλέοιεν ἐκ Μυὸς ὅρμου πρὸς τὴν Ἰνδικὴν, πρότερον ἐπὶ τῶν Πτολεμαϊκῶν βασιλέων ὀλίγων πανταπάσι θαρρούντων πλεῖν καὶ τὸν Ἰνδικὸν ἐμπορεύεσθαι φόρτον.

At any rate, when Gallus was prefect of Egypt, I accompanied him and ascended the Nile as far as Syene and the frontiers of Ethiopia, and I learned that as many as one hundred and twenty vessels were sailing from Myos Hormos to India, whereas formerly, under the Ptolemies, only very few ventured to undertake the voyage and to carry on traffic in Indian merchandise: (Strab. XVII, 1, 13)

πρότερον μέν γε οὐδ' εἴκοσι πλοῖα ἐθάρρει τὸν Ἀράβιον κόλπον διαπερᾶν, ὥστε ἔξω τῶν στενῶν ὑπερκύπτειν, νῦν δὲ καὶ στόλοι μεγάλοι στέλλονται μέχρι τῆς Ἰνδικῆς καὶ τῶν ἄκρων τῶν Αἰθιοπικῶν, ἐξ ὧν ὁ πολυτιμότατος κομίζεται φόρτος εἰς τὴν Αἴγυπτον.

'In earlier times, at least, not so many as twenty vessels would dare to traverse the Arabian Gulf far enough to get a peep outside the straits, but at the present time even large fleets are despatched as far as India and the extremities of Aethiopia, from which the most valuable cargoes are brought to Egypt.'

The first passage refers to 26 BC, the year in which Strabo accompanied Aelius Gallus, then prefect of Egypt,[9] in a voyage up the Nile as far as the frontiers of the kingdom of Meroe.

The Romans therefore found the trade network which the Ptolemies, beginning with Philadelphus, had set up across the 'Red and Indian Sea' to be still in working order.[10] Already under the Ptolemies there were those who dared 'carry on traffic in Indian merchandise': only thus can we understand how the entourage of Augustus immediately grasped the prospect opened up by the possession of ports on the Red Sea.

However, during the years which immediately followed the fall of Alexandria, the Roman conquest determined a decisive change. Galvanized by an unprecedented demand which was favoured by the inflationary process connected with the arrival in Rome of Egyptian treasures, trade with India grew to the extent of making the previous Ptolemaic experience appear almost insignificant,[11] and of turning Egypt into the 'port of India'.[12] Only a few years would elapse before the remarkable presence of Western merchants along India's coasts was to lead several Indian kings to send embassies to Augustus.[13]

Following this new burst in interest, the Indian coasts were explored even as far north as the mouth of the Ganges, as attested by Strabo in a passage often ignored by scholars.[14] But the ports upon which Western merchants mainly focused their interest were those of India's south-western coast, the Limyrike.[15] Why this area was of greater importance than that of other areas of the Indian subcontinent must now be investigated.

THE *COMPENDIA* AND THE LIMYRIKE

The reason for directing our research towards the ports of the Limyrike will immediately transpire from a correct interpretation of the data provided by our two main sources, Pliny and the *Periplus Maris Erythraei* (hereafter *PME*).

Let us begin with the celebrated passage of Pliny, *N.H.* VI, 100-1:

[...] *Sic Alexandri classis nauigauit; postea ab Syagro Arabiae promunturio*

Patalen fauonio, quem hypalum (Mazzarino *hipalum* E'g *hypilum* Fa *ipilum* R *pypylum* D *hi<p>palum* edd. plerique)[16] *ibi uocant, peti certissimum uidebatur* XIII *(centena milia)* XXXII *(milia) p. aestimatione. Secuta aetas propiorem cursum tutioremque iudicauit, si ab eodem promunturio Sigerum portum Indiae peteret, diuque ita nauigatum est, donec compendia inuenit mercator lucroque India admota est: quippe omnibus annis nauigatur, sagittariorum cohortibus inpositis; etenim piratae maxime infestabant.*[17] *Nec pigebit totum cursum ab Aegypto exponere nunc primum certa notitia patescente: digna res, nullo anno minus* HS D *(centena milia)*[18] *imperii nostri exhauriente India et merces remittente, quae apud nos centiplicato ueneant.*

[...] Such was the route followed by the fleet of Alexander; but subsequently it was thought that the safest line was to start from Syagros eape (Ras Fartak) in Arabia with a west wind (the native name for which in those parts is Hypalus) and make for Patale, the distance being reckoned as 1332 miles. The following period considered it a shorter and safer route to start from the same cape and steer for the Indian harbour of Sigerus, and for a long time this was the course followed, until a merchant discovered *compendia*, and for the *lucrum* India was *admota*; indeed, the voyage is made every year, with companies of archers on board, because these seas used to be very greatly infested by pirates. And it will not be amiss to set out the whole of the voyage from Egypt, now that reliable knowledge of it is for the first time accessible. It is an important subject, in view of the fact that in no year does India absorb less than fifty million sesterces of our empire's wealth, sending back merchandise to be sold with us at a hundred times its prime cost.

It is natural that the interest of all those who have studied relations between India and the classical world should have been focused on this passage. We believe, however, that one major point has escaped the attention of scholars.

The doctrine, once widespread, according to which Roman authors did not possess any historical alertness to economic phenomena needs to be abandoned.[19] It is generally believed, for example, that the sequence of the three routes described by Pliny[20] (the first route leading to Patale; the second to port Sigerus, and the last leading to Muziris) was the result of consecutive stages of progress in navigational techniques.[21] What is not taken into consideration are the economic reasons which Pliny wished to emphasize (together with the closely related problem of protecting the convoys).

It is actually possible to show that at least in one case (in the deviation of trade routes from Sigerus to Muziris) it was not the progress made in terms of navigational techniques, but the requirements of the ancient 'capitalist'[22] economy, which lay at the heart of Pliny's interest.

One of the earliest Italian translations renders for part of the passage in question as follows:

chosì fu la nauichatione d'Alexandro. Dipoi da Syagro promontorio d'Arabia si ua con fauonio el quale quiui chiamano Hypalo a Patale è el uiaggio per estimatione .XIII.XXXII migla. L'età sequente dimostrò corso più brieue et più sichuro se dal decto promontorio s'andassi a Zigero fiume, porto d'India. Et lungho tempo si nauichò in questo modo insino a che e mercatanti trouorono più brieui tragecti et in India uanno per guadagno.[23]

In this translation, as in all others up to the most recent ones,[24] *compendia* is attributed the meaning of 'shorter route'. When this term bears the meaning of *uia breuior, rectior,* however, either tends to be followed by a genitive or an explicative attribute, or at any rate is placed in a context in which the notion of *uia breuior* appears implicit, even though *compendium* is used without specification.

Examples of the first case (*compendium, -a* +genitive) include, among others, passages by Pliny himself, *N.H.* II, 245: *cursus compendiis maris breuior fieri potest* and *ibid.* V, 38: *compendium uiae quadridui deprehensum.* As an example of the second case (*compendium, -a* + attribute) we can quote Tac. *Ann.* XII, 28: *qui dextris et propioribus compendiis ierant.* As examples of *compendium* used on its own, but in an extremely clear context, we can adduce passages such as Iust. II, 10, 24: *quaedam ad nauigationis commodum per compemdium ducebat.*

But here, in Plin. *N.H.* VI, 101, *compendia inuenit mercator* is not a context in which the notion of *uia breuior* appears to be implicit. A *mercator* discovers *compendia* in that he is able to obtain greater profit. And indeed the term *compendium* necessarily indicates the notion of earning:[25] a notion which in this case may be applied, in accordance with its original meaning, to earning as profit.

But above all, Pliny's passage must be considered as a whole. While it is true that he attributed the purpose of attempting a *propior cursus* to the second of the three phases, Pliny already described this second phase as *tutior*. A change in the route, therefore, was also determined by security reasons. The third phase was certainly not *tutior* as compared to the second.[26] Is it possible, then, that the prospect of a shorter route alone was responsible for leading the *mercatores* to alter their itineraries? And was the third route actually the shortest?

At this point it is useful to discuss the passage *PME* 57, p. 19, 7-12 Fr.:

ἀφ' οὗ μέχρι καὶ νῦν τινὲς μὲν εὐθὺς ἀπὸ Κανῆ, τινὲς δὲ ἀπὸ τῶν 'Αρωμάτων ἀφιέντες, οἱ μὲν εἰς Λιμυρικὴν πλέοντες ἐπὶ πλεῖον τραχηλίζοντες, οἱ δὲ εἰς Βαρύγαζαν οἵ τε εἰς Σκυθίαν οὐ πλεῖον ἢ τρεῖς ἡμέρας ἀντέχουσι καὶ τὸ λοιπὸν † παρεπιφέρον πρὸς ἴδιον δρόμον ἐκ τῆς χώρας ὑψηλοὶ διὰ τοῦ ἔξωθεν γῆς παραπλέουσι τοὺς προειρημένους κόλπους.

Since then right up to the present, some leave directly from Kane and some from the Promontory of Spices, and whoever are bound for Limyrike hold out with the wind on the quarter for most of the way, but whoever are bound for Barygaza and whoever for Skythia only three days and no more, and carried along (?) the rest of the run on their own proper course, away from the shore on the high seas, over the [?ocean] off the land, they bypass the aforementioned bays.

Does this passage confirm the conclusion that the route followed during the third phase (Ocelis-Becare) is a 'shortcut' (in other words a *compendium uiae*), compared to the itineraries of the first and the second phase (Syagros promontory to Patale and Syagros promontory to port Sigerus, respectively)?

The problem of the difference, in terms of navigational techniques, between the route taken by vessels travelling to the Limyrike and that heading towards Σκυθία or Barygaza has been recently analysed by L. Casson.[27] Although the explanation given by Casson for the verb τραχηλίζειν raises a few questions, I agree with his criticism of those who believe that the actions of τραχηλίζειν and of ἀντέχειν imply sailing against the wind: actually 'all heading for the Malabar coast had the wind on the starboard quarter the whole way'.[28] Yet, as Casson himself later states, the ships directed towards Σκυθία or towards Barygaza, after three days of ἀντέχειν, 'were able to steer directly for their destination with the wind more aft, in the case of Scythia almost astern. Some such meaning must have been conveyed by what the scribes transformed into † παρεπιφέρον'.[29]

Thus the ships heading towards Σκυθία or Barygaza, merely making use of a wind which was 'more aft' or 'almost astern' for a large part of the voyage, made faster progress than those which headed towards the Limyrike and had the wind 'on the starboard quarter the whole way'. If to this we add the fact that the distance between the Arabian coasts and the Limyrike is greater than that between the Arabian coasts and Σκυθία or Barygaza, we conclude that the route to the Limyrike could not have been shorter than those for Σκυθία or Barygaza.[30]

We are consequently led to seek a different interpretation of Pliny's passage than that generally accepted. In our opinion *compendia* in Plin. *N.H.* VI, 101 connotes not *uia breuior, rectior,* but *lucrum, commodum,*[31] as examplified in Tib. I, 3, 93: *nec uagus ignotis repetens compendia terris/presserat externa nauita merce ratem.* ('The sailor roving across unknown lands in search of profit had not yet filled his ship with foreign merchandise.')

The expression *lucroque India admota est* may perhaps be considered rather obscure. But even those who think so cannot deny that in using it, Pliny's thought is dominated by the idea of the profit made by the *mercatores*—just as it is, in our view, in the case of the preceding *compendia inuenit mercator.* Thus, even if we were to attribute to *admota est* the connotation given by *Th.l.L.*, namely '*facere ut compendio itineris celerius ad ea perueniatur*',[32] we would still need to underline the emphasis given by Pliny to the notion of *lucrum,* profit. It is however preferable to ascribe to the term either the meaning (cf. Landino) 'one goes to India for the profit', or better still—though the metaphor may appear a rather bold one—'India was drawn closer to the profit'.[33] In other words, was 'involved' in the realization of a high profit.

Finally, in contrast to others,[34] I share Landino's opinion, that the word *mercator* used in Plin. *N.H.* VI, 100, means not 'a' merchant, but 'the' merchant: in short, a case of *singularis pro plurali.*

Once again the essential point is the *mercator*'s discovery of a way to make profit. 'For a long time sailing occurred in this way (along the route from Syagros to Sigerus) until the merchant was able to find (the way of realizing) his gains and India was brought closer to the profit (or: one goes to India for the profit).'

In short, the merchants who took the sea-route to Becare could obtain profits which had been (and still were) impossible for those who sailed towards Patale or port Sigerus. One circumstance needs to be borne in mind: only in the ports of the Limyrike was it possible to purchase certain products which had a wide diffusion, or at any rate for which there was a strong demand, in Rome. Thanks to the detailed lists of commodities published in the *PME* we know what types of merchandise were severally imported from the mouth of the Indus,[35] from Barygaza and from the Limyrike.

Let us begin with the merchandise imported from Minnagar, *metropolis* of Σκυθία. *PME* 39, p. 13, 9-12 Fr.: ἀντιφορτίζεται δὲ κόστος, βδέλλα, λύκ<ι>ον, νάρδος καὶ καλλεανὸς λίθος καὶ σάπφειρος καὶ Σιρικὰ δέρματα καὶ ὀθόνιον καὶ νῆμα Σιρικὸν καὶ Ἰνδικὸν μέλαν. ('As return cargo it [sc. Minnagar] offers: costus; bdellium; *lykion*; nard; *calleanos* stone; sapphire; Chinese pelts, cloth, and yarn; Indian black').

Secondly the goods imported from Barygaza are listed as follows *PME* 49, p. 16, 28-31 Fr.: φέρεται δὲ ἀπὸ τῶν τόπων νάρδος, κόστος, βδέλλα, ἐλέφας, ὀνυχίνη λιθία καὶ σμύρνα [μουρρίνη Müller] καὶ λύκιον καὶ ὀθόνιον παντοῖον καὶ Σηρικὸν καὶ μολόχινον καὶ νῆμα καὶ πέπερ<ι> μακρὸν καὶ τὰ ἀπὸ τῶν ἐμπορίων φερόμενα. ('This area [sc. the region of Barygaza] exports: nard; costus; bdellium; ivory; onyx; murrine; *lykion*; cloth of all kinds, Chinese cloth included, *molochinon*, yarn; long pepper; and items brought here from the ports of trade').

Thirdly, let us consider the merchandise imported from the Limyrike. *PME* 56, p. 18, 22-28 Fr.:

φέρεται δὲ πέπερι, μονογενῶς ἐν ἑνὶ τόπῳ τούτων τῶν ἐμπορίων γεννώμενον πολύ, λεγομένῃ Κοτταναρικῇ. φέρεται δὲ καὶ μαργαρίτης ἱκανὸς καὶ διάφορος καὶ ἐλέφας καὶ ὀθόνια Σηρικὰ καὶ νάρδος ἡ Γαγγιτικὴ καὶ μαλάβαθρον ἐκ τῶν ἔσω τόπων εἰς αὐτὴν καὶ λιθία διαφανὴς παντοία καὶ ἀδάμας καὶ ὑάκινθος καὶ χελώνη ἥ τε Χρυσονητιωτικὴ καὶ ἡ περὶ τὰς νήσους θηρευομένη τὰς προκειμένας αὐτῆς τῆς Λιμυρικῆς.

('They export [sc. from the Limyrike] pepper, which only grows, and abundantly, in the region of these ports of trade, which is called Kottonarike. They also export good supplies of fine-quality pearls;

ivory; Chinese cloth; Gangetic nard; *malabathron* brought here from the interior; all kinds of transparent gems; diamonds; *hyakinthos*; tortoise shell, both the kind from Chryse island and the kind caught around the islands lying off the Limyrike itself.')

A comparison of the three lists enables us to clearly distinguish Minnagar, *metropolis* of Σκυθία, and Barygaza from the ports of the Limyrike, Muziris and Nelkynda.

The main articles exported from Minnagar and Barygaza were nard, costus, bdellium, *lykion* and cloths, whereas the major exports from Muziris and Nelkynda were malabathron and pepper. The great quantities of these latter products imported made it necessary to use big ships.[36] Pearls too should not be overlooked: southern India was their greatest producer and the quality of Indian pearls was among the best.[37] Diamonds are also worth noting—the most precious material according to Pliny[38]—and *lithía diaphanès pantoía*, that is, beryl[39] which we shall return to later.

Pearls and pepper: the revolution in the lifestyle of Rome at the beginning of the Augustan period, which Tacitus identified in the luxury of banqueting (*luxus mensae*) and Fenestella in the diffusion of the use of pearls, was in many respects based on imports from the Limyrike; the outflow of coins lamented by Pliny[40] and Tacitus[41] occurred mostly in the direction of the ports of the Limyrike. As the *PME* confirms, προηγουμένως χρήματα πλεῖστα ('essentially a large number of coins') were exported to Muziris and Nelkynda:[42] it is not by chance that the finds of Roman coins in the Indian subcontinent have preponderantly come from southern India,[43] nor that the most vivid memories of this trade are preserved in Tamil poetry.

THE PORTS OF THE LIMYRIKE

(a) Naoura, Nitriai and Tyndis.

The Limyrike began, according to the *PME*, at Naoura and Tyndis. *PME* 53, p. 17, 24-27 Fr.:

εἶτα Σησεκρείεναι λεγόμεναι νῆσοι καὶ ἡ τῶν Αἰγιδίων καὶ ἡ τῶν Καινειτῶν κατὰ τὴν λεγομένην Χερσόνησον, καθ' οὓς τόπους εἰσὶν πειραταί, καὶ μετὰ ταύτην Λευκὴ νῆσος. εἶτα Νάουρα καὶ Τύνδις, τὰ πρῶτα ἐμπόρια τῆς Λιμυρικῆς κτλ.

Then come the Sesekreienai Islands as they are called, the Isle of the Aigidioi, the Isle of the Kaineitoi near what is called the Peninsula, around which places there are pirates, and next White Island. Then come Naura and Tyndis, the first ports of trade of the Limyrike etc.

It is worth comparing the situation described in the *PME* with that presented by Ptolemy. Ptol. *Geogr.* VII, 1, 7-8:

Ἀνδρῶν Πειρατῶν· Μανδάγαρα ριγ ιδ L′, Βυζάντιον ριβ γ′ ιδ, Χερσόνησος ριδ γ′ ιδ L′ γ′, Ναναγούνα ποταμοῦ ἐκβολαί ριδ L′ ιε γ′, Ἀρμαγάρα ριε ιδ γ′, Νιτραίαι ἐμπόριον ριε ϛ′ ιδ γ′. Λιμυρικῆς· Τύνδις πόλις ριϛ γ′ ιδ, Βραμαγάρα ριϛ L′ δ′ ιδ γ′, Καλαικαρίς ριϛ γ′ ιδ, Μούζηρις ἐμπόριον ριζ ιδ, Ψευδοστόμου ποταμοῦ ἐκβολαὶ ριζ L′ γ′ ιδ κτλ.

In the land of pirates: Mandagara 113° 14° 30', Byzantion 112° 20' 14°, Chersonesos 114° 20' 14° 50', mouth of the river Nanagouna 114° 20' 15° 20', Armagara 115° 14° 20', emporium of Nitriai 115° 10' 14° 20'. In the Limyrike: city of Tyndis 116° 14° 10', Bramagara 116° 45' 14° 20', Kalaikaris 116° 20' 14°, emporium of Mouzeris 117° 14°, mouths of the river Pseudostomos 117° 50' 14°.

Whereas in the *PME* the Limyrike started at Naoura (an emporium which did not belong to the Cēralar kingdom, but at the same time was situated outside the area controlled by the pirates), in Ptolemy Tyndis *polis* marked the beginning of both the Cēralar kingdom and the Limyrike, and the pirates appear to have extended their dominion southwards towards the kingdom of the Cēralar as far as the emporium of Nitriai. In short, the buffer zone which lay to the north of Tyndis and to the south of the Chersonesos; which was annexed to Naoura; and which was already considered to be part of the Limyrike in the *PME*, appears to have vanished, occupied by pirates.

The strategic importance of this area is shown by Pliny's passage *N.H.* VI, 104: *non expetendum* (sc. *emporium Muzirim*) *propter uicinos piratas, qui optinent locum nomine Nitrias.* ('not a desirable port of call on account of the neighbouring pirates, who occupy a place called Nitriae'). Nitriai, according to Ptolemy, lay immediately to the north of Tyndis; it has been thought, therefore, and with good reason, that if Nitriai is not exactly the Naoura mentioned in the *PME*, it must have been situated very close to it.[44] Thus at the time of Pliny's informants the pirates had reached the borders of the Cēralar kingdom, and, using Nitriai as a base, were able to cause enough disruption to the trade with Muziris, to the extent that it became no longer advisable for Western merchants to dock in that port.

The pirates to the north of the Cēralar kingdom had always represented an obstacle to the commercial ventures of Western merchants,[45] but following the occupation of the emporium of Nitriai the situation became truly critical. The picture provided by the *PME*, with pirates occupying the Sesekreinai Islands, the Isle of the Aigidioi, the Isle of the Kaneitoi, and the Chersonesos, is not very far removed from the one presumed by Pliny, except in one essential point: at the time of Pliny's informants the pirates occupied Nitriai and were even threatening Muziris.[46]

We will return to the consequences that piracy had on Roman commercial policy later. But let us now consider the sources relating to Tyndis. Tyndis, according to the *PME*, marked the beginning of the Cēralar kingdom. *PME* 54, p. 17, 29-30 Fr.: βασιλείας ἐστὶν ἡμὲν Τύνδις Κηπροβότου κώμη παραθαλάσσιος ἔνσημος ('Tyndis, a well-known village on the coast, is in the kingdom of Keprobotos'). Ptolemy defines it as *polis* and claims it is the point where the Limyrike begins;[47] Pliny's silence is in some way compensated by the numerous testimonies in the *Caṅkam Ilakkiyam*. It may be useful to consider some of them.

Certain formulae[48] confirm that Toṇṭi (= Gr. Tyndis) belonged to the kingdom of the Cēralar: *tiṇ tērp poṟaiyaṉ toṇṭi*, ('Toṇṭi which belongs to the *Poṟayaṉ* with the solid carriage')[49] *ceṅkōṟ kuṭṭuvaṉ toṇṭi*, ('Toṇṭi which belongs to the *Kuṭṭuvaṉ* with the righteous sceptre');[50] *viṟaṟ pōrk kuṭṭuvaṉ teṇ tiraip parappiṉ toṇṭi muṉtuṟai*, ('the port of Toṇṭi, the sea with its white surf, belongs to the *Kuṭṭuvaṉ* whose war is victorious').[51]

In the *Aiṅkuṟunūṟu* an entire decade, the *Toṇṭipattu*,[52] takes its name from Toṇṭi. In each of the ten short poetic compositions Toṇṭi is in fact mentioned. More often than not the anonymous heroine of the Tamil love poem (*talaimakaḷ*) is compared to the city, so that 'she' resembles Toṇṭi,[53] has the same perfume as that of the fresh and fragrant flower of Toṇṭi,[54] shares the same qualities possessed by Toṇṭi,[55] and so on.

In *Puṟanāṉūṟu* 17, 9-13 we find a suggestive description of the landscape of Toṇṭi:

kulai iṟaiñciya kōṭ tāḻai
akal vayal malai vēli
nilavu maṇal viyaṉ kāṉal
teṉ kaḻimicait tīp pūviṉ
taṉ toṇṭiyōr aṭu poruna !

O king of Toṇṭi slayer of foes! Your city is surrounded by mountains and the sand of its vast beaches is the colour of the moon. In its immense fields grow coconut trees laden with fruit, in the marshes grow flowers which are the colour of red fire!

Certain passages underline the importance of fishing, for example, *Akanāṉūṟu* 10, 8-13:

[...] koṇṭaloṭu
kurūut tiraip puṇari uṭaitarum ekkarp
paḻan timil koṉṟa putu valaip paratavar
mōṭṭu maṇal aṭaikaraik kōṭṭumīṉ keṇṭi
maṇam kamaḻ pākkattup pakukkum
vaḷam keḻu toṇṭi aṉṉa ivaḷ nalaṉē.

Her beauty is like the rich Toṇṭi, where in the fragrant seaside villages the fishermen who still have new nets, and whose old boat was removed in the sand heaps, broken by the glittering waves of the ocean ruffled by the east-wind, having caught the shark in the high sand shore, divide it into parts.

From the testimonies gathered here, Toṇṭi, the 'well-known village on the coast' of the *PME*,[56] appears to have mainly supported itself on agriculture and fishing. We must emphasize, however, that the *PME* itself defines it as an emporium[57] and that the *Akanāṉuṟu* confirm the existence of a *muṉtuṟai*, a port, in Toṇṭi.[58] Certainly its importance could in no way be compared with that of Muziris and Becare. Moreover, at the time of Pliny's informants, when pirates were occupying Nitriai, contacts with the Western merchants were very much reduced, thus accentuating a trend which even the *PME* had noted.[59]

(b) *Muziris*

Next we have Muziris, undoubtedly the most famous port of the Limyrike, *primum emporium Indiae* as Pliny defines it.[60] let us begin be examining the relevant passage *PME* 54, p. 17, 30-18, 3 Fr.:

ἡ δὲ Μούζιρις βασιλείας μὲν τῆς αὐτῆς, ἀκμάζουσα δὲ τοῖς ἀπὸ τῆς Ἀριακῆς εἰς αὐτὴν ἐρχομένοις πλοίοις καὶ τοῖς Ἑλληνικοῖς· κεῖται δὲ παρὰ ποταμὸν ἀπέχουσα ἀπὸ μὲν Τύνδεως διὰ τοῦ ποταμοῦ καὶ διὰ θαλάσσης σταδίους πεντακοσίους, ἀπὸ δὲ τοῦ <**> (<στόματος τοῦ ποταμοῦ τοῦ> e. gr. Müller in comm.) κατ' αὐτὴν εἴκοσι.

Muziris in the same kingdom [sc. of Keprobotos], owes its prosperity to the shipping from Ariake that comes there as well as to Greek shipping. It lies on a river 500 stadia distant from Tyndis by river and by sea, and from [? the river mouth] to it is 20 stadia.

Muziris, therefore, was a great centre for 'international' trade, and merchants came there not only from the Roman empire but also from the Ἀριακή, that is, from the north-western coast of India. This point must be underlined: Muziris was not only the main bridgehead for Roman commerce in India, but had already become one of the most active centres in the commercial relatioships between south and north of the Indian subcontinent. These intercourses had already begun to take place during the third century BC[61], simultaneously with the migration of Buddhist and Jain monks towards the south, which had been encouraged also by the Mauryan monarchy. At the time of the journey made by Eudoxus of Cyzicus, in the latter years of the second century BC, the coasts of India were already linked by active commercial networks with fully developed centres of trade, and it is into this well-developed commercial organization that little by little the Western merchants introduced themselves. This, in essence, is the meaning of the succession of Pliny's three routes.

Several passages of the *Caṅkam Ilakkiyam* allow us to grasp other aspects of the wide-ranging activities of a port like Muziris. Let us begin with the *Puṟanāṉūṟu* 343, 1-10:

mīn noṭuttu nel kuvaii
micai ampiyiṉ maṉai maṟukkuntu
maṉaik kuvaiiya kaṟi mūṭaiyāl

kalic cummaiya karai kalakkuṟuntu
kalam tanta poṟ paricam
kaḻit tōṇiyāṉ karai cērkkuntu
malait tāramum kaṭal tāramum
talaip peytu varunarkku īyum
pu'al am kaḻḻiṉ polan tārk kuṭṭuvaṉ
muḻaṅku kaṭal muḻaviṉ muciṟi aṉṉa

like Muciṟi (= Gr. Mouziris; Lt. Muziris), of the sea which roars like a drum, which belongs to the *Kuṭṭuvaṉ* with the golden garland, who offers toddy as if it were water to those who come to pour there the goods from the mountains and those from the sea, to those who bring ashore in the lagoon boats the 'gifts' of gold brought by the ships, and to those who crowd the port in the turmoil created by the sacks of pepper piled up in the houses, and finally to those who return home having sold the fish and having heaped the paddy on the boat.[62]

The riches offered in exchange for a damsel's hand are compared with the rich merchandise of Muziris, and offer the poet a chance to describe the bustling activities of his port. What emerges is a rather precise picture of the commercial exchanges in Muziris, and the economic system on which they were based. The text appears to divide those frequenting the port of Muziris into four different categories:

(a) Those who come to pour the goods of the mountain and those of the sea;[63]

(b) Those who bring ashore in the lagoon boats the 'gifts' of gold[64] brought in by the ships;[65]

(c) Those who crowd the port in the turmoil created by sacks of pepper which had been piled up in the boxes;

(d) Those who return home having sold fish and having heaped rice on the boat.

Points (a) and (d) suggest internal trade within the Cēralar kingdom, for which Muziris became the point of convergence of two economies:[66] the coastal economy, based on fishing and trade, and the inland economy, essentially based upon agriculture (rice and pepper), but also on other activities, such as the extraction of beryl in the quarries at Padiyur, in the district of Coimbatore.[67]

This exchange between the coast and the inland areas represented, on the one hand, the means of which basic commodities such as rice and fish could be diffused throughout the kingdom, and on the other, the presupposition for 'international' trade, since some of the most sought after goods imported from the Limyrike, such as beryl and pepper, came precisely from the inland areas. It is not by chance that Muziris, Becare and Nelkynda, the most important ports of the Limyrike, was situated on the banks of rivers which allowed easy communication with the territories further inland.[68]

As mentioned above, one of the 'goods of the mountain' exchanged for the 'goods of the sea', and eventually imported by Western merchants, was beryl. The attention of scholars became focused on the trade of this gem due to the vast quantity of Roman coins found in the district of Coimbatore; their findspots were located in the vicinity of the ancient beryl quarries, which must have been skirted by the road leading inland from the coast, i.e. the road which led from Muziris, to Karoura capital in the kingdom of the Cēralar.[69]

To the twelve finds cited by Gupta[70] we must now add two new hoards, one found in Polachi and the other in Velatavalan, the exact size and composition of which unfortunately remain unknown. In addition to these we also have a single *denarius* of Tiberius found in Sulur.[71]

Some of these hoards are of exceptional size and importance. Among them are the three recovered in Vellalur: the first included 522 *denarii*, of which 134 were of Augustus, 378 of Tiberius, 7 of Caligula and 3 of Claudius. The second included 547 *denarii*, of which 189 were of Augustus, 329 of Tiberius, 3 of Drusus, 2 of Antonia, 8 of Caligula, 14 of Claudius, and 1 of Nero and Agrippina. The third find consisted of 121 *denarii*, all of Augustus.

The importance of this area in terms of precious stones is also confirmed by a Tamil inscription in Brahmī characters found at Araccalur, recording that Tevan Cattan, *maṇi-y-vaṇṇakkaṉ*, built seven beds for anchorites—it is not known whether Buddhist or Jain—in a cave.[72] The term *maṇi-y-vaṇṇakkaṉ* is translated by the most distinguished scholar of these inscriptions as 'a dealer in or a tester of precious gems, a lapidary'.[73]

Beryl was very popular in Rome during the Julio-Claudian period:[74] its importance in Roman life and fashion is clearly attested by literary and epigraphic sources,[75] as well as by archaeological evidence. It is therefore probable that Tacitus is at least partly referring to beryl in *Ann.* III, 53: [...] *promiscas uiris et feminis uestes atque illa feminarum propria, quis lapidum causa pecuniae nostrae ad externas aut hostilis gentis transferuntur.* ('The promiscuous dress of male and female—and the specially female extravagance by which, for the sake of jewels, our wealth is transported to alien and hostile countries ?').[76]

There is therefore a relation between the outflow of coins *lapidum causa* lamented by the Tiberius of Tacitus and the treasures of Roman coins found in the district of Coimbatore, where it is precisely the Tiberian types that predominate.

It must be said, however, that other factors may have contributed towards the exceptional concentration of Roman coins in the latter district, not least the favour enjoyed by beryl among the Indians themselves. A favour which was explicitly attested in Pliny, *N.H.* XXXVII, 76-9:

> *India eos* (sc. *berullos*) *gignit, raro alibi repertos* [...] *Indi mire gaudent longitudine eorum solosque gemmarum esse praedicant, qui carere auro malint; ob id perforatos elephantorum saetis subligant. Conuenit non oportere perforari quorum sit absoluta bonitas, umbilicis tantum ex auro capita conprehendentibus. Ideo cylindros ex iis malunt facere quam gemmas, quoniam est summa commendatio in longitudine.* [...] *Indi et alias quidem gemmas crystallum tinguendo adulterare inuenerunt, sed praecipue berullos.*[77]

Beryls are produced in India and are rarely found elsewhere [...] The Indians are extraordinarily fond of elongated beryls and claim that they are the only precious stones that are preferably left without a gold setting. Consequently they pierce them and string them on elephants' bristles. They are all agreed that a stone of perfect quality should not be pierced, and in this case they merely enclose the head of the stone in a convex gold cap. They prefer to shape beryls into long prisms rather than into gems simply because length is their most attractive feature [...] The Indians have found a way of counterfeiting various precious stones, and beryls in particular, by staining rock-crystal.

The employment of beryl as building material for monumental complexes is attested in the inscription of Khāravela which mentions (1.16) *chaturo cha veḍūriya-gabhe thaṁbe* 'four columns with a beryl core'.[78]

Due caution is therefore needed in the interpretation of the Roman coin hoards found in the district of Coimbatore, since their concentration in this area could be largely the result of internal transactions among the Indians themselves:[79] judging from the *PME*, pepper and malabathron must have been more important than beryl as goods imported from the Limyrike by the Romans.[80] There is no doubt, too, that the *lapides* to which Tiberius refers, also (and perhaps especially) included pearls and diamonds,[81] and that in Rome these were appreciated a great deal more highly than beryl.

(c) Poṉṉoṭu/Kaṟiyoṭu, *the prices of pepper in Pliny*

We are now able to reconsider *Purānāṉūṟu* 343; in point (b) as we have seen, mention was made of those who 'bring ashore in the lagoon boats the gifts of gold brought by the ships'. It is worth comparing this testimony, which would otherwise remain rather obscure, with that of *Akanāṉūṟu* 149, 7-11:

[...] cēralar
cuḷḷi am pēriyāṟṟu veṇ nurai kalaṅka
yavaṉar tanta viṉai māṇ naṉ kalam
poṉṉoṭu vantu kaṟiyoṭu peyarum
vaḷam keḻu muciṟi

> [...] the rich Muciṟi where ships, the perfect and wonderful constructions of the Yavaṉar, having come with gold (*poṉṉoṭu*), returned carrying pepper (*kaṟiyoṭu*), churning the white surf of the great Cuḷḷi river which belongs to the Cēralar.[82]

Thus, it is to the Yavaṉar[83] that the vessels (*kalam*) belong and it is above all *kaṟi* (or *milaku*[84]) they seek. *Kaṟi* and *milaku* are the two Tamil words used for *piper nigrum* (black pepper), the fruit of a climbing plant which grows abundantly in the forests on the mountain ranges situated inland in present-day Kerala.[85] It will not be irrelevant at this point to provide a brief historical and etymological account of the word πέπερι / *piper*, a name which the Westerners of the first century AD used also for *piper nigrum*. Obviously we shall limit our history of *piper* to data significant for the history of Roman merchants in India. These data provide us in fact with a hitherto ignored—albeit not entirely well-defined—evaluation of the development in the commercial activities of the Western merchants in India. The history of *piper* in the Celtic, Germanic, Slavonic and Chinese languages is therefore beyond the scope of the present work.

At the origin of the Gr. πέπερι lies *pippalī*, a Sanskrit word connoting *piper longum*, which penetrated into the Greek lexicon[86] through Iranian mediation at a rather early date. As may be easily inferred from the few testimonies we possess in this connection, there was no clear-cut and well-defined idea about πέπερι during the Hellenistic period, since this name was also used for other spices with a totally different provenance.[87] Theophrastus is aware of two kinds of πέπερι, but if the πρόμηκες μέλαν can apparently be identified as *piper longum*, the identification of στρογγύλον remains obscure; in any case the possibility that it may connote *piper nigrum* must be rejected.[88] In order to explain how the merchants of the late Hellenistic and/or Roman period ultimately came to call πέπερι/*piper* what the Tamils called *kaṟi* or *milaku*, it has been assumed that foreign merchants applied to *piper nigrum* the name given to *piper longum*.[89]

It is perhaps possible to be more precise on this point, thanks to a text which is not normally taken into account. This is the Amarasiṁha, *Nāmaliṅgānuśasānaṃ*, II 4, 97-8, p. 104 Sh.:

kṛṣṇopakulyā vaidehī māgadhī capalā kaṇā/uṣaṇā pippalī śauṇḍī kolā, 'tha karipippalī // kapivallī kolavallī śreyasī vaśirah (pumān) / cavyaṃ tu cavikā, kākaciñcī-guñce tu kṛṣṇalā //.

In these two verses the lexicographer, who lived during the fifth-sixth century AD, lists various names of spices which are more or less similar to pepper. Let us focus our attention on the term *karipippalī*. Indu, an author quoted by Kṣirasvamin, an eleventh century commentator of the work of Amarasiṁha, explains it with the words *bṛhattvād gajayogyā vā* 'due to its size or because related to elephants'. In other words he interprets *karipippalī* as a compound of *kariṇ* 'elephant' + *pippalī* 'pepper' (linked to this interpretation are also the compounds *hastipippalī*, *kuñjarapippalī* and *gajapippalī* quoted in other sources of Kṣirasvamin). I prefer, instead, to see in the first term of the compound the Tamil *kaṟi*, rather than the Sanskrit *kariṇ*. In this case *karipippalī* would be the name given by non-Dravidian India to this product which was so typical of southern India,[90] in some ways assimilating it to the *pippalī* of northern India, but specifying its nature by using the word *kaṟī*.

If this hypothesis is correct, we must infer that the Western merchants became acquainted with *kaṟī* in non-Dravidian areas, where it could be assimilated to *pippalī*. In fact, the Yavaṉar's fondness for *kaṟī* was noticed even outside the Dravidian world, as shown by the compounds *Yavanapriya* and *Yavaneṣṭha*, 'loved by the Yavana', both synonyms of *piper nigrum*.

To understand all this we must once again return to Pliny. As we have seen, according to Pliny, the north-western coast of India represented for a long time (*diu*) the Western merchants' destination. There they found *karipippalī*, imported from southern India,[91] which they called simply πέπερι. All this *donec compendia inuenit mercator*, that is, until the merchants discovered the markets of southern India,[92] where incidentally *kaṟi* must have been cheaper than in the markets of the north-western coast of India. But by that time the use of the term πέπερι to indicate *piper nigrum* had become well-established. Indeed it should be noted that the author of the *PME* calls *piper nigrum* πέπερι tout court and uses the formula πέπερι μακρόν for the *piper longum* from Barygaza, the original *pippalī*: *kaṟi*, in other words, had become the πέπερι par excellence and the most popular species of pepper.[93] Furthermore, if we consider that black pepper was less expensive than the long and the white varieties,[94] and bear in mind the great use that was made of it in Roman cuisine,[95] the discovery of the husks of black peppercorns in a deposit left by a Roman *castrum* at Oberaden on the Lippe in Germany comes as no surprise.[96]

In the history of prices, the indications given by Pliny relating to these three species of *piper* (the *longum*, the *album* and the *nigrum*) must once again be emphasized. We can establish a ratio of 46.6 per cent between the price of the *album* variety and that of the *longum* variety; and a ratio of 26.6 per cent between the price of the *nigrum* variety and that of the *longum* variety, as set out below:

longum : 1
album : 0.466
nigrum : 0.266

This remarkable differential in the price of the various species of *piper*, which we are able to deduce from Pliny, refers in our opinion to the price at the point of arrival. But clearly we must expect a quite similar differential in the price at the point of departure: i.e. in the export centres themselves. The prices applied were in any case rather high. The most significant comparison is offered by an event which occurred more than three centuries later, and which is to be seen within the greater drama of the Roman state (Alaric's imminent threat to Rome in 408, following Stilicho's downfall and his death in Ravenna on the 22 August 408—a threat which ended with the sack of Rome in 410). Towards the end of the year 408, in an attempt to appease Alaric, a decree of the senate decided to pay ransom to the barbarian: the tributes—among which there were 5000 lb of gold and 30 000 lb of silver—included also 3000 lb of πέπερι (Zosim. V, 41,4). This information must no doubt be accepted and even Maenchen-Helfen (p. 459), who is generally sceptical about the figures in Olympiodorus, adduces no argument against it.

In 408, thirty years after the battle of Hadrianople, and no doubt even before it, the prices of pepper revealed a tendency towards ever greater increases, and, despite the deflationistic policies introduced by Julian and later followed (with important mitigations) by his successors, proved impossible to stop it, precisely because pepper was largely an imported product.

When Pliny's work was completed, Titus was (or had been) consul for the sixth time; the work, therefore, was completed in 77 (Titus' sixth consulate), or at the latest in 78. The merchants who provided him with information on their voyages to the ports of the Limyrike must have met him several years earlier. Unfortunately, we do not know how many years earlier. The question is linked to the problem of the *castrense contubernium* of Pliny with Titus; we must remember, too, that book XII in which the series of prices for *piper* appears (ch. 28 cit.) had already been outlined in its content when Pliny wrote VI, 161 (cf. in fact VI, 161 11.16-17 M. with XII, 66 and 69). So when the decree of the senate was issued in 408 and the delivery of 3000 lb of πέπερι to Alaric was deliberated, approximately 330 (331) years had elapsed from the presentation of the *Natural History* to the emperor Titus. Yet even then pepper continued to be considered a merchandise of great value and prestige. Neither piracy, nor other events which had characterised, or jeopardized, the relationship between the merchants coming from the Roman empire and the *emporia* of the Limyrike, had been able to dampen the great demand for pepper.

(d) *Indian piracy and Yavaṉar soldiers*

Let us now return to the problem of piracy. As we have seen, Pliny's text reflects a time when the Cēralar state was seriously jeopardized by piracy, to the point that it was not advisable for Western merchants to land in Muziris.[97] We have seen that from the data in the *PME* and in Ptolemy it is possible to reconstruct other phases (and we must bear in mind the time lapse between the *PME*, close to the age of Pliny, and Ptolemy) of the struggle between the kingdom of the Cēralar and the pirates. Thanks to the *Caṅkam Ilakkiyam*, it is possible to ascertain a decisive moment of this struggle and to name the pirates in question.

Of Neṭuñcēralātaṉ, a Cēra king, it is in fact said in *Patiṟṟuppattu* 20, 1-5:

num kō yār ? eṉa viṉaviṉ, em kō
iru munnīrt turuttiyuḷ
muraṇiyōrt talaicceṉṟu
kaṭampu mutal taṭinta kaṭuñ ciṉa muṉpiṉ
neṭuñcēralātaṉ; vāḻka avaṉ kaṇṇi !

If I were asked: 'Who is your king?'. My king, I would reply, is Neṭuñcēralātaṉ, who has strength and frightening anger. Having gone amidst his enemies, on the islets of the great sea, he cut the trunk of the *kaṭampu*. Long live his victorious wreath!

In *Cilappatikaram* XXIII, 81-2, the Cēra king Ceṅkuṭṭuvaṉ, son of Neṭuñcēralātaṉ is hailed as *kaṭaṟ kaṭampeṟinta kāvalaṉ*, 'the guardian who has uprooted the *kaṭampu* from the sea'.[98]

As we learn from several medieval inscriptions,[99] the *kaṭampu*, was the totem-tree of the Kaṭampar, 'those of the kaṭampu, the sons of the *kaṭampu'*. The phrases *kaṭampu mutal taṭinta* and *kaṭampu eṟinta*, respectively 'to cut the trunk of the *kaṭampu*' and 'to uproot the *kaṭampu*' allude apparently to victories of Neṭuñcēralātaṉ and Ceṅkuṭṭuvaṉ over their enemies, the Kaṭampar.[100] The fact that these victories were obtained at sea renders entirely feasible the hypothesis that the Kaṭampar in some ways threatened or disturbed the trade of the kingdom of the Cēralar; and that the pirates mentioned by Pliny, in the *PME* and by Ptolemy, and the Kaṭampar mentioned in the *Caṅkam Ilakkiyam*, posed similar problems to the Cēralar. Moreover it should be noted that both these groups were based on small islands.

If these assumptions are correct, we will then be able to fix an important moment in the long struggle of the kingdom of the Cēralar against piracy. During the reigns of Neṭuñcēralātaṉ and Ceṅkuṭṭuvaṉ the Cēralar kingdom reacted vigorously against the Kaṭampar (the pirates of Western sources), culminating in the 'cutting' of the *kaṭampu*. Fortunately, we are able to suggest a date, albeit vague, for this important event thanks to the contemporaneity established in the *Cilappatikaram* between Ceṅkuṭṭuvaṉ and Gajabāhu, king of Ceylon. According to computations worked out on the basis of the Sinhalese chronicles *Dīpavaṁsa* and *Mahāvaṁsa*, it seems, in fact, that the twenty-two years of reign which tradition assigns to this king should be placed between AD 174 and 196.[101]

The fact that the merit for having 'cut' the *kaṭampu* is attributed to both these kings, prompts the assumption either that the war was fought during the latter part of the reign of Neṭuñcēralātaṉ and in the first years of the reign of Ceṅkuṭṭuvaṉ, or that Ceṇkuṭṭuvaṉ, commander of the fleet, defeated the Kaṭampar on behalf of his father.[102] In either case, it is clear that the 'cutting' of the *kaṭampu* occurred in a period postdating—though perhaps not by long—that of Ptolemy,[103] who still presents a situation very similar to that of Pliny, with Nitriai occupied by pirates. As attested by Pliny, from Nitriai it was possible to threaten Muziris, and it is natural therefore, that the Cēralar aspired to conquer those coasts to the north of their kingdom, on which the safety of their trade depended. The 'cutting' of the *kaṭampu* had as immediate consequence the annexation by the Cēralar kingdom of the 'Naṟavu with its cool marine breeze',[104] which corresponds to the Naoura of the *PME* and almost certainly to the Nitriai mentioned by Pliny and Ptolemy.[105]

The point that needs to be emphasized, however, is that the Western merchants also found themselves involved in this struggle. We know that already in Pliny's times (and even earlier, ever since the beginning of Pliny's third phase), these merchants took with them cohorts of archers, in order to defend their ships from the pirates. All this had remarkable consequences. Some of these mercenaries, once they had accompanied the Western merchants, apparently decided to stay on in India at the courts of the Indian kings. In the *Cilappatikaram* the Yavaṉar are mentioned as guards at Maturai, the capital of the kingdom of the Pāṇṭiyar. *Cilappatik.* XIV, 66-7:

> *kaṭimatil vāyil kāvaliṟ ciṟanta*
> *aṭalvāḷ yavaṉark kayirātu pukkāṉ*

> He (se. Kōvalaṉ) entered without being suspected by the Yavaṉar with the murderous swords, excellent as guards at the gate of the bastion of defence.[106]

Are we able to establish—if only hypothetically—how this situation developed? We have on the one hand the *sagittarii* who protected the trade between the Cēralar and the merchants coming from the Roman empire; and on the other the Yavaṉar who guarded the gates at Maturai: between the *sagittarii* and the Yavaṉar there is obviously a link. And that link was the interest of Western merchants in ensuring the necessary stability for the conduct of trade.

But Pliny's *sagittarii* and the reign of Cenkuṭṭuvaṉ are separated by a period of approximately one hundred years, and more importantly, by a change in the trade policies of the Roman merchants: Muziris, which according to the *Tabula Peutingeriana* was the site of a *templum Augusti*, had been the *primum emporium Indiae* from the very beginning of trade relations between the Roman empire and southern India right up until the age of Vespasian and Titus (we should recall *N.H.* VI, 104). When necessary, Western merchants helped to defend it from the pirates; but already Pliny's informants noted that at that time the merchants ought to have preferred to divert their trade at the 'other more serviceable port, belonging to the Neacyndes tribe, called Becare': this port was in the kingdom of the Pāṇṭiyar.

The Cēralar no longer represented a reference point for Western merchants; the ships which in the absence of the dangers posed by the piracy would have turned towards Muziris to exchange, e.g., gold for pepper, instead turned increasingly to the *utilior portus Becare* further south. The Yavaṉar tended to avoid the uncertain struggle against piracy, travelling further south to discover markets which were not only safer, but also richer in goods and more convenient in terms of the loading and unloading operations.[107] The mercenaries who continued to accompany merchants now enrolled in the service of the Pāṇṭiyar kings.

All this led to a cooling of relations between the Cēralar and the Western merchants. The Neṭuñcēralātaṉ who 'cut' the *kaṭampu* was the same king who put in chains the 'rough-speaking Yavaṉar';[108] this occurred during the second half of the second century AD but the roots of the problems this Cēra king had to tackle can be traced back to the period of the *PME* and of Pliny. In short, already then, in the Flavian period, relations between the Cēralar and merchants coming from the Roman empire had been placed within a different framework.

(e) Becare and Nelkynda

Becare and Nelkynda marked the beginning of the kingdom of the Pāṇṭiyar, who already in the Augustan age had followed with great interest the development of commercial relations between the Roman empire and India.[109] Unfortunately the only sources which provide information on these emporia are the Greek and Latin ones: classical Tamil literature provides us with no help.[110]

A few meagre details are provided by Pliny, *N.H.* VI, 105:

Alius utilior portus gentis Neacyndon, qui uocatur Becare. Ibi regnabat Pandion, longe ab emporio in mediterraneo distante oppido quod uocatur Modura. Regio autem, ex qua piper monoxylis lintribus Becaren conuehunt, uocatur Cottonara.

Another more serviceable port, belonging to the Neacyndes tribe, called Becare. Here reigned Pandion in a city by the name of Modura which is situated inland, very far from the emporium. But the region from which pepper is brought to Becare in monoxyl boats [made from a single block of wood] is called Cottonara.

A somewhat more detailed picture is presented by the *PME* 54-5, p. 18, 4-11 Fr.:

ἡ δὲ Νελκύνδα σταδίους μὲν ἀπὸ Μουζίρεως ἀπέχει[ν] σχεδὸν πεντακοσίους, ὁμοίως διά τε ποταμοῦ [καὶ πεζῇ] καὶ διὰ θαλάσσης, βασιλείας δέ ἐστιν ἑτέρας, τῆς Πανδίονος. κεῖται δὲ καὶ αὐτὴ παρὰ ποταμὸν ὡσεὶ ἀπὸ σταδίων ἑκατὸν εἴκοσι τῆς θαλάσσης. ἑτέρα δὲ κατ' αὐτὸ τὸ στόμα τοῦ ποταμοῦ πρόκειται κώμη Βακαρή εἰς ἣν ἀπὸ Νελκύνδων ἐπὶ τῆς ἀναγωγῆς προκαταβαίνουσι τὰ πλοῖα· ἐπὶ σάλῳ διορμίζεται πρὸς ἀνάληψιν τῶν φορτίων διὰ τὸ τὸν ποταμὸν ἕρματα **(Müller: ἄλματα** cod.) **και** διάπλους ἔχει<ν> ἐλαφρούς.

Nelkynda is just about 500 stadia from Muziris, likewise by river and by sea, but it is in another kingdom, Pandion's. It too lies on a river, about 120 stadia from the sea. Another settlement lies at the very mouth of the river, Bakare, to which vessels drop downriver from Nelkynda for the outbound voyage; they anchor in the open roads to take on their cargoes because the river has sandbanks and channels that are shoals.

In Pliny's language should be noted immediately the equivalence of the expression *gens Neacyndon* with Νελκύνδα. This is extremely interesting from a sociological point of view. Nelkynda, as an emporium, occupied a position fixed by the *PME* at 120 stadia from the sea on the banks of a river which, as we know from Ptolemy, was the Baris;[111] on other respects, however, Nelkynda might appear as a community, roughly speaking, of tribal type (the term *gens* could be perhaps read in this way). In other words, there must have been a sort of polarity between the commercial centre, born of the new needs dictated by trade with the Yavaṉar, and the pre-existing tribal-type structure.[112] The relationship between Nelkynda and Becare at any rate appears to be fairly straightforward. Situated at the mouths of the river upon which Nelkynda lay, Becare was the *portus gentis Neacyndon*, in the same way that Ostia was the port of Rome.

Due to the sandbanks and shoals at the mouth of the river, ships were forced to moor at Becare, where the goods destined for the West were loaded.[113] Communications with the interior were however facilitated by river navigation, thanks to which several of the goods requested by the Yavaṉar (pepper being the most important) were able to reach Becare.[114] Loading and unloading operations were in any case easier than in Muziris. Moreover, an abundance of merchandise was available at Becare which was not to be found at the other port.[115]

The fact that these two cities displayed very similar characteristics in terms of commerce (both were very important in the pepper trade), that the two ports were situated relatively close to one another,[116] but belonged to two different kingdoms, may suggest some of the economic causes for the wars between the Pāṇṭiyar and Cēralar kingdoms. We learn of these battles in the *Caṅkam Ilakkiyam*, and it is clear that they were determined by the conflict of interests between Muziris and Becare. I would like to draw attention to one particular war, as it culminated in the siege of Muciṟi (Muziris) at the hands of the Pāṇṭiyar army. Twice the *Caṅkam Ilakkiyam* alludes to this war. The first allusion is found in *Akanāṉūṟu* 57, 14-17:

koy cuvaṟ puravik koṭit tērc celiyaṉ
mutunīr muṉtuṟai muciṟi muṟṟi
kaḷiṟu paṭa erukkiya kalleṉ ñāṭpiṉ
arum puṇ uṟunariṉ varuntiṉal

she has suffered like the warriors who received a mortal wound and were killed by the elephant when the Celiyaṉ [epithet of the Pāṇṭiyar king[117]] on his flag-bearing chariot and horse with decorated mane besieged the port of Muciṟi with its abundant water.

The heroine's suffering for the beloved's departure is compared to that of the warriors who die in battle during the siege of Muciṟi. A second allusion is found in a passage which has in part been considered already, *Akanāṉūṟu* 149, 7-13:

[...] cēralar
cuḷḷi am pēriyāṟṟu veṇ nurai kalaṅka
yavaṉar tanta viṉai māṇ naṉ kalam
poṉṉoṭu vantu kaṟiyoṭu peyarum

vaḷam keḻu muciṟi ārppu eḻa vaḷaii,
aruñ caman kaṭantu, paṭimam vavviya
neṭu nal yāṉai aṭupōrc ceḻiyaṉ

the Ceḻiyaṉ who conquers in battle with his great and good elephant and who snatched the sacred images, having won the difficult battle after having surrounded the rich Muciṟi, where the ships of the Yavaṉar, arriving with gold, returned with pepper, churning the white surf of the great river Cuḷḷi, which belongs to the Cēralar.

The above two passages are extremely interesting. They inform us, in fact, that a war between the Pāṇṭiyar, lords of Becare, and the Cēralar, lords of Muziris culminated in the siege of the latter city at the hands of the Pāṇṭiyaṉ. The fact that in the second of the passages the mention of Muziris should almost automatically evoke the trade with the Yavaṉar, is useful in understanding this conflict. By besieging the *primum emporium Indiae,* the Pāṇṭiyaṉ aimed to destroy the only port which could in any way rival that of Becare. The aim, in other words, was to monopolize the trade with the Yavaṉar.

Unfortunately our present state of research does not allow us to work out even an approximate date for the war referred to in the two poems. Notwithstanding the efforts of various scholars[118] we still await a satisfying historical elucidation and interpretation of the great mass of information contained in the *Caṅkam Ilakkiyam.*

PORTS OF THE SOUTH-EASTERN COAST

As may be safely deduced from Pliny and the *PME,*[119] Western merchants in the mid-first century AD, did not usually sail for purpose of trade beyond the ports of the Limyrike, that is India's south-western coast: it cannot be excluded of course that some enterprising mariners may have occasionally pushed beyond Cape Comorin, along the eastern coast of India. Already in Strabo's time, as we have seen, several merchants had reached the estuary of the Ganges,[120] but this does not alter (at least with regard to the Julio-Claudian age) the general picture which sees the Western merchants concentrated above all in Muziris and Becare. And yet, anyone who fails to take into account the role played by the ports of India's south-eastern coast, will have difficulty in grasping how the ports of the Limyrike could have stocked such a wide variety of goods.

The list of commodities available to merchants in the ports of the Limyrike[121] quoted in the *PME* includes several varieties of goods which were in turn imported from the ports of the south-eastern coast, or via these from the Ganges emporium and the island of Chryse.[122] Among these were ὀθόνια Σηρικά (Chinese cloth [silk]), νάρδος ἡ Γαγγιτική (Gangetic nard), μαλάβαθρον ἐκ τῶν ἔσω τόπων εἰς αὐτὴν (malabathron, brought here from the interior), χελώνη ἡ Χρυσονητιωτική (tortoise shell from the island of Chryse), and μαργαρίτης ἱκανὸς καὶ διάφορος (good supplies of fine quality pearls) which came mostly from Kolchoi.[123]

Research on trade relations between the Roman empire and the Limyrike must therefore necessarily take into consideration the trade which linked the Limyrike to India's south-eastern coast, and through it to the mouth of the Ganges and beyond.

(a) *Kolchoi*

According to Pliny, Muziris did not display such an abundance of goods as was to be found in Becare.[124] It is probable indeed that the kingdom of the Pāṇṭiyar, to which Becare belonged, derived a certain advantage (even over the Cēralar) in terms of trade with the eastern coast on account of its more favourable geographical position. Moreover, we must consider a very important point: the kingdom of the Pāṇṭiyar also included Kolchoi, a great emporium in the region characterized by the use of convicts as pearl-divers. The fundamental passage is in *PME* 59, p. 19, 22-4 Fr.:

ἀπὸ δὲ τοῦ Κομαρεὶ ἐκτείνουσα χώρα μέχρι Κόλχων, ἐν ᾗ κολύμβησις τοῦ πινικοῦ ἐστίν, ἀπὸ δὲ κατακρισίμων κατεργάζεται πρὸς τὸν νότον (haec uerba ante uerbum χώρα posuit Müller: ut mihi uidetur, fortasse recte; del. Frisk, quippe quae ex 19, 14 deprompta sint) ὑπὸ τὸν Πανδίονά ἐστιν.

Beyond Komar the region extends [south?] as far as Kolchoi, where diving for pearls goes on; it is carried out by convicts. The region is under King Pandion.

When the author of the *PME* recorded these brief notes, the pearls of the Pāṇṭiyar had been famous throughout India for centuries. The first reports date back as far as Megasthenes. FGrHist. 715 F 13 (= Arr., *Ind.* 8):

τὴν σκευὴν δὲ οὗτος ὁ Ἡρακλέης ἥντινα ἐφόρεε, Μεγασθένης λέγει ὅτι ὁμοίη ἦν τῷ Θηβαίῳ Ἡρακλεῖ, ὡς αὐτοὶ Ἰνδοὶ ἀπηγέονται. καὶ τούτῳ ἄρσενας μὲν παῖδας πολλοὺς κάρτα γενέσθαι ἐν τῇ Ἰνδῶν γῇ—πολλῇσι γὰρ δὴ γυναιξὶν ἐς γάμον ἐλθεῖν καὶ τοῦτον τὸν Ἡρακλέα—θυγατέρα δὲ μουνογενέην. οὔνομα δὲ εἶναι τῇ παιδὶ Πανδαίην, καὶ τὴν χώρην ἵνα τε ἐγένετο καὶ ἧστινος ἐπέτρεψεν αὐτῇ ἄρχειν Ἡρακλέης, Πανδαίην <καλεῖσθαι> τῆς παιδὸς ἐπώνυμον. καὶ ταύτῃ ἐλέφαντας μὲν γενέσθαι ἐκ τοῦ πατρὸς ἐς πεντακοσίους, ἵππον δὲ ἐς τετρακισχιλίην, πεζῶν δὲ ἐς τὰς τρεῖς καὶ δέκα μυριάδας. καὶ τάδε μετεξέτεροι Ἰνδῶν περὶ Ἡρακλέους λέγουσιν, ἐπελθόντα αὐτὸν πᾶσαν γῆν καὶ θάλασσαν καὶ καθήραντα ὅ τι περ κακόν, καινὸν εἶδος ἐξευρεῖν ἐν τῇ θαλάσσῃ κόσμου γυναικηίου [...] τὸν μαργαρίτην δὴ τὸν θαλάσσιον οὕτω τῇ Ἰνδῶν γλώσσῃ καλεόμενον. τὸν γὰρ Ἡρακλέα ὡς καλόν οἱ ἐφάνη τὸ φόρημα, ἐκ πάσης τῆς θαλάσσης ἐς τὴν Ἰνδῶν γῆν συναγινέειν τὸν μαργαρίτην δὴ τοῦτον, τῇ θυγατρὶ τῇ ἑωυτοῦ εἶναι κόσμον.

Megasthenes also says that the garb which this Heracles wore was like that of the Theban Heracles, as also the Indians themselves record; he also had many sons in this country for this Heracles too wedded many wives; he had only one daughter, called Pandaea; so the country in which she was born, and to rule which Heracles educated her, was also called Pandaea after the girl; here she possessed five hundred elephants given by her father, four thousand horsemen, and as many as a hundred and thirty thousand foot-soldiers. This also some writers relate about Heracles: that he traversed all the earth and sea, and when he had rid the earth of evil monsters he found in the sea a new kind of jewel for women [...] the sea pearl, as it is called in the Indian tongue; and since the jewel appeared to him charming, Heracles collected this kind of pearl from all the seas of India, to adorn his daughter.

This tradition of Megasthenes on Pandaea, the only female among the offspring of the Indian Heracles, eponymous queen of her kingdom and founder of a royal lineage,[125] has been linked directly to traditions relating to the kingdom of the Pāṇṭiyar:[126] she has thus been identified with the *kula mutal* or *Maturāpati* (the 'goddess founder of the lineage',[127] 'she who protects Maturai' the capital of the kingdom of the Pāṇṭiyar).

The description of 'the patron of Maturai' at the beginning

of canto XXIII of the *Cilappatikaram*, reveals a highly poetic imagination and a precision rare in Western poetry: the reader will not forget her image, imbued with an aura of religious wonder and enveloped in an atmosphere of pure dream, which suggests to the historian a careful consideration of the richness by which the representation is inspired (*Cilappatik.* XXIII, 1-15):

caṭaiyum piṟaiyum tāḻnta ceṉṉik
kuvaḷai uṇkaṇ tavaḷavāḷ mukatti
kaṭaiyeyiṟu arumpiya pavaḷaccev vāytti
iṭainilā virinta nittila nakaitti
iṭamaruṅ kiruṇṭanīla māyiṉum
valamaruṅku poṉṉiṟam puraiyu mēṉiyaḷ
iṭakkai polam pūn tāmarai yēntiṉum
valakkai am cuṭark koṭuvaḷ piṭittōḷ
valakkāl puṉaikaḻal kaṭṭiṉum iṭakkāl
taṉiccilampu araṟṟun takaimaiyaḷ paṉittuṟai
koṟkaik koṇkaṉ kumarit tuṟaivaṉ
poṟkōṭṭu varampaṉ potiyiṟ poruppaṉ
kulamutaṟ kiḻatti ātaliṉ alamantu
orumulai kuṟaitta tirumā pattiṉi
alamaru tirumukat tāyiḻai naṅkaitaṉ.

And further on in verse 22:

mā peruṅ kūṭal maturā patiyeṉpēṉ.

She, the lady with the sacred visage was confused; the divine, chaste and faithful woman was troubled, she who had deprived herself of one of her breasts, she who possessed the ancient science, the beautiful *mutal* of the royal house who possesses mount Potiyil, golden frontier, who possesses the port of Kumari, who reigns upon Koṟkai with its cool harbour; a *cilampu* tinkled round her left ankle and a *kaḻal* round her right one; in her right hand she held a tremendous sword which glinted brightly, in her left a golden coloured lotus flower; her colour resembled that of the gold on her right side, but faded into dark blue on her left; with the splendid pearl jewel blossomed from the rays of the full moon, with her coral-red mouth with its sparkling teeth, with her white and luminous face, her eye painted like a water lily, her head adorned by a crescent moon over her matted hair [...] She said: 'I am the protectress of the great and beautiful city of Maturā'.

One of the attributes of the 'goddess founder of the lineage' is the *iṭainilā virinta nittila nakai*, 'the splendid pearl jewel blossomed from the rays of the full moon'—particularly interesting is the subtle taste for the light emanated by the pearl jewel. In a similar manner, in the fragment by Megasthenes quoted above (FGrHist 715 F 13), the importance of the fabulous jewel belonging to Pandaea, given to her by her father Heracles, was underlined by Megasthenes' Indian sources. The close parallel between the passage by Megasthenes on 'a new kind of jewel for the women' and *Cilappatik.* XXIII, 4 is clear: the great interest for the pearls found in the seas of southern India is evident in both texts.[128] Undoubtedly this was one of the causes which led the Magadha empire to enforce its 'Südpolitik' which, under the converted king Aśoka, would have its most remarkable success in the transplantation of the tree sacred to Buddhism from Bodh Gaya to Ceylon.[129]

About the results of such policies on the commercial level the author of the *Arthaśāstra* is clear, *Arthaśāstra* VII, 12, 22-4:

sthalapathe 'pi haimavato dakṣiṇāpathācchreyān, hastyaśvagandha-dantājinarūpyasuvarṇapaṇyāḥ sāravattarāḥ ityācāryāḥ / neti kauṭilyaḥ / kambalājināśvapaṇyavarjāḥ śaṅkhavajramāṅimuktāsuvarṇa paṇyāśca prabhūtarā dakṣiṇāpathe/.

Regarding the overland route: 'That of the Himalaya (*Haimavat*) is preferable to that of the South (*Dakṣiṇa*[130]); in fact merchandise such as elephants, horses, spices, ivory, hide, silver and gold are the more precious.' So think the masters. But not so Kauṭilya. Although in the Road to the South goods such as woollen blankets, hide and horses are not available, commodities such as shells, diamonds, precious stones, pearls and gold are more abundant there.

The author of the *Arthaśāstra* also has a very clear idea of where the pearls came from. *Arthaśāstra* II, 11, 2:

tāmraparṇikaṃ pāṇḍyakavāṭakaṃ pāśikyaṃ kauleyaṃ caurṇeyaṃ māhendraṃ kārdamikaṃ srautasīyaṃ hrādīyaṃ haimavataṃ ca mauktikam. ('A pearl may be *tāmraparṇika, pāṇḍyakavāṭaka, pāśikya, kauleya, caurṇeya, māhendra, kārdamika, srautasīya, hrādīya and haimavata*.')[131]

Thus, we may in part conclude that the fanciful colouring of the legend of Pandaea which is so striking to Megasthenes' readers and so splendidly assimilated into India's <Hellenistic> mythology, like the description of the beautiful *mutal* which must have no less struck the readers of the *Cilappatikaram*, does have an historical foundation. It reflects on a mythological level the commercial importance of the 'Road to the South', which enabled merchants to embark upon the great adventure of the purchasing of pearls.

Another reference, this time epigraphic, to the pearls found in the kingdom of the Pāṇṭiyar, is found in the above-mentioned inscription of Khāravela.[132] In line 13 it is said of the Kaliṅga king that: *Paṃḍarājā* [*ch=edāni anekāni*] *m*[*u*]*tamaṇi-ratanāni āharāpayati.* ('He has had many pearls, precious gems and jewels brought from king Paṃḍa'.)

As we have seen, according to the *PME*, diving for pearls occurred mostly along the coast from Cape Comorin to Kolchoi,[133] and the *Cilappatikaram* attests to the existence of *tuṟai* both in Kumari and Koṟkai (= Gk. Kolchoi).[134] Kumari, however, was honoured above all as a religious centre,[135] whereas Koṟkai was linked by Dravidian poetry to the glory of the pearls of the Pāṇṭiyar. Its site has been identified on the banks of the river Tāmraparṇī; on account of the receding of the sea it is now situated some five miles from the coast.[136] Excavations on the site, carried out rather unsystematically, have brought to light heaps of oyster shells here and there.

At this point it will be useful to look at the various testimonies relating to Koṟkai in the *Caṅkam Ilakkiyam.* Quite often, the splendour of the beloved's teeth is compared to that of the pearls from Koṟkai,[137] but a more interesting picture is in *Akanāṉūṟu* 130, 8-11:

[...] pū nāṟu parappiṉ
ivar tirai tanta īrṅ katir muttam
kavar naṭaip puravi kāl vaṭut tapukkum
nal tēr vaḻuti koṟkai muṉ tuṟai

In the port of Koṟkai, which has the fragrance of the strongly scented flower and which belongs to king Pāṇṭiyaṉ of the good chariot, the horse that would wish to tread upon the pearls with the moist light which the wave has brought, would ruin its hoof with a scar.

We can follow this up with *Akanāṉūṟu* 201, 3-7:

viṉai navil yāṉai viṟaṟ pōrp pāṇṭiyaṉ
pukaḻ mali ciṟappiṉ koṟkai muṉtuṟai,
avirkatir muttamoṭu valampuri corintu,
taḻai aṇip polinta kōṭu ēntu alkul
paḻaiyar makaḷir paṉit tuṟaip parava

In the port of Koṟkai, pride of the Pāṇṭiyaṉ victorious in battle with his trained elephants, the fishermen's wives with their rounded hips and resplendent waists, with dresses made of leaves, having offered *valampuri* and shining pearls, pray in the cool ghat.

Finally Maturaikkāñci 135-8:

viḷaintu mutirnta viḻumuttiṉ
ilaṅkuvaḷai iruñcēri
kaṭkoṇṭik kuṭippākkattu
ṅaṟkoṟkaiyōr nacaipporuna

Oh king, beloved by the good citizens of Koṟkai, who drink *kaḷ* in the wide roads of the villages, as a reward for the shell resplendent with the marvellous pearl which has completely ripened.

In these passages is expressed with poetic grace the proud opulence of this city, derived from the age-old activity, i.e. pearl fishing, which had earned it its fame and importance among the cities of the kingdom of the Pāṇṭiyar, as Koṟkai was the seat of several members of the royal family.[138] Though sporting a different name, it maintained all its grandeur even in Marco Polo's times.[139]

Unfortunately it is not possible to investigate further the fascinating claim made by the *PME*, that diving for pearls was carried out by convicts:[140] it may, however, be related to the widespread use of slave labour in ancient India.[141]

(*b*) *Kamara, Podouke, Sopatma*

Paṭṭiṉappālai 184-93:

cellā nal icai amarar kāppiṉ,
nīriṉ vanta nimir parip puraviyum,

kālin vanta karuṅ kari mūṭaiyum,
vaṭamalaip piranta maṇiyum poṉṉum,
kuṭamalaip piranta āramum akilum,
teṉ kaṭal muttum, kuṇa kaṭar tukirum,
kaṅkai vāriyum, kāvirip payaṉum,
īlattu uṇavum, kāḻakattu ākkamum,
ariyavum, periyavum, neriya īṇṭi,
vaḷam talaimayaṅkiya naṉan talai marukiṉ.

Under the protection of the gods of immortal and good fame, agile jumping horses are transported by sea, sacks of black pepper taken upon the wheels of carts; precious gems and gold which are born in the northern mountain; sandalwood and *akil* born in the western mountain; pearls which come from the southern seas, coral which comes from the eastern seas; the prosperity of the Ganges, the produce of the Kāviri; the foodstuffs of Ceylon and the artefacts of Kāḻakam and other rare and precious merchandise are accumulated, compressed, in the wide streets where wealth lies in disarray.

Thus, by the end of the second century AD,[142] Pukār, also known as Kāvirippūmpaṭṭinam, capital of the kingdom of the Cōḻar, identifiable with the *Chabēris empórion* in Ptolemy[143] and the *Kamára* of the *PME*, was one of India's most important centres of trade. Displayed on its streets one could find goods coming from the Ganges, from Ceylon, and from Kāḻakam;[144] pearls from Korkai, and coral from the eastern seas,[145] as well as gold, precious gems and pepper from the interior.[146] Yet already by the first century AD Kāvirippūmpaṭṭinam had gained a position which was certainly not secondary in the context of the trade conducted in the Bay of Bengal and in the seas of southern India. *PME* 60, p. 20, 4-10 Fr.:

τῶν δὲ καὶ † τούτων ἐμπορίων τε καὶ ὅρμων, ἐς οὓς οἵ τε ἀπὸ τῆς Λιμυρικῆς καὶ ἀπὸ ἄρκτου πλέοντες κατάγονται, ἐπισημότερα καὶ κατὰ τὸ ἑξῆς κείμενά ἐστιν ἐμπόρια Καμάρα καὶ Ποδούκη καὶ Σωπάτμα, ἐν οἷς τοπικὰ μέν ἐστιν πλοῖα μέχρι Λιμυρικῆς παραλεγόμενα τὴν γῆν, ἕτερα δ' ἐκ μονοξύλων πλοίων μεγίστων ἀφαῖς ἐζευγμένα, λεγόμενα σάνγαρα· τὰ δὲ εἰς τὴν Χρυσῆν καὶ εἰς τὸν Γάγγην διαίροντα κολανδιοφωντα τὰ μέγιστα.

Of the ports of trade and harbours [in these parts?] at which vessels sailing from both Limyrike and the north call, the more important are in sequence the ports of trade of Kamara, Poduke, and Sopatma. They are the home ports for local boats that sail along the coast as far as Limyrike and other boats, called *sangara*, that are very big Kolandiophonta (?) that sail across to Chryse and Ganges emporium.

Kamara, Podouke and Sopatma were the most important ports of the south-eastern coast of India. The function of these ports is clear: on the one hand they represented ports of call for the long-distance trade with the Ganges emporium and the 'island' (as the *PME* calls it) of Chryse, on the other they helped develop the small-scale local trade, redistributing the goods imported from the north along the numerous small ports of India's southern tip, up to the Limyrike. Hence the different types of vessels which so impressed the author of the *PME*.[147] It is precisely in the context of trade links between the Limyrike and the south-western coast of India, that the Roman pottery found at some sites along the coast of modern-day Tamilnadu should, in my view, be interpreted.

One of the most sensational archaeological discoveries in the Indian subcontinent was the excavation of several sherds of Arretine ware and 'mediterranean' amphorae at Arikamedu near Pondicherry.[148] The presence of this pottery, dating to the Augustan period[149] has been variously explained. Publishing the results of the excavation, R.E.W. Wheeler argued, on the basis of a passage of the *Cilappatikaram*,[150] that the remains found at Arikamedu were the vestiges of an 'Indo-Roman Trading Station', where the Roman merchants had their warehouses.[151] M.P. Charlesworth, recognising that the *PME* had a good knowledge of the Indian coasts only up to Cape Comorin, maintained that the Arretine ware must have been brought to Arikamedu aboard Indian ships.[152] Wheeler's later reassessment of the problem led him to conclude that the Roman trading stations which had been set up in the ports of the eastern coasts under Augustus and Tiberius, constituted for Westerners the 'termini of trans-peninsular routes';[153] i.e. that the pottery reached Arikamedu overland by the road which ran from the western to the eastern coast through the district of Coimbatore.

Material similar to that found at Arikamedu has more recently been excavated at Vasavasamudra,[154] situated just to the north of the former site, and at Ramanathapuram[155] at the mouths of the Vaikai (the river which flows through Maturai, the capital of the Pāṇṭiyar), further to the south. The phenomenon, therefore, is neither casual nor sporadic and cannot be ignored or minimized, but should be interpreted in the light of the Latin and Greek sources of the first century, while the *Cilappatikram* cited by Wheeler reflects, as we have seen, a reality which dates back at least to the late second century AD:[156] in other words, to a time when the Yavaṉar merchants had penetrated much deeper into southern India. It would therefore be anachronistic to refer to this text in order to explain the presence of Arretine ware of the Augustan period at the site of Arikamedu.

In the last analysis, the problem posed here relates to the trade routes of Roman merchants in India in general: were they exclusively maritime, or part maritime, part-overland? The first of these two hypotheses seems by far the more preferable: that Western merchants had penetrated into the interior of southern India in the pursuit of their trade is attested by no literary source.[157] The silence of Pliny, commander of the Roman fleet and so very well-informed about the characteristics of these trade routes, is eloquent on this point. On the basis of the information he provides, in conjunction with the data in the *PME*, it is difficult to believe in a combination of maritime and overland routes. The Roman pottery found at Ramanathapuram, Arikamedu and Vasavasamudra can be most naturally explained in terms of the small-scale coastal trade which linked the ports of the Limyrike to those of India's south-eastern coast.

In this respect we must consider a crucial passage, *PME* 60, p. 20, 10-13 Fr.:

προχωρεῖ δὲ εἰς τοὺς τόπους τούτους πάντα τὰ εἰς τὴν Λιμυρικὴν ἐργαζόμενα, καὶ σχεδὸν εἰς αὐτοὺς καταντᾷ τό τε χρῆμα τὸ ἀπ' Αἰγύπτου φερόμενον τῷ παντὶ χρόνῳ κα<ὶ> τὰ πλεῖστα γένη πάντων τῶν ἀπὸ Λιμυρικῆς φερομένων <καὶ> διὰ ταύτης τῆς παραλίας ἐπιχορηγουμένων.

Into these places are [re-]exported all the trade goods sent into [or: exchanged in] the Limyrike, and almost as far as there arrive the cash [or: commodities] exported from Egypt in all time and most kinds of all the goods brought from Limyrike and supplied along the coast.

The interpretation of this is disputed. While Müller thought it referred in general to the goods exported from the Limyrike: ('*Importantur in haec loca quaecumque in Limyricen negotiandi causa mittuntur, et omnes fere species quovis tempore ex Aegypto afferri solitae, plurimaeque eorum quae e Limyrice exportantur et per tractum hunc litoralem suppeditantur.*')[158] Frisk instead considers the translation by Müller 'un peu douteuse'. Concerning the interpretation of the expression εἰς τὴν Λιμυρικὴν ἐργαζόμενα he does not amend its text as had been suggested by Fabricius, but approves the latter's translation 'alles was in Limyrike produciert wird'.[159] Moreover, he attributes to χρῆμα the meaning of 'argent',[160] and not that of '*species*' given by Müller.

It is perhaps possible that in εἰς τὴν Λιμυρικὴν ἐργαζόμενα the construction εἰς + acc. is intended (as Frisk maintained) as conveying a locative sense; but in any case ἐργαζόμενα seems more likely to have here the meaning of 'traded', all the more appropriate coming from the pen of a merchant. It is possible too that χρῆμα here means only 'coins', and not (as Müller believed) 'goods'. But if the author of the *PME* was particularly interested in the occurrence of the Roman coins in the emporia of the south-east coast of India, it does not follow that only coins, among the Western goods, were re-exported. Coins and, as we have good reason to think, also goods coming from Egypt were therefore re-exported together with the products of the Limyrike, along the south-eastern coast of India. Those carrying out this trade are simply named οἱ ἀπὸ τῆς Λιμυρικῆς—πλέοντες opposite to them are (οἱ) ἀπὸ ἄρκτου πλέοντες. These are the two opposite routes from the west (Limyrike) and from the east and north (Ganges emporium and 'island' Chryse), which join at the emporia of India's south-eastern coast:[161] this would seem to show that this was a trade mainly conducted among Indians.

The ports of India's south-western and south-eastern coasts complemented each other. Those of the south-western coast were the the point of arrival of the ships coming from the Roman empire and from the north-western coast of India.[162] Those of the south-eastern coast maintained trade relations with the 'island' of Chryse, with the Ganges emporium and, through the latter, with the '*polis*' of Thina.[163] All that was imported through the ports of both coasts became the object of a short-distance coastal trade which linked all the ports of the southern coasts of India. The organization which allowed Western merchants to purchase in the Limyrike goods which came from the Ganges emporium and the 'island of Chryse', is the same as that which brought the Roman amphorae full of wine to Arikamedu.[164]

Throughout the first century AD, the ports of the Limyrike remained the main if not the only bridgeheads of Roman trade in India. It was only in the second century that the Roman merchants, for reasons which still remain to be explained, shifted their attention to the south-western and south-eastern coasts of India. Increasingly they came to use the trade routes of the Bay of Bengal. That was also the period during which the Yavaṉar possessed palaces in Pukār, the capital of the kingdom of the Cōlar,[165] and had embassies as far afield as the Chinese court.[166]

THE EFFECTS OF TRADE BETWEEN ROME AND SOUTHERN INDIA ON THE ECONOMY AND POLITICS OF ROME

What were the effects of trade with India and what consequences did it have on the economy and politics of Rome during the Julio-Claudian period? An attempt to answer these questions may begin with some remarks on the deficit in the empire's trade balance. As is well-known, an annual deficit of 50,000,000 HS in trade with India is lamented by Pliny in the above-cited passage *N.H.* VI, 101: [...] *digna res nullo anno minus HS D (centena milia)*[167] *India exhauriente et merces remittente quae apud nos centiplicato ueneant.*[168]

Although this figure is only an approximate one, I do not share the scepticism with which it has been treated by some scholars.[169] Without being excessively inquisitive as to their nature and origin,[170] I do believe the indications given by Pliny, *praefectus classis*, to have at least some degree of reliability. Pliny in fact claims to have had *certa notitia* ('sure knowledge') about Roman trade with India. Whoever asserts that 'personal experience and acquaintance [...] appear to be unlikely sources for Pliny's figures'[171] would then have to explain why Pliny in some respects succeeds in being even more accurate than the *PME*. However, the figure of 50,000,000 HS given by Pliny can only represent an indicative value if one wishes to estimate the outflow of precious metals in the form of coinage towards India during the Julio-Claudian period. One cannot be sure that the expression *nullo anno* extends back to the first years of the Augustan age. Nor do we know by how much the minimum of 50,000,000 HS could have been increased.

The only evidence which could help to define the extent of the Roman empire's deficit during the Julio-Claudian period, is represented by the Roman coin hoards found in southern India. However, the exceptional preponderance of coins of Tiberius (the most significant finding that emerges from the analysis of these hoards)[172] suggests the possibility that due to an intensification of trade under this emperor, a predilection for coins struck by him[173] became widespread throughout southern India, and that a part of these coins was exported to India only after his death. The results of a statistical calculation carried out on the basis of the number of Roman coins found to this day in India would therefore be even more uncertain. Yet even if a considerable percentage of coins of Tiberius found in India were only exported following his death, the importance of this emperor's rule in terms of trade with southern India would remain unaffected; it must be seen in relation to the observations of Tacitus on the expansion of *luxus* in the years AD 16 to 22, to which we shall return later.

As for the consequences which this outflow was to have on monetary circulation in the Roman empire, the opinions of scholars are divided. On the one hand, we have the hypotheses of T. Frank[174] who saw this 'outflow of gold and silver' as an important factor in the 'contraction of currency' which determined, among other things, the economic crisis in AD 33. On the other, we have the theories of G. Mickwitz,[175] who maintained that 'du moment que l'empire romain comprenait des régions productives d'or, une exportation d'or était une chose parfaitement naturelle, tout comme dans les pays productifs d'or actuellement. Vouloir prétendre que, par là, la quantité d'or serait devenue trop faible est naturellement absurde'.

The problem may be examined by comparing the deficit in the balance of payment to India (let us accept, for the sake of convenience, the 50,000,000 HS indicated by Pliny) with other data relating to the Roman economy. The comparison which is generally drawn in this regard is with the assets of certain exponents of the senatorial order, who were the main beneficiaries of the luxury items imported from India. One can but note the exiguousness of the Roman deficit as compared to the wealth of some senators.[176] Considering that Seneca alone possessed assets worth 300,000,000 HS, a deficit of a mere 50,000,000 HS would tend to corroborate the 'tenuità effettiva del volume assoluto di questi commerci'.[177] Yet we still lack indispensable data for evaluating the volume of Roman trade with India from Pliny's figure. For example, we still lack more precise information concerning the purchasing power of Roman coins in India—the only indication we possess, and that a rather vague one, is that the price of Indian goods in the Roman empire (*apud nos*) was a hundred times more than in India. We do not actually know the extent of the 'outflow' of Roman coins other than the figure of 50,000,000 HS pointed out by Pliny, or the amount of exported goods. The most significant evidence concerning the volume of trade are thus the one hundred and twenty ships which, according to Strabo, left for India in 26 BC.[178]

Returning to Pliny's text, what rendered the trade with India worthy (*digna res*) of detailed description, was not only the trade deficit of 50,000,000 HS per year, but also the goods which were sold within the Empire at a price one hundred times greater. Both phenomena need to be analysed in context. The round figure prevents us from taking Pliny's text too be literally. Yet even so, it cannot be very far from the truth. In Rome the prices of certain articles were truly very high, and it was natural for them to have been subjected to steep price rises as compared to their Indian prices.[179] We may cite in this connection Plin. *N.H.* IX, 117:

Lolliam Paulinam [...] *uidi smaragdis margaritisque opertam, alterno textu fulgentibus toto capite, crinibus, auribus, collo, digitis, quae summa quadrigentiens HS colligebat, ipsa confestim parata mancupationem tabulis probare. nec dona prodigi principis fuerant, sed auitae opes, prouinciarum scilicet spoliis partae.*

I have seen Lollia Paulina, [...], not at some considerable or solemn ceremonial celebration but actually at an ordinary betrothal banquet, covered with emeralds and pearls interlaced alternately and shining all over her head, hair, ears, neck and fingers, the sum total amounting to the value of 40,000,000 sesterces, she herself being ready at a moment's notice to give documentary proof of the purchase at such a price. That parure was not the gift of a lavish emperor, but it was purchased with hereditary riches, accumulated by plundering provinces.

Lollia Paulina's parure (40,000,000 HS) must have been exceptional, just like her 'hereditary riches'. But her case may help us all the same to understand how the 'passion for magnificence' (in which so significant a role was played by the goods imported from the Limyrike), fuelling a business worth billions of sesterces within the empire, not only caused the ruin of the 'noble and illustrious families', but led to the immense enrichment of all those who exploited the fashion of the time by trading in luxury goods.[180] It is clear, in any case, that if India with its exported goods was able to absorb (*exhaurire*) approximately 50,000,000 HS of the Roman empire (*imperii nostri*) every year, the *luxus* must have cost the old senatorial families far more, both economically and politically.

The question of *luxus* in fact was to have political repercussions, since it posed a major problem to a state such as the Roman one: that of the stability of its ruling class. This problem was clearly posed under Tiberius[181], following the calls for sumptuary laws made by several senators. Tac. *Ann.* II, 33:

Proximo senatus die multa in luxum ciuitatis dicta a Q. Haterio consulari, Octauio Frontone praetura functo; decretumque ne uasa auro solida ministrandis cibis fierent, ne uestis Serica uiros foedaret. Excessit Fronto ac postulauit modum argento, suppellectili, familiae: erat quippe adhuc frequens senatoribus, si quid e re publica crederent, loco sententiae promere. Contra Gallus Asinius disseruit: auctu imperii adoleuisse etiam priuatas opes, idque non nouum, sed e uetustissimis moribus: aliam apud Fabricios, aliam apud Scipiones pecuniam et cuncta ad rem publicam referri, qua tenui angustas ciuium domos, postquam eo magnificentiae uenerit gliscere singulos. Neque in familia et argento quaeque ad usum parentur nimium aliquid aut modicum nisi ex fortuna possidentis. Distinctos senatus et equitum census, non quia diuersi natura, sed ut locis (*ut sicut locis* Url.), *ordinibus, dignationibus antistent ita iis* (Rup.: *talis*) *quae ad requiem animi aut salubritatem corporum parentur, nisi forte clarissimo cuique plures curas, maiora pericula subeunda, delenimentis curarum et periculorum carendum esse. Facilem adsensum Gallo sub nominibus honestis confessio uitiorum et similitudo audientium dedit. Adiecerat et Tiberius non id tempus censurae nec, si quid in moribus labaret, defuturum corrigendi auctorem.*

At the next session, the ex-consul, Quintus Haterius, and Octavius Fronto, a former praetor, spoke at length against the national extravagance; and it was resolved that table-plates should not be manufactured in solid gold, and that Oriental silks should no longer degrade the male sex. Fronto went further, and pressed for a statutory limit to silver, furniture and domestics: for it was still usual for a member to precede his vote by mooting any point which he considered to be in the public interest. Asinius Gallus opposed—'With the expansion of the empire, private fortunes had also grown; nor was this new, but consonant with extremely ancient custom. Wealth was one thing with the Fabricii, another with the Scipiones; and all was relative to the state. When the state was poor, you had frugality and cottages; when it attained a pitch of splendour such as the present, the individual also throve. In slaves or plate or anything procured for use there was neither excess nor moderation except with reference to the means of the owner. Senators and knights had a special property qualification, not because they differed in kind from their fellow-men, but in order that those who enjoyed precedence in place, rank, and dignity should enjoy it also in the easements that make for mental peace and physical well-being. And justly so—unless your distinguished men, while saddled with more responsibilities and greater dangers, were to be deprived of the relaxations compensating those responsibilities and those dangers'.—With his virtuously phrased confession of vice, Gallus easily carried with him that audience of congenial spirits. Tiberius, too, had added that it was not the time for the censor, and that if there was any loosening of the morality, a reformer would be forthcoming.

In this session of the senate held in AD 16 two distict positions were enunciated. The first, supported by Q. Haterius and Octauius Fronto, demanded norms to regulate several aspects of the *luxus* in Rome. The second, represented by Asinius Gallus, affirmed the principle that 'in slaves or plate or anything procured for use there was neither excess nor moderation except with reference to the means of the owner'.

The problem, presented as ethical, was in reality essentially an economic and political one. We can imagine that the speeches of Q. Haterius and Octauius Fronto in the senate must have been filled with appeals to ancient simplicity, but their substance was altogether different. The senatorial order consisted of families whose fortunes differed greatly: if a limit were not fixed to the frenetic pursuit of luxury and magnificence, those senators who had difficulty in maintaining such a life-style would have been relegated to a secondary position, if not altogether condemned to exclusion from the senatorial order for having squandered their patrimony in the vain attempt to keep up with their more affluent colleagues.[182] Precisely for these reasons many senators began to be assailed by the problem of *census* during these years.[183] This attempt to establish equality between the members of the senatorial aristocracy was opposed by those who, like Asinius Gallus, based their political prestige precisely on the magnificence and their economic power on the practice of usury.

Faced with this opposition between the two senatorial camps, Tiberius showed prudence: he reassured Asinius Gallus and his supporters ('it was not the time for the censor'), but at the same time gave guarantees to the proponents of austerity, ('if there was any loosening of the morality, a reformer would be forthcoming'). Let us now analyse the events of AD 22. Tac. *Ann.* III, 52:

C. Sulpicius D. Haterius consules sequuntur, inturbidus externis rebus annus domi suspecta seueritate aduersum luxum, qui immensum proruperat ad cuncta, quis pecunia prodigitur. Sed alia sumptuum, quamuis grauiora, dissimulatis plerumque pretiis occultabantur: uentris et ganeae paratus adsiduis sermonibus uulgati fecerant curam, ne princeps antiquae parsimoniae durius aduerteret. Nam incipiente C. Bibulo ceteri quoque aediles disseruerant sperni sumptuariam legem uetitaque utensilium pretia augeri in dies, nec mediocribus remediis sisti posse et consulti patres integrum id negotium ad principem distulerant.

The consulate of Gaius Sulpicius and Decimus Haterius followed: a year of quiet abroad, though at home there was uneasiness at the prospect of stern measures against the luxury which had broken all bounds and extended to every object on which money could be squandered. But other extravagances, though actually more serious, could as a rule be kept private by concealing the prices paid. It was the apparatus of gluttony and intemperance which had become the eternal theme of gossip and had awakened anxiety lest a prince of old-fashioned thriftiness might adopt too harsh measures. For when the point was mooted by Gaius Bibulus, it had been maintained by his fellow-aediles also that the sumptuary law was a dead letter; that the prices for articles of food were unlawfully rising daily; and that the advance could not be checked by moderate methods. The senate too, when consulted, had referred the question without any discussion to the emperor.

Thus the *luxus* which Tiberius had not considered worth subjecting to *censura* in AD 16 had spread in an uncontrollable manner in the following years. In Rome this had given rise to a strange kind of inflation which had been originally fuelled by the high price of luxury goods, but which gradually spread to *utensilia* too.[184] And it was precisely this rise in the price of foodstuffs which brought about protests from the populace as well as the resentment of the *princeps*.[185]

The fear of a harsh reaction on Tiberius' part must have given fresh heart to the party of 'rigour'. In AD 22, at any rate, D. Haterius Agrippa, son of Q. Haterius, was elected consul together with C. Sulpicius.[186] On the initiative of C. Bibulus the aediles[187] submitted the closely interlinked problems of the infringement of the sumptuary law and rising prices to the examination of the senate. The senators in turn referred them back to Tiberius. After lengthy consideration, the emperor was forced to go back on his word and forsake the *censura* which he had promise, but which had now become impossible;[188] any attempt to introduce it would have been inevitably vain and ended up by discrediting the emperor himself and the institutions.[189] Embittered and disappointed, Tiberius ultimately gave his reluctant approval to the economy of the senatorial order, characterized by *luxus* and usury, and destined to resist throughout the Julio-Claudian period.

Having outlined the context in which the trade relations with India must be visualized, let us now try to answer the question posed at the beginning of this chapter by pointing out what we believe were the main consequences of this trade on Roman economic and political life.

The first consequence on the economy—the one usually pointed out—was the 'outflow of gold and silver' towards southern India. This certainly must have had some importance, if the figure actually approximated to 50,000,000 HS mentioned by Pliny: a sum which corresponds to half the total which Tiberius made available to the banks in order to solve the serious financial crisis in AD 33.[190] The second consists in the huge sums which poured into the state coffers as a result of the imposition of high taxes on the kind of imported luxury goods we are considering.[191] The third consequence was the impetus given to the reinforcement of the enormous capital, the capital, that is, that financed the trade with India and the associated sumptuary expenses of the aristocratic families.

All three forces contributed, and not, we believe, marginally, to determine the imbalances typical of the Julio-Claudian period. In AD 33 the greater part of the capital in question was in the hands of the money-lending senators and of the state treasury.[192] Tiberius solved the financial crisis which occurred that year by making available 100,000,000 HS. By the time of his death four years later the state treasury had accumulated resereves of 2,700,000,000 HS.[193]

As far as the political repercussions are concerned, the responseof Tiberius to the question raised by the aediles in AD 22 marked a turning-point in the history of the Julio-Claudian period. It spelt the ultimate defeat of those who, by opposing the rage for *luxus*, had sought to curb the political and economic ascendancy of the richest senators and to ensure the preservation and survival of impoverished noble families.

Yet not even the supporters of *luxus* and of Asinius Gallus whose 'greatness of fame meant death', emerged as victors in this contest. Their political power was fatally weakened by informers and their possessions were eventually absorbed by the state treasury.

Throughout the Julio-claudian period, therefore, the great senatorial families were exposed on the one hand to the risks of financial ruin determined by too high a standard of living, and on the other to the crises deriving from the difficult relationship with an ever-suspecting monarchy. Despite 'legal penalties and threats', the situation only changed in the Flavian period, by which time the ruling class had been renewed in manpower and customs. The trade with India of course continued; indeed, in some respects, it even increased. But it did so within a different economic 'cycle' of the Mediterranean world.

I would like to conclude by quoting in its entirety the passage of Tacitus which has inspired this research right from the outset. My only hope is that I may have stimulated the reader to reflect on this subject more fruitfully than I did. Tac. *Ann.* III, 55:

Auditis Caesaris litteris remissa aedilibus talis cura: luxusque mensae a fine Actiaci belli ad ea arma, quis Seruius Galba rerum adeptus est, per annos centum profusis sumptibus exerciti paulatim exoleuere. Causas eius mutationis quaerere libet. Dites olim familiae nobilium aut claritudine insignes studio magnificentiae prolabebantur. Nam etiam tum plebem, socios, regna colere et coli licitum; ut quisque opibus, domo, paratu speciosus, per nomen et clientelas inlustrior habebatur. Postquam caedibus saeuitum et magnitudo famae exitio erat, ceteri ad sapientiora conuertere. Simul noui homines, e municipiis et coloniis atque etiam prouinciis in senatum crebro adsumpti, domesticam parsimoniam intulerunt, et quamquam fortuna uel industria plerique pecuniosam ad senectam peruenirent, mansit tamen prior animus. Sed praecipuus adstricti moris auctor Vespasianus fuit, antiquo ipse cultu uictuque. Obsequium inde in principem et aemulandi amor ualidior quam poena ex legibus et metus.

Nisi forte rebus cunctis inest quidam uelut orbis, ut quem ad modum temporum uices, ita morum uertantur;[194] *nec omnia apud priores meliora, sed nostra quoque aetas multa laudis et artium imitanda posteris tulit. Verum haec nobis <in> (Lips.) maiores certamina ex honesto maneant.*

When the Caesar's [Tiberius'] epistle had been read, the aediles were exempted from such a task; and luxury of banqueting, after being practised with extravagant prodigality throughout the century between the close of the Actian War and the struggle which placed Servius Galba on the throne, went gradually out of vogue. The reasons for that change are worth examining. Old rich families, noble and illustrious, were often ruined by a passion for magnificence. For it was still legitimate in those to court or be courted by the populace, by the provincials, by dependent princes; and the more handsome the fortune, the palace, the establishment of a man, the more imposing his reputation and his clientèle. After the merciless executions, when greatness of fame meant death, the survivors turned to wiser paths. At the same time, the self-made men, repeatedly drafted into the senate from the municipalities and colonies, and even from the provinces, introduced the plain-living habits of their own hearths; and although by good fortune or industry very many arrived to be rich in later life, they retained their former habits. No one promoted simplicity more than Vespasian, with his own old-fashioned way of life. For deference to the emperor and the wish to emulate him were more effective than legal penalties and threats. Or should we rather say there is a kind of cycle in all things, so that habits revolve like season?

Nor, indeed, were all things better in the old time before us; but our own age too has produced much in the sphere of true nobility and much in that of art which posterity well may imitate. In any case, may the honourable competition of our present with our past long remain!

NOTES

1. Regarding the *uexata quaestio* relating to the dating of the *Periplus Maris Erythraei*, here for obvious reasons we will be able to consider it only in terms pertinent to our theme. For bibliography it will be sufficient to refer to Raschke 1978, pp. 663-6.

   Of the works published after Raschke's study we recall the paper of F. Pauli, *NAHAPĀNA/MANBAN.Σ vor 78 n.Chr.? Ein epigraphischer Neufund aus Indien und seine Bedeutung für die antike Südasien-Chronologie*, in *Studien zur alten Geschichte Siegfried Lauffer zum 70. Geburstag am 4 August 1981 dargebracht von Freunden, Kollegen und Schülern*, Roma 1986, II pp. 744-53, which has the merit of having shown that in the epigraphs of Nahapāna the year of reign is indicated instead of that of the Śaka era.The dating of Nahapāna which may be deduced from it would, together with the dating of Maliku, suggest a period comprised between AD 40 and 70: a dating supported by the considerations made in the present work, pp. 90-93.
2. Warmington 1928, p. vii.
3. M. Rostovzeff, *Foreign Commerce of Ptolemaic Egypt* in *Journal of Economic and Business History*, 4 (1931/29), pp. 728-96; id., *The Social and Economic History of the Hellenistic World*, Oxford 1941, pp. 927 ff.; Otto/Bengtson 1938, pp. 194-223; Thiel 1966. Other relevant studies will be cited *infra*.
4. Cf. W. Reese, *Die griechischen Nachrichte über Indien*, Leipzig 1914, pp. 39-40; trade with India during the Achaemenid age occurred as a result of explorations carried out by Skylax of Karyanda, cf. Hdt. IV, 44: μετὰ δὲ τούτους περιπλώσαντας Ἰνδοὺς τε κατεστρέψατο Δαρεῖος καὶ θαλάσσῃ ταύτῃ ἐχρᾶτο, although it obviously fulfilled the general requirements of the Achaemenid state (cf. for example, P.J. Junge, *Dareios I. König der Perser*, Leipzig 1944, pp. 75 ff.).

   Skylax's acute sense of observation with regard to Indian political structures (regarding the distance between the sovereign and his subjects: FGrHist 709 F 5; A. Peretti, *Il periplo di Scilace*, Pisa 1979, p. 62) must be compared with the accuracy shown by

Hecataeus in his study of Asia (and here it must be said that the widespread opinion that he was unaware that the Caspian is an inland sea, is an erroneous one: cf. Mazzarino 1965, pp. 73 ff.). Such a sense of observation also has an economic foundation. It may be interesting to recall Deinon's tradition regarding the Persian king's attitude to food and drink originating from areas which were not under Persian control. Is it a problem which may be related to the import of merchandise? Cf. Mazzarino 1966a, p. 14 and n. 331. As for Dravidian India, it must be underlined that a first reference to it is made already in Herodotus III, 101, on which cf. I. Puskás, *Herodotus and India*, in *Oikumene*, 4 (1983), pp. 201-7.

For the existence during the Achaemenid age of a maritime route linking Egypt to Persia which required a journey of approximately forty days, see the fragment of Damastes FGrHist 5 F 8 and Mazzarino's interpretation in *Le vie di comunicazione fra impero achemenide e mondo greco*, in *Atti del convegno sul tema: La Persia e il mondo greco-romano*, Roma 1966, pp. 81-3 (cf. also Mazzarino 1965, n. 194). That these sea voyages, were made taking advantage of the monsoon, once Bab el-Mandeb had been passed, may be deduced from the fact that excursions only took forty days, a very short interval of time indeed when one considers that it took the same time for rowing boats to cross the Red Sea (cf. Hdt. II, 11), whereas other vessels needed about thirty days for the distance Berenice-Muza (cf. Plin. *N.H.* VI, 104).

5. The idea that the discovery of the monsoon occurred 'in stages' is already present in Warmington 1928, p. 44: '[...] the discovery was made in successive stages, developing in a natural manner from voyages to North-West into voyages to Malabar'. I, however, would argue as follows: the wind taken advantage of along all three routes mentioned by Pliny *N.H.* VI, 100-1 is always the same. But the way it was utilized certainly changes, simply because the merchants preferred the new markets of the Limyrike to those of India's north-western coast. The new requirements of commerce, therefore, determined changes, by no means revolutionary, in the navigational techniques—and not *vice versa.*

For a 'complete discovery' of the monsoon and therefore a development of trade with India occurring only during the Julio-Claudian period, cf. Rawlinson 1916, p. 109; Warmington 1928, pp. 42-7; M.P. Charlesworth, *Some Notes on the Periplus Maris Erythraei*, in *Classical Quaterly*, 22 (1928), pp. 94-5; J. Filliozat, *Les échanges de l'Inde et de l'Empire remain, aux premiers siècles de l'ère chrétienne*, in *Revue Historique*, 201 (1949), pp. 5-6; Tarn 1951, pp. 368-9; for a 're-discovery' cf. J. Schwartz, *L'empire romain, l'Egypte et le commerce oriental*, in *Annales (ESC)*, 15 (1960), pp. 24-5. On the problem cf. Raschke 1978, pp. 660-3.

6. Fenestella's testimony is very interesting since it derives from a historian who showed a lively interest in changing customs during his times. Cf. F 24 Pet. on togas, F 25 Pet. on *triclinia* (under Tiberius these became ornate with tortoise-shell scales, the best quality arriving from India), F 27 Pet. on the *tripatinium* (B.S. -*num* v. *tispatiniū* r.). On the different traditions in Pliny and Jerome regarding Fenestella's death, which occurred according to Pliny *nouissimo Tiberii Caesaris principatu*, and according to Jerome in AD 19 cf. Wissowa, *R.E.* VI, II, 2177-8.
7. Cf. Suet. *Aug.* 41, 1; Cass. Dion. 51, 21; Oros. VI, 19, 19; on these passages cf. G. Billeter, *Geschichte des Zinsfusses im griechisch-römischen Altertum bis auf Justinian*, Stuttgart 1898 (rpt Wiesbaden, 1970), pp. 165-7; and Lo Cascio 1978, pp. 250-1.
8. Cf. Verg. *Georg.* II, 116-24: Mazzarino 1965, p. 509, detects in this passage an allusion to a Roman commercial policy.
9. Cf. PIR[2] I, pp. 27 ff., n. 179; S. Jameson, *Chronology of the Campaigns of Aelius Gallus and C. Petronius*, in *Journal of Roman Studies*, 58 (1968), pp. 71-84.
10. Cf. W.W. Tarn, *Ptolemy II*, in *Journal of Egyptian Archaeology*, 14 (1928), p. 251; id., *Ptolemy II and Arabia*, in *Journal of Egyptian Archaeology*, 15 (1929), pp. 9-25; Kortenbeutel 1931; Otto/Bengtson 1938, pp. 194-223; Mooren 1972, pp. 127-32; on the στρατηγὸς ἐπὶ τῆς Ἐρυθρᾶς καὶ Ἰνδικῆς θαλάσσης, cf. H. Bengtson, *Die Strategie in der ellenistischen Zeit*, München 1952, III, pp. 118-19; E. van't Dack, *L'évolution de l'épistratégie dans la Thébaide au Ier siècle av. J. C.*, in *Miscellanea in honorem J. Vergote* (1975/6), pp. 577-87; Raschke 1978, pp. 971-3.
11. Slightly excessive are the observations by Raschke 1978, p. 662, who speaks of 'Strabo's disparagement of the accomplishments of the Ptolemaic period'. Undoubtedly one must bear in mind the laudatory tone used for the Romans, but this must not lead us to doubt the essential veracity of the picture provided by Strabo. In particular the data regarding one hundred and twenty ships setting sail for India appears to be too precise for it not to 'be considered reliable'. As Raschke himself points out, there were in fact excellent reasons for a 'relatively low volume of late Ptolemaic commerce'. 'Strabo's disparagement' refers precisely to the last Ptolemies (the Auletes, cf. Strab. XVII, 1,13).
12. The expression is that of Flavius Josephus, *B. I.* II, 16, 4. (But codices V and C give the reading ὅμορος instead of οὕρμος).
13. Cf. *R. G.* 31; Strab. XV, 1,4; 73; Suet. *Aug.* 21,3; Cass. Dion. LIV.

9, 8; Eutrop. VII, 10,1; Vict. Caes. I, 7; Epit. de Caesaribus I, 9; Oros. VI, 21, 19; Hieron. *Chron.*, ol. 188; on these embassies, cf. Kortenbeutel 1931, p. 57.

14. Cf. Strab. XV, 1, 4:

καὶ οἱ νῦν δὲ ἐξ Αἰγύπτου πλέοντες ἐμπορικοὶ τῷ Νείλῳ καὶ τῷ 'Αραβίῳ κόλπῳ μέχρι τῆς 'Ινδικῆς σπάνιοι μὲν καὶ περιπεπλεύκασι μέχρι τοῦ Γάγγου κτλ.

'As for the merchants who now sail from Egypt along the Nile and the Arabian Gulf as far as India, only a small number have sailed as far as the Ganges etc.'

15. The comparison of the form Limyrike in the *PME* and in Ptol. *Geogr.*, VII, 1,8; 85 with *Dymirice* (but cf. also *Damirice*) in the Tabula Peutingeriana, seg. XII and *Dimirica* in the Cosmographus Ravennas II, 1,2,3 is familiar. These two forms (*L-*, *D-*) are parallel and both correct; the correction proposed by Schoff 1912, p. 205 and by Huntingford 1980, p. 116, is therefore unacceptable.

The term Limyrike, which in the *PME* and in Ptolemy refers exclusively to the Malabar coast (and will be used with this meaning also in the present work), derives, as is the case for *Dimirica* and *Damirice*, from a Prakrit rendering of the Dravidian *tamiḻ* : it can be compared to the Tamil concepts of *tamiḻakam* and *tamiḻkūṟu*, 'the land of the Tamils', a geographical definition of which is found in the ancient grammatical treatise *Tolkāppiyam*, *Pāyiram: vaṭa vēṅkaṭam teṉ kumari āyiṭait tamiḻkūṟu nallulakam*, 'the good earth comprised between mount Vēṅkaṭa (in the vicinity of Tirupati) to the north, and Cape Comorin to the south, this is the *tamiḻkūṟu*'. Here *tamiḻkūṟu* denotes the linguistic area (cf. K. Ramamurthy, *The Linguistic Area of Tamil Nad*, in *Tamil Culture* [1952] p. 165) and its extension is much vaster than that of the Limyrike since it includes the entire southern extremity of the Indian subcontinent. The corresponding political concept is to be found in the inscription at Hāthīgumphā of the king of Kalinga Khāravela (cf. K.P. Jayaswal, R.D. Banerji, in *Epigraphia Indica*, XX, pp. 72 ff.) in which line 11 reads: *janapasa-bhāvanaṁ (sic) cha terasa vas-satikaṁ ābhi[ṁ]dati tramira-desha-saṁghātaṁ* ('defeated the confederation of the Tamil region, which was 113 (or 1300?) years old and had endangered the *janapada*'). The dating of the inscription is controversial: some date it to the middle of the second century BC, others to the early first century AD, cf. D.C. Sircar, *Select Inscriptions bearing on Indian History and Civilization*, Calcutta 1942, p. 206. Unfortunately it is not possible to ascertain the relationship between this 'confederation of the Tamil region' and the three great kingdoms—already attested in the well known R.E. of Aśoka II and XIII—of the Cēralar, Pāṇṭiyar and Cōḻar; it would be interesting to ascertain whether they were all members of this confederation, in other words, whether the *tramira-desha* was one with the *tamiḻ-kūṟu*.

16. We accept the reading *hypalum*, in agreement with the conclusions drawn by S. Mazzarino, *On the name of the hipalus (hippalus) wind in Pliny*: in the present volume, pp. 72-79.
17. Mayhoff 1906, pp. 554-5, remarks: 'tempus praeteritum *infestabant* aliter ferri uix potest quam inserto aut *prius* post *positis* (sic!) aut *nunc* ante *nauigatur*'. This is however unacceptable: the expression *omnibus annis nauigatur* refers to an action which while still continuing in the present, had begun in the past. The imperfective *infestabant* takes us back to the time when Western merchants decided for the first time to take archers with them. In those times pirate attacks must have been more frequent (*maxime*) than later on, at the time when Pliny was writing. It should be noted that Pliny in *N.H.* VI, 104 advises not heading for Muziris so as to avoid the attacks of pirates; further remarks on this will be made later in the paper.

    An echo of the Yavanāḥ merchants' fighting of Indian piracy is also found in the Daśakumāracarita of Daṇḍin VI, 16.
18. For this reading, cf. *infra* n. 167.
19. Cf. Mazzarino 1965, p. 17; 454 ff.; 613; Mazzarino 1966a, pp. 123 ff.; p. 217; Mazzarino 1966b, pp. 205; 231; 365 ff.; Mazzarino 1986, pp. 96; 141; 146; E. Gabba, *Progetti di riforme economiche e fiscali di uno storico dell'età dei Severi*, in *Studi in onore di A. Fanfani*, I, Milano 1962, pp. 41-68; Cavallaro 1984, pp. 198 ff.
20. Plin. *N.H.* VI, 100-1 must be compared with the *PME* 57, p. 19, 8-9 Fr.:

    οἱ μὲν εἰς Λιμυρικὴν πλέοντες ἐπὶ πλεῖον τραχηλίζοντες, οἱ δὲ εἰς Βαρύγαζαν οἵ τε εἰς Σκυθίαν κτλ

    whoever are bound for Limyrike hold out with the wind on the quarter for most of the way, but whoever are bound for Barygaza and whoever for Skythia etc.

    As A. Dihle, *Die entdeckungsgeschichtlichen Voraussetzungen des Indienhandels der römischen Kaiserzeit*, in *Aufstieg und Niedergang der Römischen Welt*, II.9.2. Berlin-New York 1978, p. 549, correctly notes: 'Plinius und der Autor des Periplus zählen übereinstimmend drei Routen auf, über die der Indienhandel im I Jh.n.Chr. abgewickelt wurde: Die eine endete im Gebiet der Indusmündung, die zweite an der Küste des heutigen Gujerat und die dritte, zu jener Zeit wichtigste, die Plinius ausfürlich beschreibt, an der Malabarküste im heutigen Kerala.'

21. Cf. Warmington 1928, p. 44.
22. In the present work the term is used here and elsewhere, in the limits within which it may be applied to ancient Roman society. For a discussion on ancient capitalism, cf. G. Salvioli, *Il capitalismo antico*, Roma 1985 (reprint edited by A. Giardina), pp. 157-89; M. Rostovzev, *Storia economica e sociale dell'impero romano*, Firenze 1933, pp. 401-4; 615-17; on the controversy between 'modernists' and 'primitivists', cf. for example, H.W. Pearson, *The secular debate on economic primitivism*, in K. Polanyi, C.M. Arensberg (eds.), *Trade and Market in the Early Empires. Economics in History and Theory*, New York 1957, pp. 3-12.
23. *Historia Naturale di G. Plinio Secondo, Tradocta di Lingua Latina in Fiorentina per Cristophoro Landino al serenissimo re di Napoli*, 1476.
24. *Caio Plinio Secondo. La Storia Naturale tradotta in 'napolitano misto' da G. Brancati.* Inedito del XV sec. a cura di S. Gentile, Napoli 1974, vol. III, pp. 575-6: 'Et longo tempo <......>, mentre che lo mercante trovò le abreviatione et la India per lo lucro fo facta vicina'; A. Brucioli, *Historia Naturale di G. Plinio Secondo*, Venezia 1548, p. 143: 'Et lungamente si è così nauigato infino a che un mercatante, trouò più breue camino, et pel guadagno si è appressata l'India'; L. Domenichi, *Historia Naturale di G. Plinio Secondo*, Venezia 1561, p. 160: 'Et lungamente s'è nauicato in questo modo, infin che i mercatanti hanno trouata la uia più breue, et che l'India s'è accostata al guadagno'; E. Littré, *Histoire Naturelle de Pline*, Paris 1883, p. 256: 'Longtemps on a navigué ainsi, jusqu'à ce qu'un négociant eût trouvé une voie abrégée, et que l'amour du gain eût rapproché l'Inde'; H. Rackham, *Pliny Natural History*, II, London 1969, p. 415: '[...] for a long time this was the course followed, until a merchant discovered a shorter route and the desire for gain brought India nearer'; André-Filliozat 1980, p. 53: '[...] et ce fut pendant longtemps la route suivie jusqu'à ce qu'un marchand en découvrît une plus courte et que l'appât du gain rapprochât l'Inde'; A. Barchiesi, R. Centi, M. Corsaro, A. Marcone, G. Rannuci, *Gaio Plinio Secondo. Storia Naturale*, I, Torino 1982, p. 711: 'Essa (sc. la seconda rotta) fu seguita a lungo sino a che un mercante ne scoprì una ancora più breve e la brama di richezze non ci avvicinò all'India'.
25. Cf. S. Mazzarino, *Antico, tardoantico ed èra costantiniana*, I, Bari 1974, p. 52.

26. Cf. Pliny's phrase *piratae maxime infestabant.*
27. Casson, 1984, pp. 473-9. Cf. also D. Schlingloff, *Indische Seefahrt in römischer Zeit,* in: H. Müller-Karpe, *Zur geschichtlichen Bedeutung der frühen Seefahrt,* München 1982, p. 70.
28. Casson, 1984, p. 476.
29. Ibid., p. 478.
30. Pliny maintains that the crossing took forty days, *N.H.* VI, 104: *inde uento hippalo nauigant diebus XL ad primum emporium Indiae Muzirim.* This figure is considered by Casson, in *Rome's trade with the East; the sea voyage to Africa and India*, in *Transactions and Proceedings of the American Philological Association*, 110 (1980), pp. 32-3, as 'a mistake'. If it were otherwise the average speed of ships heading to Limyrike would have been only two knots, whereas according to calculations made by Casson himself on the basis of data provided by Pliny and other authors (for which cf. Casson, *Ships and Seamanship in the Ancient World*, Princeton 1971, pp. 282-8) ancient sailing boats aided by favourable winds in the Mediterranean were able to reach a speed of four to six knots; thus Pliny 'by a slip [...] wrote 40 instead of 20'. A somewhat dubious conclusion.
31. Cf. *Th.l.L.*, s.v. *compendium,* III, 2038.
32. A connotation accepted by Brancati, Brucioli, Littré, Rackham, André-Filliozat, Barchiesi-Centi-Corsaro-Marcone-Ranucci.
33. Thus Domenichi.
34. Brucioli, Littré, Rackham, André-Filliozat, Barchiesi-Centi-Corsaro-Marcone-Ranucci.
35. In actual fact the first two lists examined specify the merchandise imported from Minnagar and Barygaza, as opposed to Patale and Sigerus, the ports mentioned by Pliny. However, considering the geographical proximity of Patale to Minnagar and of Sigerus to Barygaza, we may safely assume that from a commercial point of view Patale and Sigerus can be considered equivalent to Minnagar and Barygaza respectively.
36. Cf. *PME* 56, p. 18, 16-17 Fr.:

    πλεῖ δὲ εἰς τὰ ἐμπόρια ταῦτα μεγάλα πλοῖα διὰ τὸν ὄγκον καὶ τὸ πλῆθος τοῦ πιπέρεως καὶ τοῦ μαλαβάθρου

    'Great ships sail in these ports due to the vast quantities of pepper and malabathron'.
37. Cf. *PME* 36, p. 12, 9-10 Fr.:
    εἰσφέρεται δὲ ἀπὸ ἑκατέρων τῶν ἐμπορίων εἴς τε Βαρύγαζαν καὶ εἰς Ἀραβίαν πινικὸν πολὺ μὲν χεῖρον δὲ τοῦ Ἰνδικοῦ κτλ.

'Large quantities of pearls are exported from both ports of trade [sc. Apologos and Omana] to Barygaza and Arabia. They are however of inferior quality as compared to the Indian ones etc.'

Pliny's judgement differs *N.H.* IX, 106:

Indicus maxime has (sc. *margaritas*) *mittit Oceanus* [...] *praecipue autem laudantur circa Arabiam in Persico sinu maris Rubri.*

'They [sc. the pearls] are produced above all by the ocean close to India's coasts [...], but the most praised are those found around Arabia, in the Persian Gulf.'

According to Pliny, Indian pearls exceeded all others in size, cf. *N.H.* IX, 113.

38. Cf. Pliny *N.H.* XXXVII, 55:

Maximum in rebus humanis, non solum inter gemmas, pretium habet adamas, diu non nisi regibus et iis admodum paucis cognitus.

'The highest price, among human things, not only among gems, is that of diamonds, known for a long time only to very few kings.'

On Indian diamonds see Plin. *N.H.* XXXVII, 56; *Arthaśāstra,* II, 11, 89; cf. Gy. Wojtilla, *Indian precious stones in the Ancient East and West,* in *Acta Orientalia,* 27 (1973), p. 216; 223.

39. Schoff 1912, p. 222, identifies the 'transparent stones' with 'principally the beryls'.
40. Plin. *N.H.* VI, 101; XII, 84.
41. Tac. *Ann.* III, 53.
42. *PME* 56: to be rejected is the emendation χρυσώματα suggested by Fabricus and adopted by Rodewald 1976, p. 121.
43. Cf. Raschke 1978, p. 665: 'Of the approximately 5,400 *denarii* which have come to light on the Indian subcontinent, over 99.9% occur in hoards in the southern states of Mysore, Kerala, Madras (Tamilnadu), and the southern portion of Andhra Pradesh. In fact, with the exception of the large Akkempalle hoard, no large find has come from the region north of the Kistna River. Similarly 98% of the approximately 800 *aurei* have been found south of the Kistna'.
44. Cf. Müller 1853, p. 300. On the location of Tyndis, cf. O. Stein, *R.E.* VII, A^2 1791-2.
45. Cf. n. 17.
46. Cf. Plin. *N.H.* VI, 104; *Non expetendum* (sc. *emporium Muzirim*) *propter uicinos piratas, qui optinent locum nomine Nitrias.*

47. Compare the Κηπροβότος of *PME* 54 (but C. Lassen, *Indische Alterthumskunde*, III, Bonn 1873, p. 193 emends the reading to Κηροβότρου) with *Caelobothras* in Plin. *N.H.* VI, 104 and with Κηροβόθρος in Ptol. *Geogr.* VII, 1, 86; all these forms go back to *Keralaputra*, 'son of Kerala', epithet of the Cēralar kings, which appears already in the R.E. XIII of Aśoka.
48. On the formulae of the *Caṅkam Ilakkiyam*, K. Kailasapathy, *Tamil Heroic Poetry*, Oxford 1968, pp. 147-87.
49. *Akanāṉūṟu* 60, 7; *Naṟṟinai* 8, 9; *Kuṟuntokai* 128, 2. On the epithet *Poṟaya*' ('the one from the mountains'), peculiar to the Cēralar, cf. Subrahmanian 1980, p. 41; Dorai Rangaswamy 1968, p. 111; according to the latter scholar it was used to identify a particular branch of the Cēralar.
50. *Aiṅkuṟunūṟu* 178, 2-3. On the cēra epithet *Kuṭṭuva*' ('the western one') again compare Subrahmanian 1980, p. 41; Dorai Rangaswamy 1968, pp. 110-11.
51. *Akanāṉūṟu* 290, 12-13.
52. *Aiṅkuṟunūṟu* 171-80.
53. Id. 171, 4.
54. Id. 173, 3-4.
55. Id. 175, 4.
56. *PME* 54, p. 17, 29-30. Fr.
57. *PME* 53, p. 17, 27 Fr.
58. Cf. n. 51.
59. Cf. *PME* 53, p. 17, 27-28 Fr.: [...] Μούζιρις καὶ Νελκύνδα αἱ νῦν πράσσουσαι, 'Muziris and Nelkynda, which are now the active ones'. Müller 1853, p. 296, quotes the interpretation by Salmasius, *Cl. Salmasii Plinianae Exercitationes*, Parisiis 1629, p. 835: 'i.e. quae nunc negotiantur et frequentatur mercibus'. Frisk 1927, p. 100, believes, albeit with some reservations, that in this case an equivalence between πράσσειν and εὖ πράσσειν can be established.
60. Plin. *N.H.* VI, 104. On the location of Muziris, cf. A. Hermann, *R.E.* XVI 989.
61. On this point cf. my observations in n. 91 and *infra* in the text with regard to the fragment by Megasthenes FGrHist 715 F 13. On the migration of Buddhist and Jain monks towards the south, cf. Mahalingam 1967, pp. 161-92.
62. The interpretation of the passage is disputed. The present translation slightly differs from both that of Meile and that of Zvelebil. The translation of Meile 1940 reads as follows, p. 93: 'Avec ses rues ses maisons, ses barques couvertes, où l'on vend le poisson, où l'on entasse le riz,-avec le remue-ménage de sa

rive bruyante, où les sacs de poivre s'amoncellent, -avec ses livraisons d'or, apportées par les vaisseaux, et amenées à la rive par les bateaux de la lagune, la cité du Kuttuvan au collier d'or, qui donne aux arrivants, pêle-mêle, et les marchandises de la montagne, et les marchandises de la mer, la ville où la liqueur abonde, oui cette Muciri, où gronde l'Océan bruyant, même si l'on me donnait une merveille, un trésor pareils [...]'. Compare with the translation of Zvelebil 1956, p. 403: 'Fish has been sold and paddy piled up on boat and pepper, filling the house, has been heaped in bags in the house and having been thrown, mixed, on the very noisy beach, the gold brought in ships as donation, gathered on shore has been brought in boats ploughing the backwaters. The products of the mountain and the products of the sea having been mixed and heaped and given to the newcomers (in) Mucuṟi resounding with the roar of the sea, belonging to the Kuṭṭuvaṉ with the garland of gold, where toddy flows like water [...]'.

63. On the word *taram*, translated here as 'goods', cf. Meile 1940, p. 94.
64. On the word *paricam*, cf. n. 79.
65. The term *kalam* here takes on the specific connotation of 'ship, vessel' as compared to its more common meaning of 'vase, vessel'. The fact that in Muziris big ships had to anchor from the shore and all operations of loading and unloading were carried out by means of small boats, is confirmed by Pliny *N.H.* VI, 104: *praeterea longe a terra abest nauium statio lintribusque adferuntur* (*efferuntur* va.*II*) *onera et* (DFR*H*. *-ret* E^s *-rat* a *-ra quae* v) *egeruntur*.
66. Cf. Meile 1940, p. 94.
67. On the beryl quarries in the district of Coimbatore, see Ptol. *Geogr.* I, 86: Πουννάτα ἐν ᾗ βήρυλλος 'Pounnata, where beryl (quarries are found)'. (Cf. Vaidyanathan 1983, p. 78); and Buddhabhaṭṭa, *Ratnaparīkṣā* 199: *avidūre vidūrasya girer uttuṅgarodhasaḥ/koṅgavālikasīmānte maṇes tasyākaro* (sc. *vaiḍūryasya*) *bhavat*, ('not far from mount Vidūra with its high slope, within the boundaries between the *koṅga* and the *vālika* is located the quarry of this stone'). Cf. Finot 1896, p. XLVI, who denies the identity between *vaiḍurya* and beryl; for the identification of βήρυλλος/*berullus* with beryl, cf. Blümmer, *R.E.*, III, 1, 320).

The Greek term βηρύλλιον, attested for the first time in the translation of the Septuagint, derives perhaps through a Prakrit form *verūliya*, from the Sanskrit *vaiḍurya*, cf. G.R. Cardona, *I nomi del berillo*, in *Incontri linguistici*, 6 (1980/1981), p. 80.

68. Cf. *PME*, 54, p. 18,1-5 Fr.; Plin. *N.H.* VI, 105; *Akanāṉūṟu*, 149, 8.
69. Cf. Vaidyanathan 1983, pp. 76-7.
70. Gupta 1965, pp. 41-3. Lists of finds of Roman coins in India can be found in R. Sewell, *Roman Coins Found in India*, in *Journal of Royal Asiatic Society*, 1904, pp. 591-637; Wheeler, Ghosh, Deva 1946, pp. 116-21; Wheeler 1951, pp. 375-81; for updating see cf. Rodewald 1976, n. 378; and *Journal of the Numismatic Society of India*, 42 (1980) pp. 11-17; 46 (1984) pp. 37-46.
71. This information was received personally on 10/2/1985 from Dr. Y. Subbarayalu, Professor of Epigraphy and Archaeology of the Tamil University, Thanjavur, to whom I am greatly indebted.
72. Mahadevan 1966, n. 72.
73. Ibid., p. 67; id., *Tamil-Brahmi Inscriptions of the Sangam Age*, in *Proceedings of the Second International Conference Seminar of Tamil Studies*, I, Madras 1971, p. 100; a different reading is given by Mahalingam 1967, p. 296: *māṟaiya vaṇṇakkam* 'a tester of coins and a native of Māranāḍu'.
74. On the diffusion of beryl during the age of Augustus, cf. A. Furtwaengler, *Die antike Gemmen*, Leipzig-Berlin 1900, III, p. 395; G.M.A. Richter, *Catalogue of the Engraved Gems Greek, Etruscan and Roman in the Metropolitan Museum of Art*, Roma 1956, p. XXVII.
75. The most detailed information is found, as usual, in Pliny, *N.H.* XXXVII, 76-9; beryl, together with other precious stones, became widespread in those milieux which had an interest in such exotic luxury items: cf. Maec. *Carm.* F2:

    lucentes, mea uita, nec smaragdos beryllos neque, Flacce mi, nitentes nec percandida margarita quaero.

    'Oh my Flaccus, my life, I search not for shining emeralds, nor resplendent beryl, nor candid pearls etc.'

    Cf. also the letter of Augustus to Maecenas, given in Macr. *Sat.* II, 4,12:

    uale, mi ebenum Medulliae, ebur ex Etruria, lasar Arretinum, adamas Supernas, Tiberinum margaritum, Cilniorum smaragde, iaspi Iguuinorum (Jahn, *ficulorum* M *figulorum* cett.), *berulle Porsenae, carbunculum Hadriae,* ἵνα συντέμω πάντα, μάλαγμα, *moecharum.*

    'Hail, my ebony of Medullia, ivory of Etruria, *lasar* of Arretium, Adriatic diamond, pearl of the Tiber, emerald of the Cilnii, iaspis of Igurium, beryl of Porsenna, carbunculus of Adria. In a word, cataplasm of prostitutes!'

Famous artists would engrave their gems on beryl, cf. *Anth. Pal.* IX, 544 (on Tryphon, cf. EAA, s.v.); beryl stones enhanced the beauty of rings worn by Roman matrons, cf. Prop. IV, 7, 9; a *collaris ex gemmis beryllis* mentioned in CIL XIV, 2215, is probably part of a set of jewellery associated with the cult of Isis. An extraordinary archaeological confirmation regarding the diffusion of beryl has been obtained recently from the excavation at Oplontis, cf. A. D'Ambrosio, *Gli ori di Oplontis,* Napoli 1987, nn. 8, 9, 14, 23, 50.

76. Cf. K. Nipperdey, *P. Cornelius Tacitus erklärt von K. Nipperdey*, Berlin 1892, p. 268: 'quis bezieht sich auf *illa propria*: "wodurch", "infolge wovon".'
77. On the counterfeiting of beryl, cf. also Buddhabaṭṭa, *Ratnaparīkṣā* 205:

girikācaśaiśupālau kacasphaṭikaś ca dhūmanirbhinnāḥ vaiḍūryāṇām ete vijātayaḥ saṃnibhā bhānti, '*girikāca, śaiśupāla,* glass and crystal impregnated with smoke, these are the counterfeits'.

78. On the inscription of Khāravela, cf. n. 15.
79. Here it is necessary at least to raise the issue of the use of Roman coins in southern India. The discussion can take as its starting point the expression, in *Puṟānāṉūṟu* 343, 5, *poṟ paricam,* 'the gifts of gold'. Although there is no doubt that the *poṟ paricam* were coins, the expression had appeared rather obscure (cf. Meile 1940, p. 93). Useful in clarifying the phrase, in my opinion, is the comparison with a text which strangely enough has escaped the attention of scholars so far. It is the *Patikam* in the seventh decade of the *Patiṟṟuppattu.* It is said here that:

pāṭip peṟṟa paricil: ciṟupuṟam eṉa nūṟāyiram kāṇam koṭuttu, naṉṟā eṉṉum kuṉṟu ēṟi niṉṟu, taṉ kaṇṇiṟ kaṇṭa nāṭu ellām kāṭṭik koṭut tāṉ ak kō.

'Having sung he obtained this gift: the king offered one hundred thousand gold coins called *ciṟupuṟam*; and what is more, having climbed mount Naṉṟā, from its summit he presented him with all the land which could be seen from its peak.'

Thus, the gifts (*paricil,* it should be noted, has the same root and the same meaning as *paricam*; for a derivation of *paricam* from the Skt. *sparśa,* cf. Meile 1940, p. 93) which king Celvakkaṭuṅkō Vāḻiyātaṉ Kuṭṭuvaṉ Irumpoṟai offered the poet Kapilar, included 100,000 gold coins called *ciṟupuṟam.* The expression *poṟ paricam* in *Puṟānāṉūṟu* 345, 5 refers then to the Tamil sovereigns' use of Roman coins as gifts for their subjects and it is natural that a court poem such as the *Caṅkam Ilakkiyam* should underline this aspect. The possibility that this may not be the only use the Roman coins had, is, however, suggested by a Tamil-Brahmi inscription which mentions *karu-ūr poṉvāṅikaṉ atti*, ('Atti, gold merchant of Karu-ūr'). Cf. Mahadevan 1966, n. 66.

Some attention should also be given to the Tamil name of these coins: *ciṟupuṟam*. In Tamil *Ciṟupuṟam* signifies the nape of the neck, and it would probably be safe to read in this word a reference to the effigy of the emperor found on Roman coins (for the importance of the relationship between coin and *sacer uultus*, we should recall the well-known *logion* of Jesus relating to the payment of tribute: the coin belongs to the emperor as it has his effigy, cf. Mazzarino 1986, p. 167). Two trends can thus distinguished in India: the first recognizing in the emperor's 'nape of the neck' the characteristic feature of Roman coins, the other denying it by the act of defacement (on the defacement of Roman coins in India, cf. Gupta 1965, pp. 68 ff.).

80. Cf. *PME* 56, p. 18, 16-17 Fr.
81. However, the dual possibility which Tacitus allows us to glimpse (*ad externas aut hostilis gentis*) must lead us to take into account other *lapides* of different provenance.
82. On the importance of rivers for the ports of Limyrike, cf. *supra*, p. 96.
83. For the Yavaṉar in the *Caṅkam Ilakkiyam*, cf. Meile 1940; Zvelebil 1956: in this and in analogous contexts they are identified with the merchants coming from the Roman empire. On the Yavanāḥ in the Indian inscriptions and in other literatures of the Indian subcontinent, cf. S. Levi, *Quid de Graecis ueterum Indorum monumenta tradiderint*, Paris 1890 and by O. Stein, *Yavanas in Early Indian Inscriptions*, in *Indian Culture*, I (1935), pp. 346-57. For a more complete history of the name, cf. R. Soraci, *L'unità dei Greci e il nome Yauna*, Catania (s.d.).
84. *Milaku* is the gloss of the medieval commentators.
85. Cf. J. Innes Miller, *The Spice Trade of the Roman Empire*, Oxford 1969, pp. 80-3.
86. Attested for the first time in [Hippokrat.] *morb. mul.* I, 81:

    ἰνδικοῦ φαρμάκου [...] ὃ καλέεται πέπερι; ibid. II, 205: τὸ ἰνδικὸν, ὃ καλέουσι οἱ Πέρσαι πέπερι.
87. Tarn 1951, p. 370.
88. Theophr., *Hist. Plant.* IX, 20,1; cf. Steier, *R.E.* XIX, 2,1421; K. Ziegler, *Kl. Pauly*, IV, 681.
89. Cf. H. Yule, A.C. Burnell, *Hobson-Jobson. A Glossary of Anglo-Indian Colloquial Words and Phrases*, 1903², p. 697.

90. Cf. *PME* 56, p. 18,22-23 Fr.:

φέρεται δὲ πέπερι, μονογενῶς ἐν ἑνὶ τόπῳ τούτων τῶν ἐμπορίων γεννώμενον πολύ, λεγομένη Κοτταναρικῇ.

'They export pepper, grown for the most part in only one place connected with these ports of trade, that called Kottanarike.'

91. In Barygaza, together with the local products it was also possible to obtain τὰ ἀπὸ τῶν ἐμπορίων φερόμενα (*PME* 49). These emporia also—indeed preeminently—included those of the Limyrike; in fact, as we have seen, in Muziris alongside the 'Hellenic' ships there were also those coming from Ariake (*PME* 54). These exchanges began long before the Western merchants arrived to trade along the Indian coasts, cf. *infra* our observations on the pearls of Pāṇṭiyar.
92. The *terminus ante quem* for this discovery is Strabo's claim that the merchants of his age had—albeit rarely—reached the Ganges via a sea route [cf. n. 14]. Something which implies *a fortiori* a thorough knowledge of southern India.
93. We must remember that the author of the *PME* was a merchant and his language presents 'nombreuses ressemblances avec la κοινή plus populaire' (Frisk 1927, p. 102).
94. Cf. Plin. *N.H.* XII, 28:

Emitur (sc. *piper longum*) *in libras* * XV, *album* * VII, *nigrum* * IIII. Long pepper is bought for 15 *denarii* a pound, white pepper for 7, black pepper for 4. This passage will be further commented upon *infra*. The reading presents no great difficulties (* *XV* as the price for the *longum* variety seems to me indisputable: *XXVI* of R[s] is evidently the corrupt form of * *XVI*, in which in turn the corrupt form XVI is due to attraction from *libras* * *VI* of 1. 17 M.). In the comparison we will draw with the situation in the age of Alaric (*infra*, pp. 100-102) we rely on, alongside the great works by Gibbon, Seeck, E. Stein and other fundamental works, the synthesis by O.J. Maenchen-Helfen, *The World of the Huns*, Berkeley, Los Angeles, London 1973. On deflationistic tendencies in the late fourth century, cf. S. Mazzarino, *Aspetti sociali del IV secolo*, Roma 1951, pp. 89; 107; 115 ff.

95. It is enough to think, in this connection, of Apicius.
96. Cf. *Frankfurter Allgemeine Zeitung für Deutschland*, 27/7/1984. The castrum at Oberaden was occupied only from the 9 to the 8 BC, cf. C. Albrecht, K. Regling, A. Oxé, *Das Römerlager in Oberaden*, Dortmund 1938, pp. 9-10.
97. Cf. Plin. *N.H.* VI, 104; cf. 101.
98. Other references to Neṭuñcēralātaṉ's 'cutting' of the *kaṭampu*

are found in *Patiṟṟuppattu* 11, 12-16; 12, 2-3; 17, 4-7; for Ceṅkuṭṭuvaṉ instead cf. *Cilappatikaram* XXV, 187.

99. Cf. *Epigraphia Carnatica* VII Sk 117; VII Sk 176; VIII Sb 262; IX Dg 35. Cf. also G. M. Moraes, *The Kadamba Kula. A History of Ancient and Medieval Karnataka*, Bombay 1931, pp. 9-11.

100. The 'cutting' of the *kaṭampu* should be compared with the 'cutting' of the *vēmpu* in *Patiṟṟuppattu* 44,15, alluding to another of Ceṅkuṭṭuvaṉ's victories, the one over Paḻaiyan of Mōkūr (Cf. Subrahmanian 1980, p. 92).

101. For the contemporaneity between Gajabāhu and Ceṅkuṭṭuvaṉ, cf. *Cilappatik., Patikam* 3; XXX, 160: *kaṭal cūl ilaṅkaikkayavāku* 'Kayavāku (king of) Laṅka surrounded by the sea', who takes part together with Ceṅkuṭṭuvaṉ, in the consecration of a temple dedicated to Kaṇṇaki-Pattiṉi at Vañci. The Kayavāku of the *Cilappatikaram* has been identified with Gajabāhukagāmaṇi of the *Dīpavaṁsa* 22,14,28 and *Mahāvaṁsa* 35,115 by Kanakasabhai Pillai 1904, p. 6. The reign of Gajabāhukagāmaṇi is placed between AD 174 and 196 by W. Geiger, *The Cūlavaṁsa*, II, Colombo 1953, Introd. X; other scholars bring it forward by approximately sixty years, for example, G.C. Mendis, *The Chronology of the Early Pali Chronicles of Ceylon*, in *University of Ceylon Review*, 5 (1947), p. 54.

102. For the first hypothesis, cf. Sivaraja Pillai 1984, p. 124; for the second, Balasubramanian 1980, pp. 20-1.

103. The Γεωγραφίας ʿΥφήγησις was composed only after AD 147: cf. B. L. v.d. Waerden, Der Kleine Pauly IV, 1224.

104. Cf. *Patiṟṟuppattu* 60, 11-12; 85, 7-8; Sivaraja Pillai 1984, p. 137; p. 172, though here Neṭuñcēralātaṉ is dated around AD 25.

105. Cf. n. 44.

106. This tradition of the *Cilappatikaram* on the Yavaṉar as guardians of the gate of Maturai, capital of the kingdom of the Pāṇṭiyar, may be compared with the one contained in the *Gārgī saṁhitā*, on the Yavanāḥ as conquerors of Mathurā in northern India (cf. Tarn 1951, pp. 452-6). It seems improbable, however, that the first is a mere literary echo of the second. We should remember, in fact, that the author of the *Cilappatikaram* also is aware (cf. n. 149) of the image, prevalent in ancient Tamil literature (cf. *Akanāṉūṟu* 149; *Puṟanāṉūṟu* 56), of the Yavaṉar as merchants and sailors; the presence of Yavaṉar guards in the Maturai described in the *Cilappatikaram* must therefore be linked with the needs of Roman trade in southern India. There is no doubt that the Yavaṉar merchants of Pukar were closer to the mind of the author and of the readers of the *Cilappatikaram*,

than the Yavanāḥ conquerors of Mathurā in northern India.

Another testimony on the employment of the Yavaṉar as bodyguards may be found, if one accepts the interpretation offered by Kanakasabhai Pillai 1904, pp. 37-8, in *Mullaippāṭṭu* 59-62:

mattikai vaḷaiiya maṟintuvīṅku ceṟivuṭai/meyppai pukka veruvarun tōṟṟattu/valipuṇar yākkai vaṉkaṇ yavaṉar/pulittoṭar viṭṭa puṉaimā ṇallil/.

'In a tent (with double walls of canvas) firmly held by iron chains, guarded by powerful Yavanas, whose stern looks strike terror into every beholder and whose long and loose coats are fastened at the waist by means of belts.'

On the problem of the interpretation of this passage, cf. Meile 1940, pp. 106-12. Fascinating in this context is the hypothesis that the Tamils learned to use certain war instruments such as catapults from the Yavaṉar, cf. Balasubramanian 1980, p. 53.

The obvious comparison is that with *miles Crassi,* imprisoned in Carrhae and forced to serve in the Parthian army (cf. H.H. Dubs, *An Ancient Military Contact between Romans and Chinese*, in *American Journal of Philology*, 62 [1941], pp. 322-30); Crassus' soldiers were no doubt exponents of a realistic and 'popular' culture (Mazzarino 1966b, p. 125, who incidentally manifests doubts on the well-known hypothesis by H.H. Dubs, *A Roman Influence upon Chinese Painting*, in *Classical Philology*, 38 [1943], pp. 13-19).

107. Cf. Plin. *N.H.* VI, 104.

108. Cf. *Patiṟṟuppattu*, 2 *Patikam* 7-10:

pēr icai marapiṉ āriyar vaṇakki/nayaṉ il vaṉ col yavaṉarp piṇittu/ ney talaip peytu kai piṟ koḷii/aru vilai naṉkalam vayiramoṭu koṇṭu/

'Having subdued the glorious dynasty of the Āriyar and having put in chains the rough-speaking Yavaṉar, he poured oil upon their heads and keeping their hands tied behind their backs he seized the good and precious jewels and the diamonds.'

109. Cf. Strab. XV, 1, 4.

110. It is perhaps possible, however, to see a reference to Nelkynda in *Maturaikkāñci* 75-88:

vāṉ iyainta iru munnīrp/pēem ṇilaiiya irum peḷavattu/koṭum puṇari vilaṅku pōla/kaṭuṅ kāloṭu karai cēra/neṭuṅ koṭi micai itai eṭuttu/iṉ icaiya muracam muḻaṅka/poṉ malinta viḻup paṇṭam/nāṭu āra naṉku iḻitarum/ātu iyaṟ peru nāvāy/ maḻai muṟṟiya malai puraiyat/tuṟai muṟṟiya tuḷaṅku irukkai/teṉ kaṭal kuṇṭu akaḻi/cīr cāṉṟa uyar nelliṉ/ ūr koṇṭa uyar koṟṟava !

'Oh noble victor, [you] who possess the noble town of Nel full of the noise of the deep moat which leads to the southern sea: its houses are resplendent, surrounded by the port just as a mountain is resplendent, surrounded by clouds. Here the big ships descend bearing the town's splendid prosperity, the excellent *paṇṭam* ("gold", "riches", "goods") which makes the *pōn* grow ("riches", "gold"); here the roaring war drum resounds; here the sails unfurl and, above them, the high banner; and they reach the shore with a strong wind having broken the tall waves in the great sea which makes fear last, in the ocean which joins the sky.') Usually (for example, Kanakasabhai Pillai 1904, p. 23) *nelliṉ ūr* 'the city of *nel*', is identified with Cāliyūr 'the city of *cāli*' (corresponding to the Σήλουρ ἐμπόριον of Ptol. *Geogr.* VII, 1, 11), seeing in the text a pun using the words *nel* and *cāli* which both mean 'rice' in Tamil. It is perhaps more natural however, to see Nelkynda in *nelliṉ ūr.* On the name Nelkynda, formed by the name Nel+kynda, as in Gol+conda, cf. Müller 1853, p. 297. The propriety of maintaining in Pliny the reading *Neacyndon*, has been insisted upon by André-Filliozat, p. 138; on the problem of the identification of the site of Nelkynda, cf. Kanakasabhai Pillai 1904, pp. 19-20; O. Stein, *R.E.*, XVI, 2, 2281-5; and again André-Filliozat 1980, p. 138.

111. Cf. Ptol. *Geogr.* VIII, 1, 8.
112. A comparison here may not be entirely unwarranted: namely that of *gens Neacyndon*- Νελκύνδα with the well-known case of the Gallo-Roman cities which during the medieval and modern periods took on their Celtic ethnic names, thus abandoning their Roman names, cf. O. Hirschfeld's classic work, *Kleine Schriften*, Berlin 1913, pp. 734 ff.
113. Cf. *PME* 55, p. 18, 10-11 Fr.
114. Cf. Plin. *N.H.* VI, 105.
115. Cf. Plin. *N.H.* VI, 104.
116. They were situated approximately five hundred stadia apart, cf. *PME* 54, p. 18, 4-5 Fr.
117. Cf. Dorai Rangaswamy 1968, pp. 104-5.
118. Kanakasabhai Pillai 1904; P.T. Srinivasa Aiyangar, *History of the Tamils from the earliest Times to 600 A.D.*, Madras 1929; Sivaraja Pillai 1984: K.G. Sesha Aiyar, *Cera Kings of the Sangam Period*, London 1937; S. Vaiyapuri Pillai, *History of Tamil Language and Literature*, Madras 1956.
119. Pliny does not mention at all the ports of the south-eastern

coast; as for the *PME* cf. Müller's observation, p. 300: '[...] *quae post Nelcynda emporium sequuntur neque ipse vidit auctor, neque ab aliis accuratiora accepit, adeo ut admodum vaga sit descriptio*'.

120. Cf. n. 14.
121. Cf. *PME* 56, pp. 18, 22-8, quoted *supra* in the text.
122. The so-called 'island of Chryse'–actually a peninsula–was already known to Pomponius Mela and to Pliny's sources and corresponds to the Sanskrit *Suvarṇadvīpa.* In the age of Ptolemy, when a much greater knowledge of the Bay of Bengal had been acquired than that available to the author of the *PME,* the toponym Chryse was applied to a *chersónēsos,* that is the Malay peninsula, cf. P. Wheatley, *The Golden Khersonese,* Kuala Lumpur 1961, pp. 127 ff.
123. Cf. *infra.*
124. Cf. n. 115.
125. Cf. FGrHist 715 F 13:

'Ηερακλέα ὀψιγόνου οἱ γενομένης τῆς παιδός, ἐπεί τε ἐγγὺς ἔμαθεν ἑαυτῷ ἐοῦσαν τὴν τελευτήν, οὐκ ἔχοντα ὅτῳ ἀνδρὶ ἐκδῷ τὴν παῖδα ἑωυτοῦ ἐπαξίῳ, αὐτὸν μιγῆναι τῇ παιδὶ ἑπταέτει ἐούσῃ, ὡς γένος ἐξ οὗ τε κἀκείνης ὑπολείπεσθαι 'Ινδῶν βασιλέας,

'Heracles whose daughter was born to him late in life, realizing that his own end was near, and having no man of his own worth to whom he might give his daughter, copulated with her himself when she was seven, so that their progeny might be left behind as Indian king.'

On the work of Megasthenes, see the recent study of A. Zambrini, *Gli Indiká di Megastene,* in *Annali della Scuola Normale Superiore di Pisa,* ser. III 12,1 (1982) pp. 71-149.

126. Cf. Kanakasabhai Pillai 1904, pp. 54-5; for a reference to the kingdom of the Pāṇṭiyar in the account by Megasthenes, cf. also V.A. Smith, *The Early History of India,* Oxford 1908[2], p. 407 and André-Filliozat 1980, pp. 156 ff.
127. In the remaining two passages of the *Cilappatikaram* (IV, 22; XIII, 17-18) where reference is made to the *teṉṉar kulamutal,* 'goddess founder of the lineage of the Southerners (Pāṇṭiyar)', she is identified with the moon (it should be noted that the *piṟai,* 'waxing moon' adorns the head of the *kulamutal* described in XXIII, 1 ff.). The *kulamutal* of the Pāṇṭiyar must be placed within the context of female deities (*Ammā,* 'mother', 'woman'), typical of Dravidian India (cf. J. Gonda, *Die Religionen Indiens. II. Der jüngere Hinduismus,* Stuttgart 1963, pp. 5-7). On the cult of

an otherwise unspecified *malai uṟai kaṭavuḷ kulamutal* 'the *kulamutal* who dwells in the mountain', we have the delicate testimony of the *Aiṅkuṟunūṟu* 259, in which a maiden who has fallen in love offers flowers and honey, so that the goddess may grant her to be wedded soon.

We should also draw attention to the word *mutal* which together with *kulam* 'family, tribe', makes up the compound *kulamutal. Mutal* connotes 'God as prime cause', but also takes on the meaning of 'trunk (of a tree)' (cf. T. Burrow-M.B. Emeneau, *A Dravidian Etimological Dictionary*, Oxford 1961, nn. 4053 and 4054). This point is worth underlining as in southern India it is not rare for a tree to represent a family or tribe's totem, as we have seen for the Kaṭampar and their *katampu mutal.* It is possible, therefore, to grasp even at a linguistic level the close link (on which cf. Gonda) between the worship of female deities and the worship of trees (on tree worship in ancient Dravidian India cf. G. Subrahmania Pillai, *Tree Worship and Ophiolatry*, Annamalai 1948). Lastly, extremely interesting is the fact that *kulamutal* is also a title for the queen of the Pāṇṭiyar, cf. *Cilappatik.* XVI, 136 in which the wife of Netuñceḻiyaṉ is named *kulamutal tēvi.*

128. On this point cf. also another fragment by Megasthenes, FGrHist 715 F 26, in which with reference to Taprobane it is said:

Megasthenes flumine diuidi (sc. *Taprobanem*), *incolasque Palaegonos apellari, auri margaritarumque grandium fertiliores quam Indos.*

'Megasthenes maintains that Taprobane is divided by a river, that its inhabitants are called *Palaegoni,* and are richer than the Indians in terms of of gold and big pearls'.

Cf. F.F. Schwarz, *Onesikritos und Megasthenes über den Tambapaṇṇidīpa,* in *Grazer Beiträge* 5 (1976), pp. 252 ff.

129. The memory of an important moment in this 'Südpolitik' of the Mauryas is preserved (if the Vampa Mōriyar are to be identified with the Mauryas) in *Akanāṉūṟu* 251 which mentions an attack of the Vampa Mōriyar on the lord of Mōkūr. On this passage cf. M.G.S. Narayanan, *The Mauryan Problem in Sangam Works in Historical Perspective,* in *Journal of Indian History,* 1975, pp. 243-54: it must be said however, that this scholar's reconstruction is unacceptable. In fact, having postulated the contemporaneity (or virtual contemporaneity) of Māmūlanār, author of *Akanāṉūṟu* 251, with the Nanda and Maurya dynasties, he is led not only to deny the chronology of *Ceṅkuṭṭuvaṉ* established on the basis of the *Cilappatikaram* and of the

Mahāvaṁsa (cf. n. 101), but also to ignore the suggestions which may be gleaned from the comparison between classical literature and the *Caṅkam Ilakkiyam* concerning the latter work's chronology.

Regarding Aśoka's 'Südpolitik' it would be impossible to give a full bibliography here, cf., e.g. Thapar 1961, pp. 132-36. For our purposes it will suffice to underline that Aśoka also (although only to a certain extent) fell within the pale of Hellenistic culture (on relations between Hellenistic culture and Aśoka's preaching on the Victory of the Law, cf. Mazzarino 1966a, p. 330. Other literature includes K.R. Norman, *Note on the Greek Version of Aśoka's Twelth and Thirteenth Rock Edicts*, in *Journal of the Royal Asiatic Society*, (1972) 2, pp. 111-18; D. Schlumberger, *De la pensée grecque à la pensée bouddhique* in *Comptes Rendus de l'Académie des Inscriptions et Belles-Lettres*, 1972, pp. 1-198; P. Eggermont, *India en de hellenistische rijken. Totalbee van een maatschappij tussen ca. 550—ca. 150 v. Chr.*, in *Kleio*, 1978, pp. 145-53; G. Pugliese Carratelli, *Sull'editto di Asoka da Kandahar*, in *Parola del Passato*, 1984, pp. 147-9).

The culture of Aśoka which we call 'Hellenistic' (though only for certain aspects, as I say), is to be considered in roughly the same way that the Aksumitic culture might, cf. S. Mazzarino, *Antico, tardoantico ed èra costantiniana*, II, Roma 1980, pp. 104-18. For some of these manifestations one could talk of 'peripheral' Hellenistic culture.

130. The concept of *dakṣiṇāpatha* 'the road towards the South', 'the land of the South', was known also to the author of the *PME*, cf. *PME* 50, p. 17, 1-3 Fr.:

μετὰ δὲ Βαρύγαζαν εὐθέως ἡ συναφὴς ἤπειρος ἐκ τοῦ βορέου εἰς τὸν νότον, διὸ καὶ Δαχιναβάδης καλεῖται ἡ χώρα· δάχανος γὰρ καλεῖται ὁ νότος τῇ αὐτῶν γλώσσῃ.

'Immediately beyond Barygaza the coast runs from north to south. Thus the region is called Dachinabades, for the word for south in their language is *dachanos.*'

131. On this passage, Bhaṭṭasvāmin comments as follows:

tatra tāmraparṇikaṃ pāṇḍyeṣu tāmraparṇyākhyā nadī, samudrasaṅgamasamutpannaṃ, pāṇḍyakavāṭakam tatraiva malayakoṭiparvatotpannaṃ cañcatkoṣṭhāgārakoṭimācakṣeta/pāśikyaṃ pāśādikānadīnam, kauleyaṃ simhaladvīpe mayūragrāmasamīpe kulā nāma nadī tadutpannaṃ, caurṇeyaṃ keraleṣu muracīpattanasamīpe cūrnī nāma nadī tasyāṃ jātaṃ, māhendraṃ mahendragirisamīpe samutpannam, kārdamikaṃ pārasīkeṣu kardamā nāma nadī tadut-

pannaṃ, (srotasīyaṃ barbarakūle srotasī nāma nadī tadutpannaṃ), hrādīyaṃ barbarakūla eva samudraikadeśe srīghaṇḍābhidhāno hradaḥ tadutpannaṃ, haimavataṃ himavadgirijaṃ/.

'*tāmraparṇika.* River by the name of Tāmraparnī in the country of the Pāṇḍyāḥ. This pearl is born of the encounter (of the said river) with the ocean. *pāṇḍyakavāṭaka.* This is the pearl which is born on the mountain, extreme limit of the Malaya (this is to be understood as the extreme limit of the seat which trembles [?]). *pāśikya* is the pearl of the river Pāśādikā. *kauleya.* River Kulā in the vicinity of Mayura village in the island of Siṁhala (Ceylon). This pearl is born here. *caurṇeya.* River by the name of Cūrṇi near the city of Muracī in the country of the Keralāḥ. This pearl is born here. *māhendra.* This pearl is born in the vicinity of mount Mahendra. *Kardamika.* River by the name of Kardamā in the country of the Pāraśīkāḥ. (*srotasīya.* River in *barbarakūla* by the name of Srotasī. This pearl is born here.) *hrādīya.* In the oceanic land of *barbarakūla, hrada,* mentioned by Śrī Ghaṇḍa. This pearl is born here. *haimavata.* It is the pearl which is born on mount Himavat.'

Of the ten places of origin listed by the author of the *Arthaśāstra,* three were situated in the kingdom of the Pāṇḍyāḥ, that is, the river Tāmraparṇī, the river of Kolchoi (in the image of the pearl being born of the encounter of the TāmraparĪī with the ocean Bhaṭṭasvāmin echoes Kālidāsa, *Raghuvaṁśa* IV, 50); the district of the Pāṇḍyāḥ (*pāṇḍīyakavāṭa*) where mount *Malayakoṭi* is situated (for the identification of this mountain with 'the southern part of the Western Ghats' cf. A.B.L. Avasthi, *Studies in Skanda Purāṇa*, Lucknow 1965, p. 134; for the reading *pāṇḍyaka-vāṭa* instead of *pāṇḍya-kavāṭa,* cf. O. Stein, *Pāṇḍyakavāṭa,* in *Indian Historical Quarterly* 4 [1928], pp. 778-82); and finally mount Mahendra, to be identified with Mahendrāchala in the district of Tinnevelly (cf. Avasthi, p. 134). Also situated in the southern part of the Indian subcontinent are the river Kulā in the island of Ceylon (on pearls from Ceylon cf. the fragment by Megasthenes FGrHist 715 F 26 quoted in n. 127 and Mahāvaṁsa IX) and the river Cūrṇī which flows in the vicinity of the *muracīpattana*: *curnī* and *muracī* in Bhaṭṭasvāmin in fact are none other than the *cuḻḻi* and *muciṟi* found in Tamil literature (cf. *Akanāṉūṟu* 149 quoted *supra*), Pseudóstomos and Moúzēris in Ptol. *Geogr.* VII, 1, 8.

132. Cf. n. 15.

133. Cf. *PME* 59, p. 19, 22-23 Fr.

134. *Cilappatik.* XXIII, 11.
135. Cf. *PME* 58, p. 19, 17-21 Fr.:

ἀπὸ δὲ ταύτης ἐστὶν ἕτερος τόπος τὸ Κομὰρ λεγόμενος, ἐν ᾧ τόπῳ φρούριόν ἐστιν καὶ λιμήν, εἰς ὃν οἱ βουλόμενοι τὸ μέλλοντα αὐτοῖς χρόνοις ἱεροὶ γενέσθαι ἐρχόμενοι ἀπολούονται καὶ χῆροι μένουσιν αὐτοῦ· τὸ δ'αὐτὸ καὶ γυναῖκες. ἱστορεῖται γὰρ τὴν θεὸν ἐκεῖ ἐπιμεῖναι κατά τινα χρόνον καὶ ἀπολελοῦσθαι.

'After this comes another place called Komar, where there is a stronghold and a port; in it men who wish to lead a holy life for the rest of their days come there and they perform ablutions. Women, too, do the same. For it is said that at one time the goddess remained there and performed ablutions.'

Allusions to this rite of ablution at Komarei are also found in *Cilappatik.* XXVII 68-9, where Matalan the Brahmin says: *māmuṉi potiyil malaivalaṅ koṇṭu/ kumariyam perun tuṟai yāṭi mīḷ vēn,* ('I have circled round mount Potiyil, sacred to the great sage and I have been purified by dipping into the great *tuṟai* of Kumari'); and in *Maṇimēkalai* XIII, 3-7:

vāraṇāciyōr maṟaiyōṟ paḷaṉ/āraṇa uvātti, apañcikan eṉpōṉ/pārppaṉi cāli kāppukkaṭai kaḻintu/koṇṭōṟ piḷaitta taṇṭam añcit/teṉticaik kumari yāṭiya varuvōḷ.

'At Vāraṇāsi there was a teacher of the Law, his name was Apañcika. His brahmin wife Cāli transpassed the boundary of safety and since she feared the punishment of one who sins in behaving like a prostitute, she went to bath in the southern Kumari.'

On the eponymous goddess Kumārī, at times identified with the goddess Durgā (*Bhagavata Purāṇa* X, 79, 17), cf. *Skanda Purāṇa* I, 2, 39. It is not possible to quote here the numerous testimonies relating to this *tīrtha,* offered by Sanskrit literature, for which readers are referred to P.V. Kane, *History of Dharmaśāstra,* Poona 1953, IV, pp. 763; 772.

136. Cf. Kanakasabhai Pillai 1904, p. 23. For the excavations at Koṟkai see *Excavations at Koṟkai, District Thirunelveli,* in *Damilica* 1 (1970) pp. 50-4.
137. Cf. *Akanāṉūṟu* 27, 8-10; *Aiṅkuṟuṉūṟu* 185, 1-2.
138. Cf. *Cilappatik.* XXVI, 127 ff. Veṟṟiverceḻiyaṉ, 'prince of the lunar dynasty', resident at Koṟkai, succeeds king Neṭunceḻiyaṉ (his brother?) when the latter commits suicide.

139. Further details in André-Filliozat, 1980 p. 116. For a history of Koṟkai from prehistoric to medieval times, cf. Sundaraj, *Rise and Fall of Korkai*, in *Journal of Tamil Studies* 19 (1981) pp. 55-63.
140. A reference to this detail can perhaps be seen in the statement that the fishermen 'drink *kaḷ*, as a reward for the resplendent shell'. This occurs twice in *Maturaikkāñci*, quoted in the text, and in *Akanāṉūṟu* 296, 8-10.
141. On slavery resulting from a judicial sentence, cf. Dev Raj, *L'esclavage dans l'Inde Ancienne d'après les textes palis et sanskrits*, Pondichery 1957, p. 74; on slavery in ancient India, cf. Thapar 1961, pp. 89 ff.; D. Chanana, *Slavery in Ancient India*, 1960; with regard to southern India cf. Subrahmanian 1980, pp. 296-7.
142. This is the date usually attributed to the *Paṭṭiṉappālai*, cf. K.V. Zvelebil, *Tamil Literature*, Wiesbaden 1974, p. 22.
143. Ptol. *Geogr.* VII, 1,13.
144. The identification of this place is rather problematic, cf. K.A. Nilakanta Sastri, *Kaṭāha*, in *Journal of the Greater India Society*, 5 (1938), p. 128.
145. K.A. Nilakanta Sastri, *The Colas*, Madras 1955, I, pp. 99-100, translates: 'the coral of the western sea' (reading *kuṭakaṭal* instead of *kuṇakaṭal*?). In that case it would be coral imported from the Roman empire.
146. At Kāvirippūmpaṭṭinam the same exchange of goods between the coast and the interior took place as that we have already noted at Muziris.
147. On the κολανδιοφωντα τὰ μέγιστα, cf. A. Christie, *An Obscure Passage from the Periplus*: κολανδιοφωντα τὰ μέγιστα in *Bulletin of the School of Oriental and African Studies*, 19, 2 (1957), pp. 345-53.

The corrupt form καὶ in p. 20, l. 4 Fr. has been emended in various ways:

τούτων δὲ τῶν ἐμπορίων Bernhardy, τῶν δὲ ἀπὸ τούτου ἐμπορίων uel τῶν δὲ ἀπὸ τούτων ἐμπορίων Müller *in comm., qui tamen in textu* τῶν δὲ τοπικῶν ἐμπορίων maluit, τῶν δὲ κατὰ τοῦτον ἐμπορίων Frisk. None of these emendations can be considered certain, nor do there appear to be other feasible ones; therefore I have simply mentioned the *crux*. The general picture, however, remains clear, and it is in this sense that I have indicated the function of the three emporia. The essential point lies in the expression οἵ τε ἀπὸ τῆς Λιμυρικῆς καὶ ἀπὸ ἄρκτου πλέοντες; I shall return to οἵ τε ἀπὸ τῆς Λιμυρικῆς— πλέοντες later on in this paragraph.

148. Wheeler, Ghosh, Deva 1946; J. M. Casal, *Fouilles de Virampatnam-Arikamedu*, Paris 1949; J. M. and G. Casal, *Site urbain et sites funéraires des environs de Pondichéry*, Paris 1959; on Arikamedu see now the intelligent re-examination by V. Begley, *Arikamedu reconsidered*, in *American Journal of Archaeology*, 87 (1983), pp. 461-81, which dates the most ancient settlement at Arikamedu to the third to second century BC and places it within the broader context of the development of trade relations between the Mauryan empire and southern India.
149. L. Ohlenroth, *Zur Datierung der Funde von Arikamedu*, in *Germania*, 30 3/4 (1952) pp. 389-92, concludes that the Arretine ware at Arikamedu cannot be dated later than the final period of Augustus' reign.
150. *Cilappatik.* V, 9-10:

    kayavāy maruṅkiṟ kāṇpōrt taṭukkum/payaṉaṟa vaṟiyā yavaṉa rirukkaiyum.

    'Towards the mouth of the river the gaze of the observer was attracted by the abode of the Yavaṉar whose richness has no limits.'
151. Wheeler, Ghosh, Deva 1946, pp. 18-21.
152. Charlesworth 1951, pp. 135-6.
153. Wheeler 1954, pp. 144-5; cf. also Wheeler 1951, pp. 365-6.
154. R. Nagaswamy, A. Abdul Majeed, *Vasavasamudra: A Report on the Excavation conducted by the Tamil Nadu State Department of Archaeology*, Madras, 1978.
155. My thanks to Dr. Thulasiraman of the Tamilnadu State Department of Archaeology, who provided this information on 20/2/1985.
156. Cf. n. 101.
157. Plin., *N.H.* VI 105: *ibi* [Becare] *regnabat Pandion, longe ab emporio in mediterraneo distante oppido quod uocatur Modura*, is a confirmation, rather than a refutation, of this view.
158. Müller 1853, p. 301.
159. Frisk 1927, pp. 73-4.
160. Ibid., 97.
161. Cf. *supra*, n. 147.
162. Cf. *PME* 54, p. 17, 30—p. 18, 1 Fr.
163. Cf. *PME* 64, p. 21, 11-15 Fr.:
    μετὰ δὲ ταύτην τὴν χώραν ὑπ' αὐτὸν ἤδη τὸν βορέαν, ἔξωθεν εἴς τινα τόπον ἀποληγούσης τῆς θαλάσσης, παράκειται [δὲ] ἐν αὐτῇ πόλις μεσόγειος μεγίστη, λεγομένη Θῖνα ἀφ' ἧς τό τε ἔριον καὶ τὸ νῆμα καὶ ὀθόνιον τὸ Σηρικὸν εἰς τὴν

Βαρύγαζαν διὰ Βάκτρων πεζῇ φέρεται καὶ εἰς τὴν Λιμυρικὴν πάλιν διὰ τοῦ Γάγγου ποταμοῦ. εἰς δὲ τὴν Θῖνα ταύτην οὐκ ἔστιν εὐχερῶς ἀπελθεῖν· σπανίως γὰρ ἀπ' αὐτῆς τινὲς οὐ πολλοὶ ἔρχονται.

'Beyond this region by now at the northernmost point, where the sea ends somewhere on the outer fringe, there is a very great inland city called Thina from which silk floss, yarn, and cloth are shipped by land via Bactria to Barygaza and via the Ganges river back to Limyrike. It is not easy to get to this Thina; for rarely do people come from it, and only few.'

On the toponym Θῖναι indicating China, cf. A. Herrmann, in *Reallexicon für Antike und Christentum*, II, 1078-9. This route from China to the Roman empire, partly overland (as far as Barygaza or the Ganges), and partly maritime, must be connected with the problems of how to by-pass the Parthian 'barrier'. These problems proved to be unavoidable after Nero's abortive attempt to open a direct line of overland communication with Bactria by means of an alliance with the Hyrkanians (to the detriment of the Parthians), cf. W. Schur, *Die Orientpolitik Kaisers Nero*, Leipzig 1923, pp. 80-5.

164. Cf. Wheeler, Ghosh, Deva 1946, p. 41; on importing wine into India see *PME* 39; 49; 56. and also Puṟanāṉūṟu 56, 18-21:

yavaṉar naṉ kalam tanta taṇ kamaḻ tēṟal/poṉ cey puṉai kalattu ēnti nāḷum/oṇ toṭi makaḷir maṭuppa makiḻ ciṟ antu / āṅku iṉitu oḻukumati [...]

'[...] live each day with pleasure, increasing the joy which is had from the women with the shining bangle, who pour into the beautiful cup decorated with gold the sweet, cool wine brought by the perfect ship of the Yavaṉar.'

For the rendering of the term *tēṟal* with 'wine', cf. Meile 1940, pp. 103-5. To be interpreted in this context is also the Greek farce in P. Oxy. 413. Some of the sentences in the 'barbarian' language contained in this farce have been traced to a Dravidian context (more specifically, Kannaḍa) by E. Hultzsch, *Zum Papyros 413 aus Oxyrhynchos*, in *Hermes*, 39 (1904), pp. 307-11.

165. Cf. n. 150.

166. Cf. Hirth 1885, espec. pp. 42; 47-8; 64; 82; 94-5; 173 ff. It should be underlined that both the embassy of An-tun in AD 166 and that of Ts'in-lun in AD 226 reached China via Indo-China and must therefore have had India (most probably southern India)

as their original starting point.

167. This is the reading generally accepted; *D* is reading of codices E^{s}p; other offer the *DL (milia)*. In the present work I shall continue to talk of 50,000,000 HS, while considering *DL (centena milia)* a plausible reading for this passage.

168. Cf. Plin. *N.H.* XII, 84:

> [...] *minimaque computatione miliens centena milia sestertium annis omnibus India et Seres et paeninsula illa* (sc. *Arabia*) *imperio nostro adimunt.*

'And by the lowest reckoning India, China and the Arabian peninsula take from our empire 100 million sesterces every year'.

Veyne 1979, pp. 211-44, maintains that these figures do not refer to the quantity of precious metal which was needed every year to balance the importation of goods from India, but rather to their value overall. Pliny, it is argued, deliberately ignored the value of exported goods, which in Veyne's opinion were worth as much as the imported goods. Roman exports should not be underestimated, but at least in the Limyrike they cannot have balanced the goods which were imported. We have seen that in *Akanāṉūṟu* 149 (cf. *supra*, p. 98) the Yavaṉar arrived with gold and returned with pepper, and this is confirmed to a certain extent by the *PME* (ch. 56, cf. *supra*, pp. 89-90). It does not appear therefore that 'les espèces romaines elles-même n'étaient qu'une marchandise parmi les autres exportations romaines en Inde, et non pas l'instrument qui servait à payer les cent millions d'importations'. Equally unacceptable seems the statement: 'il devait arriver aussi que l'Inde paie les marchandises romaines en or non monnayé'. What would the merchants have gained by returning with gold when ample profits were to be made by selling Indian goods within the empire? Moreover, such an eventuality appears to be excluded by Pausan. III, 12,4:

οἱ δὲ ἐς τὴν 'Ινδικὴν ἐσπλέοντες φορτίων φασὶν 'Ελληνικῶν τοὺς 'Ινδοὺς ἀγώγιμα ἄλλα ἀνταλλάσσεσθαι, νόμισμα δὲ οὐκ ἐπίστασθαι, καὶ ταῦτα χρυσοῦ τε ἀφθόνου καὶ χαλκοῦ παρόντος σφίσι.

'Those sailing to India say that Indians give other merchandise in exchange for Hellenic goods as coins are unknown to them, even though they possess gold and bronze in large quantities.'

Finally, the juxtaposition in Pliny's passage of the *quingenties sestertium* and the Indian *merces* suggests that the 50,000,000 HS did include the value of goods exported from Rome, but that the latter was negligible compared to that of the gold which was exported. Or, better still, that the 50,000,000 HS represented the effective deficit in the Roman balance of payments in trade with India.

169. Cf. Warmington 1928, p. 276; Charlesworth 1951, p. 137; M.I. Finley, *The Ancient Economy*, Berkeley-Los Angeles, p. 132, n. 20.

170. However it may be noted that whereas the 50,000,000 HS in *N.H.* VI, 101 appear to rest on official or at least ascertained data [this impression would be greatly reinforced if the reading *DL (centena milia)* were to be adopted], the 100,000,000 HS in *N.H.* XII, 84 are the result of a *computatio,* that is of an approximate estimate.

171. Raschke 1978, p. 635. His efforts to demonstrate that Pliny's figures have no value do not seem to me convincing.

172. For the lists of finds cf. n. 70. Another peculiarity of the Indian hoards is the scant number of Republican *denarii* despite the fact that even in the Julio-Claudian period they constituted the bulk of *denarii* in circulation. This phenomenon appears to be related to the tendency to export the good coins to India (cf. Lo Cascio 1980, p. 451). Now, the very fact that Roman coins destined to be exported to India were carefully selected, must lead us to believe that among those involved in this trade there were people who were able to provide good coins in great quantity, choosing them from among the ones in circulation; and that the *negotiatores,* in short, were able to draw on considerable financial resources. This could also have occurred in an indirect manner, as suggested by Petron. *Satyr.* 76:

Postquam coepi plus habere quam tota patria mea habet, manum de tabula: sustuli me de negotiatione et coepi libertos fenerare.

'When I came to have more than the entire revenue of my own country, I threw up the game: I retired from active work and began to finance freedmen.'

This passage can perhaps help to elucidate the relationship existing between Annius Plocamus *redemptor* of the *uectigal maris Rubri* and his freedman who engaged in trade in the Arabian ports up to the Persian Gulf (cf. Plin. *N.H.* VI, 84). [On Petron. *Satyr.* 76 I disagree to some extent with P. Veyne, *Vie de Trimalcion,* in *Annales (ESC),* 16 (1961), pp. 213-47, who interprets the last phase of the 'career' of Trimalchio as a 'métamorphose de l'homme d'affaires en proprietaire terrien' (p. 237). On the contrary, it is precisely Chapter 76 of the *Satyricon* which appears to emphasize the activity of the *libertos fenerare.* This activity cannot fail to be considered a 'capitalistic' investment, if one recognizes, as Veyne does (p. 229), the importance of the role played by the freedmen as craftsmen and traders in Rome and in Italy]. What should also be noted is that after Nero the export of *denarii* ceased almost completely. This is an extremely important phenomenon since prior to Nero's reform the *denarius* had supported (at times very successfully, for example during the time of Tiberius) the gold coinage in the difficult task of balancing the value of imported goods. But now, with the sudden fall of its weight, it was protected and no longer exported to India, in the same way as the old Republican *denarii*. The reform provided an impulse for the 'bourgeois' economy, emancipating it and placing it in opposition to that characterised by the *luxus* of the *dites familiae* of the senatorial order. Cf. Mazzarino 1986, pp. 221 ff.

173. Ibid., p. 252.
174. Frank 1935.
175. G. Mickwitz, *Le problème de l'or dans le monde antique*, in *Annales (ESC)*, 6 (1934), p. 247.
176. Cracco Ruggini 1968, pp. 750-1; A.H.M. Jones, *The Roman Economy*, Oxford 1974, p. 144.
177. Cracco Ruggini 1968, p. 751. For other assets of exceptional size, cf. Duncan-Jones 1978, pp. 343-4.
178. Cf. Strab. II, 5,12, quoted *supra*, p. 83.
179. In Rome the actual prices of luxury items were kept secret, cf. Tac. *Ann.* III, 52:

sed alia sumptuum quamuis grauiora, dissimulatis plerumque pretiis occultabantur [...].

'But other extravagances, though actually more serious, could as a rule be kept private by concealing the prices paid.'

Factors affecting the cost of Indian goods included the tax to which the goods were subject (cf. Raschke 1978, p. 670), the high cost of transport and the risks which this trade involved, as well as the bold speculations of those selling such luxury items to a wealthy clientele. Cf. Pliny's observations concerning the prices of purple dye, *N.H.* IX, 138:

Pretia medicamento sunt quidem pro fertilitate litorum uiliora, non tamen usquam pelagii centenas libras quinquagenos nummos excedere et bucini centenos sciant qui ista mercantur immenso.

'The prices for dyestuff vary in cheapness with the productivity of the coasts, but those who buy them at an enormous price should know that the deep-sea purple nowhere exceeds 50 sesterces and trumpet-shell 100 sesterces per 100 lbs.'

180. For the patrimony of Lollia Paulina cf. Tac. *Ann.* XII, 22:

ita quinquagies sestertium ex opibus immensis exuli (sc. *Lolliae Paulinae*) *relictum.*

'Thus, from amongst immense riches 5,000,000 sesterces were left to the exile.'

Large parts of family fortunes were squandered on the *instrumenta uitiorum*, cf. Tac. *Hist.* I, 20:

Bis et uicies milies sestertium donationibus Nero effuderat: appellari singulos iussit (sc. *Galba*), *decuma parte liberalitatis apud quemque eorum relicta. At illis uix decumae super portiones erant, isdem erga aliena sumptibus quibus sua prodegerant, cum rapacissimo cuique ac perditissimo non agri aut faenus, sed sola instrumenta uitiorum manerent.*

'Twenty-two hundred million sesterces had been squandered by Nero in gifts. It was voted that individuals should be summoned, and that a tenth part of the gifts which Nero had made them should be left with each. But Nero's favourites had hardly one-tenth left, for they had wasted the money of others on the same extravagances as they had their own; the most greedy and depraved had neither lands nor principal, but only what would minister to their vices.' Cf. also Plut. *Galba,* 15.

181. Yet it was not first under Tiberius that demands for sumptuary legislation were made: provisions to curb the rage for *luxus* had already been taken under Augustus, cf. Cavallaro 1984, pp. 189-90.

182. *Luxus* and political prestige is explicitly correlated by Tacitus, *Ann.* III, 55:

nam etiam tum plebem, socios, regna colere et coli licitum; ut quisque opibus, domo, paratu speciosus per nomen et clientelas inlustrior habebatur.

'It was still legitimate to court or to be courted by the populace, by the provincials, by dependent princes; and the more handsome the fortune, the palace, the establishment of a man, the more imposing his reputation and his clientèle.'

Pliny's expression *lictor feminae* is significant in this regard, Plin. *N.H.* IX, 114:

cupiuntque iam et pauperes lictorem feminae in publico unionem esse dictitantes.

'Now even women who are poor have a desire for pearls, and they repeat that the great pearl is the lictor befitting a woman appearing in public.'

The political action of Q. Haterius and his calls for sumptuary legislation, would acquire added prospective resonance if one could be sure that, apart from being the father of D. Haterius Agrippa, consul in AD 22, he was also the grandfather of Q. Haterius Antoninus, consul in AD 53 (on these three personages, cf. PIR^2 IV, pp. 49-50, nn. 24, 25, 26). Q. Haterius Antoninus received annual sums of money from Nero from AD 58 onward, having squandered his father's patrimony on a life of luxury (Tac., *Ann.*, XIII, 34). The family, which had led the 'resistence' to the *luxus* of Rome under Tiberius, thus found itself in grave financial difficulties under Nero, precisely as a result of its *luxus* expenses. All this would provide added corroboration to the above interpretation of the speeches of Q. Haterius and Octauius Fronto in the senate in AD 16: namely, that they were inspired not by empty moralistic concerns, but by real political and economic motives. As for Asinius Gallus, it should be recalled that he had, for other reasons, already clashed with D. Haterius Agrippa, then tribune of the plebs, in the senate in the previous year (Tac. *Ann.* I, 77). On the political personality of Asinius Gallus, cf. D.C.A. Shotter, *Tiberius and Asinius Gallus*, in *Historia*, 20 (1971), pp. 443-57.

183. Cf. Vell. Pat. II, 129:

[...] *senatorumque censum, cum id senatu auctore facere potuit, quam libenter expleuit, ut neque luxuriam inuitaret neque honestam paupertatem pateretur dignitate destitui !*

'[...] and how gladly, whenever he could do so with the senate's sanction, did he [se. Tiberius] raise to the required rating the fortunes of senators, but in such a way as not to encourage extravagant living, nor yet to allow senators to lose their rank because of honest poverty !'

Tac. *Ann.* I, 75:

Propertio Celeri praetorio ueniam ordinis ob paupertatem petenti decies sestertium largitus est, satis comperto paternas ei angustias esse. Temptantis eadem alios probare causa<*s*> (Sir.) *senatui iussit, cupidine seueritatis in iis etiam quae rite faceret acerbus. Vnde ceteri silentium et paupertatem confessioni et beneficio praeposuere.*

'When Propertius Celer, the ex-praetor, requested to be excused from his senatorial rank on the score of poverty, he [se. Tiberius] gave him 1,000,000 sesterces as it was known that he had inherited his patrimonial difficulties from his father. Others who tried a similar experiment were ordered to make out a case before the senate; for in his passion for austerity even when he acted justly he contrived to be harsh. The rest therefore, preferred silence and poverty to confession and charity.'

Cf. also Sen. *Ben* II, 7, 2; Tac. *Ann.* II, 37-38; 48; Suet. *Tib.* 47; Cass. Dion. LVII, 10,4. The attitude of Tiberius to the problem of the senators' *census,* considered contradictory by some, is in fact typical of this emperor. The conflicting claims which determined it were on the one hand his sense of duty as *princeps* towards the *res publica,* and on the other his loyalty to the old senatorial families which in the eyes of the patrician Tiberius incarnated the essence of Roman spirit. Therefore, if his devotion to the senate was an impediment to the 'loss of rank because of honest poverty', his 'old-fashioned thriftiness' prevented him from 'encouraging extravagant living'. On the above cf. F.B. Marsh, *The Reign of Tiberius,* London 1931, pp. 131-3; E. Koestermann, *Cornelius Tacitus. Annalen,* Band I, Heidelberg 1963, p. 246; R. Seager, *Tiberius,* London 1972, pp. 134-6; P. Veyne, *Le pain et le cirque,* Paris 1976, p. 635. On the problem of the senatorial *census,* cf. A. Chastagnol, *La naissance de l' 'ordo senatorius',* in *Mélanges de l'École Française de Rome,* 85 (1973), p. 586 ff.; C. Nicolet, *Le cens senatorial sous la République et sous Auguste,* in *Journal of Roman Studies,* 66 (1976), pp. 20-38; Cavallaro 1984, pp. 214-19. Together with the monographs on Tiberius quoted in the present work and elsewhere, readers are referred to E. Ciaceri, *Tiberio successore di Augusto,* Roma 1944[2]; E. Kornemann, *Tiberius,* Stuttgart 1960; B. Levick, *Tiberius the Politician,* London 1976.

184. Tac. *Ann.* III, 52: [...] *uetitaque utensilium pretia augeri in dies,* cit.

185. Tac. *Ann.* III, 52: *Ventris et ganeae paratus* etc., cit.; Suet. *Tib.* 34:

[...] *tresque mul<l>os triginta milibus nummum uenisse grauiter conquestus.*

'He gravely lamented the fact that three *mulli* (a kind of fish) had been sold for 30,000 sesterces.'

All this appears all the more significant when one considers that it occurred only a year after the Gallic revolt which had broken out *ob magnitudinem aeris alieni*, and was exacerbated by the *grauitas faenoris* (cf. Lo Cascio 1978, p. 244). For a discussion of prices in Rome during the principate, cf. Duncan-Jones, pp. 345-7.

186. Cf. n. 179.

187. Cf. Suet. *Tib.* 34:

dato aedilibus negotio popinas ganeasque usque eo inhibendi, ut ne opera quidem pistoria proponi uenalia sinerent.

'[...] While the aediles were instructed to put such restrictions on cook-shops and eating-houses as not to allow even pastry to be exposed for sale.'

188. Tac. Ann. III, 53:

Quid enim primum prohibere et priscum ad morem recidere adgrediar? Villarumne infinita spatia? Familiarum numerum et nationes? Argenti et auri pondus? Aeris tabularumque miracula? Promiscas uiris et feminis uestes atque illa feminarum propria, quis lapidum causa pecuniae nostrae ad externas aut hostilis gentis transferuntur?

'For on what am I to make my first effort at prohibition and rentrenchment to the ancient standard? On the infinite expanse of our villas? The numbers—the nations—of our slaves? The weight of our silver and gold? The miracles of bronze and canvas? The promiscuous dress of male and female—and the especially female extravagance by which, for the sake of jewels, our wealth is transported to alien or hostile countries ?'

However, the fact that Tiberius' *antiqua parsimonia* was not alien to a certain taste for artistic *miracula*, for the σπήλαια ὑπερμεγέθη, κατοικίας μεγάλας καὶ πολυτελεῖς δεδεγμένα ('the huge caves which host large and luxurious residences'), and for the luxury of banquets, is elegantly shown by A.F. Stewart, *To entertain an emperor: Sperlonga, Laokoon and Tiberius at the Dinner-table*, in *Journal of Roman Studies*, 67 (1977) pp. 76-90.

189. Tac. Ann. III, 54:

Tot a maioribus repertae leges, tot quas diuus Augustus tulit, illae obliuione, hae, quod flagitiosius est, contemptu abolitae securiorem luxum fecere.

'All the laws our ancestors discovered, all which the deified Augustus enacted, are now buried, those in oblivion, these—to our yet greater shame—in contempt. And this it is that has given luxury its greater boldness.'

190. On the financial crisis of AD 33 readers are referred to W.F. Allen, *The monetary crisis in Rome, A.D. 33*, in *Transactions and Proceedings of the American Philological Association*, 18 (1887), pp. 5-18; Frank, 1935 (cf. id., *Economic Survey of Ancient Rome. V. Rome and Italy of the Empire*, Paterson 1959, pp. 32 ff.); Rodewald 1976, spec. p. 1-17; Lo Cascio 1978, pp. 241 ff. For an interpretation of the suicide of the jurist Cocceius Nerva in the context of the financial crisis in AD 33, cf. G. Crifò, *Studi sul quasi-usufrutto romano I, Problemi di datazione*, Padova 1977, pp. 26-37; a general perspective in Mazzarino 1986, pp. 96 ff.

191. Strab. XVII, 1, 13:

νῦν δὲ καὶ στόλοι μεγάλοι στέλλονται μέχρι τῆς Ἰνδικῆς καὶ τῶν ἄκρων τῶν Αἰθιοπικῶν, ἐξ ὧν ὁ πολυτιμότατος κομίζεται φόρτος εἰς τὴν Αἴγυπτον, κἀντεῦθεν πάλιν εἰς τοὺς ἄλλους ἐκπέμπεται τόπους· ὥστε τὰ τέλη διπλάσια συνάγεται, τὰ μὲν εἰσαγωγικά, τὰ δὲ ἐξαγωγικά· τῶν δὲ βαρυτίμων βαρέα καὶ τὰ τέλη.

'At the present time even large fleets are despatched as far as India and the extremities of Aethiopia, from which the most valuable cargoes are brought to Egypt, and thence sent forth again to the other regions, so that double duties are collected on both imports and exports; and on goods that cost heavily the duty is also heavy.'

Cf. Raschke 1978, p. 670. The attempt made by Nero to abolish indirect taxes in AD 58, and the tax relief which benefited the *negotiatores* who possessed ships in the same year (Tac. *Ann.* XIII, 50-1), were linked to the need to lower the prices of luxury items, thus benefiting the senatorial class, cf. Mazzarino 1986, pp. 219-20.

192. Cf. Tac. *Ann.* VI, 17:

hinc inopia rei nummariae commoto simul omnium aere alieno et quia tot damnatis bonisque eorum diuenditis signatum argentum fisco uel aerario attinebatur.

'This resulted in a dearth of liquid money, as all credits were asked for at the same time and due to the fact that once the possessions of those who had been condemned were sold off the money lay in the state treasury.'

193. Suet. *Cal.* 37, 3. Different figures are given by the sources of Cassio Dione LIX, 2, 6, cf. Cavallaro 1984, p. 187.

194. On this passage cf. Mazzarino 1966b, pp. 80 ff.

Romanukharaṭṭha and Taprobane: Relations between Rome and Sri Lanka in the First Century AD

FEDERICO DE ROMANIS

EGYPTIAN TIME-RECKONING AND ROMAN MERCHANTS: A NEW READING OF A GREEK INSCRIPTION FROM EGYPT (*AÉ* 1954, N. 121A)

It is well known that in Roman Egypt, in addition to the Julio-Alexandrian fixed year of 365 and a quarter days, probably introduced by Octavian in 30 BC[1] and called by Theon of Alexandria[2] ὁ καθ' Ἕλληνας ἤτοι κατὰ 'Αλεξανδρέας – ἐνιαυτός, the use of the old revolving year, consisting of only 365 days, continued in several regions for at least some time; this latter calendar year was defined by Censorinus as the *annus ciuilis*[3] and by Theon as ὁ κατ' Αἰγυπτίους (sc. ἐνιαυτός).[4]

The difference of a quarter day per year between these two ways of measuring time inevitably determined the fact that every four years the ἀποκατάστασις would occur: the revolving year was brought forward by one day with respect to the Julio-Alexandrian fixed year, as well as to the Roman Julian year, which also consisted of 365 and a quarter days.[5]

Several documents have a double dating (according to the Egyptian revolving year and the Julio-Alexandrian fixed year, or otherwise according to the Egyptian revolving year and the Roman Julian calendar) and some even show a triple dating (the Egyptian revolving year, the Julio-Alexandrian fixed year and the Roman Julian calendar), which allows us to calculate the discrepancy between the two dating systems (the fixed one and the revolving one) during certain years. The following are some examples.

The first is a bilingual (Greek and demotic) inscription of the seventeenth year of Tiberius, found at Abydos.[6] In the demotic version the dating 'according to the Egyptians' (*pe-rem-kemau*) fixed on the first day of Mechir, is set against the dating 'according to the Ionians' (*pe-uinen)* fixed on the 18th day of the month of Tybi. This inscription therefore registers a thirteen-day discrepancy between the date of the Egyptian revolving year and that of the Julio-Alexandrian fixed year for the AD 13 January 31.

The second document is a horoscope preserved on papyrus and dated AD 1 April 81 by means of a triple dating system: here the discrepancy between the date of the Egyptian revolving year (second of the month of Pachon) and that of the Julio-Alexandrian fixed year (sixth of the month of Pharmouthi) has increased to 26 days—and the same between the Egyptian revolving year and the Roman Julian year.[7]

Then we have the dates of two more horoscopes, both for AD 4 December 137: the equivalence between the eighth day of the month of Hadrian (Choiak) in the Julio-Alexandrian fixed year and the eighteenth day of the month of Tybi in the Egyptian revolving year denotes a forty-day gap between the dates of the two years.[8]

Finally, a forty-day gap between the Egyptian revolving year and the Roman Julian year for the year AD 139 is attested in a well-known passage of Censorinus, which also shows how in the year AD 238 the discrepancy between the dates of the Egyptian revolving year and of the Roman Julian year had increased to 65 days.[9]

Other documents could be cited, but the principle is clear: every four years (for those years of the Christian era, whose number divided by four gives a remainder of three) 29 August of the Roman-Julian year, which corresponded to the sixth of the Julio-Alexandrian *Epagomenai*, the Egyptian revolving year would 'gain' one day with respect to the Julio-Alexandrian fixed year; and once every four years (for those years of the Christian era whose number can be divided by four), on the thirtieth day of Mechir during the Julio-Alexandrian fixed year, which corresponded to the *bisextus kal. Mart.* of the Roman Julian year, the Egyptian revolving year would 'gain' one day with respect to the Roman Julian calendar. The evidence concerning the use of the Egyptian revolving year in Roman Egypt will help us to elucidate two important passages in the *Natural History* of Pliny.

The first of these—deriving from information which Pliny had received from merchants of his time—takes us to Muziris and Becare, the renowned emporia of southern India, whence the ships of Roman merchants set sail for Egypt before the ides of January, taking advantage of the North-Easterly monsoon. The deadline for departure is expressed by Pliny as follows: *ex India renauigant mense Aegyptio Tybi incipiente, nostro Decembri, aut utique Mechiris Aegyptii intra diem sextum, quod fit intra idus Ianuarias nostras,* ('Travellers set sail from India on the return voyage at the beginning of the Egyptian month of Tybi, which is our December, or at all events before the sixth day of the Egyptian Mechir, which works out at before 13 January in our calendar.').[10]

As Ideler correctly suggested as early as 1825, in this case the sixth day of the month of Mechir must be worked out according to the Egyptian revolving year.[11] We can thus establish in which quadriennium the merchants who later informed Pliny travelled to India, their reports being the source of chapters 101-6 of book VI of the *Natural History*.[12]

The equivalence of the *idus Ianuariae* with the sixth day of the month of Mechir in fact shows an eighteen-day discrepancy between the dates of the Egyptian revolving year and the Roman Julian year. If we begin by taking into consideration the twenty-six day gap ascertained for the quadriennium AD *V kal. Mart.* 80/*VI kal. Mart.* 84, by means of a simple calculation we can discover the four-year period within which Pliny's informants found themselves in the ports of southern India waiting to set sail for Arabia and Egypt: that is, 80/84—[(26—18) x 4] = AD *V kal. Mart.* 48 / *VI kal. Mart.* 52. The Roman merchants consulted by Pliny had travelled to India during the principate of Claudius (to be more precise between AD 48/49 and 51/52), exactly 25/30 years before the *Natural History* was dedicated to Titus. This was a period, as we shall see below, which was extremely important for the development of relations between the Indian subcontinent and the Roman empire.

Let us set aside our merchants for a moment, and examine instead another passage of the *Natural History* in which there is a reference to the Egyptian revolving year. This time it is in connection with the description of some Egyptian magico-religious rituals related to ailments of the eyes. The rituals are of great interest linked as they are on the one hand with the widespread diffusion of eye ailments in ancient Egypt,[13] and on the other with motifs typical of Egyptian folklore, which believed eye ailments to be divine punishments.[14] Pliny's commentary runs as follows, *N.H.* XXVII, 105:

myosota siue myosotis leuis herba, caulibus pluribus ab una radice, aliquatenus rubentibus, concauis ab imo, foliis angustis, oblongis, dorso acuto, nigris, per interualla adsidue geminatis, tenuibus cauliculis ex alis prodeuntibus, flore caeruleo. Radix digitali crassitudine multis capillamentis fimbriata. Vis ei septica et exulceratrix ideoque aegilopas sanat. Tradunt Aegypti, mensis, quem Thoti uocant, die XXVIII fere in Augustum mensem incurrente si quis huius herbae suco inungatur mane, priusquam loquatur, non lippiturum eo anno.

'Myosota or Myosotis is a smooth plant with several stems growing from one root, these are red for a portion of their length and hollow at the bottom; they grow narrow, longish leaves which are arranged in pairs at regular intervals and have a dark spine along the back. There are slender stalks growing from the axils, and the blossom is blue. The root, the thickness of a finger, is fringed with many filament-like hairs. It has septic and ulcerating properties, and therefore heals lacrimal fistulas. The Egyptians say that if on the twenty-eighth day of the month they call Thoti (a day falling about in our August), a person rubs himself over in the morning with the juice of this plant before speaking to anyone, he will not in that year suffer from ophthalmia.

The information digested in these notes by Pliny on the *myosota* or *myosotis*, comes from two different sources. A comparison between Dioscorides II, 183 and the first part of Pliny's chapter (*myosota—sanat*) suggests that both derived from a common source, identified by Wellmann as Sextius Niger-Crateuas.[15] The last part of the passage (*tradunt—anno*), if not derived from first-hand information and if the formula *die XXVIII fere in Augustum mensem incurrente* was not adapted by Pliny, must relate to a text published after AD 76. In this case too, *pace* De la Nauze,[16] the twenty-eighth day of the month of Thoth can only refer to the Egyptian revolving year.

By contrast with *N.H.* VI, 106, in *N.H.* XXVII, 105 Pliny (or his source) refrains from giving a definite date corresponding to the twenty-eighth day of Thoth, simply saying that it falls approximately in the month of August. However, the twenty-eighth day of Thoth began to fall in the month of August only from AD 76 onward, in which year it coincided with the Julian 31 August. It is obvious that if Pliny scrupulously followed his written source, as was his habit, the latter must date from after AD 76. Hanslik, using a different argument, believed he could recognize the source of the second part of *N.H.* XXVII, 105 in Xenocrates of Aphrodisias,[17] a physician who lived during the age of Galen's grandparents and who was, in Galen's view, 'in many ways rather superstitious and above all not alien to magic'.[18] A man not alien to magic could well have taken an interest in Egyptian magico-cum-religious rituals and if he is the same 'Xenocrates [...] who wrote very recently and is still living',[19] Hanslik's hypothesis gains in probability.

Returning to *N.H.* VI, 106, the dates relating to the return journey from India of Pliny's informants are not the only inference we are able to make from this valuable passage of Pliny. In the formulation *Mechiris Aegyptii intra diem sextum, quod fit intra idus Ianuarias nostras* ('before the sixth day of the Egyptian Mechir, which works out at before January 13th in our calendar'), we can glimpse and reconstruct the encounter, on the banks of the Nile, on the caravan routes in the south-eastern desert of Egypt and in the ports of the Red Sea and India, between two different cultures with two different systems of calculating time.

The first culture is that of the agents of the Roman 'capitalists', who invested their good coins to acquire India's fabulous merchandise; the second, that of the seafaring Egyptian crews whose life was regulated by the rising of Sothis (the star of Sirius, α *Canis Maioris*).[20] This heralded the imminent flooding of the Nile and gave a warning to those ships, that had lingered in the ports of the Red Sea, to set sail immediately so as to be on time for their annual rendezvous with the South-Westerly monsoon, off the shores of the Arabian coasts past the straits of Bab el-Mandeb.[21] I believe the two inscriptions discussed below are to be interpreted in the context of this characteristic encounter between Roman and Egyptian culture.

Pliny's *excursus* on trade with southern India (*N.H.* VI, 102-6) also includes a description of the lines of communication which linked Alexandria to Berenice, one of the two ports in the Red Sea—the other being Myos Hormos—whence merchants used to set sail for India. Setting off from Juliopolis, merchants would sail up the Nile for twelve days, benefiting from the favourable Etesian winds until they reached Coptos. From here the caravan route headed for Berenice. Plin. *N.H.* VI, 102-3:

a Copto camelis itur, aquationum ratione mansionibus dispositis: prima appellatur Hydreuma XXII,[22] *secunda in monte diei itinere, tertia in altero Hydreumate a Copto LXXXV, deinde in monte; mox ad Hydreuma Apollinis a Copto CLXXXIIII, rursus in monte; mox ad Nouum Hydreuma a Copto CCXXXVI. Est et aliud Hydreuma uetus—Trogodyticum nominatur—ubi praesidium excubat deuerticulo duum milium; distat a Nouo Hydreumate VII. Inde Berenice oppidum, ubi portus Rubri maris, a Copto CCLVII p. Sed quia maior pars itineris conficitur noctibus propter aestus et statiuis dies absumuntur, totum a Copto Berenicen iter duodecimo die peragitur.*

From Coptos the journey is made with camels, stations being placed at intervals for the purpose of watering; the first stage of 22 miles is called Hydreuma; the second is *in monte*, a day's journey on; the third at a second Hydreuma 85 miles from Coptos; the next is *in monte*; next we come to Apollo's Hydreuma, 184 miles from Coptos; again followed by a station *in monte*; then we reach New Hydreuma, 230 miles from Coptos. There is also another old Hydreuma it is called Trogodetieum where a guard is stationed on outpost duty down a side road, two miles away; it is seven miles from New Hydreuma. Then comes the town of Berenice, where there is a harbour on the Red Sea, 257 miles from Coptos. But as the greater part of the journey is made at night because of the heat and the days are spent at stations, the whole journey from Coptos to Berenice takes twelve days.

The journey from Coptos to Berenice thus took twelve days, and provision was made for seven (or eight, if we also include the *Hydreuma Vetus*) *mansiones* (stations); of these, however, only four (or five) halts were made in proximity to a water cistern, the others were *in monte*. To clarify this latter expression, which might otherwise remain somewhat ambiguous, it might be argued that the term *mons* in *N.H.* VI, 102 is a calque of the Greek ὄρος, which in Egypt[23] corresponds to the hieroglyph *h 3st* and often takes on the meaning of 'desert'. The *mansiones in monte*, therefore, would represent halting places in 'the middle of the desert', far away from the water cisterns (*hydreumata*). This would also explain why Pliny does not specify their exact distance in miles from Coptos (only for the first *mansio in monte* does he state that it was one day's journey from the first *hydreuma*). In actual fact they were not located at precise places like those near the *hydreumata*, even though the exigence of travel ultimately determined the choice of preferential areas.

However, even if we do not accept the hypothesis that the expression *in monte* in *N.H.* VI, 102, is a poor translation of ἐν ὄρει—whether by Pliny or perhaps simply unwittingly accepted by him—the *mansiones in monte* were self-evidently not situated near places with water reserves. The reason for these necessary halts was, of course, to provide rest, possibly in the shade, for members of the caravan worn-out by the long march and by the oppressive heat of the desert in June-July.

The first *mansio in monte* was situated a day's journey from the first *hydreuma*. The first *hydreuma* is probably identifiable with modern-day el-Laqeita.[24] Approximately forty kilometres from there the caravan route from Coptos to Berenice crossed a site on the Wadi Menih, where the numerous Greek, Latin and Arabic inscriptions, the many graffiti and especially the constant shade offered by a little cave, suggest that it was here that the caravans used to wait for dusk before resuming their journey to Berenice.

On this site in 1936, H.A. Winkler saw, among others, two inscriptions (a Greek and a Latin one),[25] which were subsequently published by D. Meredith in 1953, on the basis of a photograph of the Latin inscription and Winkler's transcription of the Greek one, as follows:[26]

Λυσᾶς Ποπλίου 'Αννίου Πλοκάμου/ ἥκωι L λε
Καίσαρος ἐπεὶφ η̄.
Lysa P. Anni Plocami ueni anno XXXV/III non. Iul.

The Greek text says: 'I, Lysas (slave) of Publius Annius Plocamus, came (here) in the 35th year of Caesar, on the 8th day of the Egyptian month of Epeiph.' The Latin text says: 'I, Lysa (slave) of Publius Annius Plocamus, came (here) in the 35th year, the third day before the nones of July, i.e. the 5th of July.'

Meredith dates the Greek inscription to the AD 2 July 6—apparently interpreting the date ἐπειφ η̄ according to the Julio-

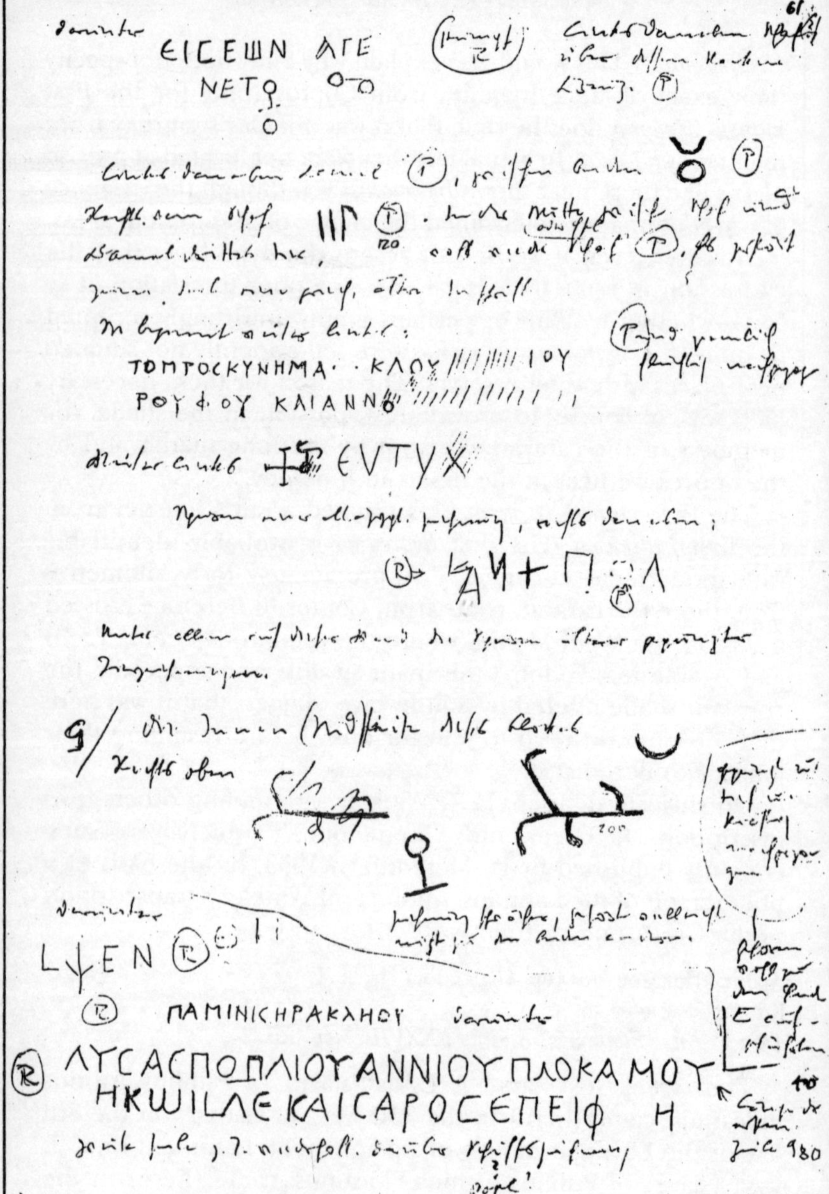
ΕΙϹΕѠΝ ΑΓΕ
ΝΕΤΟ
ΤΟΜΠΡΟϹΚΥΝΗΜΑ · ΚΛΟΥ ΙΟΥ
ΡΟΥΦΟΥ ΚΑΙΑΝΝΟ
ΕΥΤΥΧ
ΠΑΜΙΝΙΚΗΡΑΚΛΗΟΥ
ΛΥϹΑϹΠΟΠΛΙΟΥΑΝΝΙΟΥΠΛΟΚΑΜΟΥ
ΗΚѠΙΛΑΕΚΑΙϹΑΡΟϹΕΠΕΙΦ Η

Plate I: The Greek inscription by Lysas (*A. É.* 1954, nº 121a), in the transcription by H.A. Winkler, with annotation by the latter.

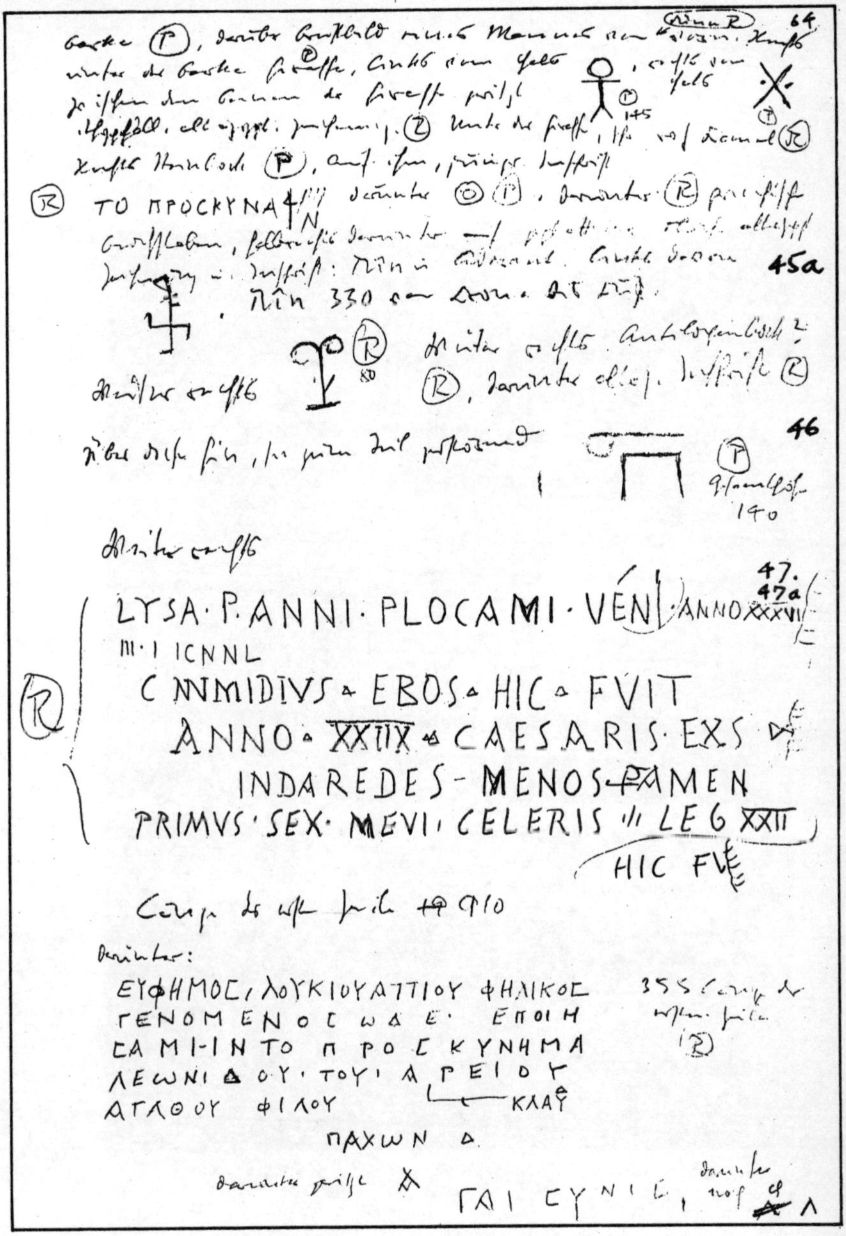

LYSA · P. ANNI · PLOCAMI · VEN · ANNO XXXVII

C NUMIDIUS · EBOS · HIC · FUIT

ANNO · XXIIX · CAESARIS · EXS

INDAREDES · MENOS · FAMEN

PRIMUS · SEX · MEVI · CELERIS · LEG XXII

HIC FU

ΕΥΦΗΜΟΣ ΛΟΥΚΙΟΥ ΑΤΤΙΟΥ ΦΗΛΙΚΟΣ

ΓΕΝΟΜΕΝΟΣ ΩΔΕ ΕΠΟΙΗ

ΣΑΜΗΝ ΤΟ ΠΡΟΣΚΥΝΗΜΑ

ΛΕΩΝΙΔΟΥ ΤΟΥ ΑΡΕΙΟΥ

ΑΓΛΟΟΥ ΦΙΛΟΥ ΚΛΑΥ

ΠΑΧΩΝ Δ

Plate II: The Latin inscription by Lysas (*A.É.* 1954, n⁰ 121b), in the transcription by H.A. Winkler, with annotations by the latter.

Plate III: *A.É.* 1954, n⁰ 121b (Photo by Prof. H.T. Wright)

Alexandrian fixed year. The Latin inscription he dates to 5 July of the same year. The implications of Meredith's reading and interpretation are, if true, rather unsettling: one would need to imagine that, upon reaching the Wadi Menih on AD 2 July 6, the slave Lysas recorded for posterity his passing through that place by carving a Greek inscription dated by the Julio-Alexandrian fixed year, and that three days later he engraved the same text, in the same place, but this time in Latin and with a date according to the Roman Julian year.[27] According to the Egyptian revolving year system of dating, the Greek inscription would date back to AD 25 June 6 and this would still leave us with a problem.

Our perplexity concerning the reading η̄ is not at all dispelled by the copy of the inscription produced by Winkler, which is the only source on which Meredith's edition is based (Plate I).[28] We may assume that the Greek inscription was accurately transcribed by Winkler.[29] If so, then the unusually large gap between the letter Φ of ἐπείφ and the letter H, might perhaps be explained by the need to highlight the numerical value of H. It should be noted, in fact, that in Winkler's copy there is no such horizontal stroke, even though he marked one over ΛΕ). That, however, does not exclude the possibility that in the crucial space before H a letter may have become illegible.

In short, Pliny's formulation in *N.H.* VI, 106, attests that the merchants who frequented the ports of southern India used a double dating system: one according to the Egyptian revolving year, and the other according to the Roman Julian year. In much the same mercantile context we find two complementary inscriptions, one in Greek, the other in Latin, carved out in the 'sands through which is the route to the commerce of the Indian sea'[30] by the slave of a personage related to the man contracted to farm the *uectigal maris Rubri* ('the Red Sea tax') in the age of Claudius and patron of the 'discoverer' of the island of Taprobane (Sri Lanka).[31] The difficulties deriving from Meredith's reading of the Greek inscription, the excessively wide space between the letters Φ and H in Winkler's transcript, concur, it seems to me, in suggesting that the reading ἐπεὶφ [τ]η̄ is more probable than Meredith's proposal ἐπεὶφ η̄—that is to say, the numeral was 18 not 8. The two dates recorded by the Wadi Menih inscriptions must in short be the same:

according to the Egyptian revolving year, the eighteenth day of the month of Epiphi in AD 6 would in fact correspond to AD 5 July 6, the same day on which the Latin inscription was carved.[32] If this conjecture is correct, the same correlation between the Egyptian revolving year and the Roman Julian year as that recorded by Pliny in the ports of southern India would be corroborated by the inscriptions of the slave of Annius Plocamus in the cave of Wadi Menih.

It is striking—and revealing with regard to the social environment to which the readers of the work belonged—that the author of the *Periplus Maris Erythraei* should only refer to the Julio-Alexandrian fixed year and the Roman Julian year, and in an approximate and rough-and-ready manner at that.[33] It is also striking that Pliny's informants and subsequently Pliny himself, and (if our suppositions are correct) also Lysas, the slave of P. Annius Plocamus, should have showed an interest in and a respect for local Egyptian culture, greater than that shown by the author of the *PME*.

ROMANUKHARAṬṬHA AND TAPROBANE: THE IMAGE OF THE PARTS OF THE WORLD

The dynamism which, in many respects, characterized the Roman society during the Julio-Claudian period is also reflected in its particular conception of the world, its mode of understanding the oecumene. During the late Julio-Claudian period, the Augustan vision—anticipated by Polybius, and connected with the old idea of universal empire[34]—of an *orbis terrarum subiectus imperio populi Romani*, of an oecumene, in short, subjected to Roman imperialism, was combined with (and opposed by) a conception of the world as a sphere of action for Roman merchants, resulting from the new commercial routes which extended from the Atlantic to the Indian Ocean.[35]

It is precisely during the middle decades of the first century AD that we notice a growing interest in the accounts of journeys written by those merchants who travelled to the most disparate and distant parts of the world. We have stressed the contacts, during the principate of Claudius (or at least those which referred to journeys undertaken during that period), between

Pliny and the Roman merchants who frequented the ports of southern India, but we should not overlook the merchants who ventured along the Atlantic coast to the south of Mauretania, who penetrated into the Baltic sea, or who sailed along the Horn of Africa, Arabia and Persia. It is during the course of this sudden and dramatic expansion of the geographic (and economic) horizon, which led to the forecast that the day was not far distant when the Ocean would dissolve the *uincula rerum* a reveal new continents,[36] that we must place the event examined in the present study: the 'discovery'[37] of Taprobane (Sri Lanka) by a freedman of a certain Annius Plocamus. Once again, the event is recorded by Pliny, *N.H.* VI, 84-5:

hactenus a priscis memorata. Nobis diligentior notitia Claudi principatu contigit legatis etiam ex ea insula (sc. Taprobane) *aduectis. Id accidit hoc modo. Anni Plocami, qui maris Rubri uectigal a fisco redemerat, libertus circa Arabiam nauigans aquilonibus raptus praeter Carmaniam, XV die Hippuros portum eius inuectus, hospitali regis clementia sex mensum tempore inbutus adloquio percunctanti postea narrauit Romanos et Caesarem. Mirum in modum in auditis iustitiam ille suspexit, quod pari pondere denarii essent in captiua pecunia, cum diuersae imagines indicarent a pluribus factos, et hoc maxime sollicitatus ad amicitiam legatos quattuor misit principe eorum Rachia.*

So far the facts stated have been recorded by the early writers. We however, have obtained more accurate information during the principate of Claudius, when an embassy actually came to Rome from the island of Taprobane. The circumstances were as follows: Annius Plocamus had procured a contract from the Treasury to collect the taxes of the Red Sea; a freedman of his, while sailing round Arabia, was carried by gales from the north beyond the coast of Carmania, and after a fortnight made the harbour of Hippuri in Taprobane, where he was entertained and shown kind hospitality by the king and in a period of six months acquired a thorough knowledge of the language. Subsequently in reply to the king's enquiries, he gave him an account of the Romans and their emperor. Of all that he heard, the king was remarkably struck by Roman equity because among the money found on the captive the denarii were all equal in weight, although the various images on them showed that they had been coined by several emperors. This most of all persuaded him to extend his friendship, and he sent four envoys, the chief of whom was Rachias.[38]

Several important details of this well-known text still await a more precise evaluation.

(a) Aquilonibus raptus: Indian Ocean winds and Graeco-Roman science

Let us examine first the freedman's voyage. Nothing in Pliny's account gives us reason to connect the adventurous crossing of the freedman of Annius Plocamus with the discovery of the monsoons or with the development of navigation in the Indian Ocean.[39] Yet in spite of this, a comparison between the voyage of Annius Plocamus' freedman and the route described by Pliny in *N.H.* VI, 102-6, the one followed in his time by Western merchants, will help to clarify the difference between the two sea voyages, above all with respect to the different winds utilized.

According to Pliny, the wind exploited by western merchants for the voyage from Arabia to India was the westerly *fauonius* (or *hypalus/hippalus*),[40] whereas the journey back (from India to Arabia) benefited, he says, from the impetus of the *uolturnus* wind.[41] In this last statement Warmington[42] perceived an error by the naturalist. In fact, the *uolturnus* is—according to the more usual wind rose, which Pliny himself knew and refers to[43]—the *ab oriente brumali* wind, that is, the wind blowing from ESE, and such a description does not fit the North-Easterly winter monsoon used by ships leaving India between December and mid-January. Böker[44] explained the anomaly by recalling that in the ancient sources the *uolturnus* is sometimes used in substitution for the καικίας, a wind blowing from the north-east. Pliny, therefore, in *N.H.* VI, 106, supposedly followed a source which named the north-easterly wind as *uolturnus*.

In my opinion, this explanation is insufficient, as it does not explain two further anomalies which are linked to that noted by Warmington. The first is the name *fauonius* (described as a wind *ab occasu aequinoctiali*, that is, coming from the West) given to the South-Westerly monsoon;[45] the second is the definition of *africus* or *auster* (winds described respectively as *ab occasu brumali* [i.e. WSW] and *a meridie* [i.e. S]) as the winds which would favour the merchants' return journey on entering the Red Sea[46] where the prevailing winds are south-east in the winter months.[47]

We are therefore faced with a distortion (with clockwise rotation, in all three cases) of the cardinal points.[48] The incorrect orientation by Pliny of the winds in the Indian Ocean and in the Red Sea appears all the more interesting if we recall that at least some of the mariners familiar with the sea routes of the Indian Ocean in the first century AD were able to indicate the direction of the monsoon winds more or less correctly. The author of the *Periplus Maris Erythraei*, for example, defines the South-West monsoon as λιβόνοτος,[49] a wind, blowing from SSW. In attempting a reconstruction of the genesis of the errors committed by Pliny, I believe it may be useful to recall some of the stages in the investigation carried out by the ancients on the regime of the winds in the Indian Ocean.

As shown by S. Mazzarino, the historians of Alexander grasped that the peculiarity of the monsoons especially consisted in the fact that one of them (the South-Westerly monsoon) was ὕφαλος, i.e. a (sub)marine wind, whereas the other (the North-Easterly) monsoon was ἀπόγαιος, i.e. a land wind. This conception was combined with an albeit timid attempt at orientation, at least for the South-Westerly monsoon.[50] The memory of these first empirical observations of the monsoons, and of the conception of two monsoons, one being a wind from the sea, the other from the land, still survived, in Pliny's time, in the name *hypalus/hippalus* attached to the South-Westerly monsoon. But if we wish to understand Pliny's definitions of the monsoon winds, we must turn to another author who exerted a strong influence on subsequent investigation in this field, namely Posidonius.

I think that the solution of the problem lies in the definition of the SW monsoon as ζέφυροι by Posidonius. We find it when he describes the third journey of Eudoxus of Cyzicus to India: [...] πλεῖν ἐπὶ τὴν Ἰνδικὴν μετέωρον ζεφύροις συνεχέσι ('he (sc. Eudoxus) sailed in the open sea towards India with the favour of continuous Zephyrs').[51]

This definition by Posidonius, which implies the adoption of the simple Homeric wind rose with only four (groups of) winds[52] and most probably refers back to the Aristotelian anemography of the 'southern sea beyond Libye (Africa)', characterized by the alternation of Zephyrs and Euroi, westerly and easterly winds,[53] was translated by Pliny as *fauonius*. This is evident from another fragment of Posidonius preserved in the *Natural History*, which refers to effects of the SW monsoon on the Indian climate.[54] *N.H.* VI, 57 (= FGr Hist 87 F 100 = F 212 E.-K. = 69a Th.):

Posidonius ab aestiuo solis ortu ad hibernum exortum metatus est eam, aduersam Galliam statuens, quam ab occidente aestiuo ad occidentem hibernum metabatur, totam a fauonio. Itaque aduersam (-*o* R^2 -*um* rell.) *eius uenti adflatu iuuari Indiam salubremque fieri haut dubia ratione docuit.*

Posidonius places India opposite to Gallia, betwwen summer and winter sunrise, and accordingly he shows by an unqestionable line of argument that India has the advantage of being exposed to the current of the west wind (*fauonius*), which gives it a healthy climate.

In this case, too, *fauonius* goes back, perhaps indirectly, to an original ζέφυροι. But if the plural form ζέφυροι (which generically indicates the winds ἀπὸ δύσεως, 'from the West') was sufficiently ambiguous to include even a SW wind, then the term *fauonius* exclusively indicates, within an eight-wind wind rose, the wind *ab occasu aequinoctiali*, that is the wind from due West. Nevertheless we can understand why Pliny (or his eventual Latin source) translated ζέφυροι as *fauonius*. In an eight-wind wind rose, the ζέφυρος (singular) is a wind which blows ἀπὸ τῆς ἰσημερινῆς δύσεως, just as the *fauonius* does *ab occasu aequinoctiali*: both the Greek and the Latin designations mean that the wind is from due West. Exactly in the same way, within an eight-wind wind rose, the εὖρος is ἀπὸ τῆς χειμερινῆς ἀνατολῆς, just as the *uolturnus* is *ab oriente brumali*: both mean it is a South-Easterly wind.

It becomes clear that Pliny's error in *N.H.* VI, 100 and 106 consists in having interpreted Aristotelian and Posidonian designations ζέφυροι and εὖροι, which he probably found in his source, Iuba,[55] according to the eight-wind wind rose used by Posidonius,[56] whereas these in fact referred to the simple Homeric four-wind wind rose. This meant, in effect, that the SW monsoon became a wind from the West, and the NE monsoon one from East-South-East. The result, therefore, was not only the distortion of the cardinal points, but also that of the angle formed by the direction of the two winds, which worked out to be a mere 150^0 as compared to the actual 180^0. The same error must have been committed by Pliny (or by his

Latin source) in *N.H.* VI, 57, where the SW monsoon is also called *fauonius.*

If the origin of Pliny's designation of the monsoon winds as *fauonius* and *uolturnus* is the result of a misinterpretation of Posidonius' terms ζέφυροι and εὖροι, the same cannot be said of the terms *africus uel auster* applied to the SE winds which prevail at the entrance of the Red Sea during the winter months, since the reference to *africus* excludes the possibility of a misunderstanding of the original Greek form. However, this definition also proved wrong in a manner similar to that of the monsoon winds, with a discrepancy which varies between 60° and 120° from the true direction.

The formula *africus uel auster* cannot be attributed to Posidonius, nor can it be attributed to those merchants (such as the author of the *PME*) who described the SW monsoon as a λιβόνοτος. In fact, they would have called these SE winds εὖρος or εὐρόνοτος, translated into Latin as *uolturnus,* not as *africus uel auster.*

The origin of this double definition is unclear. But we can at least make a conjecture. Let us assume the probability that the monsoon winds constituted for merchants of old not only a means of sailing to and from India, but also, considering the perseverance and relative invariability of these winds, the simplest device for taking a bearing. If indeed this is so, the definition *africus uel auster* could be the result of an evaluation of the SE winds on the basis of the *fauonius-uolturnus* 'monsoon angle'. In other words, the merchants knew perfectly well that between the direction of the NE monsoon and that of the Red Sea there was an angle of approximately 90° in a clockwise direction, and that between the direction of the SE Red Sea winds and that of the SW monsoon there was a further 90° angle, also in a clockwise direction.

If the interpretation of the Red Sea winds stemmed from the equation SW monsoon = *fauonius,* then by the same process, the SE winds were interpreted as *auster.* But if the equation NE monsoon = *uolturnus* was used as the starting point, it followed that these same winds were *africus.* This would also explain the uncertain direction of the formula *africus uel auster, africus* or *auster.* 'Pliny', said Mazzarino 'is a scholar who bases himself upon the *auctores*—but also upon direct information'. If our hypothesis is correct, then the definition *africus uel auster* would show how Pliny correlated Aristotelian and Posidonian anemography, probably known to him through the work of Iuba, with the first-hand accounts of the merchants he had heard.[57]

Doubts remain, however. Among other things, did the merchants from whom Pliny had derived his information about trade with India, and who had perhaps informed him about the angles between the direction of the Red Sea winds and those of the monsoon winds, also tell him that the SW monsoon was a λιβόνοτος (or, in Latin, *africus*) and not a *fauonius*? In short, did Pliny ignore the information supplied by the merchants if (in his view) it contradicted his source Iuba, which depended in turn on Aristotle and Posidonius ? Or did he resort to literary sources because the merchants he consulted were unable to identify the directions of the monsoon winds ? Or had the merchants themselves read Iuba's remarks on the monsoon winds, and derived from them the conviction that the SW monsoon was a *fauonius* and the NE monsoon a *uolturnus*, and therefore considered the SE winds at the entrance of the Red Sea to be *africus uel auster*?

After this digression, let us now return to the voyage of Annius Plocamus' freedman. Obviously, it differed from what constituted the normal crossing between Arabia and India and back favoured by the monsoon winds. Pliny summed it up in three participial clauses: *circa Arabiam nauigans aquilonibus raptus praeter Carmaniam, XV die Hippuros portum eius inuectus* ('While sailing round Arabia, having been driven by gales from the north beyond the coast of Carmania, and after a fortnight having made the harbour of Hippuri in Taprobane.') From Pliny's account we are able clearly to distinguish two phases in the voyage: the first consisting of coastal navigation round the Arabian peninsula, which was probably for trade; and the second culminating in the freedman landing in Taprobane (Sri Lanka) as a result of a storm after fifteen days' at sea.

The key to understanding the freedman's journey lies in the expression *aquilonibus raptus*. As had already been observed by Harduinus,[58] the plural *aquilonibus* certainly does not oblige us to identify the wind which 'captured' the freedman's vessel with a NE wind, nor do I consider it possible to identify the *aquilones* in question with one of the two monsoon winds. It is hard to believe, in fact, that an expert helmsman would have allowed himself to be 'captured' by seasonal winds which were regular and well known by any sailor who had sailed beyond the straits of Bab el-Mandeb. Another consideration is that the NE monsoon is certainly not a storm wind, and had he been driven by a SW wind, it is difficult to see how he could have reached Sri Lanka from the Arabian coast.

We must remember, on the other hand, that storms and shipwrecks in the eastern part of the Gulf of Aden are quite frequently recorded in ancient literature: the *PME* says that the 'Αρωμάτων ἐμπόριον (the 'Spice Port') is dangerous at times because it is exposed to the north wind;[59] and Marinus of Tyre mentions a certain Diogenes, who, when he arrived at Cape Guardafui on his return voyage from India, was driven by a northerly wind down the East Coast of Africa, probably as far as Tanzania.[60]

It seems to me that in attempting to identify the *aquilones* in *N.H.* VI, 84, the following premises need to be borne in mind: (1) it must have been a very violent and sudden wind, such as would have taken an expert pilot unawares, causing the vessel to stray far off its course; (2) the events of the voyage show that the *aquilones* struck the freedman's vessel off the shores of the Arabian coast, blowing approximately in an easterly direction.

Taking these considerations into account, it seems probable that Pliny's *aquilones* are to be identified with the *Belat*, a name given to

> northwesterly winds which sometimes blow off the southern coast of Arabia in the period December to March. They are especially strong in Kuria Muria bay. These winds usually commence at night and within about an hour may increase to Force 7, raising dust and sand. They usually reach their maximum in the latter part of the morning and cease by about midday, sometimes occurring on several days in succession. They are liable to be dangerous to vessels near the shore on account of violent squalls which may blow down from the hills.[61]

If Pliny's *aquilones* really were the *Belat*, then we would have to deduce that the freedman's vessel was blown southeast of the Arabian coast (which would fit with the phrase *praeter*

Carmaniam—raptus) during a period of the year in which the Indian Ocean is dominated by the NE monsoon.

We don't know for how many days the freedman sailed under the impetus of the *aquilones*, but it seems to me legitimate to infer, from the semantic disjunction between the two participles *raptus* and *inuectus*, that the latter part of the voyage was completed under the impetus of another, less violent wind: this could only have been the NE monsoon, which has the capacity, in March-April, to *inuehere* a vessel adrift in the Indian Ocean between Arabia and India all the way to Ceylon.[62]

Thus, after a storm off the coast of southern Arabia and a period adrift in the midst of the Indian Ocean, the freedman of Annius Plocamus landed at last, as if by a miracle, on the marvellous island of Taprobane. Welcomed and given hospitality by the king, he was able to learn the local language in six months and 'to give an account of the Romans and their emperor'. There was one thing in particular that the king admired: the unvarying (*iustitia*) of the Romans and of Caesar[63] reflected in the equity weight of the *denarii*, although they bore different images and had therefore been struck by several emperors.

(b) Denarii pari pondere: Sinhalese kings and Roman coins

The Sinhalese king's admiration for the constant weight of the Roman *denarii*, evidently a currency hitherto unknown to him, has struck some as a suspicious detail.[64] There are however several considerations, which should make us have greater confidence in Pliny's words. First of all, the great surprise shown by the Sinhalese king on ascertaining the constant weight of the *denarii* cannot be considered on the same level as the literary distortions found in the following passage by Pliny, giving 'more accurate information' about Taprobane. These latter distortions in fact have the clear inten-tion of depicting Taprobane— once known as 'alternative-earth' (*Antichthones*) and 'confined by nature beyond the world'—as a land of justice and virtue.[65] I think it improbable, therefore, that a detail that turned the terms of praise the other way round could have been completely invented: the Sinhalese king's reaction ran counter to the ideological colouring of the 'more accurate information' on Taprobane (and hence, as Pliny says, strangely—*mirum in modum*), and ended up by applauding the *iustitia* of the Romans and of Caesar.

Similarly, it appears improbable that this detail could have been invented in order to make a veiled criticism of Nero's monetary reform. For an interpretation of this kind one would have to assume that Pliny drew on a literary source[66] dated after AD 64, and compiled, therefore, more than ten years after Rachias' legation, when the event had lost much of its topicality. Moreover, if the praise for the constant weight of the *denarii* implicitly voiced disapproval of a monetary system in which *denarii* of different standards circulated, it is difficult to understand why this admiration for the 'just' currency of the Claudian period did not include the *aurei*, the weight of which was also reduced by Nero.

Nor should it be a matter for much surprise that the Sinhalese king should have been so unfamiliar with Roman coins, in spite of the fact that Western merchants had already been frequenting the ports of India's western coast, particularly those of Limyrike (present-day Malabar), for about seventy years and had been exporting large quantities of Roman coins to them. Indeed a few merchants had even pressed as far north in their explorations as the mouth of the Ganges in the age of Strabo, but subsequent commerce was largely concentrated on the ports of the Limyrike (especially Muziris and Nelkynda, αἱ νῦν πράσσουσαι, 'now the active ones').[67] From this trade Taprobane was excluded: the island was isolated from the usual routes taken by Western merchants, as numismatic finds would also appear to confirm.[68] In all likelihood, therefore, Roman coins were not well known in Taprobane during the Claudian period.

Scepticism about the Sinhalese king's admiration for the Roman *denarii* seems to me therefore misplaced. No less inappropriate, it seems to me, is to consider it a *topos* celebrating the sovereignty of Rome.[69] The scrutiny to which the Sinhalese king subjected the Roman coins and, even more so, his admiration for the equity displayed by the constant weight of the *denarii* are, in my view, to be explained in the light of the very real problems of monetary circulation in ancient India. Even if one wanted to see in it an invention of Pliny's source, one would nevertheless have to admit that the invention is based on the direct observation of several characteristics of the monetary economy of ancient India.[70]

We know very little about monetary circulation in Taprobane during the Claudian period.[71] We are, therefore, unable to comprehend fully the astonishment shown by the Sihalese king—assuming this is, as we have reason to believe, a genuine element in the account. Two essential points should, however, be underlined: (*a*) the examination of currency was a fairly common practice in the daily life of ancient India; it represented the key moment when the *rūpasutta* ('science of coinage') was applied, the importance of which was brilliantly illustrated in Bhandarkar's classic study;[72] (*b*) among the money found on the captive, it was the silver *denarii* in particular which drew the king's attention: in other words, those Roman coins which, more than any other kind of currency, could be compared with the silver punch-marked coins, the *signatum argentum* which, according to Curtius Rufus, was donated to Alexander by the king of Taxila,[73] and which at that time circulated throughout the whole of India.[74] Let us take each of these points in turn.

According to Buddhagosa, who lived in Sri Lanka during the reign of Mahānāma (fifth century AD),[75] *rūpasuttaṃsikkhantena kahāpaṇā parivattetvā parivattetvā passitabā honti.* ('Those who wish to learn the *rūpasutta* must look at the *kahāpaṇa* (the coins) by turning them over again and again.')[76] The aim of this art is explained in a passage of the *Visuddhimagga*, in which Buddhaghosa himself describes the skill of the *heraññika* (money-changer), who is greatly versed in the *rūpasutta*, as compared to the naivety of the child and the lack of experience shown by the *gāmikapurisa*, the villager, *Visuddhimagga* XIV:[77]

yathā hi heraññikaphalake ṭhapitaṃ kahāpaṇarāsiṃ eko ajātabuddhidārako eko gāmikapuriso eko heraññiko ti tīsu janesu passamānesu, ajātabuddhidārako kahāpaṇānam cittavicittadīghacaturassaparimaṇḍalabhāvamattam eva jānāti; idaṃ manussānaṃ upabhogaparibhogaṃ ratanasammatan ti na jānāti. Gāmikapuriso cittavicittādibhāvaṃ jānāti, idaṃ manussānaṃ upabhogaparibhogaṃ ratanasammatan ti ca; ayaṃ cheko, ayam kūṭo, ayam addhasāro ti imaṃ pana vibhāgaṃ na jānāti. Heraññiko sabbe pi te pakāre jānāti, jānanto ca kahāpaṇaṃ oloketvā pi jānāti, ākoṭitassa saddaṃ sutvā pi gandhaṃ ghāyitvā pi rasaṃ sāyitvā pi hatthena dhārayitvā pi: asukasmiṃ nāma gāme vā nigame vā nagare vā pabbate vā nadītīre vā kato ti pi asukācariyena kato ti vijānāti.

Suppose there were three people, a child without discretion, a villager, and a money-changer, who saw a heap of coins lying on a money-changer's counter. The child without discretion knows merely that the coins are figured and ornamented, long, square or round; he does not know that they are reckoned as valuable for human use and enjoyment. And the villager knows that they are figured and ornamented, etc., and that they are reckoned as valuable for human use and enjoyment; but he does not know such distinctions as 'This is genuine, this is false, this is half-value'. The money-changer knows all those kinds of things, and he does so by looking at the coin, and by listening to the sound of it when struck, and by smelling its smell, tasting its taste, and weighing it in his hand, and he knows that it was made in a certain village or town or city or on a certain mountain or by the banks of a certain river, and that it was made by a certain master. (trans. Malalasekera)

As is natural in the case where most of the coins in circulation were made from noble metals, even in ancient India techniques for the assay of coins had been devised.[78] The *herañññika*'s skills may be compared to those of the ἀργυρογνώμων ('coin-tester') described by Epictetus.[79] But in Pliny's passage there is something more: the acknowledgment of the justice displayed by Caesar and the Romans in terms of the fact that the *denarii* had a constant weight while showing different images. This can only be read in relation to the monetary system of ancient India in which such an undeviating standard did not obtain.

The mass of money in circulation in ancient India—and the same holds true for that of medieval and (in part) modern times—must have been made up of a very varied combination of coins of different age,[80] of different materials,[81] of different provenance[82] and consequently of different weight.[83] As trade intensified, the problems posed by these disparities became exacerbated, and were tackled in a variety of ways. It is not difficult to imagine the problems of monetary circulation and the social tensions implicit in such a system. But it may be not out of place to quote from a contemporary account of the difficulties (above all in relation to the paying of taxes) posed by similar monetary system in Bengal as recently as the end of the eighteenth century AD:

The coinage, the refuse of twenty different dynasties and petty potentates, had been clipped, drilled, filed, scooped out, sweated, counterfeited, and changed from its original value by every process of debasement devised by Hindu ingenuity during a period of four hundred years. The smallest coin could not change hands, without an elaborate calculation as to the amount to be deducted from its nominal value. This calculation, it need hardly be said, was always in favour of the stronger party.[84]

For example, the treasury officers, and the tax collectors used to deduct three per cent from the value of coins which had been circulating for a year and five per cent from those which had been circulating for two years, irrespective of whether there had actually been a loss in their intrinsic value or not. In addition, the criteria for valuation, or of what currencies were acceptable, were not uniform: 'at some treasuries cowries were taken, at others they were not. Some collectors accepted payment in gold; others refused it; others, again, could not make up their minds either way'. In such uncertainty 'the miserable peasant never knew whether the coin for which he sold his crop would be of any use to him when he came to pay the rent'.[85]

It is within a similar context that we should place and interpret the contrast drawn by Buddhaghosa between the *gāmikapurisa* (who does not allow for distinctions, such as 'This is good, this is counterfeit, this is half-counterfeit') and the *heraññika* (who acknowledges all these different distinctions). The picture is confirmed by the complexity of the monetary system in India during the fifth century AD, upon which Buddhaghosa himself insists,[86] and by the functions which the *Arthaśāstra* assigns to the *rūpadarśaka* ('coin-tester'), functions which hint at grave monetary problems, precisely in relation to the state's fiscal policies.[87]

We know very little about the monetary and fiscal systems of Taprobane during the Claudian period, but there is no doubt that the measurement of the weight of the *denarii* brought by Annius Plocamus' freedman, and the king's scrutiny of the different images they bore, were linked with the traditional art of the *rūpasutta*. Nor is there any doubt that deducing justice from the constant weight of the *denarii* betrayed a situation of confusion in the Indian silver currency of the period. The absence of monetary frauds and the agreement of several rulers to a single weight were enough to characterize, in the eyes of the king of Taprobane, the homeland of the shipwrecked freedman as a land of justice, from which the swindles of the *rūpasutta* had been banished.

The importance of this comparison between the Indian monetary system and the coins exported from the West (which did not at all reflect the reality of monetary circulation within the Roman empire),[88] should not escape us. It should be recalled that the *rūpasutta* had been familiar in India, and taught to crown princes and to the sons and heirs of the well-to-do, long before the Claudian period.[89] Whether stimulated or not by problems of fiscal policy, the king of Taprobane's recognition of the *denarii* of the freedman of Annius Plocamus as the tokens and guarantee of justice by their undeviating weight, assumes an enormous importance in the light of the age-old swindles perpetrated by the *heraññika* and the no less age-old sufferings caused to the *gāmikapurisa*, the village man, who was ignorant of the sophisticated tricks of the *rūpasutta* and hopelessly enmeshed in the tangles of a treacherous monetary system.

In Pliny's account, the king's admiration for the social justice inferred from the constant weight of the *denarii* is adduced as the main reason for Rachias' subsequent embassy to Rome (*et hoc maxime sollicitatus*). We have already argue that the episode should be taken on its face value. Indeed, that Pliny would have attached such importance to it if it had been invented is difficult to imagine. But it might just be conceivable that Pliny's source did invent it on the basis of the accounts of Western merchants from southern India, who might have spoken in general terms of the Indians' admiration for the constant weight of Roman *denarii* (reinforced by the fact that the merchants tended to export good money). But if that is so, the episode, wrenched from its precise and localized historical context, would assume an even greater significance: the *denarii* exported by Western merchants satisfied, in short, the need for justice which the Indian monetary system was incapable of satisfying.

Earlier I cited the passage of the *Visuddhimagga* which said that, 'Those who wish to learn the *rūpasutta* must observe the *kahāpaṇa*, turning them over again and again.' There is no doubt that not only the king of Taprobane mentioned by Pliny, but also the Sinhalese king who was the protagonist of the episode narrated by Cosmas Indicopleustes in the sixth century

AD, was well versed in this art. *Top. Chr.* XI, 17-19:

αὕτη οὖν ἡ Σιελεδίβα, μέση πως τυγχάνουσα τῆς Ἰνδικῆς, ἔχουσα δὲ καὶ τὸν ὑάκινθον, ἐξ ὅλων τῶν ἐμπορίων δέχεται, καὶ ὅλοις μεταβάλλει, καὶ μέγα ἐμπόριον τυγχάνει. ποτὲ γοῦν τις ἀπὸ τῶν ἐνταῦθα πραγματευομένων ὀνόματι Σώπατρος, ὃν ἴσμεν πρὸ λε´ ἐτῶν τελευτήσαντα, εἰσελθὼν ἐν τῇ Ταπροβάνῃ νήσῳ πραγματείας ἕνεκα, ἔτυχεν καὶ ἀπὸ Περσίδος ὁρμῆσαι πλοῖον. κατῆλθον οὖν οἱ ἀπὸ Ἀδούλης, μεθ' ὧν ἦν ὁ Σώπατρος, κατῆλθον καὶ οἱ ἀπὸ Περσίδος, μεθ' ὧν ἦν καὶ πρεσβύτης Περσῶν. εἶτα κατὰ τὸ ἔθος οἱ ἄρχοντες καὶ οἱ τελῶναι, δεξάμενοι τούτους, αποφέρουσι πρὸς τὸν βασιλέα. ὁ δὲ βασιλεὺς δεξάμενος καὶ προσκυνηθεὶς κελεύει αὐτοὺς καθεσθῆναι· εἶτα ἐρωτᾷ "πῶς αἱ χῶραι ὑμῶν καὶ πῶς τὰ πράγματα;" οἱ δὲ εἶπον "καλῶς". εἶτα ὡς ἐν τῷ μεταξὺ ἠρώτησεν ὁ βασιλεὺς "ποῖος τῶν βασιλέων ὑμῶν μειζότερος καὶ δυνατώτερος;" ὁ δὲ Πέρσης ἁρπάσας τὸν λόγον ἔφη "ὁ ἡμέτερος καὶ δυνατώτερος καὶ μειζότερος καὶ πλουσιώτερος καὶ βασιλεὺς βασιλέων ἐστίν. καὶ εἴ τι θέλει, δύναται. ὁ δὲ Σώπατρος ἐσιώπα. εἶτα φησὶν ὁ βασιλεὺς "σύ, Ῥωμεῦ, οὐδὲν λαλεις;" ὁ δὲ Σώπατρος "τί ἔχω εἰπεῖν, τούτου ταῦτα εἰπόντος; εἰ θέλεις μαθεῖν τὴν ἀλήθειαν, ἔχεις ἀμφοτέρους τοὺς βασιλέας ἐνταῦθα· κατανόησον ἑκάστῳ καὶ ὁρᾷς ποῖος λαμπρότερος καὶ δυνατώτερος ἐστιν. ἐκεῖνος ἀκούσας ἐξενίσθη λέγων "πῶς ἔχω τοὺς ἀμφοτέρους βασιλέας ἐνταῦθα;" ὁ δὲ εἶπεν "ἔχεις ἀμφοτέρων τὰς μονήτας, τοῦ μὲν τὸ νόμισμα, τοῦ δὲ τὴν δραχμὴν, τουτέστιν τὸ μιλιάρισιν· κατανόησον τῇ εἰκόνι ἑκάστου, καὶ ὁρᾷς τὴν ἀλήθειαν. ὁ δὲ ἐπαινέσας καὶ ἐπινεύσας, ἐκέλευσεν ἐνεχθῆναι ἀμφοτέρα. ἦν οὖν τὸ νόμισμα ὄβρυζον, λαμπρὸν, εὔμορφον· τοιαῦτα γαρ ἐκλεκτὰ προχωροῦσιν ἐκεῖ· ἦν δὲ καὶ τὸ μιλιάρισιν, ἅπαξ εἰπεῖν, ἄργυρος, καὶ ἀρκεῖ μὴ συγκρινόμενος τῷ χρυσίῳ. στρέψας δὲ ὁ βασιλεὺς καὶ ἀντιστρέψας, καὶ κατανοῶν ἀμφότερα, ἐπαινέσας πάνυ τὸ νόμισμα, ἔφη "ὄντως οἱ Ῥωμεῖς καὶ λαμπροὶ καὶ δυνατοὶ καὶ φρόνιμοι". ἐκέλευσεν οὖν τὸν Σώπατρον τιμηθῆναι μεγάλως, καὶ καθίσας αὐτὸν εἰς ἐλέφαντα, μετὰ τυμπάνων τὴν πόλιν περιῆγεν ἐν τιμῇ πολλῇ.

'Sielediba (=Taprobane, Sri Lanka), which is in the middle of the Indian region and possesses the hyacinth, exchanges merchandise with every port of trade and she is herself a large port of trade. One day one of the merchants active there, by the name of Sopatros—who we know died thirty-five years ago—came for the purpose of trading to the island of Taprobane, and a vessel from Persia also docked there. When the merchants from Adulis were disembarking—Sopatros was among them—also merchants from Persia disembarked. An old Persian man was with them. So, as normal the officials and the customs officers greeted them and escorted them before the king. The king, after having received them and accepted their homage, ordered them to be seated and asked 'How do your countries and things fare?'. They replied, 'Well'. Then the king after a while asked 'Which of your two kings is the mightiest, and the most powerful?'. The Persian subject jumped in and said, 'Ours is the mightiest, the greatest and the richest. He is king of kings and obtains all that he wishes'. Sopatros for his part remained silent. So the king asked, 'And you, Roman, why do you say nothing?'. Sopatros replied, 'What should I say, if this man says such things? If you wish to learn the truth, you have before you both kings, consider them both and you can see who is the most distinguished and powerful'. The king listened and was baffled. Then he said 'What do you mean by saying that I have before me both kings?'. Sopatros replied, 'You have the coins of both, the *nomisma* (the solidus) of one, of the other the drachma, that is, the *miliarisin*. Consider the image of each one and you can see the truth'. Having praised and approved the suggestion, the king ordered that both coins be brought before him. The *nomisma* was made of pure gold, shone and was beautiful to look at; since only such selected coins circulate there. The *miliarisin* was, in a word, a piece of silver, and that was enough to prevent its comparison with the gold coin. The king turned over the two coins again and again considering them both, and praising the *nomisma* without reserve he said, 'Truly the Romans are splendid, powerful and wise'. He then ordered that Sopatros be honoured with great magnificence and, placing him upon an elephant, had him escorted through the city with great honours, to the beating of drums.

The Sopatros episode has been wrongly interpreted as the tired repetition of an 'old traveller's tale'.[90] Once again, behind the comparison between the Roman solidus and the Persian drachma, lies the *rūpasutta.* But the aim with which the coins are examined is different: what is expected from them is not that they should be a proof of justice, but that they should reveal which of the two kings is the greatest and the most powerful. The different aim implies a different political situation, strongly influenced by Persian expansion within the Indian Ocean. Already in the course of the fifth century, if not earlier,[91] Roman prestige and influence had been dealt a severe blow by the Persian initiative in the Indian Ocean, and it is precisely in the island of Taprobane that the Persians succeeded in establishing a mercantile colony. Cosmas himself recognized the conspicuous presence of the Persian merchants in

Taprobane and informs us that the Christian church in the island was headed by a presbyter elected in Persia. The excellence of the *nomisma,*[92] however, was still a source of justifiable pride for the Byzantine merchants in the presence of the kings of Taprobane who were used to judging the justice and power of a state on the basis of its coinage.

(c) Coral from Romanukharaṭṭha

Doubts have been expressed about the chronology of the events narrated in Pliny's passage, despite the circumstantial detail packed into its concision. In particular, it has been suspected, and argued, that two entirely separate episodes have been conflated in Pliny's text: the arrival of the freedman of Annius Plocamus in Taprobane, which is thought to have occurred in the Augustan age, and the embassy of Rachias to Rome *Claudi principatu* (during the principate of Claudius), i.e. AD 41-54.[93] This reconstruction, however, seems to me unacceptable. Firstly, that a relatively short period of time, possibly no more than twelve months,[94] had elapsed between the arrival of the freedman of Annius Plocamus in Taprobane and Rachias' embassy to Rome seems to me clearly implied by Pliny's account.

Secondly, it seems entirely arbitrary to antedate the arrival of Annius Plocamus' freedman in Taprobane to the Augustan age, on the basis of the two inscriptions found in Wadi Menih—discussed above—which attest to the presence of a slave of P. Annius Plocamus on the caravan route between Coptos and Berenice in the year AD 6. The lapse of time between the two inscriptions (AD 6) and the adventure of the freedman of Annius Plocamus *Claudi principatu* (or immediately prior to it) does not preclude the possibility of the identification of P. Annius Plocamus master of Lysas, author of the inscriptions at Wadi Menih, with the Annius Plocamus mentioned in Plin. *N.H.* VI, 84; at any rate, it is also possible to assume the existence of two successive generations of Annii Plocami who both had dealings of an economic nature in the Red Sea.[95]

As for Pliny's silence regarding the subsequent fate of Annius Plocamus' freedman, this does not mean that his ideas were confused, or his information defective. Rather, he simply assumed that the reader had sufficient perspicacity to infer that the freedman and his crew escorted Rachias and three other members of the Sinhalese delegation to the West. It is hardly plausible that Pliny, admiral of the Roman fleet and illustrious historian, who had most probably taken an interest in trade with India already during the Claudian period, could have 'clumsily connected [...] two originally differentiated episodes', that is, Rachias' legation in the West during the Claudian period and the arrival of the freedman of Annius Plocamus in Taprobane, which allegedly occurred half a century earlier. In short, there are no elements authorizing us to doubt the chronology provided by Pliny for Rachias' legation *Claudi principatu* and for the adventure of Annius Plocamus' freedman shortly before.

I have already emphasized the Sinhalese king's lack of familiarity with Roman *denarii*, and I explained this by the Taprobane's isolation from the commercial routes which connected India's western coast with the Roman empire. In marked contrast to this, there are some remarkable Sinhalese texts which show how Taprobane not only grew to know and appreciate Western merchandise and its merchants, but also acquired an intuition concerning the Western world in its political unity and in its Roman character.

In the long history of the *Mahāthūpa*, a *stūpa* annexed to the monastery of the *Mahāvihāra* and built, according to the Sinhalese historical tradition, by the warrior King Duṭṭhagāmaṇī,[96] the reign of Bhātikābhaya was of great importance. The *Dīpavaṃsa* and the *Mahāvansa*, the two most ancient historical works of Sri Lanka's buddhist tradition to have come down to us,[97] narrate in great detail the acts of devotion of the king Bhātikābhaya to the *Mahāthūpa* they include the offering of a *pavāḷajāla*, a 'coral net'.

Dīp. XXI, 13: *pavāḷamayajālañ ca kārāpesi anagghikaṃ/ Mahāthūpe paṭimukka cīvaraṃ iva pārutaṃ.* ('He (sc. Bhātikābhaya) caused to be made an invaluable net made up of corals, the *Mahāthūpa* was clothed like in a *cīvara*.')

Mah. XXXIV, 47: *pavāḷajālaṃ kāretvā taṃ khipāpiya cetiye.* ('He (sc. Bhātikābhaya) had a coral net made and placed it upon the *cetiya*.')

Finally the *Vaṃsatthappakāsinī*, a commentary on the *Mahāvaṃsa*, written not earlier than the seventh century and not later than the thirteenth century AD[98] provides interesting details on the *pavāḷajāla* in question. Commenting upon the words *pavāḷajālaṃ kāretvā* in *Mah.* XXXIV, 47, its author remarks (p. 630 ed. Malalasekera): *pavāḷajālaṃ kāretvā ti paratīre romanukharaṭṭhaṃ*[99] *nāma pesetvā surattapavāḷaṃ āharāpetvā sabbāvantaṃ parikkhepārahaṃ mahantaṃ pavāḷacchikajālaṃ*[100] *kārāpetvā.* ('He (sc. Bhātikābhaya) had a coral net made, that is, he sent someone to the so-called *romanukharaṭṭha*, beyond the sea, had the red coral brought and had a great net made out of coral, so that it could be placed all around (the *cetiya*).')

The net made from the coral acquired from the *romanukharaṭṭha* and placed on the *Mahāthūpa* marks the point of encounter between Sinhalese buddhism and merchants from the West. The export of Western coral to Central Asia and the Far East is, in fact, among the most remarkable phenomena of trade relations between East and West in the ancient world. Echoes of it are found in Greek and Latin literature, as well as in the literatures of India and China.[101] From the Mediterranean, the Red Sea and the Persian Gulf[102] coral used to be exported by sea, to Arabia and above all to India, where, partly due to male vanity and partly due to superstitious beliefs which attributed magical virtues to coral,[103] it came to have the same 'precious authority'[104] which Indian pearls acquired within the Roman empire, thus becoming a source of extraordinary high earnings for western merchants.

The volume of export of coral was so enormous, and the trade in it so intensive, that the barriers between one continent and the other fell. Plin. *N.H.* XXXII, 23: *prius quam hoc notesceret, Galli gladios, scuta, galeas adornabant eo. Nunc tanta paenuria est uendibili merce, ut perquam raro cernatur in suo orbe.* ('Before the Indian love of coral became known, the Gauls used to ornament with coral their swords, shields and helmets. Now it is a saleable merchandise and such is the shortage of it, that it is very rarely seen in its region.')

From the emporia of India's north-western coast Western coral continued on its journey up into Kashmir.[105] From southern India, in the second century AD, it would be exported to the Indochinese peninsula.[106] The final destination of both routes—the overland one through Kashmir, and the maritime one—was the same: the Chinese empire. The information provided from the *Vaṃsatthappakāsinī*, therefore, joins an already rich collection of documents. But it also presents other interesting aspects. As far as I know, this is in fact the only instance in Pāli literature, in which the *pavāḷa* is linked to the term *romanukharaṭṭha*. This in itself is a point of considerable significance. But even more significant is the fact that it is the only instance of a compound word such as *romanukharaṭṭha* to mean the Roman Empire occurring within the ancient literatures of India.

Elsewhere we find recurring synthetic expressions, which underline the political unity of the empire under Rome. For example, *romakaviṣaya* is located by the astronomer Āryabhaṭa at a point 90⁰ west of Sri Lanka, or *romavisaya* in the *Lokapaññatti* is described as a country in which all working activities are carried out by automatons.[107] But in the case of *romanukharaṭṭha* the compound word exhibits an effort to reproduce the grammatical structures of the Latin language which is unparalleled and really rather surprising. The first element of the compound, *romanukha*, is the Indianization of the Latin adjective *Romanus*, something which constitutes a *hapax* in Indian literatures.

Since this is the only instance in Pāli literature in which the Roman empire and coral are explicitly associated with one another and since the use of the formula *romanukharaṭṭha* is so original, we can exclude the possibility that this mission to *romanukharaṭṭha* was a late and fanciful invention of the commentator of the *Mahāvaṃsa*, devised on account of the popularity of Roman coral in India and on a par with the legend of the *romavisaya* robots, handed down to us in the *Lokapaññatti*. On the contrary, the memory of this mission and the formula *romanukharaṭṭha* preserved in the *Vaṃsatthappakāsinī*, are a genuine and precious relic of folk memory; all the more precious, if one considers that Sri Lanka's Buddhist historiography has not preserved any record of the thriving relations between the kingdom of Taprobane and the Chinese empire, of which we would know nothing were it not for the Chinese sources.[108]

(d) Remarks on Sinhalese chronology

Finally we come to the chronology of Bhātikābhaya, that is, of the king who ordered the mission to *romanukharaṭṭha* in search of the beautiful red coral. Some scholars regard him as a contemporary of Augustus;[109] others, instead, a contemporary of Caligula, Claudius and Nero.[110] It will be useful to clarify the reasons for this divergence of opinion.

The problem of the chronology of the kings of Taprobane during the period between the third century BC to the thirteenth century AD may be summarized briefly in the following terms: on the one hand, the *Dīpavaṃsa* and the *Mahāvaṃsa* date Aśoka's *abhiseka* as 218 years after the Buddha's *parinibbāna*;[111] on the other, a Sinhalese inscription, found in Polonnaruva, dates the consecration of Sāhasa Malla to the 23 August of the 1743 year from the *Buddha-varṣa* ('year of the Buddha', that is, of his *nirvāṇa*), a year which, however, corresponds not to 1269 or thereabouts, but to the year 1200 of the Christian era.[112]

Clearly, the two dates are irreconcilable: the first shows that in Sri Lanka, at a relatively early period (about the fourth century AD), only 218 years were computed between the Buddha's *parinibbāna* and the emperor Aśoka's *abhiseka*, which occurred in 268 BC.[113] This might prove the existence, during the period and in the place where the *Dīpavaṃsa* and the *Mahāvaṃsa* were composed, that is, in Sri Lanka during the fourth to the sixth centuries AD, of a date for the death of the Buddha, in the second decade of the fifth century BC). The second passage, however, shows the establishment, during the medieval period, of a Buddhist era beginning a year after the *parinibbāna* in 544/3 BC, which would remain in use in Sri Lanka, Siam, Burma and Cambodia until the present day.

This means that somewhere in the Sinhalese historical tradition there must have been a break-down. Approximately 60 years have been unduly inserted between king Devānam Piya Tissa, a contemporary of Aśoka,[114] and king Sāhasa Malla. This projected the traditional date of the Buddha's *parinibbāna* backwards to 544/3 BC. An error of approximately 60 years over a span of fourteen centuries of history cannot be minimized. But it cannot be over-emphasized either. The years of the reigns which the *Dīpavaṃsa*, the *Mahāvaṃsa* and the

Cūḷavaṃsa[115] attribute to each of the kings of Sri Lanka between Devānam Piya Tissa and Sāhasa Malla cannot be considered absolutely trustworthy, although the tradition maintains overall a certain reliability.

Attempts have been made to solve the chronological problem by trying to identify the 60 surplus years, within the years of reign which tradition attributes to the kings of Sri Lanka between the third century BC and the thirteenth century AD. In particular, two different views have emerged. Some scholars believe that the 60 surplus years are to be found between the reigns of Devānam Piya Tissa and Duṭṭhagāmaṇī (that is, between 236 and 382 of the Buddhist era). According to these scholars, the beginning of the reign of Duṭṭhagāmaṇī ought to be dated back to 161 BC, and from then onwards the chronology of the kings of Sri Lanka, fixed on the basis of the years of reign provided by the *Dīpavaṃsa, Mahāvaṃsa* and *Cūḷavaṃsa,* would be essentially correct. Those who follow this line of argument would have to consider the reign of Bhātikābhaya as occurring during the age of Augustus. Others prefer to locate the error within the 129-30 years which, according to tradition, separated the accession to the throne of Siri Meghavaṇṇa (year 836 or 834 of the Buddhist era) from the death of Mahānāma (year 964 or 962 of the Buddhist era). This hypothesis leads to the reing of Bhātikābhaya being dated between the principate of Caligula and Nero.

Those who support the first solution base their reasons above all upon an inscription found at Anurādhapura which was placed there by a *Budadasa-ma[ha]rajah puta Upati [sa- -] /nami-maharaja* during the twenty-eighth year of his reign, 941 years after the Buddha's *nirvāṇa.*[116] The king was identified by the editor of the inscription, S. Paranavitana, as Upatissa, who, according to the *Cūlavaṃsa,*[117] reigned for 42 years, 66 years after the death of Mahāsena. The *Dīpavaṃsa* records this latter event as having occurred 836 years after the Buddha's *nirvāṇa.* According to the *Mahāvaṃsa,* on the other hand, the event took place after 834 years, while the *Pūjāvali*[118] records it as occurring after 844/846 years.

Since we know from the Chinese annals that in AD 428 the king of Sri Lanka, Mahānāma (brother and successor of Upatissa), sent a diplomatic mission to the Chinese court,[119]

Paranavitana believed he had found in this inscription the ultimate and irrefutable proof that the Buddhist era, which begins from 544/3 BC, was already in use in the island by the end of the fourth century AD. Moreover, he believed it would also prove that the chronology of the *Cūlavaṃsa* was correct, despite Geiger's doubts, and that therefore the approximately 60 surplus years should be sought between the reigns of Devānaṃ Piya Tissa and Duṭṭhagāmaṇī.[120]

However, these conclusions lead to a number of difficulties. First of all, in order to compute that the reign of Upatissa began in the year 913 following the Buddha's *nirvāṇa*, Paranavitana had to resort to the chronology of the *Pūjāvali*, a work compiled much later than the *Dīpavaṃsa*, which is by contrast more or less contemporary with the inscription in question. The *Pūjāvali* places the end of the reign of Mahāsena approximately ten years later than the *Dīpavaṃsa* and the *Mahāvaṃsa*. Secondly, if we assume the 60 surplus years can be placed between the reigns of Devānaṃ Piya Tissa and Duṭṭhagāmaṇī, a whole range of synchronisms will then be out of phase. For example:

(*a*) Bhātikābhaya, who imported Roman coral, would then be a contemporary of Augustus; the supporters of a 'high' chronology have to deny the Plinian chronology (*Claudi principatu*) for Rachias' legation, and tend to antedate the arrival of Annius Plocamus' freedman in Taprobane to the Augustan age:[121] both assumptions I have argued to be incorrect.

(*b*) Wang Hiuen-ts'e maintains the contemporaneity of the Indian monarch *San-meou-to-lo-kiu-to* with the king of Sri Lanka *Chi-mi-kia-po-mo*. The former personage is commonly identified with Samudragupta, the latter with Siri Meghavaṇṇa.[122] Those who accept the high chronology are forced to deny the second identification, since Samudragupta must have reigned between AD 340 and 375/380,[123] whereas Siri Meghavaṇṇa was the successor of Mahāsena (see above pp. 189-190).

(*c*) The Buddhist pilgrim Fa-hsien, who visited Sri Lanka in the years AD 410-11, mentions the ascetic *Ta-mo-kiu-ti*: in all probably he is the Mahādhammakathin referred to in the *Cūḷavaṃsa*, contemporary of king Buddhadāsa, whose reign, according to the *Cūḷavaṃsa*, began approximately 37 years after the death of Mahāsena.[124]

But most important of all is the following consequence: if we exclude the possibility that in Sri Lanka during the fifth century AD the Buddha's death was dated sometime during the second decade of the fifth century BC, the Buddhist era assumed by the so-called 'Dotted Record'[125] would then represent a real enigma. This Chinese tradition which claims (though it is highly unlikely) to date back to the year of the Buddha's *nirvāṇa* and of the compilation of the *Vinaya Piṭaka,* is undoubtely linked, through the translation of the *Samanta-pāsādikā,* to the work of Buddhaghosa and to the Buddhist school in Sri Lanka. It gives the seventh year of Young-ming (AD 489)[126] as corresponding to the 975th year of the era following the death of the Buddha.[127] In other words, it referred to a Buddhist era which began from 486 BC.

If we interpret the inscription of the *Budadasa ma[ha]rajah puta* as starting from the dating of the *nirvāṇa* according to the 'Dotted Record'—which represents a chronographic tradition that is much closer to the Sinhalese one of the fifth century than the one which led to the calculation of the year of Sāhasa Malla's coronation as the 1743 following the Buddha's *nirvāṇa*— we obtain a date for the accession of Buddhadāsa's son, author of the dedication at Anurādhapura (calculating in terms of current years), as occurring within a period stretching from the month of *Vesākha* (February-March) AD 427 to the month of *Citta* (January February) of thc following year. Therefore, assuming the year 486 BC as the year in which the author of the inscription at Anurādhapura dates the Buddha's *nirvāṇa,*[128] the *mahārājan* mentioned in the inscription would be Mahānāma, brother and successor of Upatissa, the *Ts'a-li Mo-ho-nan* who sent a diplomatic mission to the Chinese court. The inscription does not perhaps pose insurmountable obstacles to the identification of the *mahārājan* with Mahānāma. Even accepting the uncertain reading *Upati,* we could then integrate [*sa raja bhata mahanama tiripali*]/; or more simply, if the first two *akṣara* of 1. 2 are to be read *nama,* instead of *nami,*[129] [*sa raja bhata maha*]/ *nama maharaja,* etc.

An objection may be raised to my identification of the *mahārājan* in the inscription at Anurādhapura, with Mahānāma. According to the *Cūḷavaṃsa,* Mahānāma reigned 98 years after the death of Mahāsena, and only for a period of 22 years.[130] But the point is precisely that, for its most ancient part, the

Cūḷavaṃsa cannot be considered, with respect to chronology, a reliable source.[131]

If my suggestions on the chronology of the reign of Mahānāma are correct, the dates of his immediate successors would then be at least twenty years later than those generally accepted by scholars today. This appears to be confirmed by two points which certainly cannot be overlooked. The first must be dealt with at slightly greater length, since it has hitherto gone unnoticed.

The so-called eleventh book of the *Topographia Christiana* of Cosmas Indicopleustes[132] contains an ample description of the island of Sielediba (=Sri Lanka), based largely on information which the author derived from Sopatros, a merchant who had travelled there, and who had been dead for thirty-five years at the time when Cosmas was writing his work.[133] In Cosmas' description one very important detail stands out. The island of Sielediba is divided into two kingdoms: δύο δὲ βασιλεῖς εἰσιν ἐν τῇ νήσῳ, ἐναντίοι ἀλλήλων· ὁ εἷς ἔχων τὸν ὑάκινθον, καὶ ὁ ἕτερος τὸ μέρος τὸ ἄλλο, ἐν ᾧ ἐστιν τὸ ἐμπόριον καὶ ὁ λιμήν, ('The island has two kings who oppose one another; one of them occupies the hyacinth mines and the other the remaining part of the island in which the emporium and port are situated').[134]

Whatever value we may wish to attribute to the expression ἐναντίοι ἀλλήλων—in other words, whether the kings 'opposed' one another in a political or in a geographical sense[135]—it is clear that at the time when Sopatros reached Sielediba the Sinhalese kingdom was experiencing a profound crisis, so much so as to give a foreigner the impression that the island was divided into two kingdoms. The reference is precise and allows one to draw a parallel with the Sinhalese historical tradition. In fact, in our opinion the situation described by Cosmas must be identified with the one which, according to the *Cūḷavaṃsa*, was created as a result of the invasion of the northern part of the island by the Tamil king Paṇḍu. *Cūḷavaṃsa* XXXVIII, 11-12:

Mittasenaṃ raṇe hantvā Damiḷo Paṇḍunāmako
āgato paratīramhā Laṅkārajjaṃ akārayi
Janā kulīnā sabbe pi Rohanam samupāgatā
oragaṅgāya isseraṃ Damiḷā eva kappayuṃ.

The Damiḷa named Paṇḍu had slain Mittasena (previous king of Sri Lanka) in battle and now having come over from the opposite coast, held sway in Laṅkā. All the kinsmen of the noble families betook themselves to Rohaṇa (the southern part of the island), on this side of the stream (of the Mahaveligaṅga) the Damiḷas ruled.

The partition between the northern part of Sri Lanka, ruled by Tamil kings, and the south, controlled by Sinhalese noblemen who ultimately gathered round Dhātusena, lasted for twenty-seven years according to the *Cūḷavaṃsa*. *Cūḷavaṃsa* XXXVIII, 29-34:

Paṇḍu rājā pi katvāna rajjaṃ vassamhi pañcame
cuto, putto Parindo pi tatiye tassa bhātuko
kaniṭṭho Khuddapārindo kubbaṃ rajjaṃ mahāmahiṃ
Dhātusenānuge sabbe viheṭhesi mahājane.
Saṃgahesi jane Dhātuseno, yujjhittha rājinā,
so soḷasahi vassehi puññapāpakaro mato.
Tīritaro tato āsi rājā, māsadvayena taṃ
Dhātuseno vināṇesi tena katvā mahāhavam.
Hate tasmiṃ mahīpāle Dāṭhiyo Damiḷo tato
rājā vassattaye hutvā Dhātusenahato, tato
Pīṭhiyo Damiḷo sattamāsena nidhanaṃ gato;
Dhātusenena yujjhitvā vaṃso pacchijji Dāmiḷo.

After reigning, King Paṇḍu died in the fifth year, likewise his son Parinda in the third year. Parinda's youngest brother, Khuddapārinda, then ruled the wide earth and persecuted all those who attached themselves to Dhātusena. Dhātusena won over the people for himself and fought against the King. The latter, after accomplishing works both meritorious and evil, died at the end of sixteen years. Hereupon Tīritara became king; two months later he was destroyed by Dhātusena who fought a great battle with him. After this prince had been killed, the Damiḷa Dāṭhiya became king, but was slain at the end of three years by Dhātusena. Hereupon there followed the Damiḷa Pīṭhiya who after seven months went to his destruction. The race of the Damiḷas was annihilated in battle with Dhātusena.

It is evident that the situation described by Cosmas, characterized by two opposing kings, the one who controlled the *emporion* of Sri Lanka, and the other who controlled the centre for the production of the *hyakinthos*, is to be identified with the one described in *Cūḷavaṃsa* XXXVIII, 12 and assumed in *Cūḷavaṃsa* XXXVIII, 29-34. This is the only time in which the Sinhalese historical tradition relating to the age of Sopatros and Cosmas records the island of Sri Lanka as divided into two parts.[136] There is no doubt that Sopatros the merchant was in Sielediba at a time of violent hostility between the two ethnic groups in Sri Lanka; a distant antecedent of the ethnic clashes which still divide and embitter the island to this day.[137]

According to the *Cūḷavaṃsa,* Paṇḍu, founder of the Tamil dynasty which controlled the northern part of Sri Lanka (up to the Mahaveligaṅga) for twenty-seven years, began to rule only two years after the death of Mahānāma. If the latter, as Paranavitana reckons, reigned from AD 413 to 435 (or from AD 409 to 431, according to Geiger), one would have to believe that Sopatros visited Sri Lanka sometime in the mid-fifth century AD, which although not impossible, is highly improbable. The death of Sopatros is in fact mentioned by Cosmas as having occurred approximately thirty-five years before the time in which he wrote what was later included as book XI in the *Topographia Christiana.*[138] As we know, in book VI of this latter work, Cosmas mentions two eclipses which have been identified with those of AD 6 February and 17 August 547.[139] Therefore, if book VI and the so-called book XI of the *Top. Chr.* had been written more or less contemporaneously, the death of Sopatros would fall around the second decade of the sixth century AD. But if the so-called book XI of the *Top. Chr.* is in fact an extract of the geographical work by Cosmas (quoted in the *Top. Chr.* and therefore written before it),[140] which was then added to the Laurentianus and Sinaiticus manuscripts of the *Top. Chr.*, the death of Sopatros would then anticipate the dating suggested above by a number of years, which though undetermined would certainly not be very high. Cosmas, in fact, recalls having been to Adoulis πρὸ τούτων τῶν ἐνιαυτῶν εἴκοσι πέντε πλέον ἔλαττον, ἐν τῇ ἀρχῇ τῆς βασιλείας Ἰουστίνου τοῦ Ῥωμαίων βασιλέως ('approximately twenty-five years ago, at the beginning of the reign of Justin, Roman emperor').[141] If in the year AD 518 he was in Adoulis for business and in AD 547 he was still active as a writer, it would then be difficult to date his birth before AD 470 and consequently it would be difficult for him to have met Sopatros before AD 480-90. The fact that Cosmas was able to meet not only Sopatros but also those merchants from Adoulis who had been to Sielediba with him,[142] leads us to believe that Sopatros' journey cannot have been so very distant in time from his encounter with Cosmas.

In short, even if we wished to attribute the encounter between Cosmas and Sopatros (and the latter's visit to Sielediba) to the earliest among the possible datings, it would work out in any case as too late for the chronologies current nowadays for Paṇḍu and his descendants (AD 436-63 according to Paranavitana). On the other hand, by dating the beginning of the reign of Mahānāma back to the year AD 427 and allowing him more than the twenty-two years attributed for his reign by the *Cūḷavaṃsa*, the traditional twenty-seven years of the Tamil dynasty would then all fall within the second half of the fifth century AD. This is more like the probable dating for Sopatros' visit.

It seems that the current chronology for Kassapa I, son and successor of the Dhātusena who overthrew the Tamil dynasty in Sri Lanka, should be postdated by *c.* 30 years: Chinese sources in fact record for the year AD 527 an embassy sent from Sri Lanka by *Kia-che Kia-lo-ha-li-ya.*[143] Although the second word remains uncertain, the first, *Kia-che* (=skt. Kassapa), suggests the identification with Kassapa I, son of Dhatusena.[144]

It appears, then, from the coincidences between Cosmas Indicopleustes and the Chinese sources, that we can place the years of the reigns of the Tamil monarchs Mahāsena and Kassapa I (whether they be 63 as the *Cūḷavaṃsa* records, or not) sometime between the second half of the fifth century and the third decade of the sixth century AD.

To conclude: the chronology of the Sinhalese kings from Mahānāma to Kassapa I, which I have suggested, differs both from Geiger's reconstruction and from that elaborated by Paranavitana, since it assumes that even by the early sixth century Sinhalese tradition had not yet accumulated all the *c.* 60 surplus years evident in the inscription of Poḷonnaruva, which dates Sāhasa Malla's accession to 1473 after the Buddha's *nirvāṇa.* This means that the 60 years were not the result of one great error but the sum of several errors, the most important of which must be traced back to the years of the kings who ruled after Siri Meghavaṇṇa.

So much for Sinhalese chronology. But even if my proposals for the chronology of the kings between Mahānāma and Kassapa I prove unacceptable, the contextual interpretation Pliny's passage and the report in the *Vaṃsatthappakāsinī* will still remain ineluctable. Pliny's information cannot be refuted or twisted by basing one's argument on the uncertain Sinhalese chronology. In short, it is Pliny who provides a *terminus post quem* for the mission to *romanukharaṭṭha* in search for coral. He also provides a decisive element for the dating of Bhātikābhaya, which cannot precede the age of Claudius (or at most Caligula's). For if, as there is no serious reason for doubting, the king of Taprobane encountered by the freedman of Annius Plocamus was so ignorant of the Roman world as not even to be acquainted with its coins, it is hard to see how Bhātikābhaya's familiarity with the *romanukharaṭṭha* could have dated back to the Augustan period. The only way to preserve an Augustan dating for Bhātikābhaya would be to deny the historicity of the mission to *romanukharaṭṭha* in search of coral; and this, for the reasons set forth above, seems to me questionable. The various phases of relations between Rome and Taprobane in the first century AD, as we may reconstruct them from numismatic finds and from Pliny *N.H.* VI, 84, lead to the conclusion that the mission to *romanukharaṭṭha* ordered by Bhātikābhaya should not be dated anterior to the arrival in Taprobane of the freedman of Annius Plocamus, who, in turn, immediately preceded the legation of Rachias to the West *Claudi principatu*, during the reign of Claudius.

Bhātikābhaya's subjects, it should be stressed, gained a notion of the Western world comparable to (and in some ways deeper than) that attained by Indian astronomers through the study of Western astronomy.[145] Only a direct acquaintance with the Western world would justify the term *romanukharaṭṭha*.

The *pavāḷajāla* made from Roman coral, and more especially the term *romanukharaṭṭha* itself, must be considered among the most striking effects—the former on the economic-commercial, the second on the cultural level—of the legation of Rachias,[146] a kind of Marco Polo in reverse. The mission to *romanukharaṭṭha* ordered by Bhātikābhaya (who must be the same king as the one mentioned by Pliny) must therefore postdate the legation of Rachias, unless, that is, they were not one and the same.

The hypothesis that Pliny and *Vaṃsatthappakāsinī* were referring to the same event should not be rejected. Sinhalese historiography, insensitive, as we have seen, to the diplomatic events in the kingdom of Sri Lanka, may have grasped only those aspects of a more complex event which were more directly related to the religious and cultural sphere. We may assume, in other words, that Rachias' legation *ad amicitiam* returned to Sri Lanka with coral (the Western merchandise especially dear to the Indians' hearts) which was later used in the *pavāḷajala* of the *Mahāthūpa* and became fixed in the historical memory of the pious Buddhist monks.

Admittedly, Pliny's passage, too, is not devoid of distortions and embellishments of various kind, ranging from projection onto the island of Taprobane of ideals of elective and non-hereditary monarchy,[147] to the Herodotean literary motifs of 'the sun on the right'[148] and of silent barter.[149] And yet this should not lead us to doubt in the historical reality of Rachias' embassy to Rome. Rather, it should help us to identify the sources on which Pliny drew. There is no doubt, in fact, that the source from which Pliny derived the *diligentior notitia* ('more accurate information') about Taprobane was very different from those which provided him the *certa notitia* ('certain information') about trade in southern India. These latter, as I believe I have shown by my observations on the double dating according to the Egyptian revolving year and the Roman Julian year in Plin. *N.H.* VI, 106,[150] were the Roman merchants themselves who traded in the ports of southern India in the years AD 48/49-51/52.

By contrast, the source from which Pliny derived his account of the adventure of the freedman of Annius Plocamus, albeit close to the merchants (not only chronologically, emphasizing as it does the enterprise of the freedman of the man appointed to farm the tax of the Red Sea), is more disposed to give to the historical event extraneous connotations—reactions of the Roman culture to the exploits of the merchants, which had not only economic and commercial, but also cultural consequences. *Dedit uentos ad ulteriora noscenda* ['He (sc. God) gave the winds to know the furthest ends of the earth']: both Pliny's narrative and the data of the *Vaṃsatthappakāsinī* are linked, each in its own way, to a crucial moment in the encounter between East and West in antiquity: the moment in which the great Western empire and the Buddhist kingdom of Taprobane were revealed to each other.

We have already pointed out that the oecumene as a field of action of Roman merchants in the first century AD no longer coincided with the idea of the universal Roman *imperium*. Whereas to those who had yearned for a universal empire Hibernia (Ireland) and Taprobane would always remain the unattainable goals of a millenaristic utopia,[151] to the Roman merchants in the first century AD they already become the object of daily experience.[152]

During the principate of Claudius a merchant freedman became the ambassador of Caesar and of the Romans at the court of the king of Taprobane. He became the medium through whom the concept of the *imperium populi Romani-romanukharaṭṭha* was disseminated. Outside the Polybian framework, in Asia, the *imperium populi Romani* confronted with the rest of the known world, where other empires, no less great, jostled for power and influence. On this basis Indian thought elaborated those polycentric visions of the world, which would meet such success both in China and the West.[153] The universal empire of the *cakravartin* would be replaced by the four kings of the world (the 'four sons of the heaven' mentioned in the Chinese sources), and the more or less abstract design of the four *lokapada* (the four parts of the world *Pubbavideha, Jambūdīpa, Aparagoyāna, Uttarakuru*)[154] would be materialized in the four great empires of the world.

ADDENDUM

The autopsy of the Greek inscription *A.É.* 1954, n. 121a, which I had attempted without success on 31/12/1988, was made almost a year later on 25/11/1989.[155]

The inscription is situated inside a small cave, along the western side of the Wadi Menih in the position indicated by Winkler on his map as 24B,[156] at a distance of approximately forty kilometres from el-Laketa.

The cave which is formed by a jutting rock and a large slab propped up against it, is rather small in size. Its dimensions allow access to not more than half a dozen people. It represents, nevertheless, a comfortable and cool shelter in the shade throughout the day.

The two inscriptions of Lysas, slave of P. Annius Plocamus, *A.É.* 1954 nn. 121a and 121b are both engraved inside the cave. The first inscription is found on the right-hand wall at a height of approximately 1.8 m above the ground. The second is found on the left-hand wall at a height of approximately 1.7 m above the ground.

I shall be broaching further problems relating to the cave of Wadi Menih and its inscriptions more extensively in a paper to come, here I wish to simply update my discussion on the Greek inscription *A.É.* 1954, n. 121a.

Let us first of all analyse its dimensions. The first line is 96 cm in length, and the second is 86 cm in length, whereas the height of the letters is approximately 4 cm. The 'third' line (see *infra*) of the inscription extends over 54 cm and the height of the letters is again approximately 4 cm.

Compared to the original, Winkler's copy of *A.É.* 1954, n. 121a, which so far represents the only source upon which all editions of the inscription are based, appears overall to be quite precise with the exception of a few details.

(1) Exactly beneath the second line, engraved less deeply, we find repeated part of the text of the second line of the inscription. More specifically, the words ΗΚΩΙ ΛΛΕ ΚΑΙΣΑΡΟ. Winkler had not reproduced this 'third' line, although the note included in his copy could well refer to it (I am only able to recognise the words 'wiederholt', 'darunter', 'dopl?').

(2) In Winkler's copy the numeral H does not bear the horizontal accent above it which is typical of numerals. This is in fact present and quite visible in the original, although it is engraved less deeply.

(3) Regarding the problem which I had highlighted, that is, the greater probability in 1.2, of the reading [I]H as compared to the reading H provided by Winkler's copy and accepted by editors, we must observe that the latter copy reproduces in a more or less correct manner the space between the letter Φ

and the letter H (the space measures 5 cm), which therefore proves excessive also due to the fact that the numeral value of H is specified by the horizontal stroke.

Precisely in that space, however, the rock shows a natural undulation transverslly from the top downward and reveals traces of engravings. A rather less sharp vertical stroke beneath the undulation runs into the centre of the letter M on the line above. To the left, between the letter Φ and the vertical stroke we find something resembling a fourth circle, at the summit of which is a small hyphen (perhaps an attempt at a letter Φ ?). Finally, to the right of the vertical stroke we find traces left by a chisel.

Concerning this last point, the epigraphical information is therefore not unequivocally clear and suggests caution, also due to the fact that in other places the rock shows the work of different hands, to which could be attributed the strokes in question.[157]

Despite the presence of other engravings alongside it the meaning of which is unclear, it is possible to make out to the left of the letter H a vertical stroke. Although this is not as sharp as the other letters of the inscription, it can only be recognised as the letter I.

As a consequence, the reasons which had led me to think, before having seen the inscription, that the reading ΕΠΕΙΦ Η in Winkler's copy should be corrected to ἐπεὶφ [τ̅]η̅,[158] now lead me to see that vertical stroke which Winkler did not believe to be a letter, as standing for the letter I. My reading of 1. 2 of *A.É.* 1954 n. 121a is therefore ἥκω{ι} L λ̅ε̅ Καίσαρος ἐπεὶφ ι̣̅η̅.[159]

Plate IV: Wadi Menih rock-shelter (Photo by F. De Romanis)

Plate V: *A.É.* 1954, n⁰ 121a (Photo by F. De Romanis)

NOTES

1. Cf. W.F. Snyder, *When was the Alexandrian Calendar established?*, in *American Journal of Philology*, 64 (1943), pp. 385-98; R. Böker, *R.E.*, IX, A² 2445-6. An attempt to introduce a fixed year of 365 and a quarter days had already been made during the reign of Ptolemy III; cf. OGIS 56.
2. Theonis Alexandrini, εἰς τοὺς προχείρους κανόνας (editio minor), p. 203 of the edition by A. Tihon, *Le «Petit Commentaire» de Théon d'Alexandrie aux Tables Faciles de Ptolémée*, Città del Vaticano 1978. The corresponding passage of the editio maior is quoted by H. Usener, *Fasti Theonis Alexandrini a. CXXXVIII-CCCLXXII*, in Th. Mommsen, *Chronica Minora*, III (MGH AA) 1897, pp. 372-3.
3. Cens. *de die natali*, 18.
4. Cf. *supra*, n. 2. On the use of the revolving year during the Roman age, cf. e.g. U. Wilcken, *Griechische Ostraka aus Aegypten und Nubien*, I Berlin 1899, pp. 786-806; Hohmann 1911, pp. 48-62.
5. Although they are both made up of 365 and a quarter days, it is best to make a distinction between the Julio-Alexandrian fixed year and the Roman Julian year, since the additional day which is inserted into the Julio-Alexandrian fixed year after the fifth day of the 'Epagomenai' (i.e. after 28 August of the Julian calendar) of the years AD 3, 7, 11 etc.; in the Roman Julian year, as we known, it came after 24 February of the years AD 4, 8, 12 etc.
6. H. Brugsch, *Ueber eine bilingue Inschrift im Museum zu Bulaq*, in *Zeitschrift fur ägyptische Sprache und Altertumskunde*, 10 (1872), pp. 27-9.
7. Pap. Lond. 130, 37-48:

   ἔτους τρίτου θεοῦ Τίτου Φαρμοῦθι τῇ ἐπιφωσκούσῃ ἕκτηι ἐπὶ τρίτης τῆς νυκτὸς ὥρας, ὡς δὲ ʽΡωμαῖοι ἄγουσι καλάνδαις ʼΑπριλίαις [-λειας pap.] κατ'ἀρχαίους δὲ Παχὼν νεομηνίᾳ εἰς τὴν δευτέραν.

   For further comments, cf. O. Neugebauer / H.B. Van Hoesen, *Greek Horoscopes*, Philadelphia 1959, p. 21 et seq.; 167-9.
8. P. Paris. 19, 7-10:

   α^L ʼΑντωνίνου Καίσαρος τοῦ κυρίου μηνὸς ʽΑδρι[ανο]ῦ η̄ κατὰ τῶν ʽΕλλήνων [ʽΗλλ- pap.], κατὰ δὲ τοὺς Αἰγυπτίους Τῦβι ιη̄. P. Paris. 19 bis, 3-5 (= P. Lond. 110): α^L ʼΑντωνίνου Καίσαρος τοῦ κυρίου μηνὸς ʽΑδριανοῦ η̄ κατὰ δὲ τοὺς ἀρχαίο(υς) Τῦβι ιη̄.

9. Cens. *de die natali*, 21:

sed horum (sc. annorum Ναβονναζάρου) *initia semper a primo die mensis eius sumuntur, cui apud Aegyptios nomen est Thouth, quique hoc anno fuit ante diem VII kal. Iul., cum abhinc annos centum imperatore Antonio Pio II Bruttio Praesente Romae consulibus idem dies fuerit ante diem XII<I> kal. Aug., quo tempore solet canicula in Aegypto facere exortum.*

'For this sort of year (sc. of Nabonnazaros) the beginning is considered to be the first day of that month which the Egyptians call Thouth, and which in this year [AD 238] fell on 25 June, whereas one hundred years ago when the consuls in Rome were Antoninus Pius for the second time, and Bruttius Praesens [AD 139], the same day fell on 20 June.'

I accept the correction by Scaliger XII <I>. On this passage, cf. R. Böker, *R.E.* , IX A^2, 2392. The dating in OGIS 56 of the heliacal rising of Isis on the first day of Payni (obviously according to the revolving year) in the ninth year of Ptolemy III agrees with the dating of Censorinus (heliacal rising of Sothis on the first Thoth of the year AD 139) cf. R. Krauss, *Sothis- und Monddaten. Studien zur astronomischen und technischen Chronologie Altägyptens*, Hildesheim 1985, pp. 54-60.

10. Plin. *N.H.* VI, 106. On the dependence on contemporary informants for the passage VI, 102-6, cf. Plin. *N.H.* VI, 96; 105 and p. 163 in this volume.

11. The double dating (according to both the Egyptian and Roman calendar) had already attracted the attention of Harduinus 1685, tome I. p. 356, who perceived that the correspondence between the month of January and that of Mechir was in contrast with the one between the month of February and that of Mechir which could be deduced from other sources. Although he did not realize that the contradiction was only an apparent one, since Pliny referred to the revolving year whereas the *PME* and the epigram of the *Anthologia Graeca*, which he quoted, referred to the fixed year, he nevertheless concluded by not only granting Pliny a '*liberatio culpae*', but also by conceding him a '*singularis eruditionis laus*' with respect to all other writers, ancient and profane. Subsequently, De la Nauze 1751, pp. 179-80, starting from the assumption that the entire sixth volume of the *Naturalis Historia* had been written after the second book and therefore following Titus' consulate, inferred that 'la supputation de Pline ne regarde point l'année vague égyptienne' and therefore that 'dans l'ancien calendrier alexandrin, le 1er jour de méchir

répondoit au 8ᵉ de janvier, & le premier jour de thoth au 11ᵉ d'août; & qu'ainsi l'ouverture de l'ancienne année fixe des Alexandrins concouroit avec le 11ᵉ jour du mois d'août julien'. Against this which he considered to be a 'sonst durch nichts begrundete Hypothese' Ideler 1825-6, p. 152 correctly observed that: 'Es ist aber natürlicher anzunehmen, daβ Plinius von beweglichen Monaten spricht und den 6. Mechir der damaligen Stellung des 1. Thoth gemäβ mit den Idus des Januars verglichen hat, vielleicht ohne zu wissen, daβ der Anfang des ägyptischen Jahrs im römischen seine Stelle ändert'. Committing a slight error, he then concluded: 'Ist diese Voraussetzung richtig, so muβ er, oder derjenige, von dem er die ganze Notiz entlehnt hat, in einem der Jahre 48, 49, 50, 51 n. Chr. geschrieben haben, wo der 1. Thoth mit dem 11. August zusammentraf'. As a matter of fact the passage by Pliny refers to the *idus Ianuariae,* and not to 11 August: in AD 48 the intercalary day of the Roman Julian year was placed, as usual, only after the *VI kal. Mart.*; the *idus Ianuariae* in AD 48 corresponded therefore not to the sixth but to the seventh day of Mechir of the revolving year. For a similar reason, i.e. that the intercalary day occurred only after the *VI kal. Mart.*, in AD 52 the *idus Ianuariae* still corresponded to the sixth day of the month of Mechir of the revolving year and therefore Pliny's informants found themselves in southern India waiting to set sail for Arabia and Egypt in a year comprised between AD 48/49 and 51/52. Unfortunately the passage in question (the same applies to the other passage, *N.H.* XXVII, 105, which we shall subsequently take into consideration) was overlooked by Wilcken and Hohmann during their debates on the propagation of the revolving year in the Roman age (cf. *supra,* n. 4) and ultimately misunderstood by R. Böker, *R.E.*, Supplb. IX, 411, who interprets Pliny's datum according to the Julian-Alexandrian fixed year ('Letzter Rückfahrtstermin: 6. Mech. 1. Febr.' [Böker refers us to his article *Die technische Entstehung des* ̱*naratischenî Globus,* in *Ber.u.d.Verhandl.d.Sachs. Ak.d.Wiss.math. Kl.*, Bd 99, Heft 5, 1952, p. 51, for the correspondence between 6 Mechir = 1 February as opposed to 31 January]), without quoting the different interpretations by De la Nauze and Ideler and without even commenting upon the grave error made, according to his interpretation, by Pliny.

The importance of this detail in Pliny's passage, appears to have escaped those scholars who have written on trade relations between Rome and India. I myself must confess that it would never have occurred to me when writing *Roma e i* nótia *dell'India* (cf. *supra* pp. 80-160).

12. Although subsequent addenda or revisions to chapters 101-6 are not to be excluded. For instance in Plin. *N.H.* VI, 104:

    inde uento hippalo nauigant diebus XL ad primum emporium Indiae Muzirim. Non expetendum propter uicinos piratas, qui optinent locum nomine Nitrias, neque est abundans mercibus; praeterea longe a terra abest nauium statio, lintribusque adferuntur onera et egeruntur.

    '[...] from that port, by catching the Hippalus wind, it is a forty-day voyage to the first trading station in India, Muziris—not a desirable port of call on account of the neighbouring pirates who occupy a place called Nitriae, nor is it especially rich in articles of merchandise; furthermore the roadstead for shipping is a long way from the land and cargoes have to be brought in and carried out in light boats'.

    We cannot exclude the hypothesis that the blunt specification *non expetendum,* etc., is a sort of 'correction while proof-reading' added at a later stage when Pliny received news of the conquest of Nitriai at the hands of the pirates. It should be borne in mind that according to the *PME*—written between AD 40 and 70—the area immediately to the north of Tyndis and the city of Naoura (probably Nitriai itself or at any rate a city very close to it) was not yet under the control of the pirates, cf. De Romanis, *Roma e i* nótia *dell'India, supra,* pp. 102-5.
13. Documented by the great number of forms of ophthalmic treatment handed down on papyri, cf. H. Grapow, *Grundriss der Medizin der alten Ägypten,* V, Berlin 1958, pp. 71-103; German translation in H. von Deines, H. Grapow, W. Westendorf, *Grundriss der Medizin der alten Ägypten,* IV 1, Berlin 1958, pp. 41-61; notes on IV 2, pp. 51-65. On the high esteem in which opticians were held in ancient Egypt, cf. Hdt. III, 1.
14. Together with the legend of Pheros (Hdt. II, 111) and the reference by Juvenal (XIII, 91-4), we should also remember the stelae from Deir el-Medina (cf. F. Jonckheere, *Le monde des malades dans les textes non médicaux,* in *Chronique d'Égypte,* 25 1950, pp. 217-18); cf. A.B. Lloyd, *Herodotus. Book II. Commentary 99-182,* Leiden, New York, København, Köln, 1988, pp. 38-9.
15. Cf. the apparatus of his edition of Dioscorides *ad loc.*
16. De la Nauze 1751, pp. 180-1 misunderstood the expression *fere in Augustum mensem incurrente,* ('on the twenty-eighth day—a day approximately falling in our August'), and considered the interpretation of *N.H.* XXVII, 105 to be necessary according to a fixed year beginning on 11 August (cf. *supra* n. 11). According to De la Nauze, «si Pline eût voulu parler du thoth vague, qui

commença au 4e d'août en l'année qu'il écrivoit, le 27 de thoth seroit tombé dans le courant même du mois d'août et le terme *presque* n'auroit point en lieu». De la Nauze follows the edition by Harduinus which still favoured the reading *XXVII*: Mayhoff is mistaken when he ascribes it to the v.a.H.; see the apparatus by Sillig. In actual fact Pliny's expression identifies 28 day of Thoth not with one of the first days of the month of September but rather with an unspecified day in the month of August. On the meaning of the verb *incurrere* in this passage, cf. *Th.l.L.* VII col. 1085. On the use of *fere*, to mean 'approximately' and linked to the names of months, cf., for example, Plin. *N.H.* IX, 75; XI, 35; XVIII, 135; and also *Th.l.L.* VI, col. 498.

17. *R.E.* XXXI, 375.
18. Gal. XI, 793: τἄλλα περίεργος ἱκανῶς καὶ γοητείας οὐκ ἀπηλλαγμένος.
19. Plin. *N.H.* XXXVII, 37: *Xenocrates* [...] *qui* [...] *nuperrime scripsit uiuitque adhuc.* In this sense cf. M. Wellmann, *Xenocrates aus Aphrodisias,* in *Hermes,* 42 (1907), pp. 614-29. On this question cf. M. Ullmann, *R.E.,* Supplb. XVI, 975.
20. Cf. OGIS 56:

    τῆι ἡμέραι ἐν ἧι ἐπιτέλλει τὸ ἄστρον τὸ τῆς Ἴσιος, ἣ νομίζεται διὰ τῶν ἱερῶν γραμμάτων νέον ἔτος εἶναι κτλ.

    'The day in which the star of Isis rises, which on the basis of the sacred scriptures is believed to be the new year.'
21. Plin. *N.H.* VI, 104:

    nauigare incipiunt aestate media ante canis ortum aut ab exortu protinus.

    'Travelling by sea begins at midsummer before the dogstar rises or immediately after its rising.'
22. The Plinian manuscript tradition relating to the distances of the various *hydreumata* from Coptos on the Coptos-Berenice caravan route, presents several difficulties deriving from the fact that one often notices differences between E[s] Pg (sigla of the André edition) on the one hand and DFR on the other. For further details the reader is referred to the apparatus of the editions by Sillig, Detlefsen, Mayhoff and André. We wish however, to draw attention to the distance of the first *hydreuma,* from Coptos, for which E[s] Pg offer the reading(s) $\overline{XXXII}$ (*XXXII* g), DFR *XXII.* Among the modern editors, the reading $\overline{XXXII}$ is taken up by Detlefsen (*Die goegr. Bücher d. Nat. d. C. Plin. Sec.*, Berlin 1904), Mayhoff, André, Sillig and Rackham adopt instead

reading *XXII*. Several considerations lead us to believe—against the authoritative E^s—that reading *XXII* is the genuine one, or at least the one that comes closest to it.

In the *Itinerarium Antonini* (171-3), in the *Tabula Peutingeriana* (seg. IX) and in the *Geographus Ravennas* (II, 7), the Coptos-Berenice caravan route shows a far more complex and well-organized structure as compared to the four (or five) *hydreumata* and to Pliny's three *mansiones in monte*. As many as eleven *stationes*, situated not more than twenty-eight miles apart, were to be found along the way. However, Pliny's *hydreumata*—many of which were built by the Roman troops during the early imperial age (cf. ILS 2483; Strab. XVII, 1, 45)—still constitute the main logistical support of the Coptos-Berenice caravan route. Among these we are able to recognise *Cenon (Nouum Hedreuma)*, *Apollonos (Hydreuma Apollinis)*, *Compasi* (Pliny's second *hydreuma*: the identification seems certain, considering that Compasi was situated 90 miles away from Coptos, according to the *Itin. Anton.*, and 81 miles away according to the *Tab. Peut.* Pliny locates the second *hydreuma* 85 [or 95? cf. apparatus] miles from Coptos). As for Pliny's first *hydreuma*, the most reasonable solution appears to be that of identifying it with the *statio* of *Poeniconon* (or *Phenice/Phinice*), which is located 24 miles away from Coptos. In fact: (a) given that the other three *hydreumata* remained in function for three or four centuries to follow, I would tend to exclude the possibility that Pliny's first *hydreuma* be found in a locality other than among the *stationes* mentioned by the *Itin. Ant.*, in the *Tab. Peut.* and by the *Geographus Ravennas*, since in the meantime it had fallen into disuse; (b) it is highly improbable that the first *hydreuma* may be identified with the second *statio*, Dydime, 48 miles (according to the *Itin. Anton.*) or 44 miles (according to the *Tab Peut.*) away from Coptos. Setting aside the contradiction relating to the distance suggested by Pliny (22 or 32 miles, depending upon the codiees), it would still be difficult to understand why in the course of the first 48 (or 44) miles not even one *mansio* was made, whereas in the successive 42 miles there were at least three: two in the proximity of an equal number of *hydreumata* and another *in monte*. Now, considering that both the *Itin. Anton.* and the *Tab Peut.* estimate the distance between Coptos and Poeniconon-Phenice as 24 miles, we are led, considering the different readings relating to the distance between Coptos and the first *hydreuma* *XXXII* of E^s Pg (*XXXII* g) and *XXII* of DFR, to suggest *XXII* as the reading which comes closest to being the genuine one. I hold as improbable so divergent a computation of the same distance, especially taking into account that it is the first *statio* after Coptos and that this must be identified with the site of el-Laqueita, situated at approximately 24 Roman miles from Coptos (cf., *infra*, n. 24).

23. In addition to the sources collected by H. Caddell/R. Remondon, *Sens et emplois de* τὸ ὄρος *dans le documents papyrologiques*, in *Revue des Études Grecques*, 80 (1967), pp. 343-5, see Harrauer/ Sijpesteijn 1985, pp. 130; 138; cf. also Thür 1987, pp. 229-45. On the contrast between *kmt* 'black fertile earth' and h*3st* 'desert mountains', cf. K.W. Butzer, in *Lexicon der Ägyptologie* VI, 1292-3.

24. Modern el-Laqeita is identified with certainty as Pliny's first *hydreuma* by G. W. Murray, *Roman Roads and Stations in the Eastern Desert,* in *Journal of Egyptian Archaeology*, 9 (1925), p. 144, n.1, who, perhaps unaware of the textual problems of Pliny's passage (cf. *supra* n. 22), refers to an error on Pliny's part in determining the distance of the first *hydreuma* from Coptos. S.E. Sidebotham, *Roman Economic Policy in the Erythra Thalassa. 30 B.C.- A.D. 217,* Leiden 1986, pp. 59-61 accepts the identification of Pliny's first *hydreuma* with el-Laqeita and accepts (without providing any justification), the reading *XXII* in *N.H.* VI, 102 for the distance between Coptos and the first *hydreuma.* It should be underlined that the actual distance between Coptos and el-Laqeita roughly corresponds to that estimated between Coptos and Poeniconon-Phenice by the *Itin. Anton.* and the *Tab. Peut.*

25. We may quote here the telegraphic, but vivid, description of the site and of the cave inscriptions by Winkler I, p. 7: 'West side, opposite to the entrance to the Wâdi-Menîh el-Hêr. Cave-like shelter. Full shadow all day. Ancient roads follow the Wâdi-Menîh el-Hêr. Favourite resting place. Giraffe, asses, ibexes. Boats. In one boat stands a woman with upraised arms. Men, archer, dancers.—Hieroglyphic inscriptions, boat, Min.—Greek, Latin, Himyaritic and Nabatean inscriptions, sailing-boat, cattle, Blemyan signs.—Some flints and late potsherds on the surface.'

26. Meredith 1953, pp. 38-40, including a photograph of the Latin inscription taken by Winkler and already published by him in I, pl. VIII. Inscriptions re-published without any variation in *AÉ* 1954, n. 121; V. Ehrenberg/A.H.M. Jones, *Documents illustrating the reigns of Augustus and Tiberius,* Oxford 1955[2], p. 163; *SEG* XIII, n. 614; Bernand 1977, pp. 162-4.

27. Unconvincing is Meredith 1953, p. 39: 'as there is no water at this spot, the three-day interval between the two inscriptions may be explained by a visit to the Roman station (in Wadi Menih el-Heir, the main Berenice road)'. Apart from the fact

that the reason for such a journey through the Egyptian desert would be hard to understand, it is anachronistic to imagine a 'Roman station' in Wadi Menih el-Heir being provided with a *hydreuma* in AD 6. As Pliny shows in *N.H.* VI, 102, between the first and the second *hydreuma* situated respectively 22 (?) and 85 (?) miles from Coptos, there were no other places which allowed for *aquationes.* Therefore at the time of Pliny's informants (during the principate of Claudius), and even more so in AD 6 the *statio* of Afrodito which Meredith refers to did not yet exist, at least not as a *mansio* provided with *hydreuma,* but possibly simply as a *mansio in monte.*

28. Printed here is the copy of the Greek inscription transcribed by Winkler, which is found on page 61 of a notebook marked 'Packet III Bk. 2' kept in the archives of the Egypt Exploration Society of London. I am greatly indebted to the Secretary of the Egypt Exploration Society, Dr. P. Spencer, for having helped me search for this document, and the President of the same society, Mr. T.G.H. James, for allowing its publication.

    As yet I myself have been unable to reach the site where the inscriptions are found, but I hope to have the opportunity to do so in order to examine them in a not too distant future. As regards the Greek inscription, the slides generously placed at my disposal by Prof. H.T. Wright have unfortunately not proved useful, though I am extremely grateful to him, also for having agreed to accompany me on the an abortive expedition to Wadi Menih. My thanks are also due to my friend, Prof. G. De Luca, who shared with me the hardships typical of such an enterprise, and to Professors S. Donadoni and M. Suhair who offered valuable advice.

29. It is possible to gain an idea of the accuracy with which Winkler habitually transcribed inscriptions by comparing the copy (Plate II), taken from p. 65 of the notebook (n. 28), of some inscriptions found at Wadi Menih (including the Latin one by Lysas) with the photograph of the same inscriptions (Plate III).

30. Sen. *N.Q.* IVa, 2, 4: *harenae per quas iter ad commercia Indici maris est.* It is no accident that precisely beneath the Lysas inscription the following inscription is found: *C. Numidius Eros hic fuit/anno XXIIX Caesaris exs/Ind<i>a red<i>e<n>s menos Pamen(oth).* 'Gaius Numidius Eros was here in the 28th year of Caesar, coming back from India, in the month Phamenoth'. Cf. Meredith, *Inscriptions from the Berenice Road,* in *Chronique d'Égypte,* 29 (1954), pp. 283-4; Bernand 1977, pp. 161-2.

31. On the Annius Plocamus, tax farmer of the *uectigal maris Rubri*

mentioned by Pliny (*N.H.* VI, 84), at present it is impossible to say anything more—apart from the connection (identity according to Meredith 1953, p. 40; or kinship according to Raschke 1978, p. 644) with Lysas' master, already noted by A. Stein, PIR² 115, n. 676. In other words, that he must be linked to one (or more?) of the three figures in the three important inscriptions CIL X 2389; XV 798; 7391. The *tegula* of Annius Plocamus (CIL XV 798) and the *fistula* of A. Annius Plocamus (CIL XV 7391: 'saeculi primi fere exeuntis') are important in terms of placing their respective personage within Rome's economic framework; whereas the Puteolan inscription is important because it shows P. Annius Plocamus within the framework of the port, i.e. Puteoli, in which—as on the basis of Cic. II, *Verr.* 5, 59, 154, it had been noticed by K.J. Beloch, *Campanien,* 1890², p. 115—'wer nach Sicilien ging, schiffte sich gewöhnlich—ein'. Within this same framework belonged the *homines locupletes atque honesti* ('rich and respectable men'), merchants mentioned by Cicero—among whom was M. Annius—as witnesses in the trial against Verres, 75 years before the P. Annius Plocamus mentioned in the two inscriptions of AD 6 and approximately 110 to 123 years before Rachias' embassy which immediately followed the adventure of Annius Plocamus' freedman in Taprobane discussed below.

But the opinion of those who consider that Pliny's Annius Plocamus and the P. Annius Plocamus—whether they be the same person or not—were freedmen (Camodeca 1979, p. 23), is questionable. On the contrary, the condition as freedman envisaged for the P. Annius Plocamus in CIL X 2389 (with whom Camodeca identifies both the P. Annius Plocamus of *A.É.* 1954 n. 121, and the Annius Plocamus *redemptor* of the *uectigal maris Rubri*), must be rejected for the following reasons. (1) The inscription CIL X 2389 explicitly points out the freedman status of three persons whom it mentions, and it is therefore difficult to understand why in the case of P. Annius Plocamus the name of his patron (in the genitive form followed by *l.* or *lib.* or even by *liberti* written in full, as would have been the case of a freedman patron of a freedman), should have been omitted if he had been a freedman; (2) Had Annius Plocamus *redemptor* of the *uectigal maris Rubri* been a freedman, thus making the 'discoverer' of Taprobane the freedman of a freedman, why should Pliny have mentioned the freedman status of the 'discoverer' of Taprobane, at the same time making no mention of the freedman status of the former's rich patron and thus missing an excellent chance to criticize, as he was in the habit of doing, the greed typical of freedmen in high social positions? (3) The Greek *cognomen* (upon which Camodeca bases his certainty concerning the freedmanship of P. Annius Plocamus) may be considered, with some reservations, to be on a par with Greek *cognomina* which are typical of freedmen but also of those who were free born, and even of senators (for example, Spinther, *cognomen* of a freedman in ILLRP 767, but also of the renowned consul of the year AD 57 in ILLRP 502).

32. We should remember that from 1 BC or from AD 4—in any case before AD 6—the Roman Julian calendar had, thanks to the decision of the emperor Augustus to interrupt the intercalations for twelve years, 'reabsorbed' the three days gained *uitio sacerdotalis festinationis*, cf. G. Radke, *Die falsche Schaltung nach Caesars Tode*, in *Rheinisches Museum*, 103 (1960), pp. 178-85.

33. Cf. *PME* 6: [...] ἀπὸ μηνὸς Ἰανουαρίου μέχρι τοῦ Σεπτεμβρίου ὅ ἐστιν ἀπὸ Τῦβι ἕως Θώθ; 14, 56: [...] περὶ τὸν Ἰούλιον μῆνα, ὅ ἐστιν Ἐπῖφι; 24: [...] περὶ τὸν Σεπτέμβριον μῆνα, ὅς ἐστι Θώθ; 39; 49: [...] περὶ τὸν Ἰούλιον μῆνα, ὅς ἐστιν Ἐπῖφι. We should also bear in mind that this way of correlating the months of the Roman calendar with those of the Egyptian calendar occurs also in Ptolemy and in the scholia at Aratus, cf. Ideler 1825-6, p. 141.

34. Cf. S. Mazzarino, *La fine del mondo antico*, Milano 1988 (reprint), pp. 18-19; D. Musti, *Polibio e l'imperialismo romano*, Napoli 1978, pp. 15-16. As we know, the ideology of the universal empire inspired Pompey's propaganda (cf. Plin. *N.H.* VII, 98=ORF[4] 111, V) and also that of Caesar (cf. Pan. Lat. VIII 11, 2) and persisted into the imperial period, though with different emphases, due to 'the decision to limit the empire within its frontiers' (Tac. *Ann.* I 11). We should recall for example, *R.G.* 26: 'I have extended the boundaries of all provinces belonging to the Roman people which bordered with peoples who did not obey our *imperium.*'

35. Man. IV, 169-71:

orbisque orbi bona uendere posse/totque per ignotas commercia iungere terras/atque alio sub sole nouas exquirere praedas

'be able to sell the goods of the world to the world interweaving commerce in many an unknown land and searching for new prey beneath a different sun'.

Sen. *N.Q.* I *praef.*, 13: *quantum est enim, quod ab ultimis litoribus Hispaniae usque ad Indos iacet? Paucissimorum dierum spatium, si nauem suus ferat uentus,*

'What is the distance between Spain's farthest shores and the Indians? Only a few days' sailing if a favourable wind bears the ship along' (where Seneca proposes again with renewed enthusiasm, the theoretical possibility of an Atlantic route to India—something which Aristotle, Eratosthenes and Posidonius had already surmised).

It is Seneca who reveals himself the most acute interpreter of this second conception of the world. He underlines not only the economic advantages, but also the scientific progress and the new ethical values which it entailed.

Sen. *N.Q.* IVa 2, 24: *tunc erat mendacio locus; cum ignota essent externa, licebat illis fabulas mittere; nunc uero tota exteri maris ora mercatorum nauibus stringitur, quorum nemo narrat initium Nili aut mare saporis alterius,*

'Then it was possible to lie. When that which was external was also unknown. Now instead all coasts of the external sea are surrounded by the vessels of merchants and no one among them tells of (having seen) the beginning of the Nile or that the sea has a different flavour'.

Sen. *N.Q.*, V, 18, 14: *dedit* (sc. deus) *uentos ad ulteriora noscenda: fuisset enim imperitum animal et sine magna experientia rerum homo, si circumscriberetur natalis soli fine. Dedit uentos, ut commoda cuiusque regionis fierent communia, non ut legiones equitemque gestarent nec ut perniciosa gentium arma transueherent.*

'The deity has given the winds for the things farthest away to be known. Man would be an ignorant being without experience, if he were to remain within the confines of the land of his birth. He has given the winds so that the wealth of each region might become common, and not in order to carry legions and cavalry, nor to transfer harmful arms to the peoples.'

36. Sen. *Med.*, 375-9.
37. I use this term (as I have used the term 'discoverer'), with all the reservations that the case requires. It is obvious that even before the arrival of the freedman of Annius Plocamus, merchants from the Roman empire in some way or other knew of Taprobane. Yet, as we shall see later, this was not a market they frequented—or at least not habitually. The arrival of the freedman of Annius Plocamus represents, therefore, a fundamental moment in the history of relations between Rome and Taprobane.

38. Compare the summary in Sol. 53, 8-10.
39. Cf. Dihle 1965, p. 27, nt. 24; Raschke 1978, p. 662.
40. On the reading, in Plin. *N.H.* VI, 100, *hypalum*, cf. pp. 72-9
41. Plin. *N.H.* VI, 106: *nauigant ex India uento uolturno.*
42. Warmington, 1928, p. 48.
43. Plin. *N.H.* II, 119.
44. R. Böker, *R.E.*, VIII A² 2323.
45. Plin., *N.H.* VI, 100: *postea ab Syagro Arabiae promunturio Patalen fauonio quem ibi hypalum uocant, peti certissimum uidebatur.*
46. Plin. *N.H.* VI, 106: *nauigant ex India uento uolturno et, cum intrauere Rubrum mare, africo uel austro.*
47. Cf. Great Britain Admiralty. Naval Intelligence Division 1955, p. 31.
48. For analogous cases in ancient geographical literature, cf. P. Janni, *La Mappa e il periplo. Cartografia antica e spazio odologico*, Roma 1984, pp. 102-4.
49. *PME* 57.
50. Strab. XV, 1, 17:

[...] τὴν δὲ θάλατταν ἄπλουν εἶναι τῶν ἀνέμων ἀντιπνεόντων, ἀπογαίας δὲ μηδεμιᾶς πνοῆς ἐκδεξαμένης

'and the sea was not navigable when the winds were blowing in the opposite direction, and that no land breezes succeeded them'.

Arr. *Anab.* VI, 21, 1:

οἱ γὰρ ἐτησίαι ἄνεμοι κατεῖχον, οἳ δὴ τῇ ὥρᾳ ἐκείνῃ οὐ καθάπερ παρ' ἡμῖν ἀπ' ἄρκτου, ἀλλ' ἀπὸ τῆς μεγάλης θαλάσσης κατὰ νότον μάλιστα ἄνεμον ἵστανται, ἀπὸ δὲ τοῦ χειμῶνος τῆς ἀρχῆς τὸ ἀπὸ Πλειάδων δύσεως ἔστε ἐπὶ τροπάς, ἃς ἐν χειμῶνι ὁ ἥλιος ἐπιστρέφει, πλόϊμα εἶναι ταύτῃ ἐξηγγέλλετο. τότε γὰρ κατὰ γὴν μᾶλλον οἷα δὴ πολλῷ ὕδατι ἐξ οὐρανοῦ βεβρεγμένην αὔρας ἵστασθαι μαλθακὰς καὶ ἐς τὸν παράπλουν ταῖς τε κώπαις καὶ τοῖς ἱστίοις ξυμμέτρους.

'The Etesian winds were blowing, which do not blow in that season as with us from the north, but from the great sea and from a roughly southerly quarter. But from the beginning of winter, the setting of Pleiadesto the winter solstice, navigation was reported to be possible here; for as is natural when the land is drenched with heavy rains, there are light land breezes, convenient for the coast voyage whether by oars or sails');

Arr., Ind. 21:

ὡς δὲ τὰ ἐτήσια πνεύματα ἐκοιμήθη, ἃ δὴ τοῦ θέρεος τὴν ὥρην πᾶσαν κατέχει ἐκ τοῦ πελάγεος ἐπιπνέοντα ἐπὶ τὴν γῆν καὶ ταύτῃ ἄπορον τὸν πλοῦν ποιέοντα κτλ.

'When the Etesian winds had sunk to rest, which continue blowing from the Ocean on to the land all the summer season, thus making it impossible to sail etc.'

51. FGrHist 87 F 28,12 = F 49 E.-K. = F 13 Th. No difficulty is posed by the fact that in reality Eudoxus must have been sailing in the Atlantic Ocean, along the West Coast of Africa, and that the real wind was not the SW monsoon: Posidonius thought Eudoxus was sailing straight towards India with the help of the ζέφυροι.
52. Hom. V, 295-6; Plin. *N.H.* II, 119; [Arist.], περὶ κόσμου, 394b. Other cases in which Posidonius appears to refer to Homer's wind rose in FGrHist 87 T 5b = T 22 E.-K. = F 18 Th.; FGrHist 87 F 28, 20 = F 49 E.-K. = F 13 Th.
53. Arist. *meteor.* II, 363a:

[...] ὥσπερ ἐνταῦθα οἱ βορέαι καὶ οἱ νότοι πνέουσιν, οὕτως ἐκεῖ εὖροι καὶ ζέφυροι διαδεχόμενοι συνεχεῖς ἀεὶ πνέουσι.

'In the same way that south and north winds blow here, unceasing eastern and western winds blow in the southern sea beyond Libye'.

Literature on this passage in Böker, *R.E.*, Supplb. 9, 406.

54. On the question of Posidonius' authorship of the fragment, cf. K. G. Sallmann, *Die Geographie des älteren Plinius in ihrem Verhältnis zu Varro*, Berlin-New York, pp. 71-9, who surmises (p. 73) a 'Vermittlung' of Seneca's *de situ Indiae*; and W. Theiler, *Posidonius. Die Fragmente*, II Berlin-NewYork 1982, pp. 71-2.
55. The source followed by Pliny for his account of the sea voyage of Alexander's fleet (VI, 96-100) is Iuba (cf. VI, 96). A dependence on the very same Iuba for the description of the first two routes for India (VI, 100-1), already believed probable (cf. C. Müller, HGF, III, p. 476; F. Jacoby, FGrHist 275 F 28 Komm.), is now indisputable following the observations by S. Mazzarino, pp. 72-79 of this volume, on the reading *hypalum* in *N.H.* VI, 100. The definition of the SW monsoon as *fauonius*, clearly originating from Aristotle and Posidonius, must therefore derive from an original ζέφυροι (or ζέφυρος) in the work by Iuba. Similarly, although the definition of the NE monsoon as *uolturnus* in VI, 106, is found in the text subsequent to information received from merchants of the Claudian period, it

must however relate back to an original εὖροι (or εὖρος) in the work by Iuba.

56. Cf. FGrHist 87 F 74 (= F 134a E.-K. =F 5 Th.). I would not exclude the fact that Pliny's error may have more easily occurred due to the use in the passage by Posidonius-Iuba, from which Pliny's designations of the monsoon winds as *fauonius* and *uolturnus* are derived, of singular forms, ζέφυρος and εὖρος used in the 'Homeric' sense. This usage is also found in another famous fragment by Posidonius, FGrHist 87 F 28, 20 (= F 49 E.-K. = F 13 Th.):

ὑπονοεῖ (se. Posidonius) δὲ τὸ τῆς οἰκουμένης μῆκος ἑπτὰ που μυριάδων σταδίων ὑπάρχον ἥμισυ εἶναι τοῦ ὅλου κύκλου, καθ' ὃν εἴληπται, ὥστε, φησίν, ἀπὸ τῆς δύσεως εὔρῳ πλέων ἐν τοσαύταις μυριάσιν ἔλθοι ἂν εἰς 'Ινδούς.

'and he (sc. Posidonius) suspects that the length of the inhabited world, being about seventy thousand stadia, is half of the entire circle on which it has been taken, so that, he says, if you sail from the West along a straight course you will reach India within seventy thousand stadia.'

In this case also the term εὖρος, although in the singular, should be understood according to the Homeric wind rose, that is, as a wind generally coming from the east and not specifically as ἀπὸ τῆς χειμερινῆς ἀνατολῆς (SSE), as it would be understood according to the eight-wind wind rose. Thus, if εὖρος was the designation for the wind which theoretically could have allowed one to *buscar el levante por el poniente*, this same designation could indicate the wind which permitted Arabia to be reached from India.

57. Other examples of 'updating' the geographical literature relating to Arabia and the Persian Gulf by means of information obtained by merchants, in Plin. *N.H.* VI, 139-140:

prius fuit (sc. Charax) *a litore stadiis X—maritimum etiam Vispania porticus habet—, Iuba uero prodente* $\overline{L}$ *p.; nunc abesse a litore* $\overline{CXX}$ *legati Arabum nostrique negotiatores, qui inde uenere, adfirmant.*

'It [sc. Charax] formerly was at a distance of 10 stadia from the sea, and the porticus Vipsania gives it as maritime, yet when Iuba published his work it was 50 miles inland; its present distance from the coast according to Arab envoys and to our own traders who have come from the place, is said to be of 120 miles.'

Plin. *N.H.* VI:

nostri negotitores dicunt Characenorum regi parere et Apameam, sitam ubi restagnatio Euphratis cum Tigri confluat.

'Our merchants say that the king of the Characeni also rules over Apamea, a town situated at the confluence of the overflowing of the Euphrates with the Tigris.'

Plin. *N.H.* VI:

ultra nauigationem incopertam ab eo latere propter scopulos tradit Iuba, praetermissa mentione oppidi Omanorum Batrasauaues et Omanae, quod priores celebrem portum Carmaniae fecere, item Homnae et Attanae, quae nunc oppida maxime celebrari a Persico mari nostri negotiatores dicunt.

'According to Juba the voyage beyond, on that side has not been explored because of the rocks. He omits mentioning Batrasavave, the town of the Omani, and the town of Omana which previous writers have made out to be a famous port of Carmania, and also Homna and Attana, towns said by our traders to be the most frequented ports in the Persian Gulf.'

Plin. *N.H.* VI: 157:

Nabataeis Thimaneos iunxerunt ueteres, nunc sunt Taueni, Suelleni, Araceni, Arreni oppido in quod negotiatio omnis conuenit.

'Adjoining the Nabataei the old authorities put the Thimanei, but now the Taveni, Suelleni, Araceni, Arreni are there, with a town which is a centre for all mercantile business.'

58. Harduinus 1685, I, p. 694.

59. *PME* 12:

ὁ δὲ ὅρμος ἐπίσαλος κατὰ καιροὺς ἐπικίνδυνος διὰ τὸ προσεχῆ τὸν τόπον εἶναι τῷ βορέᾳ. σημεῖον δὲ τοῦ μέλλοντος χειμῶνος τοπικὸν τὸ τὸν βυθὸν θολερώτερον γίνεσθαι καὶ τὴν χρόαν ἀλ<λ>άσσειν. τούτου δὲ γενομένου πάντες ἀποφεύγουσιν εἰς τὸ μέγα ἀκρωτήριον, τόπον καὶ σκέπην, τὸ λεγόμενον Τάβαι.

'The harbour, an open roadstead, is dangerous at times, because the site is exposed to the northern wind. Sign of the coming storm in this place is when the deep sea becomes rather turbid and changes colour; when it happens all take refuge on the big promontory—a place and a shelter—called Tabai.'

60. Ptol., *Geogr.* I, 9, 1:

ἔπειτα καὶ κατὰ τὸν μεταξὺ τῶν 'Αρωμάτων καὶ τῶν

ʽΡάπτων πλοῦν Διογένη μέν τινά φησι τῶν εἰς τὴν ʼΙνδικὴν πλεόντων ὑποστρέφοντα τὸ δεύτερον, ὅτε ἐγένετο κατὰ τὰ ʼΑρώματα, ἀπωσθῆναι ἀπαρκτίᾳ, καὶ ἐν δεξιᾷ ἔχοντα τὴν Τρωγλοδυτικὴν ἐπὶ ἡμέρας εἴκοσι πέντε παραγενέσθαι εἰς τὰς λίμνας, ὅθεν ὁ Νεῖλος ρεῖ, ὧν ἐστι τὸ τῶν ʽΡάπτων ἀκρωτήριον ὀλίγῳ νοτιώτερον.

'About the navigation between the Aromates (Cape Guardafui) and Rhapta (probably Dar es Salaam, in Tanzania) he (sc. Marinus) says that a certain Diogenes, one of the merchants who sail to India, coming back the second time arrived at the Aromates, but was driven off by a north wind. Having at his right the East Coast of Africa, after twenty-five days he reached the marshes, from where the Nile begins: the promontory of Rhapta is just a little further south.'

61. Great Britain Admiralty. Naval Intelligence Division 1955, p. 34.
62. Great Britain Admiralty. Naval Intelligence Division 1975, Diagram 19; p. 24. On the probable landing-place, cf. G. Fiaccadori, *Hippuros portus* in *La Parola del Passato*, 38 (1983), pp. 440-1.
63. I prefer to interpret the expression *in auditis* in Plin. *N.H.* VI, 85, together with Cl. Salmasius, *Plinianae exercitationes in Caii Solini Polyhistora*, Parisiis 1629, p. 1117, as masculine referring to the Romans and to Caesar, object of the freedman's narration; conversely Harduinus interprets it as neuter (ex iis quae audierat).
64. Cf., e.g., Raschke 1978, nt. 1316.
65. Cf. Plin. *N.H.* VI, 89:

seruum nemini, non in diem aut interdiu somnum, aedificia modice ab humo exstantia, annonam numquam augeri, non fora litesue esse, coli Herculem, eligi regem a populo senecta clementiaque, liberos non habentem, et, si postea gignat, abdicari, ne fiat hereditarium regnum.

'nobody kept a slave, everyone got up at sunrise and no one took a siesta in the middle of the day; their buildings were of only moderate height; the price of corn was never inflated; there were no law courts and no litigation; the deity worshipped was Hercules; the king was elected by the people on the grounds of age and gentleness of disposition and on condition that he had no offspring. In the event of a child being subsequently born to him, he would be deposed to prevent the monarchy from becoming hereditary.'

Cf. Ch. G. Starr, *The Roman Emperor and the king of Ceylon*, in

Classical Philology, 51 [1956], p. 27-30). It is worth noting also the tone of grievance in the admissions, ibid.:

sed ne Taprobane quidem, quamuis extra orbem a natura relegata, nostris uitiis caret. Aurum argentumque et ibi in pretio; marmor testudini simile, margaritae gemmaeque in honore; multo praestantior est totus luxuriae nostrae cumulus. Ipsorum opes maiores esse dicebant, sed apud nos opulentiae maiorem usum.

'Yet even Taprobane, though banished by nature beyond the confines of the world, is not without the vices that belong to us: gold and silver are valued there also, and a kind of marble resembling tortoise-shell, and pearls and precious stones are held in honour; in fact the whole mass of luxury is carried there to a far higher pitch than ours. They told us that there was greater wealth in their own country than in ours, but that we made more use of our riches.'

All this is linked to the image of the Indians as 'just' people, already present in the work of Ctesias and Megasthenes, cf. Mazzarino, 1966a, pp. 332-3.

66. Pliny's dependence on a literary source appears certain precisely in consideration of the presence of literary *topoi* in the *diligentior notitia* on Taprobane, cf. Dihle 1965, p. 27, n. 24.
67. Cf. Strab. XV, 1, 4; *PME* 53.
68. Cf., recently, Walburg 1985, p. 35.
69. So Schwarz 1975, p. 486.
70. Similarities between 'Rachias' tale' and the accounts by *nostri negotiatores* were noticed by Pliny with regard to the 'silent barter' with the Serae, cf. *N.H.* VI, 88.
71. On numismatic finds in Sri Lanka, as well as the aforementioned work (*supra*, n. 68) by Walburg, we should recall the works by J. Still in *Journal of the Royal Asiatic Society (Ceylon Branch)*, 19 (1907), pp. 161-215; the classic study by H. W. Codrington, *Ceylon coins and currency*, Colombo 1924; and Mitchiner 1973, pp. 111-15.
72. Bhandarkar 1921, pp. 124-66; cf. also Sircar 1968, pp. 95-7.
73. Curt. Ruf. VIII, 12. On the role played by coins as gifts in India cf. my observations concerning the expression *poṟ paricam* of *Puṟanāṉūṟu* 343, 5 in De Romanis, *supra*, pp. 139-40, n. 79.
74. On 'punch-marked coins', cf., e.g. Mitchiner 1973.; P.L. Gupta, *Indian silver punchmarked coins*, 1985. Bibliography prior to 1955 in: P.L. Gupta, *A bibliography of the hoards of punch-marked coins of ancient India*, Bombay 1955.
75. On the personality and works of Buddhaghosa (*Cūḷ.* XXXVII, 225-7), cf. Norman 1983, pp. 120-30.

76. Buddhaghosa, *Samantapāsādikā. Pacittiya-vannana,* 65 (11. 7-8, p. 867, vol. IV ed. J. Takakusu, Makoto Nagai, PTS, London 1934).
77. On this passage see for example, Sircar 1968, p. 96.
78. On the assay of coins in ancient times, cf. R. Bogaert, *L'essai des monnaies dans l'Antiquité*, in *Revue Belge de Numismatique*, 122 (1976), pp. 5-34; S. Mazzarino, *Antico, tardoantico ed èra costantiniana,* I Bari 1974, pp. 282-5.
79. Epict. I, 20, 8-9:

    ὁρᾶτε ἐπὶ τοῦ νομίσματος, ὅπου δοκεῖ τι εἶναι πρὸς ἡμᾶς, πῶς καὶ τέχνην ἐξευρήκαμεν καὶ ὅσοις ὁ ἀργυρογνώμων προσχρῆται πρὸς δοκιμασίαν τοῦ νομίσματος, τῇ ὄψει, τῇ ἁφῇ, τῇ ὀσφρασίᾳ, τὰ τελευταῖα τῇ ἀκοῇ· ῥήξας τὸ δηνάριον τῷ ψόφῳ προσέχει καὶ οὐχ ἅπαξ ἀρκεῖται ψοφήσαντος, ἀλλ' ὑπὸ τῆς πολλῆς προσοχῆς μουσικὸς γίνεται.

    'You all see in the matter of coinage, in which it is felt that we have some interest, how we have even invented an art, and how many means the tester employs to test the coinage—sight, touch, smell, finally hearing; he throws the denarius down and then listens to the sound, and is not satisfied with the sound it makes on a single test, but as a result of his constant attention to the matter, he catches the tune, like a musician.'
80. Cf. the remarks in the *PME* (ch. 47) on the circulation, in Barygaza, in the period during which the work was composed (between AD 40 and 70), of παλαιαὶ δραχμαὶ, γράμμασι Ἑλληνικοῖς ἐγκεχαραγμέναι ἐπίσημα τῶν μετὰ Ἀλέξανδρον βεβασιλευκότων Ἀπολλοδότου καὶ Μενάνδρου, ('old drachmas engraved with the inscriptions, in Greek letters, of Apollodotus and Menander, rulers who came after Alexander'). Cf. W.W. Tarn, *The Greeks in Bactria and India*, Cambridge 1951², p. 149.
81. D.C. Sircar, *Media of exchange in ancient and medieval India*, in *Journal of ancient Indian history*, 10 (1976/7), pp. 1-51.
82. Alongside the various ἐντόπια νομίσματα (such as the κάλτις, the gold coin circulating in the Ganges emporium, cf. *PME* 63) there were Roman coins. On 'mixed' treasures, cf. Raschke 1978, n. 1578. It should be noted that in Barygaza silver and gold Roman coins were exchanged profitably with the local coins (*PME* 49); cf. A. Gara, *Prosdiagraphomena e circolazione monetaria. Aspetti dell'organizzazione fiscale in rapporto alla politica monetaria dell'Egitto romano,* Milano 1976, pp. 167-9.
83. E.J. Rapson, *A catalogue of the Indian coins in the British Museum. Coins of the Andhra dynasty. The Western Kṣatrapas, the Traikūṭaka*

Dynasty and the 'Bodhi' Dynasty, Oxford 1967 (reprint), pp. clxxvii-clxxxii.

84. W.W. Hunter, *The Annals of Rural Bengal*, London 1868, p. 293.
85. Ibid., p. 295.
86. Buddhaghosa, *Samantapāsādikā. Suttavibhaṅga-vannana*, IV, 18 (pp. 689-90).
87. The *saṃnidhātṛ* must accept only those coins which are guaranteed by the *rūpadarśaka* (*Arth.* II, 5, 10); the latter must fix the *yatrā* of the coin, both in relation to current use and in relation to the treasury's income (*Arth.* II, 12, 25). If the *rūpadarśaka* rejects some coins which should not be rejected or, *vice versa*, does not reject some coins which must be rejected, he must pay a fine of twelve *paṇas* (*Arth.* IV, 1, 44). On the complex problem of the dating of the *Arthaśāstra*, cf., e.g. Trautmann 1971; Scharfe 1978.
88. Cf., e.g. M. Crawford, *Economia imperiale e commercio estero*, in *Tecnologia, economia e società nel mondo romano.* Atti del convegno di Como 27/28/29 Settembre 1979, Como 1980, p. 216, containing observations on treasures comprising *denarii* found in southern India. Obviously one could object that the *denarii* examined by the king of Taprobane were to be exported not to India, but to Arabia or to the emporia of the Persian Gulf, and that we are not so well informed (cf., for example, Raschke 1978, p. 632) concerning the quality of Roman coins exported to these areas (though in terms of quantity they cannot have been small, cf. Plin. *N.H.* XII, 84). We must recognize, however, that the characteristics of the *denarii* exported to Arabia and the Persian Gulf—especially if exported by a freedman of the contractor appointed to farm the Red Sea tax—could not have differed greatly from those of the *denarii* found in the treasures of southern India, amongst which we notice the conspicuous absence of the old republican *denarius* (this being among the most significant phenomena relating to the general tendency to export good coins in southern India, cf. Lo Cascio 1980, p. 451).
89. The famous inscription by Khāravela should be recalled (about the chronology of this king of Kaliṅga, oscillating between the second century BC and the beginning of the first century AD, cf. D.C. Sircar, *Select inscriptions bearing on Indian history and civilization*, Calcutta 1942, p. 206): the inscription tells us that the young prince had learned the *rūpa* (1. 2). In the tale narrated to *Mahāvagga*, I, 49, Upāli's parents consider having their son instructed in the *rūpa*, in order to secure him a peaceful life without privations of sorts, cf. Bhandarkar 1921, pp. 124-8.

90. E.O. Winstedt, *The Christian Topography of Cosmas Indicopleustes, edited, with geographical notes,* Cambridge 1909, p. 355; cf., more recently and with different nuances, Wolska 1962, pp. 7-8; Schwarz 1975, pp. 485-6.
91. Interesting in this context, is the detail we receive from a Chinese source, which appears to date back to the last quarter of the fourth century AD, and according to which the king of Po-ssû (Persia) had asked to marry the daughter of the king of Ssu-t'iao (Sri Lanka) and had sent as a betrothal gift a gold bracelet, cf. Daffinà 1983, p. 121, who expresses some doubts however, on the reliability of this testimony.
92. The numismatic finds in Sri Lanka have shown the importance of Roman bronze coins during the fourth to fifth centuries AD, but by the sixth century bronze coins had been replaced by gold ones, cf. Walburg 1985, pp. 40-2.
93. Schwarz 1974a, pp. 166-76; Schwarz 1974b, pp. 21-48; prior to Schwarz an Augustan dating had been proposed both for the arrival in Taprobane of Annius Plocamus' freedman, and for Rachias' embassy, E. Peiris, *Greek and Roman contacts with Ceylon*, in *The Ceylonese Historical Journal*, 10 (1960/1), pp. 17-18; and S. Paranavitana, *Civilization of the Early Period: Economic, Political and Social Conditions*, in H.C. Ray (ed.), *History of Ceylon*, I, Colombo 1959, p. 225.
94. Six months are indicated by Pliny as the period of time taken by Annius Plocamus' freedman to learn the local language and subsequently *narrare Romanos et Caesarem* to the Sinhalese king. The legation, however, must have waited for the καταρχή of the NE monsoon to set sail, cf. for a similar situation, P. Ox. 413, 213-15:

    κυρία Χαρίτιον καταρχὴν [βλέπω τοῦ]/ ἀνέμου ὥστε ἡμᾶς πε[ράσαντας]/ τὸ Ἰνδικὸν πέλαγος ὑπ[οφυγεῖν].

    'Lady Charition, I see the wind beginning to blow so that, we may escape by sailing across the Indian sea.'

    Western merchants used to set sail from southern India *mense Aegyptio Tybi incipiente, nostro Decembri aut utique Mechiris Aegyptii intra diem sextum, quod fit intra idus Ianuarias nostras*; that is, in the period between 9 December and 13 January (cf. *supra*). The difference of opinion with Arrian, *Anab.* VI, 21, who indicates as a time favourable for navigation from Patale, that which goes ἀπὸ δὲ τοῦ χειμῶνος τῆς ἀρχῆς τὸ ἀπὸ Πλειάδων δύσεως ἔστε ἐπὶ τροπὰς, ἃς ἐν χειμῶνι ὁ ἥλιος ἐπιστρέφει, is explained by the fact that 'the NE monsoon normally begins earlier in the N of the region [sc. of the Indian Ocean] where it is blowing fairly regularly by mid-November, than in the S, where it is not established until December' (Great Britain Admiralty. Naval Intelligence Division 1975, p. 24).

95. Cf. *supra*, n. 31.
96. *Dīpavaṃsa* XIX, 10; *Mahāvaṃsa* XXVIII, 1-43; cf. Schwarz 1974b, p. 37.
97. Cf. for example, Geiger 1908; Perera 1979; Norman 1983, pp. 114-8.
98. Cf. G. P. Malalasekera, *Vuṃsatthappakasini, commentary on the Mahāvaṃsa,* London 1935, pp. CIV-CXI.
99. This is the reading adopted by Malalasekera, according to the reading of the codices A and J of the Sinhalese group, and S, E and N, of the Cambodian; all others give the reading *ropanukha-*
100. The codices of the Sinhalese group and the N codex, in the Cambodian group, give *pavālajalam,* the reading adopted in the text (which is the one accepted by Malalasekera), is shown by all other codices of the Cambodian group and by those of the Burmese group.
101. In the *PME* mention is made of the export of Western coral to Kane (Hisn al Gurab, in southern Arabia), emporium of Saubatha (*PME* 28); to Barbarikon, emporium of Minnagar, metropolis of Skythia (*PME* 39); to Barygaza (*PME* 49); and to the ports of the Limyrike (*PME* 56). The *Arthaśāstra* (II, 11, 42) defines the coral *ālakandakaṃ vaivarṇikaṃ ca raktam padmarāgaṃ ca,* '*ālakandaka* and *vaivarṇika,* red and the colour of the *padma* respectively' (cf. Trautmann 1971, 177 ff.; Scharfe 1978, pp. 317-20). No doubt here *ālakandaka* means 'alexandrian', that is, coming from Alexandria in Egypt. Problems arise instead from the adjective *vaivarṇika,* which is interpreted by the commentator Bhaṭṭasvāmin as indicating a second *yoni* of the coral:

    yavana-dvīpe vivarṇo nāma samudraikadeśaḥ; tatra-bhavaṃ vaivarṇikaṃ; tat padma-rāgaṃ padma-varṇaṃ,

    'in the continent of the Yavanas upon the Ocean there is a land by the name of Vivarṇa; the coral which is found there is known as *vaivarṇika,* its hue is that of the *padma*'). But as V. Mazzarino (to whom I am greatly indebted) suggests, the 'land upon the Ocean, by the name of *Vivarṇa*' could simply be the result of a mistaken personal assumption on the part of Bhaṭṭhasvāmin (or of the tradition which he represents), made on the basis of the analogy with *ālakandaka* < *ālakanda,* whereas the adjective *vaivarṇika*, in *Arth.* II, 11, 42, rather than being derived from a toponym (which would escape any further identification), could mean 'without colour' or 'pale hued'. The *padma*, one among many of India's acquatic flowers, is more specifically the *Nelumbium speciosum*, the lotus flower which has a pink hue. The distinction between the two types of coral would therefore depend not so much on the *yoni*, the place of origin, but on the colour, the *ālakandaka* being *raktavarṇa*, that is 'red'; and the *vaivarṇika* being by contrast *padma-rāga*, in other words 'the colour of the *padma*'. It is however remarkable that the *vaivarṇika* has its *yoni*, according to Bhaṭṭhasvāmin, in the *yavana-dvīpa*, the continent of the Greeks.

On the export of western coral, also very important is Plin. *N.H.* XXXII, 21-3 which should in some respects be compared with Buddhabhaṭṭa, *Ratnaparikṣā*, 250-2, cf. *infra*, n. 103. For a possible reference to Western coral in Tamil literature, cf. De Romanis, *supra*, p. 150 n. 145. For Chinese literature cf. Hirth 1885, pp. 41, 47, 55, 59, 73, 94, 246-7. To be precise we must remember that in other Chinese texts coral, together with other precious articles, is said to be a product of Po-ssû, of Persia, which at one time took the place of Ta-ch'in as a country which produced and exported 'precious and rare objects', cf. Daffinà 1983, p. 151.

102. Plin. *N.H.* XXXII, 21:

gignitur et in Rubro quidem mari, sed nigrius, item in Persico—uocatur lace—, laudatissimum in Gallico sinu circa Stoechadas insulas et in Siculo circa Aeolias ac Drepana. Nascitur et apud Grauiscas et ante Neapolim Campaniae maximeque rubens, sed molle et ideo uilissimum Erythris.

'Coral is also found in the Red Sea, but this is of a darker colour; also in the Persian Gulf—this is called *lace*—the most valued is in the Gallic Gulf around the Stoechades Islands, and around Drepana. Coral also grows at Graviscae and before Naples in Campania; but that at Erythrae, which is very red indeed, is soft and therefore thought worthless.'

103. Plin., *N.H.* XXXII, 23:

auctoritas bacarum eius non minus Indorum uiris quoque pretiosa est quam feminis nostris uniones Indici. Harispices eorum uatesque inprimis religiosum id gestamen amoliendis periculis arbitrantur. Ita et decore et religione gaudent.

'Coral berries are no less valued by Indian men than are large

Indian pearls by Roman women. Indian soothsayers and seers think that coral is a very powerful amulet for warding off dangers.'

These observations by Pliny on the popularity of Roman coral in India and on the magical powers attributed to it by the Indians must be compared with a Sanskrit text, the dating of which is entirely uncertain (Finot 1896, Introd., p. VI), Buddhabhaṭṭa, *Ratnaparikṣā*, 250-2 (Finot 1896, pp. 57-8):

saṃlāsakaṃ devakaromake (Finot: codd.-*ramake*) *ca sthānāni yeṣu prathitaṃ surāgam/anyatra jātaṃ ca na tat pradhānam/mūlyaṃ bhavec chilpiviśeṣayogāt/* <**> *prassanaṃ kamalaṃ snigdhaṃ surāgaṃ vidrumaṃ hitaṃ dhanadhānyakaraṃ loke strīṇaṃ saubhāgyadāyakam/ duṣṭavyādhiharaṃ caiva viṣādibhayanāśanam*

'Saṃlāsaka, Devaka, Romaka are the places in which a beautiful red coloured coral is common; the kind which grows elsewhere does not have the same value; the price depends upon the excellence of the artist [...] Good coral is tender, smooth and shining and of a beautiful red colour. In this world it procures richness and grain, gives women marital bliss, destroys corruption and illness and wards off perils such as poison etc.'

We must bear in mind that even in Western treatises on gems, coral was reckoned to have magical powers, cf. Sol. II, 42; *Orphei lithica* 510 ff.; *Orphei lithica kerygmata*, 20; *Lapidarius nauticus*, 5; Damigeron-Evax, 7; and it is interesting to note that coral was said to be particularly useful in warding off the perils of battles fought at sea and those deriving from sea journeys. The Gallic practice of ornamenting swords, shields and helmets with coral must also have been connected with magical beliefs.

104. Plin. *N.H.* XXXII, 21-3:

quantum apud nos Indicis margaritis pretium est [...] *tantum apud Indos curalio* [...] *auctoritas bacarum eius non minus Indorum uiris quoque pretiosa est quam feminis nostris uniones Indici.*

'Coral is as valuable among the Indians as Indian pearls [...] are among the Romans [...] Coral berries are no less valued by Indian men than are large Indian pearls by Roman women.'

105. In this way I would interpret the reference found in the annals of the former Han, according to which *Ki-pin* (Kashmir) produces pearls, corals, amber and *vaiḍūrya* (beryl), cf. E. Chavannes, *Les pays d'Occident d'après le 'Heou han Chou'*, in *T'oung Pao*, 2 ser. 8 (1907), p. 182, n. 2.

106. On the Roman presence in Indochina, cf. Hirth 1885, pp. 42; 47; 74-5; 82; 94; Mazzarino 1980, pp. 405-6.
107. Āryabhaṭa, *Āryabhaṭīya* IV, 13: *udcyo yo laṅkāyāṃ so 'stamayaṃ savitur eva siddhapure/madhyāhno yamakoṭyāṃ romakaviṣaye 'rdharātraḥ syāt,* ('that which is dawn in Laṅka, is precisely sunset in Siddhapura, midday in Yamakoṭi and midnight in Romakaviṣaya'). For the tale of the automatons of *romavisaya,* cf. *Lokapaññatti* (E. Denis ed., Paris 1977, pp. 157-61; 175-7; cf. also the introduction, pp. XLVI-XLVIII). Other occurrences of the adjective *romaka* in M. S. Ch. Vidyabhusana, *Romaka or the city of Rome,* in *Journal of the Proceedings of the Asiatic Society of Bengal,* N.S. 2 (1906), pp. 1-7; cf. also P. Aalto, *Nomen Romanum,* in *Ural-Altaische Jahrbücher,* 47 (1959), pp. 1-9. *Visaya* is the term which Aśoka uses to describe his empire; *raṭṭha,* in the Sinhalese chronicles, may designate reigns such as those of the Colar (*Mah.* XXI, 13: *colaraṭṭha*), and princely states administered by the *yuvarājan* (*Mah.* V, 46: *avantiraṭṭha*), and also the districts (*kōralē*) of Sri Lanka, cf. Geiger 1953, I, p. 199. There can be no doubt, however, that here *raṭṭha* refers to the great structure of a state governed by a *rājan.* In the *Vaṃsatthappakāsinī,* the interpretation of the Roman empire as a *regnum,* may depend upon an Indian way of perceiving the constitution of the Roman empire, but it should be underlined that this found a justification in the constitutional status of the Roman state. With Augustus, in fact, the *senatus populique imperium* formally gave way to the *imperium* of the prince both within the imperial and senatorial provinces (cf. Tac. *Ann.* I, 2): the *imperium* of the prince extended to the entire empire, *imperium* as governed territory. The double meaning of the word *imperium*—on the one hand authority of government, on the other governed territory—is evident in the passage of the H.A., *Sev. Alex.* 14: *te manet imperium quod tenet imperium.* Thus, due to an evolutionary process which had its origin and partially developed its institutions during the Augustan age (one has only to think of the Cyrene edicts), the *imperium senatus populique Romani* approximated to the idea of *regnum.* The basic principle of the Roman state, according to which it is not *fas* to restore the monarchy in Rome (cf. Cic. *Phil.* II, 87; Liu. II, 8; Dion. Halic. *Ant. Rom.* V, 19; Plut. *Poplic.,* 11-12) was in fact attenuated, in that the power of the *princeps* on the provinces guaranteed the centrality of the government.
108. Levi 1900, pp. 297-341; 401-68; Senaveratne1915/1916, pp. 74-118 (English translation of the article by Levi with the addition of 'Notes' by the translator); L. Petech, *Some Chinese texts*

concerning Ceylon, in *The Ceylon Historical Journal*, 3 (1953/4), pp. 217-27.

109. H.W. Codrington, *A Short History of Ceylon*, London 1926, p. XV, places his reign between 20 BC and AD 9; G.C. Mendis, *The Chronology of the Early Pāli Chronicles of Ceylon*, in *University of Ceylon Review*, 5 (1953), p. 53, places it between 19 BC and AD 9; this same period is indicated in C.W. Nicholas/S. Paranavitana, *A concise history of Ceylon*, Colombo 1961, p. 342.

110. D.M.D.Z. Wickremasinghe, *Ceylonese Chronology*, in *Epigraphia Zeylanica*, 3, 1928-33, p. 7, dates the reign of Bhātikābhaya from AD 39 to 67; Geiger 1953, II, Introd., p. X, dates it from AD 38 to 66.

111. *Dīp.* VI, 1:

dve satāni ca vassāni aṭṭhārasa vassāni ca/sambuddhe parinibbute abhisitto Piyadassano.

'two hundred and eighteen years after the Sambuddha's *parinibbāna* Piyadassana was consecrated'.

Mah. V, 21:

jinanibbāṇato pacchā pure tassābhisekato/sāṭṭhārasaṃ vassasatadvayaṃ evaṃ vijāniyaṃ.

'after the Jina's *nirvāṇa* and before his (sc. of Aśoka) *abhiseka* there elapsed 218 years: this should be known'.

On the chronology of Aśoka, cf. Eggermont 1956; and the same author's subsequent reflections in *Persica*, 2 (1965/6), pp. 27-70; 4 (1969), pp. 77-120; 5 (1971), pp. 69-102; 8 (1979), pp. 55-93. For an analysis of the complex problem posed by the date of the Buddha's *nirvāṇa* (here we shall only deal with those aspects of the problem which are directly related to the present research), cf. A. Bareau, *La date du nirvāṇa*, in *Journal Asiatique* 241 (1953), pp. 27-62; Bechert 1986, pp. 129-84; P. Daffinà, *Senso del tempo e senso della storia: computi cronologici e storicizzazione del tempo*, in *Rivista di Studi Orientali* 61 (1987), pp. 50-71.

112. Ll. 11-13:

Buddha-varṣa ek dahas sat siya te sālis havurudu tunmas sat visi davasak giya tena Binera pura dolos vak lada Badā davas śubha nakat mohotin abhiṣeka kärä-vū.

'27 days, 3 months and 1743 years having elapsed from the *Buddha-varṣa* ('year of the Buddha'), on the 'Wednesday' (*Bada*), twelfth day of the bright half of the month of Binera, at a time when the stars were favourable, they consecrated him' (sc. Sāhasa Malla).

Cf. T.W. Rhys Davids, *Two Old Simhalese Inscriptions*, in *Journal of the Royal Asiatic Society*, 1875, pp. 356 ff.; Muller, *Ancient Inscriptions in Ceylon*, n. 156, pp. 68, 103, 136; J.F. Fleet, *The Origin of the Buddhavarsa, the Ceylonese Reckoning from the Death of the Buddha*, in *Journal of the Royal Asiatic Society*, 1909, pp. 327; 331; D.M.D.Z. Wickremasinghe, *Poḷonnaruva: Slab-inscription of Sāhasa Malla*, in *Epigraphia Zeylanica*, 2, London 1928, pp. 219-29.

113. Cf. Eggermont 1956, pp. 120-31.
114. *Dīp.* XI, 25. The *abhiseka* of Devānaṃ Piya Tissa is dated at 236 years after the *parinibbāna* in *Dīp.* XVII, 78:

dve satāni ca vassāni chattiṃsa ca saṃvacchare/sambuddhe parinibbutte abhisitto Devānaṃ Piyo.

'Two-hundred and thirty-six years after the *parinibbāna* of the Sambuddha, Devānaṃ Piya Tissa was consecrated'). Geiger 1912, p. XXXI, draws attention to the similarity in formulation in the *Dīp.* VI, 1 (cf. above, n. 111) and *Dīp.* XVII, 78. The contemporaneity of Aśoka and Devānaṃ Piya Tissa is accepted even by those scholars who are sceptical about the historical validity of the Sinhalese chronicles, for the years down to 382 of the Buddhist era.

115. *Cūḷavaṃsa* is the name which is traditionally given to the sequel of the *Mahāvaṃsa*; the most ancient of the three sections composing it, which narrates the history of the island approximately from the fourth century to the twelfth century AD, appears to have been compiled around the thirteenth century AD cf., for example, Perera 1979, pp. 73-4.
116. Paranavitana 1960, pp. 129-55.
117. *Cūḷ.* XXXVII, 179-209.
118. Sinhalese historical work written in the thirteenth century AD, cf. Geiger 1908, pp. 8-89.
119. Levi 1900, p. 412; cf. also for other diplomatic missions (or for a different dating attributed to the same mission?), pp. 413; 415.
120. Paranavitana 1960.
121. Cf. *supra*, n. 93.
122. The reference by Wang Hiuen-ts'e is in Levi 1900, pp. 316-18; and Senaveratne 1915/1916, p. 75. Paranavitana 1962, p. 283, proposes the unlikely identification of *Chi-mi-kia-po-mo* with Upatissa.
123. Cf. N.P. Joshi, *New Light on the Gupta Era and the Chronology of the*

Early Gupta Kings, in *Vishveshvaranand Indological Journal*, 14 (1976), pp. 245-60.

124. *Cūḷ.* XXXVII, 99-105. Cf. E.R. Ayrton, *Journal of the Royal Asiatic Society*, 1911, pp. 1142-4.

125. This is a register in which were entered as many 'dots' as the number of years which had elapsed from the Buddha's *nirvāṇa.* It is said to date back to the year in which the Buddha attained *nirvāṇa,* and according to tradition Upāli himself instituted the custom of adding a 'dot' to commemorate the Buddhist festival of the *pravāraṇā.* In AD 489 the 'dots' amounted to 975. It is probable that behind this tradition there lies only a *pia fraus,* particularly when the tradition claims to attribute the institution of the 'Dotted Record' to Upāli. Yet even the most severe of critics will be unable to deny that it reflects a dating for the Buddha's *nirvāṇa* which was widespread in Sri Lanka and Indochina. The texts relating to the 'Dotted Record' are translated and discussed in Eggermont 1956, pp. 132-43; cf. also, id. *Persica* 4 (1969), pp. 94-5; id. in *Persica* 5 (1970/1), p. 69. I dissent from the theories of Pachow 1969, pp. 342-9, as it appears that the 'dot' entered in Nanking by the *bhikkhunī* Ching-hsiu was inscribed upon the copy she made in Canton of the Saṅghabhadra manuscript; the manuscript of Hung-tu (master of Vinaya in Lu-shan) is also linked to the previous manuscript, independently however, from the copy of the *bhikkhunī* Ching-hsiu; nor am I in agreement with Bechert 1986, pp. 137-40, who posits *a priori* the existence of a chronological error of approximately sixty years.

126. Cf. P. Hoang, *Concordance de chronologie néoménique chinoise et eropéenne*, Shangai 1910.

127. There are grounds, I think, for suspecting that a banal error was responsible for the further specification, in the text of Fei Chang-Fang, of the year in which the last 'dot' was entered as the cyclical year Keng-wu (eighth year Young-ming: AD 490) instead of Chi-szu. In some sense dependent on this error seems to me also the calculation which led to 1028 years being estimated between the Buddha's *nirvāṇa* and the ninth year of Ta-t'ung, the cyclical year Kuei-hai (AD 543), cf. Pachow 1969, nn. 13, 14.

It should be emphasized here that, according to tradition, Upāli entered the first 'dot' in the register on the occasion of the first commemoration of the *pravāraṇā,* i.e. only seven months—and not a full year—after the Buddha's death. The tradition of the 'Dotted Record', therefore, by attaching the number 1 to the first commemoration of the *pravāraṇā* after the *nirvāṇa*, computed time according to current years (*vartamāna*), and not according to years which had actually elapsed (*gata*). On this mode of calculating time, depending on a particular way of conceiving the sacred event, cf. Mazzarino 1966a, pp. 232 ff.

128. That the year presupposed for the Buddha's *nirvāṇa* by the author of the inscription at Anurādhapura was slightly anterior to 486 BC is also conceivable. It should be borne in mind that, in the absence of a consolidated tradition, the *nirvāṇa* could only be dated by a complicated chronological process which could, within certain limits, have produced fluctuating results. It should be recalled that even more wildly diverging dates for the Buddha's *nirvāṇa* were circulating in Sri Lanka in the fifth century AD, such as the one reported by Fa-hsien: i.e. 1497 years before his stay on the island (AD 410-11).

129. The reading of the first two *akṣara* as *nama* had been given as 'distinctly visible' in a first paper by Paranavitana himself in *Archaeological Survey of Ceylon. Administration Report*, 1952, p. 33. In the first restoration suggested by me 1. 1 was found to contain 30 *akṣara*, whereas the second one only had 24. Palaeographically, 'the lines are not of equal length, and the individual letters not of uniform size'. Both the solutions offered would be therefore legitimate, since the longest line, with Paranavitana's integrations contains 29 *akṣara*, and the shorter one 19.

130. *Cūḷ.* XXXVII, 209-47.

131. This was in a sense presupposed by Geiger 1953, II, pp. VI-VII. Moreover, we should bear in mind that Paranavitana himself (Paranavitana 1962, p. 274) identifies Mahānāma with the Sinhalese king Sirinivasa Sirisaṅghabodhi, in the twenty-sixth year of whose reign the *Sadhammapajjotikā* was written. The contradiction with the chronology of the *Cūḷavaṃsa* would be explained, according to Paranavitana, by the fact that 'as there was no legitimate occupant of the throne for some years after Mahānāma, his regnal years would have been used for dating purposes even after his death'.

132. On the question of book XI of the *Topographia Christiana*, absent in the Codex Vaticanus and described within the Codex Sinaiticus as ἕτερος λόγος ἔξωθεν τῆς βίβλου, cf. Wolska 1962, p. 26.

133. Cosm. Ind. *Top. Chr.* XI, 17. Both the episode of the 'coin contest' (see above, pp. 185-8), and Cosmas' observations on the political trends of the island and on the Persian presence in

Sri Lanka (*Top. Chr.* XI, 13-14), must be based upon information received by Sopatros the merchant. Even if we wish to assume for them a different source, it could not be very distant, culturally and chronologically speaking, from Sopatros and Cosmas; in other words, from the world of merchants who between the end of the fifth century and the beginning of the sixth century AD, could still turn their gaze toward the distant seas of the Orient. It follows, therefore, that even if the source of information on Taprobane found in *Top. Chr.* XI, 13-14 was gleaned from another merchant who may have visited Taprobane at the time of Cosmas, this would not alter the validity of the deductions we are able to make from the *Topographia Christiana* with regard to the chronology of the Sinhalese kings.

134. Cosm. Ind. *Top. Chr.* XI, 13.
135. Cf. Schwarz 1975, p. 479.
136. Once again, Schwarz, considers the chronology of the Sinhalese kings elaborated by Paranavitana to be entirely reliable, and excludes that Sopatros may have visited Sri Lanka during the 'Pandu-Invasion' (Schwarz 1975, p. 484). He is therefore led to interpret in a rather inaccurate way Cosmas' reference to the island being partitioned into two (p. 480).
137. On the links between ancient Sinhalese 'nationalism' and various aspects of modern Sinhalese nationalism, and against the hypothesis of its being due to the influence of European ideas during the colonial period, cf. Perera 1979, pp. 95-8, especially 96.
138. Cf., *supra*, n. 133.
139. Cosm. Ind. *Top. Chr.* VI, 3; cf. Wolska 1962, p. 28, n. 1.
140. Cosm. Ind. *Top. Chr.*, Prol., 1. Cf., *supra*, n. 132.
141. Cosm. Ind. *Top. Chr.* II, 56.
142. Ibid., XI, 19.
143. Levi 1900, p. 415; Senaveratne 1915/1916, p. 85.
144. The identification with Silakala, commonly accepted today precisely because the one with Kassapa I appears to be chronologically impossible, rests in fact upon very weak assumptions, cf. Geiger 1953, p. XVIII; S. Paranavitana in *Epigraphia Zeylanica*, V, pp. 98-9.
145. An outstanding example of these astronomical studies is the *Yavanajātaka* of Sphujidvaja, a Sanskrit text which D. Pingree, *The Yavanajātaka of Sphujidvaja*, Cambridge Ma. & London, 1978, has shown largely to depend upon a Greek text which reached India from Roman Egypt.
146. The name Rachias has been compared to the term *ratiya/ratika*,

which in Sinhalese inscriptions in the Brahmī alphabet of the first century AD designates an 'officer administering a territorial division called a *rata*'; in Aṅguttaranikāya III, p. 76, 300 it appears instead 'in a list of high dignitaries of the state' and indicates 'a prince having the rank of general and a hereditary title to the succession'. Cf. S. Paranavitana, *Rock Inscriptions from Labuatahandigala*, in *Epigraphia Zeylanica*, III, 1928-33, p. 252; C.W. Nicholas, *Some Offices and Titles in the Early Sinhalese Kingdom*, in *University of Ceylon Review*, 8 (1950), p. 127; Schwarz 1974b, p. 39.

147. Cf. *supra*, nt. 65.

148. Cf. P. Janni, «*Il sole a destra*»: *estrapolazione nella letteratura geografica e nei resoconti di viaggio*, in *Studi Classici e Orientali*, 28 (1978), p. 98.

149. Cf. A. Giardina, *Le merci, il tempo, il silenzio. Riceche sui miti e valori sociali nel mondo greco e romano*, in *Studi Storici*, 27 (1986), p. 298-302.

150. See above pp. 161-172.

151. H.A. *Tac.* 15, 2:

> [...] *quo tempore responsum est ab haruspicibus quandocumque ex eorum familia imperatorem Romanum futurum seu per feminam seu per uirum, qui det iudices Parthis ac Persis, qui Francos et Alamannos sub Romanis legibus habeat, qui per omnem Africam barbarum non relinquat, qui Taprobanis praesidem inponat, qui ad Iuuernam* [Purser: romanā PΣ] *insulam proconsulem mittat, qui Sarmatis omnibus iudicet, qui terram omnem, qua Oceano ambitur, captis omnibus gentibus suam faciat, postea tamen senatui reddat imperium et antiquis legibus uiuat, ipse uicturus annis centum uiginti et sine herede moriturus.*

> '[...] On this occasion the soothsayers foretold that at some future time there would be a Roman emperor from their family, descended through either the male or the female line, who would give judges to the Parthians and the Persians, subject the Franks and the Alamanni to the laws of Rome, drive out every barbarian from the whole of Africa, establish a governor at Taprobane, send a proconsul to the island of Iuverna, act as judge to all the Sarmatians, make all the land which borders on the Ocean his own territory by conquering all the tribes, but thereafter restore the power to the senate and conduct himself in accordance with the ancient laws, being destined to live for one hundred and twenty years and to die without an heir.'

On this passage, cf. A. Rösger, Princeps mundi. *Zum römischen Weltherrschaftsgedanken in der* Historia Augusta, in *Bonner Historia*

Augusta Colloquium, 15 [1979/1981], pp. 268-71.

152. On the penetration of the *negotiatores* into Ireland during the first century AD, cf. Tac. *Agr.* 24, 2: *aditus* (*sc. Hiberniae*) *portusque per commercia et negotiatores cogniti*, ('its points of access and its ports were known thanks to trade and to the merchants').

153. Cf. P. Pelliot, *La théorie des quatre fils du ciel*, in *T'oung Pao*, 22 (1923), pp. 97-123; U. Monneret de Villard, *Aksum e i quattro re del mondo*, in *Annali Lateranensi*, 12 (1948), pp. 125-80. The cosmographical effects of this doctrine extend as far as Cosmas, Cosm. Indic. *Top. Chr.* II, 45:

καί φασι οἱ Ἰνδοὶ φιλόσοφοι οἱ καλούμενοι βραχμάνες ὅτι ἐὰν βάλῃς ἀπὸ Τζίνιστα σπαρτίον, διελθεῖν διὰ Περσίδος ἕως Ῥωμανίας, ὡς ἀπὸ κανόνος τὸ μεσαίτατον τοῦ κόσμου ἐστὶν, καὶ τάχα ἀληθεύουσι.

'and the Indian philosophers known as brahmins say that if one were to throw a rope from China through Persia and reaching Rumania, like a carpenter's thread, this would be the centre of the cosmos, and perhaps they are right.'

154. Cf. W. Kirfel, *Die Kosmographie der Inder nach den Quellen dargestellt*, Leipzig 1920, p. 183.

155. A debt of gratitude to my friends L. Aimone, C. Massalini and B. Para without whose help and support the Wadi Menih expedition could not have been successful.

156. Winkler 1938-9, map.

157. It is interesting to note, for example, how a later hand 'made use of the letter O in the word ΚΑΙϹΑΡΟϹ to make up the typical sign ♀ (repeated further down to the right).

158. Reasons which are now strengthened by the observation that the two inscriptions of Lysas *A.É.* 1954 nn. 121a and 121b are situated almost opposite one another, which confers a peculiar solemnity upon the verbs (ἥκω{ι}-*ueni*) used in their respective texts.

159. Those objecting that the horizontal stroke typical of numerals is found only above the letter H and does not extend to the I in question, should note that even in ΛΕ, where it is engraved much more distinctly, the horizontal stroke is found almost entirely above the letter Λ.

The fact that the letter I runs into the letter M on the line above, could be attributed to an error of the engraver. The latter, being forced to work in a downward direction because of the height of the inscription above the ground, may have lost control of the chisel, as appears to have happened in the engraving of the first E in the word ἐπείφ.

The Dromedary of the Peticii and Trade with the East[1]

ANDRE TCHERNIA

The first stamped Roman amphora handle found in India has been recently published.[2] The stamp, *M. Livi Caustri Surus*, dated from its presence on the Grand Ribaud wreck, on the French Mediterranean coast, towards the end of the first century BC, is on the top of a Dr. 2-4 amphora handle made in the vicinity of Pompei or Sorrento in Italy. It was found in Mathura, in the State of Uttar Pradesh, about 130 km south of Delhi. At the time, Mathura was an important centre, situated at the junction of the Gangetic Valley and a route which passed through Ujjain to Barygaza in the Gulf of Cambay, one of the main ports of trade with the Roman Empire.

Mathura has thus been added to the thirty odd sites in India where one or several Roman amphora fragments have been discovered. These sites are situated for the most part either on the Tamilnadu coast, where the Arikamedu excavations made and still make it possible to find several scores of fragments, or in a large circular arc around the Gulf of Cambay which includes the States of Gujarat and Maharashtra.

The great variety of the Arikamedu amphora *facies* is truly remarkable[3] and it is likely that their contents (not only wine, but also olive oil and fish sauce) were partly meant for the consumption of the few Greeks and Romans settled there. Little is known about the typology of the amphoras found on the western coast or in the hinterland. But judging by the few available drawings, they seem to be wine amphoras, especially Dr. 2-4 or Rhodian.[4] The *Periplus of the Erythraean Sea* refers three times to the export of wine from the West to India, but on a small scale. The wines which met with the most success at Barygaza were from Italy and Laodicea in Syria.[5] Accordingly, the amphora fragments found in west or central India seem to point more towards a barter trade of western and eastern Mediterranean goods. We will have to wait for a better understanding of the archaeological material to be able to speak with greater certainty.

The question also arises of the identification of the people who actually conducted this trade; knowing the origins of the amphoras is not enough to provide an answer. The route is clear: Mediterranean goods were landed in Alexandria, then loaded onto ships which went down the Nile to Coptos, from where they were carried by camel caravans to the Red Sea ports, Myos Hormos and Berenice. From there began the long sail to India, down the Red Sea and across Arabian Sea, following increasingly direct routes. The natural inclination is to assume that, from Alexandria onwards, the Greeks or sometimes the Romans settled in Egypt took charge of cargo transfers, river and road transport and the final shipping of the goods. All written accounts suggest this – the Archive of Nicanor,[6] the papyrus of Vienna published recently,[7] and even the *Periplus of the Erythraean Sea.* L. Casson said the same thing in the commentary of his edition of the *Periplus,* adding however that the money might well have come from Rome and other major western centres and that some powerful Italian trading families had perhaps agents in Egypt.[8] The most clearcut case to date is the bilingual inscription on the wall of the Wadi Menih cave between Coptos, a port on the Nile, and Berenice, a Red Sea port. This was left by *Lysas,* a freedman of *P. Annius Plocamus,* who himself was a freedman or a member of the influential *Annii* family of Pozzuoli, the great harbour of the Italian West coast, and lived in that city.[9]

I believe I can provide another piece of evidence to show that the big traders residing in Italy sometimes had a part to play in trade and transportation to the Red Sea and beyond.

In 1989,[10] P. A. Gianfrotta brilliantly related the name engraved on a *dolium* on the Diano Marina wreck in Liguria, *Peticius Marsus,* to that of *M. Attius Peticius Marsus,* inlaid in silver at the foot of a lovely bronze statuette, a replica of the Hercules Farnese, found in the sanctuary of Hercules *Curinus*

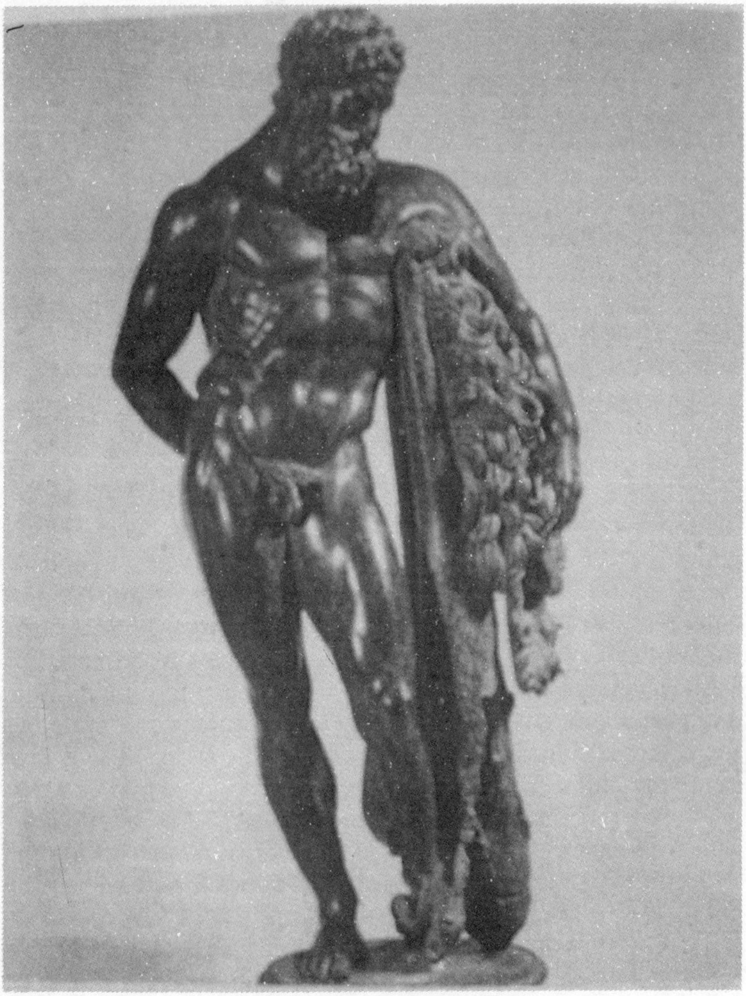

Plate 1: Silver statuette of Hercules.

near *Sulmo*[11] (Pl. 1). Both refer to the same person, and the Diano Marina wreck inscription makes us think that he was a wine merchant, around the middle of the first century AD and perhaps also a shipowner. That he donated a statue of Hercules, protector of merchants, is hardly surprising.

Towards the end of his article, Gianfrotta outlines a study of the other *Peticii* identifiable as traders. The first is the wheat merchant who, in 48 BC, soon after Caesar's victory at Pharsalia, received aboard his ship Pompey the Great as he was making his escape on a small boat. The reference to him is only through his *nomen.*[12] A *C. Peticius* appears later in the inscription painted on an amphora of the Byrsa hill 'wall' in Carthage.[13] The consular dates noted on the amphoras of this collection range from 43 to 15 BC, most of them (nine out of twelve) dating from 22 BC onwards.[14] This however does not completely exclude the possibility of the person mentioned in the inscriptions being none other than the temporary saviour of Pompey. Finally, Gianfrotta emphasizes the particularly interesting discovery of a rock inscription with the name of *C. Peticius* in the Hammamat Valley in Egypt on the route from Coptos, a port on the Nile, to Quseir-el-Qadim, a Red Sea Port, the ancient Myos Hormos.

The inscription, later printed in *CIL*, III, 1, 29, comes from Letronne's famous ancient collection.[15] More recently, it has been republished by A. Bernand.[16] In fact there is a double signature in Latin and Greek on the wall of Wadi Hammamat's *Paneion*, a rock shelter in a narrow pass where many travellers have left *proskynemas* or simply signed their name to show their obeisance to the God *Pan* and other divinities worshipped there (Pls. 2 and 3). The oldest date noted is probably AD 9 and the most recent AD 238, but the majority (twelve out of twenty-one) point to the rule of Tiberius. In any case, the absence of *cognomen* leads us to believe that the signature of *Peticius* could not be later than this period. There are few Latin inscriptions on this rockshelter. In Letronne's time, the *Peticius* inscription was the only Latin one, as against eighty-eight Greek ones. A. Bernand provided four more Latin inscriptions, making a total of five out of the hundred and two *Paneion* inscriptions he published. The only bilingual inscription is that of *Peticius.* Moreover, as A. Bernand has observed, there are on the whole

Plate 2: Latin inscription of Peticius at Wadi Hammamat
(Photo G. Réveillac, CNRS)

few bilingual Greek and Latin inscriptions in Egypt, one of which is that of the freedman of *P. Annius Plocamus.* Carefully written with punched letters, the inscriptions are 45 to 65 mm high (Pls. 2 and 3). 'The size and the care taken to repeat his name in two languages are perhaps proof of the fact that he was an important person, but he has not stated his position', concludes A. Bernand. The temptation is great to think that the name on this inscription and the *C. Peticius* on the Carthage amphora refer to the same person, in which case he was obviously a merchant.

We thus have a total of four or perhaps three individuals belonging to the *Peticius* family. A wheat merchant of the middle of the first century BC whose first name is not known; another merchant, probably a wine merchant,[17] of the triumvirate period or the beginning of the rule of Augustus; a prominent traveller between Coptos and Quseir, at the end of Augustus' rule or that of Tiberius: both the characters are called *C. Peticius*; a leading wine merchant of the middle of the first century AD, *M. Peticius Marsus,* who was adopted by one *Attius.* Chronologically the first and the second could be the same person but this would make him both a wine and a wheat merchant, a combination which epigraphical evidence so far available does not seem to attest. Two and three might have been one and the same person, provided his career lasted that long, for the Carthage amphora must be twenty to thirty years earlier than the Wadi Hammamat inscription. Perhaps this is too long a period for *C. Peticius* to be still active enough to be travelling across the Egyptian desert. I am, therefore, of the view that four generations of *Peticii* have been attested over a century, and this is quite normal. The first *Peticius* dealt in wheat, the second and fourth in wine; between the Nile and the Red Sea, the third looked after the transport of goods intended for the east. The end of Augustus and Tiberius' rule saw this trade flourish, and it is to this very period that the Mathura amphora belongs. If we stretch our imagination a little further, the *C. Peticius* of the Wadi Hammamat could well be the young son of the *C. Peticius* of the Carthage amphora, acting as an agent for his aged father who was content to stay behind in his Marsic country.

The national archaeological museum of Chieti, where the

Plate 3: Greek inscription of Peticius at Wadi Hammamat.

bronze Hercules statuette of the Sulmo temple is exhibited, also houses a bas-relief fragment depicting on the upper half—somewhat unexpectedly in the Abruzzi—a dromedary bearing two wine amphoras,[18] driven by a small figure wearing a tunic; on the lower half six men in toga (although on the right only a fragment of the sixth remains) and one woman are aligned frontally (Pl. 4).

This bas-relief, 1 m wide and 95 cm high, was published by Pietro Romanelli in 1945.[19] It was re-used in a courtyard wall of the palace of Dragonetti de Torres in L'Aquila and its exact origin is not known: Romanelli thought of Amiterno or *Peltuinum*. The pilaster element on the right delimits a space either open (a window) or closed (the epigraphical field), beneath which the line of people continued—about fifteen in total according to Romanelli—whereas another representation to the right of the bas-relief formed the matching piece to the dromedary. The entire work must have been part of a funeral monument. The close fitting togas may be put in the *Ab* category ('Pallium-Typus'), using the typology recently furnished by H.R. Goette,[20] who includes the L'Aquila bas-relief among the representations he dates from the last quarter of the first century BC.

The amphora-bearing dromedary evidently refers to the family business or to that of certain members of the family who had the funeral monument built. Romanelli rightly concluded that it must be a 'family or a corporation (but the presence of a woman makes the first hypothesis more plausible than the second) who specialized in this trade'. 'Neither the inscriptions discovered so far in Amiterno', he added, 'nor the literary texts which speak of this town shed any light on this matter'.

But the image of the amphora-bearing dromedary is a perfect illustration of the kind of transport *C. Peticius* supervised between Coptos and Myos Hormos. L'Aquila is about sixty kilometres from the temple of Hercules *Curinus*. If we base ourselves on Romanelli's hypothesis for the place of discovery of the bas-relief, Amiterno is a little further away but *Peltuinum* is much closer. All these sites are part of the Aterno and Gizio basins. Although the most likely place where the dromedary stone was found is probably not within the Marsic or Paelignian territory, it cannot have been very far from there. Moreover,

Plate 4: Bas-relief at L'Aquila (Photo Soprintendenza Archelogica dell'Abruzzo-Chieti).

though the name of the *Peticii* is particularly attested in the *Sulmo* and *Corfinium* region, it is also found at *Peltuinum*, and the *Attii* are as well represented in Amiterno as in *Corfinium* and *Sulmo*. Unfortunately, we lack evidence to put forward any theory on the *Attii* who adopted *M. Peticius Marsus* and the reasons behind this adoption. In any case, the bas-relief is prior to the time of this person. It must be contemporary with the active period of *C. Peticius* of the Carthage amphora; it may also have been contemporary with the beginning of the active period of the *C. Peticius* who left his name in the Wadi Hammamat rockshelter.

In all probability, therefore, the dromedary belonged to a funeral monument of the *Peticii* family. Otherwise, one would have to assume that another trading dynasty, settled nearby, carried out the same trade at the same time, namely transporting wine to the East.

All the documents we have reviewed complement each other and the picture that emerges is one of a rich merchant family of central Italy, which specialized in the wine trade from the time of Augustus and, among other things, wine trade with the East.[21] But, we might ask, why did they make the effort to accompany their amphoras personally across the Egyptian desert to the Red Sea? Surely it was not to sell their wine in the unimportant markets of Myos Hormos or Berenice, within a monetary economy and at a price only slightly higher than in Rome. As always, when it is a question of trade beyond the frontiers of the empire, we must not forget that the exporters were also importers. If *C. Peticius* supervised his wine amphoras in Wadi Hammamat, he must have kept a much more watchful eye on his packets of pepper and caskets of pearls that were coming along the same route from the other direction. Wine was one of the articles used to buy pepper and pearls, and the *Peticii* made their fortune out of this unequal commerce, or to be more precise, out of the value that the Tamils attached to the perfumed wines of the Yavanas, on the one hand, and from the craze for pepper and pearls among the Romans and their wives on the other. They were wine merchants in Italy and perhaps in the western Mediterranean, and that is how they were viewed by the landowners who sold them their grape crops. However, it was the trade in spices and precious stones that really accounted for their money and success. Very often we overlook this aspect of the merchants' activity, because both the sources and historians dwell on the sale of produce, and because agricultural products have, thanks to amphoras, left behind archaeological traces. But the fortune that was amassed under Augustus, which several decades later made it possible to dedicate a lovely statue to Hercules, came from trade with the East, managed directly from Italy. That is what is signified by the amphora-bearing dromedary, which is also an expression of pride for taking part in a great commercial venture whose beginnings, at the time of the bas-relief, belonged to a still very recent past.

NOTES

1. I am grateful to the archaeological superintendency of Abruzzo for having sent me a photograph of the L'Aquila bas-relief and giving me the permission to publish it. I would also like to thank in particular Miss Honor Frost, who, many years ago drew my attention to this bas-relief and sent a sketch of it to me.
2. M.C. Joshi, A.K. Sinha, *Discovery of an Amphora-handle from Mathura, in Indian Archaelogical Heritage, Shri K.V. Soundara Rajan Festschrift,* Delhi, 1990, pp. 255-8; E. Lyding Will, *The Mediterranean Shipping Amphoras of Arikamedu,* in Begley, De Puma, 1991, pp. 151-6. The correct reading is *[M.] Liui Caustri / Sur(us)*: see A. Hesnard, M.B. Carre, M. Rival, B. Dangréaux, *L'épave romaine Grand Ribaud D (Hyères, Var),* in *Archaeonautica,* 8, Paris, 1988, pp. 49-50 and pl. XXII; and H.M. Cotton, J. Geiger, *Masada II,* Jerusalem, 1989, pl. 48, no. 960 .
3. E. LydingWill, 1991, cit. and V. Begley, *New investigations at the port of Arikamedu,* in *JRA,* 6, 1993, pp. 93-108.
4. H.D. Sankalia, *Imported Mediterranean Amphorae from Kolhapur,* in *Journal of the Royal Asiatic Society,* 1957, pp. 207-8; H.D. Sankalia, S. Erhardt, *From History to Prehistory at Nevasa (1954-1956),* Poona, 1960, pp. 314-15, Figs. 45 and 46.
5. *Periplus Maris Erythraei,* 39, 49, 56.
6. *O. Petrie,* 220-304, published by J.G. Tait, *Greek Ostraka in the Bodleian Library at Oxford,* London, 1930. See A. Fuks, *Notes on the Archive of Nicanor,* in *The Journal of Juristic Papyrology,* 5, 1951, pp. 207-16.
7. Latest edition: Casson, 1990. See p. 275, n. 33.
8. Casson, 1989, pp. 31-4.

9. Meredith, 1953, Bernand, 1977, no. 65; Camodeca, 1979; De Romanis, above, pp. 167-172.
10. P. Gianfrotta, *Eracle, Peticio e il commercio marittimo*, in *Dalla villa di Ovido al santuario di Ercole*, Sulmona, 1989, pp. 177-83.
11. See in the same volume P. Moreno, *Attribuzione Lisippea del bronzo di Eracle in riposo*, pp. 159-67 (with bibliography); P. Moreno, *Vita e arte di Lisippo*, Milan, 1987.
12. Caesar, *BC*, III, 96 and Plutarch, *Pompey*, 73, 3, 6.
13. *CIL*, VII, 22640, 65.
14. A. Dclattre, *Le mur à amphores de la colline Saint-Louis à Carthage*, in *BCTH*, 1894, pp. 89-119. The inscription of *C. Peticius*: no. 20, p. 102.
15. A. Letronne, *Recueil des inscriptions grecques et latines de l'Egypte*, Paris, 1842, no. 468.
16. A. Bernand, *De Koptos à Kosseir*, Leyde, 1972, nos. 120 and 121, pp. 195-6.
17. The overwhelming majority of identifiable painted inscriptions and stamps published by Delattre refer to wine and wine amphoras.
18. It is difficult to identify the oval object behind the two amphoras. Its dimensions are such that it cannot be a third amphora upside down.
19. P. Romanelli, *Un rilievo inedito di L'Aquila*, in *BCACR*, Supplement to vol. 71, 1943-5, pp. 3-8.
20. H.R. Goette, *Studien zu römischen Togadarstellungen*, Mainz, 1990, pp. 28 and 109, no. 61.
21. This does not preclude the possibility of their having followed other activities, including those related to production: P.A Gianfrotta suggests cattle breeding, and he will come back to this question.

Winds and Coins: From the Supposed Discovery of the Monsoon to the *Denarii* of Tiberius

ANDRE TCHERNIA

Whenever there is any discussion of trade between the Greco-Roman world and India, the discovery of the monsoon is usually mentioned and generally credited to the pilot *Hippalus*, who is for many 'one of the great names in the history of navigation'.[1] The term 'discovery', however, has long been criticized. Sailors do not discover a wind and they do not invent anything when they make use of it; they merely sail with it when it takes them where they want to go. As far back as 1879, Kennedy stressed that the monsoon was common knowledge long before the disputed date when the Greeks, towards the end of the Hellenistic era or at the beginning of the Roman Empire, are supposed to have experienced it: 'The monsoons must have been known from the earliest times to all who sailed along the African and Arabian coast, and the normal trade route from the Persian Gulf to India can never have been along the inhospitable shore of Gedrosia.'[2]

The two texts on which the idea of a Greek or Roman discovery of the monsoon is built are the *Periplus of the Erythraean Sea* and the end of Book VI of the Elder Pliny's *Natural History*. A recent study of the latter, however, has thrown fresh light on the subject— of which the following are the key passages:[3]

XXVI [96] Sed priusquam generatim haec persequamur, indicari conuenit quae prodidit Onesicritus classe Alexandri circumuectus in mediterranea Persidis ex India, enarrata proxime a Iuba, deinde eam nauigationem quae his annis comperta seruatur hodie. [...]

[100] [...] Postea ab Syagro Arabiae promunturio Patalen fauonio, quem hypalum ibi uocant, peti certissimum uidebatur, XIII (centena milia) XXXII (milia) p(assuum) aestimatione.

[101] Secuta aetas propiorem cursum tutioremque iudicauit, si ab eodem promunturio Zigerum portum Indiae peteret, diuque ita nauigatum est, donec conpendia inuenit mercator lucroque India admota est: quippe omnibus annis nauigatur. [...]

[104] Indos autem petentibus utilissiumum est ab Oceli egredi; inde uento hippalo navigant diebus XL ad primum emporium Indiae Muzirim.

XXVI [96]. But before we go on to a detailed account of these countries, it is suitable to indicate the facts reported by Onesicritus after sailing with the fleet of Alexander round from India to the interior of Persia, and quite recently related in detail by Juba, and then to state the sea-route that has been ascertained in recent times and is followed at the present day. [...]

[100] [...] Subsequently, it was thought that the safest line was to start from Ras Fartak in Arabia with the favonius (the native name for which in those parts is Hypalus) and make for Patale, the distance being reckoned at 1,332 miles.

[101] The following period considered it a shorter and safer route to start from the same cape and steer for the Indian harbour of Sigerus, and for a long time this was the course followed, until a merchant discovered a shorter route and the desire for gain brought India nearer; indeed the voyage is made every year. [...]

[104] The most advantageous way of sailing to India is to set out from Ocelis. From that port, it is a 40 days' voyage, with the *Hippalus* blowing, to the first trading station in India, Muziris.

In section 100, I have followed Santo Mazzarino,[4] in adopting the reading *Hypalus*, based on the combined spelling of two manuscripts, rather than the emendation *Hippalus*, which has been wrongly accepted by all editors since Hardouin (1685), who was influenced by the double *p* in *vento hippalo* in section 104. Calling a wind '*hypalus*' means in Greek that it comes 'from under the sea', and the idea that a wind can begin from the depths of the sea (as others come from the exhalations of the earth) was not strange in Antiquity. Discussing the ways to predict the weather, the Elder Pliny says that, 'Often also the sea swells in silence and, blown up in unusually high waves, confesses that the winds are now inside it' (XVIII, 359; trans. H. Rackham). Some winds originate from greater depths than others: for this reason the *auster* whips up larger waves than the *aquilo* (II, 228). In the seventeenth century, Ralph Bohun, in an interesting *Discourse Concerning the Origin and Properties of Wind* (Oxford, 1671, p.10), once again considered the generation of winds by the sea or the land to be one of their several origins. As Mazzarino has pointed out, the idea of wind generated by the sea seems to be suitable for the southwest monsoon which blows from the open sea.

On the other hand, in section 104 the reading *hippalus* is in all likelihood the correct one. This is because Pliny's text is based on two different sources which, as was his habit, he transcribed carefully without trying to reconcile them. In section 96 Pliny announces an account divided in two parts. The first derived from Juba (first century BC), who was making use of older sources—probably Nearchus, towards the end of the fourth century, describing the return voyage of Alexander's fleet; the second is a description of the voyage towards south India in the time of Pliny. Thanks to Federico de Romanis, we know that this information was furnished to Pliny by traders between AD 49-52.[5] Between these two parts, Pliny inserts, in sections 100-1, six lines to describe two intermediate voyages which went further northwards. The first (section 100) went to the mouth of the Indus, and the other (section 101) to the western coast of the Deccan. The spelling *hypalus*, in section 100, means that this section was coupled with the earlier section (96-9), which pushes back its origin to the Hellenistic sources of Juba. Otherwise, Pliny spells it *hippalus* when he records contemporary information.

In this way Pliny's text helps us trace the transformation of a term which, because its original components were forgotten, was thought to be derived from a proper noun with a similar spelling. So was born the myth of the pilot Hippalus about whom the author of the *Periplus of the Erythraean Sea*, a Greco-

Egyptian merchant who sailed in the middle of the first century AD,[6] provides us with the other key:

In the past, smaller vessels sailed along the coast from Kanè and Eudaemon Arabia (Aden) following the coastal route that we have just described; the pilot *Hippalus* was the first, after giving thought to the location of the ports and the shape of the sea, to find the route on the high seas. Thereafter, since in this region Etesian winds coming from the sea blow seasonally just as they do in our countries, the south-west wind seems to be called Hippalos, after the first navigator to have discovered the direct sea route.[7]

This passage is an obvious clue to understanding Pliny's text and constitutes the basis of the traditional interpretation.

However, while the text indicates that Hippalus must have given his name to the wind used for the crossing, neither the existence of this wind nor the way in which it was used were regarded by the author of the *Periplus* as the discovery of the mythical pilot: his role was that he was the first to open *ton dia pelagous ploun* (or later *ton diaploun*), that is, the crossing of the open sea, after observing neither the South-West nor the North-East monsoon seasons, but the 'location of the ports and the shape of the sea'. Those who wished to interpret this passage as the discovery of the monsoon were obliged to stretch the meaning of the text.[8] That is true of the two pioneering books by Rawlinson and Charlesworth, whose influence was considerable, in which they claimed that Hippalus had observed the periodicity of the monsoon. A more recent example is the book by Sir Mortimer Wheeler,[9] another authoritative work, in which he translated *schèma thalassès* as 'the condition of the sea' (although twenty years earlier Warmington translated the phrase more literally as 'the shape of the sea') and wrote that, 'without [Hippalus'] discovery, or at least his popularization of the monsoon as a dependable aid to deep-sea voyaging, regular trade with India would have been impossible'. In reality, no ancient text has ever said any such thing. To repeat Curtin's particularly scathing criticism:[10] 'The story is obvious Roman ethnocentric nonsense'. But I would add just one correction: it was not the Romans who indulged in such ethnocentric nonsense but modern commentators.

In point of fact, the Greeks knew of the monsoon

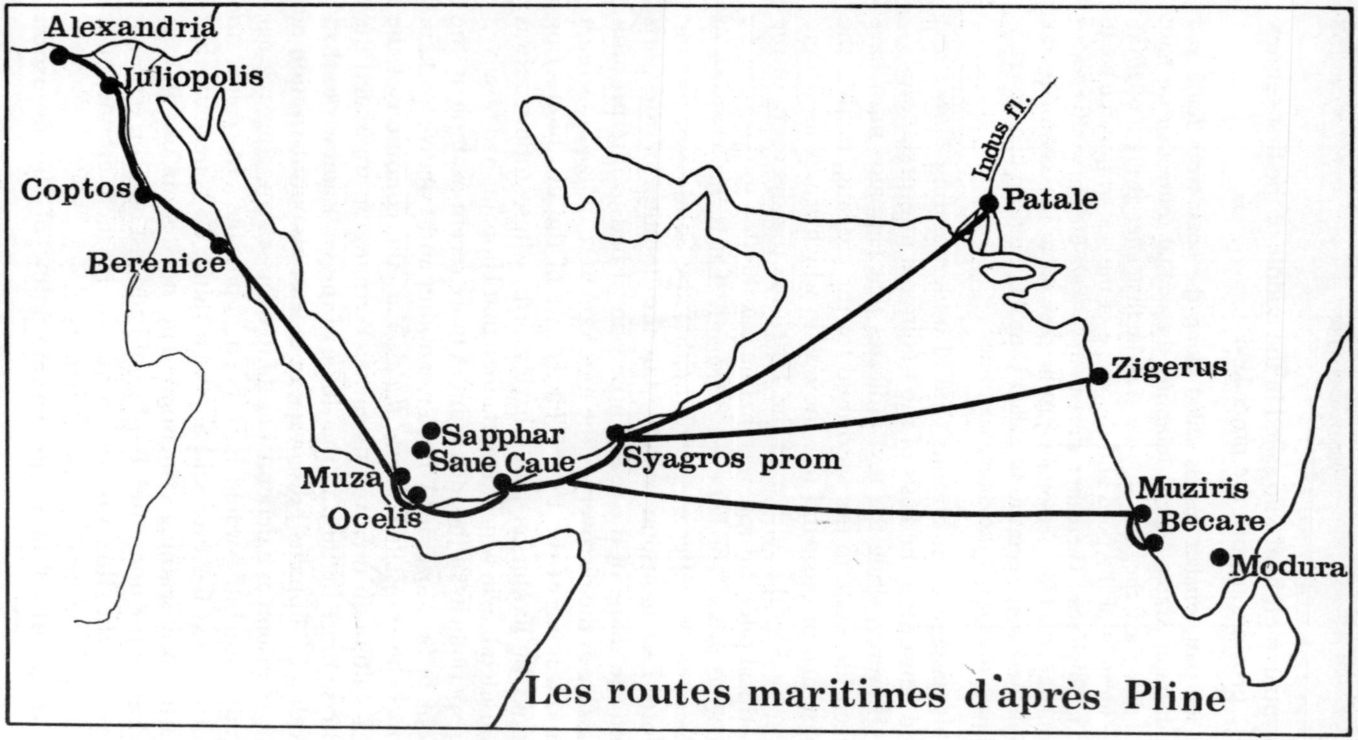

Map 1: Maritime routes according to Pliny, on a modern map.

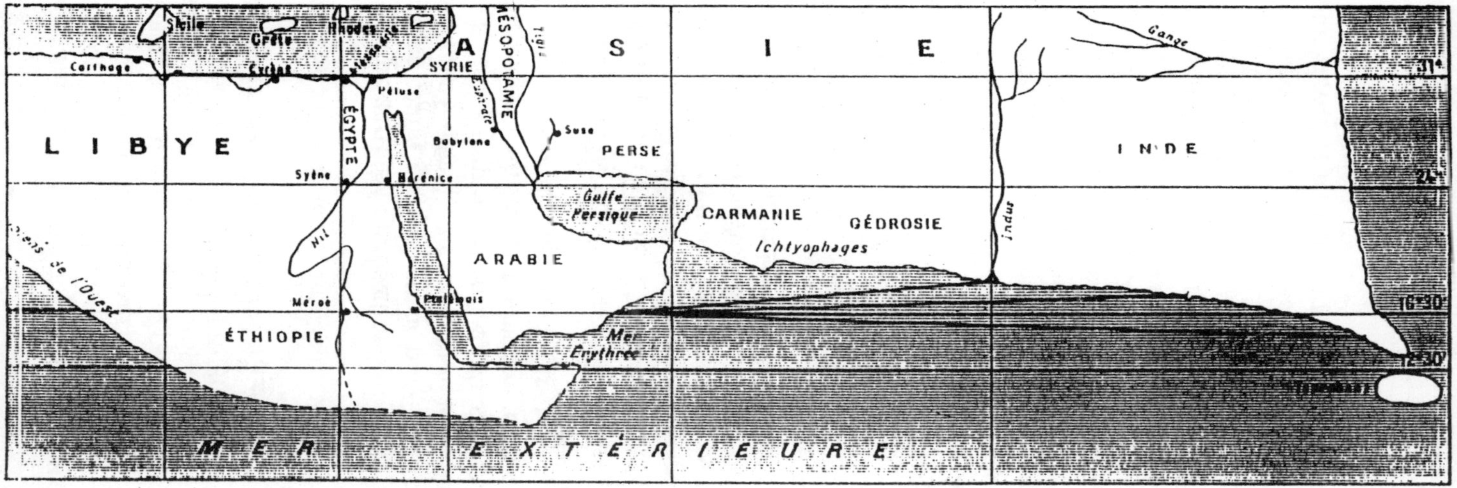

Map 2: The same, on a map according to Strabo's geography.

independently of the mythical feat of Hippalus, and the oldest Greek sources which describe it are concerned not with navigation but with the climate of India. Alexander's army experienced the monsoon while coming down from the Paropamisadae and around Taxila. Aristobulos, who took part in the expedition, made a careful study of its features as early as the end of the fourth century BC. 'In the time of the Etesian winds', he says, 'the rains pour inceasingly and violently from the clouds, both day and night, until the rising of Arcturus' [that is till mid September]. He also noticed the contrast between the rains of the Himalayan foothills and the drought in Sind. Arrian later showed that Nearchus, while bringing back Alexander's fleet, was held up at Patala on the Indus by the Etesian winds blowing from the south and the open sea, which prevented him from navigating along the Gedrosian coast.[11] Nearchus had to wait for the northeast monsoon before he could set sail.

Though the Greeks had experienced right from the start of the Hellenistic era what the *Periplus* considered an example of the Etesian winds specific to the Indian Ocean, Pliny's text, as well as the description in the *Periplus* of the transition from coastal navigation to ocean navigation and the vague portrayal of the pilot Hippalus, illustrates clearly an important event for Greco-Egyptian traders and sailors: the opening up of a sea route which no longer went all round the southern coast of Arabia. Instead of just cutting across the Gulf of Oman, it went much more directly towards the Indian coast—either to the Gulf of Cambay or to the Deccan, which meant a long crossing of the open sea—and made possible direct trading between Egypt and India without having to use Arabian ports as transit points.[12]

We need to examine the circumstances that lead to the opening of this route.

The winds do not seem to be an essential element. Sailors used them according to the techniques at their disposal. What really makes a navigator venture on the high seas along an uncharted route is the conviction that he will finally reach his destination. This was the real strength of Christopher Columbus, whom no one credits with having discovered the trade winds. Columbus never doubted for a minute that his caravels would land at Cipango or India. As Bartolomeo de Las Casas wrote, 'when he made up his mind, he was as sure of discovering what he discovered and of finding what he found as if he had kept it locked in his room'.[13] But the author of *Historia de las Indias* hints at several explanations for such a deeply rooted conviction, which have ever since been the subject of endless speculation. Was it his faith in the geographical and cartographic work that was the legacy of Marinus Tyrius, that is, the theories of Pierre d'Ailly, Martin Behaim and especially Toscanelli, which shortened the distance of the western route towards India? Or was it the secret he learnt from an 'unknown pilot'? Columbus' biographers can only speculate between these two possibilities.[14] The ancient sources present the historian of Antiquity with exactly the same kind of choice, only this time he has to choose between two figures: the mythical *Hippalus* or the adventurous explorer Eudoxus of Cyzicus.

When the author of the *Periplus of the Erythraean Sea* specifies that the direct route across the Indian Ocean came to be known after observation of the 'location of the ports and the shape of the sea', he saw a geographical reason for this new sea route. Eratosthenes towards the end of the third century BC, and even Strabo, who relied upon him, thought that the coast from the mouth of the Indus to Cape Comorin faced squarely south. Modern historians and editors have delighted in tracing on the current map of the Indian Ocean the various sea routes indicated by Pliny and the *Periplus*: the differences and advantages of each are quite obvious (Map 1). The results of such an exercise would be far less clear on the map of the world as seen by Strabo (Map 2) or even Ptolemy, who, though he was better acquainted with the location of the Gulfs of Kutch and Cambay, considered them to be the southernmost extension of India. It is important for our purpose to note that a passage of the *Periplus of the Erythraean Sea* (section 51) locates the cities more accurately than Ptolemy: Paithan is twenty days' journey south from Barygaza, the port on the Gulf of Cambay (the actual distance is about 400 km, which accords with the estimate in the *Periplus*), whereas Ptolemy thought it was a little to the north of Barygaza. Greco-Egyptian sailors and traders, therefore, had an empirical knowledge of the orientation of the Indian peninsula, something most geographers failed to record. Poseidonios was the only one to have correctly oriented the Indian coast along a north-south axis.[15] It is the acquisition of this knowledge that the *Periplus* credits the pilot Hippalus with.

Dihle[16] brought out forcefully what for him was the almost automatic effect on navigation of the knowledge of this north-south orientation of the Indian coast. The advantages of the ocean route became apparent and sailors no longer feared missing India and getting lost in the vast ocean that covered the end of the earth. He believed that with the Bactrian Greeks settling in India, such a realisation was bound to occur. Right from the early decades of the second century BC, the decline of the Mauryan Empire had made northwest India an easy prey for the Bactrian Greeks. In the middle of the second century BC and the ensuing years, Eukratides, though soon assassinated, and Menander occupied a large part of North India, initiating the creation of a number of Indo-Bactrian kingdoms which flourished for a long time after the fall of Aï-Khanoum in 145 BC.[17] Menander's kingdom spread over Sind, including the Indus port of Patala, Gujarat and perhaps Barygaza.[18] Patala and Barygaza were the Indian ports most directly in contact with the Arabian Gulf. Dihle continued with his demonstration by examining the texts for traces or proof of information gathered by the Greeks about the coast further south. Though such evidence is rather flimsy,[19] the probabilities are in favour of his hypothesis. Trade had already linked north- and south-western India.[20] Masters of the main Indus port and of a part—a sizeable part, perhaps—of the coast, the Bactrian Greeks settled in India inevitably came to know of the shores further south and they perhaps even explored them.

It remains to be ascertained how the geographical information so gathered was transmitted to the Ptolemaic kingdom. Dihle does not address the issue. On the other hand, since he considers this information to be the reason for Eudoxus of Cyzicus's expedition (to which I shall come back shortly), Dihle mixes the 'Hippalian' version of direct navigation (and its geographical origins) with that of Poseidonios, for whom the Eudoxus expedition was guided by a shipwrecked Indian. If we believe the evidence of the *Periplus* to be proof enough of the fact that the new geographical knowledge was spread chiefly among traders and navigators, we will have to look at the contacts between people of north Indian and Egyptian harbours.

The *Periplus* (section 26) describes the prosperity of Eudaemon Arabia (Aden) before the time of the direct crossings, when the port acted as a meeting point and warehouse for ships that had set sail from Egypt but were not going to India, and for ships that had left from India but were going no further than the southern coast of Arabia. Once Patala fell into the hands of the Greeks, the Indo-Bactrians must have come into contact with the Greco-Egyptians. The transmission of information, therefore, would have been only natural, as well as the desire by the Greeks to avoid Arabian ports and sailors. Exchanges in Greek between Indian and Egyptian traders and navigators lead to direct crossings which were attributed later on to the mythical Hippalus.

In contrast with the version that I have reconstructed, Poseidonios, with his strange adventures of Eudoxus of Cyzicus, puts forward the hypothesis of an 'unknown pilot'. Towards the end of the rule of Ptolemy VIII Euergetes (182-116 BC), he recounts, the coast guards of the Red Sea found a shipwrecked Indian at death's door and took him to the king. After learning Greek, he told them that, while sailing from India, his ship went off course. All his companions had died of hunger and he was the only survivor who ended up somehow at the place where they found him. Grateful to them for having saved his life, he offered to act as 'the guide of the navigators chosen by the king for the crossing to India'. Among those selected was Eudoxus of Cyzicus, who had for some time been part of the king's entourage, and had developed a keen interest, as geographer and ethnographer, in the regions of the Upper Nile. Hence the expedition has come to be named after him.[21]

Many ingredients are common to Eudoxus' adventure and to that of the 'unknown pilot', a story which was current in Hispaniola, and then in Spain, after Columbus' voyages. During Columbus' stay at Madeira, he is said to have met the captain of a ship who, having been swept along by the storm during his voyage from Portugal to England or Flanders, reached a distant western island from where he managed somehow to come back, although very ill. Despite Columbus' ministrations, the unknown pilot died, but, while breathing his last, revealed to Columbus the exact information about his route and the island he had discovered.

All in all, there are two parallel sets of explanations for the Egypt-India crossing (which, we must not forget, did not lead to a new land) and for the discovery of America. We cannot hope to reconcile them. In fact, if you take an unknown route, there are only two ways of getting to where you want to reach: either you find a guide, or, basing yourself on the information available, you try and work out the direction and the distance. Ancient history sometimes prefers the easy way out and hence there was an attempt[22]—often well received—to combine the two versions by making Hippalus the pilot of Eudoxus' expedition. 'A simple solution, too simple perhaps', as Raschke wrote, 'and one which can never be verified'.[23] The result of this was muddling up the geographical hypothesis and that of the unknown pilot, both of which had in any case been blurred by the idea of the 'discovery of the monsoon'. By making Hippalus vanish from the history of navigation, Mazzarino excludes this theory, at least in the way it is presented.

The point we need to retain is that there was established, probably during the second half of the second century BC, a sea route across the Indian Ocean. This happened when navigators realized that, by following the same parallel (even Mediterranean sailors knew how to do this by using the stars to navigate[24]), from the Masirah island (referred to as Sarapis in the *Periplus*, north of which the description of the Arabian coast becomes extremely vague), one could enter the Gulf of Cambay, or they could go from Cape Guardafui to Lymirikè.[25] This crossing had been prepared as early as the second century BC or perhaps even the third century BC by Indian and Arab navigators who had increased the number of sea routes in the northern Indian Ocean. Good evidence for this can be found in Agatharchides' passage about the Fortunate Islands (in all probability Socotra, which is derived from the Sanskrit *Sukhatara dvipa*, 'the most pleasant island'): he regards them as a place where merchant ships met from Persia, Carmania and neighbouring countries, but mostly from Patala on the Indus. The various routes did not all come into use at the same time:

there was a gradually increasing flow of traffic towards south India, where pepper, pearls and beryls were loaded. But one always sailed with the same wind,[26] and the monsoon only regulated the seasonal character of the crossings.

Several accounts attest to the fact that from the end of the second or the beginning of the first century BC relations between India and Egypt were easier and more frequent. It is not true to say that there is a complete absence of Ptolemaic coins in India. Berghaus noticed a few dozen of them, along with coins from Asia Minor, and we must not forget that most were bronze coins which caused less attention and were not as well preserved as gold or silver coins.[27] Two amphoras from Arikamedu bearing Cnidian stamps were published recently,[28] which probably date from the beginning of the first century BC. Isotopic analysis makes us think that western Mediterranean lead was used in the coins found in Central Deccan before the Satavahanas.[29] Finally, it has long been observed that the existence in the Egyptian Thebaid of an 'epistrategos of the Erythraean Sea and the Indian Sea', at the latest in 62 BC, (or maybe at the latest in 74/73),[30] furnishes a good *terminus ante quem* for Lagid interests in the Indian Ocean.

Strabo, who went to Egypt at the time when Aelius Gallus was the prefect between 27-24 BC, spoke eloquently of the second stage in the development of this trade and of the quantitative leap it took after the Roman conquest of Egypt: 'Up to a hundred and twenty ships make their way under sail from Myos Hormos for India, whereas previously, under the reign of the Ptolemies, very few people dared to launch their ships and trade in Indian goods.'[31] This is a well known text and though one might have some reservations about the figure of a hundred and twenty ships, the general tone is quite plausible in the light of the unbridled taste for luxury in Rome and the success that exotic goods—pepper, silk and pearls in particular—enjoyed there. But I believe we can identify, some thirty years after the stage so well described by Strabo, a third phase of trade, that of Italian traders and silver *denarii*, which may be none other than the last of the phases described by Pliny.

In 1979 Paul Veyne,[32] by way of introduction to his brilliant critique of the theory of an automatic return to equilibrium in international trade, examined the two well known passages of Pliny the Elder's *Natural History* concerning the haemorrhage of gold: 'In no year does India absorb less than fifty million sesterces of our empire's wealth, sending back merchandise to be sold with us at a hundred times its prime cost' (VI, 26, 101, trans. H. Rackham). 'By the lowest reckoning India, China and the Arabian Peninsula take from our Empire 100 million sesterces every year—that is the sum which our luxuries and our women cost us' (XII, 41, 84). Pliny, Veyne explains, was certainly well informed, and his figures, based on the Roman customs revenues, cannot be seriously called into question. But while keeping in mind the price of eastern merchandise entering the Roman empire, Pliny did not take into account the price of goods exported to India, since he was not concerned with the problem of balance of trade. He was thinking as a member of a society in which autarky was highly valued. That is why one cannot rely on these passages to argue that the Roman Empire was suffering from a massive haemorrhage of precious metal.

It is difficult to challenge the basic ideas of this argument. However, they can be, and have been, qualified to some extent. As Veyne has shown, Pliny's information could only have been based on what he gathered from the customs services. Ever since the publication of the Vienna papyrus *P. Vindob. G. 40822*[33], dating from the middle of the second century AD, which has preserved a part of the inventory of an Indian cargo and a part of a loan agreement in connection with its transport, we have evidence that a 25 per cent duty was levied on goods coming from India into Egypt. But we also know that this tax was applied to a conventional price fixed for each product. This was certainly not the price Western traders paid to the Indians, which probably no one on the other side of the Ocean knew exactly. The conventional price must have been closer to the price of the goods at the time they were loaded in Alexandria on Mediterranean ships heading for Rome and the Western Mediterranean, in other words, a price much higher than that paid by traders in India. However, custom taxes in the Roman Empire were levied both on imported and exported goods and there is reason to believe that Pliny's figure was based on the sum of taxes paid on Roman exports, which provided him the information he needed for his purpose. Rather than from the *portorium* accounting offices, he probably retrieved it from the amount paid out for the farming of these taxes: this, as he himself says (VI, 84), was the practice for the *portorium* of the Erythraean Sea.

Bartered goods certainly existed and the *Periplus* draws up a list of such goods. But as André and De Romanis have already stressed, the sources leave us in no doubt about the importance of coins in that period. Regarding trade with Arabia, Pliny (VI, 162) makes it clear that the Arabians sold to the Romans and the Parthians without buying anything from them in exchange and in India there is a Tamil text which speaks of Romans coming with gold and going back with pepper.[34] The *Periplus of the Erythraean Sea* mentions gold and silver coins as one of the recommended goods for trade in all the major Indian ports, especially in the southern ones: 'mainly, a great amount of money' (sections 39, 49, 56). I would add that one cannot help comparing Pliny's second text with the letter attributed by Tacitus to the emperor Tiberius, replying to the Senate in AD 22 asking him to decide on the wisdom of promulgating a new sumptuary law (*Ann.* III, 53): 'For on what am I to make my first effort at prohibition and reversion to our ancient standard? [...] The promiscuous dress of male and female—and the specially female extravagance by which, for the sake of jewels, our wealth is transported to alien or hostile countries?' Like Tiberius, Pliny too associated the luxury of jewels with the idea of a massive outflow of money, and while deploring this fact, launched a scathing attack against women. Either Pliny was directly influenced by an idea actually expressed in Tiberius' discourse or it was a *topos* widely used in the middle decades of the first century, or more precisely, an adaptation of an old *topos* on luxury and autarky to a particular set of circumstances. But in one sense Tiberius was more specific than Pliny: while the latter gives a figure in sesterces alone, which makes it possible to think that he only took into account the value of imports, Tiberius said *pecuniae nostrae transferuntur*—in other words it really was a question of money and the transfer of coins. Clearly both Tiberius and Pliny felt, rightly or wrongly, that there was a haemorrhage to the east of silver *denarii* and *aurei* from the Roman Empire.

In India about 6,000 Roman *denarii* and over 1,000 *aurei* have been found. This is not an extraordinary figure, since, for instance, about 25,000 republican *denarii* were found in Dacia. But the Roman coins which have come to the knowledge of scholars in India are a mere fraction of the actual number of coins discovered, most of which were melted down. The distribution of the dates of issue, especially for the *denarii*, is very specific and has given rise to an interesting debate.

Out of the 6,000 coins, only one is later than the debasement of weight and fineness by Nero in AD 64. In all hoards, coins of the last issue of Augustus, bearing the effigy of *C. Caesar* and *L. Caesar*, which were minted in Lyon from AD 2 onwards, and the single issue of Tiberius, constitute the overwhelming majority. Bolin added that the coins found in India were in such good condition that they could not have circulated in the Empire: according to him, the coins must have been sent when they had just been struck. Going one step further, Crawford has suggested more recently that only members of the imperial family, or at least high ranking figures, who were in direct contact with workshops where the coins were struck, could have organized this transfer of coins.[35] Recent numismatic research,[36] however, does not corroborate this provocative and stimulating hypothesis. It is not true that the Roman *denarii* and *aurei* found in India were all unworn coins; most are worn although some are in very good condition. And in the rare cases where a study has been made, there are no die links which ought to exist if Bolin's and Crawford's theories were true. We will thus have to find another explanation for the abnormal composition of the hoards found in India, of which McDowall has made a careful study. The paucity of coins of Caligula, Claudius or Nero's first issue is no more marked in India than in other hoards of the Roman West; on the other hand, the small number of coins of the end of the Republic and the absence of those of Mark Antony, which continued to circulate in large numbers in the Empire are quite surprising. By establishing a relation between the purity of the silver in the coins and their presence in India, McDowall has gone to the root of the problem. The finer coins—those dating from the end of the reign of Augustus and the Julio-Claudian dynasty until Nero's reform—are the most numerous. Coins from the end of the Republic, which are less fine, are not as frequent, and there are no others, neither those of Mark Antony which have only 90 per cent silver nor those after Nero's reform which have only 93.5 per cent silver.

This relationship between the purity of the coins and their presence in India is clarified by De Romanis' observations on the numismatic culture of the Sinhalese and Indian elite and professional money-changers, who were experts in *rūpasutta,* the science of coinage, which was a part of daily life in India.[37] Moneychangers only accepted *denarii* of the best quality. Sture Bolin had already compared the absence of *denarii* of the Flavian era in Germany and India, and assumed that the debasement had lead foreigners to refuse the new coins. The difference is that in Germany the *denarii* came back into circulation after Trajan because, Bolin says, the Germans had no choice. In India, on the contrary, silver *denarii* were completely discredited, and only *aurei* continued to come. Although their weight, like that of the *denarii,* had been reduced, they retained the same purity. Their circulation did fall off for a while, but they were reintroduced in large numbers under Antoninus Pius, as Berghaus has shown.

McDowall also put forward the paradoxical theory (inspired by Bolin's theory on Germany), that nearly all of the Roman *denarii* must have come in India after Nero's reform, where it was particularly in the interest of Roman merchants to use them as articles of trade. This theory has been partly confirmed by the most recent information Berghaus has provided us with. In the Budinatham hoard (Tamilnadu, a district of Coimbatore), one of the worn *denarii* of Augustus bore a countermark of Vespasian. This could only have come in India after the beginning of the Flavian period. But there have been also discovered very recently two hoards which consist entirely of Republican *denarii* and *denarii* of the *C.* and *L. Caesar* type, all extremely well preserved: they arrived in the time of Augustus. This leads us to the plausible conclusion that Roman coins began to be used in India in large numbers in the last decade of the Augustus' rule, first the *denarii,* then, particularly from Caligula's reign, the *aurei.* The date of the *Periplus of the*

Erythraean Sea, which was certainly written before AD 70 and more likely at around the middle of the century, and Tiberius' speech in Tacitus *Annales,* prevent us in any case from dating all Indian hoards late. The pre-Neronian *denarii,* selected by merchants after Nero's reform, continued to arrive for a time—perhaps very short—when they could be found, but certainly not after Trajan who withdrew them from circulation. After which the *aurei* were the only coins to be traded, even if in fluctuating quantities.

Lo Cascio,[38] who has made a more general study of the effect of Gresham's Law after Nero's devaluation, noticed the paucity within the empire of *denarii* of Augustus, Tiberius, Caligula and Claudius in the hoards during the Flavian era, whereas there was a large number of Republican *denarii.* The best coins, he wrote, must have disappeared, either melted or sent abroad; the hoards contained the next best available, which were preferable, despite being worn, to coins issued after the reform. The composition of the Indian hoards is practically the reverse of what Lo Cascio has described, and one cannot help thinking that the skill of the Indian moneychangers had something to do with it and that a substantial part of the missing *denarii* of Augustus and Tiberius found their way to the East.

For my purpose, I accept that in the decade before the rule of Tiberius a substantial transfer of Roman *denarii* to the other side of the Ocean took place. It seems plausible that about fifteen years later Tiberius became worried and referred the matter to the Senate. In addition, the great majority of the *denarii* have been found mainly in and around the district of Coimbatore. By means of the Ponnani and Cauvery river basins, the district links the Malabar to the Coromandel Coast, the Cera to the Cola kindgom—a geographic advantage that may well explain this concentration. But there is another explanation, which has long been known: the largest Indian beryl mine is located in this area, at Padiyar near Dharapuram. Another *denarii* hoard, found a little further to the N.E., at Koneripatty, is close to another beryl mine, the Vanayibadi mine.[39] The *Periplus* mentions beryl among articles exported from Muziris, the major port on the Malabar coast. Here we have a concrete example, perhaps, of Tiberius' remarks linking the export of coins to the luxury of jewels.

A third kind of evidence also points to the end of Augustus or Tiberius' rule. On the caravan route from the Nile to Berenice, a Red Sea port at the southern extremity of Egypt, the walls of Wadi Menih's rock shelter bear numerous inscriptions, among which are two Latin inscriptions. The first reads 'C. Numidius Eros, on returning from India, stopped there in the month of Pamenoth [between 25 February and 26 March] in the twenty-eighth year of the rule of Augustus [2 BC]'; the second, 'I, Lysas, slave of P. Annius Plocamus, came here on the third day before the nones of July in the thirty-fifth year of the rule of Augustus (AD 6 July 5).'[40] On another rock wall covered with Greek inscriptions and hieroglyphics, in the valley of Wadi Hammamat, between the Nile and the port of Myos Hormos, there are only four Latin inscriptions: three of soldiers and one of a certain *C. Peticius,* who belonged to a merchant family of the Marsi region in Central Italy, and who was probably accompanying a caravan bound for the East or on its way back.[41] This inscription is not dated but all the dated inscriptions in the rock shelter are after AD 9, and the majority belong to the rule of Tiberius. In a book just published, De Romanis provides us with a few more new inscriptions along the same lines,[42] namely the presence of Italian citizens, slaves or freedmen on the routes of the eastern Egyptian desert in the very last years of the first century BC or in the first years of the next century. Though only a handful of such inscriptions have been found so far, one is bound to note that they date from only a few years earlier than the oldest *denarii* hoards discovered in India.

The active role played by these Italian merchants in eastern trade clears up the paradox of the massive influx to India of *denarii* which were out of circulation in Egypt, compared to the paucity of coins minted in Roman Egypt. We must also remember that, in the thirty years that followed the sudden acceleration of trade noticed by Strabo between 27-24 BC, very few coins arrived in India. It is likely, therefore, that other articles were traded. Strabo, on the other hand, attributes the increase in trade to Alexandrian merchants. A new transformation of a very special type must have taken place in the period from the last few years of the first century BC and in the following fifteen years. Three clues, in less than thirty

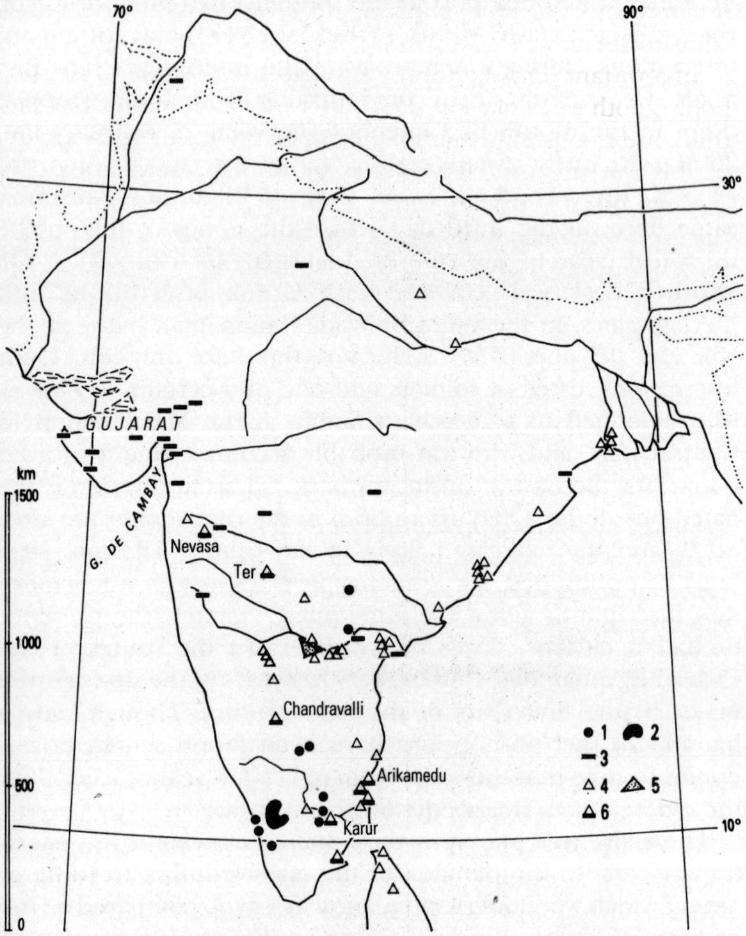

Map 3: 1 Denarii hoards, single site. 2 Denarii hoards, eight sites. 3 Greek or Roman amphora sherds. 4 Rouletted ware, single site. 5 Rouletted ware, eight sites. 6 Amphora sherds and rouletted ware on the same site.

years, point to this conclusion. They are, in chronological order, (1) the names left behind in the Egyptian desert by Italian traders, (2) the *denarii* of Augustus, followed by those of Tiberius in South India, and (3) the Emperor's fears about the drain of coins to the east.

In a distant 'crosscultural trade' (to use the title of Curtin's book), both sides play on their differences to obtain what each think are the most favourable terms of trade. A good example of this was the coral plundered by Roman merchants to be shipped off to India; soon there no was no more coral left on the Mediterranean market, for the Indians were willing to pay for it a much higher price than the inhabitants of the Empire.[43] De Romanis, confirming Pliny, showed that this article was considered a sacred gift, and even in the first half of the 16th century, coral remained the most profitable item of trade for Westerners.[44] When Italian merchants took over trade with south India, they were quick to realize that *denarii* too could secure for them good terms of trade.

This process was confined for the most part to a specific group of actors, regions and periods. There is only one Indian hoard in which we find both gold and silver coins—proof that each one had a different role to play. Though the maps showing the distribution of archaeological material in India have to be viewed with a great deal of caution, since the excavations for the period of interest to us are still very few in number, the inferences we can draw are suggestive. Vimala Begley[45] recently made a study of 'rouletted ware', a ceramic made in all likelihood in south-east India between the second century BC and the second century AD, the bottom of which is ornamented with guilloche. This pottery is spread over the Coromandel Coast as far as Orissa, and travelled up the rivers to Nashik and Nevasa among the Andhras. 'Rouletted ware' is found, on several sites on the Coromandel Coast, but also at Chandravalli, Ter and Nevasa among the Andhras, side by side with Roman amphora fragments (and even more so at Arikamedu, the only place where excavations have been carried out on a large scale). On the other hand, wherever *denarii* hoards are most frequently found, in Kerala and the Coimbatore district, 'rouletted ware' and Roman amphoras are for the moment absent.[46] Everything seems to suggest that the same articles of trade were not selected in the regions west and east of the southern part of the Deccan. Karur is the only site where *denarii* hoards, 'rouletted ware' and several (or a single) Roman amphora fragments have been discovered at the same time. The Cera capital appears to have acted as bridge between two different trading systems (Map 3). This does not mean that Italian merchants only used *denarii*, or later *aurei*, as means of exchange nor that they specially sought beryl. The use of coral, as we have seen, proves the opposite—so too, does the presence of Italian wine amphorae at Arikamedu and Nevasa, which can be compared to the bas-relief of a dromedary carrying amphorae found at L'Aquila in central Italy, which I believe can be attributed to the tomb of the Peticii, the Italian trading family who left an inscription in Egypt (see pp. 238-49). But it appears to me that in India the various goods moved along different routes and different networks.

A similar demonstration is possible in other regions. In Gujarat, for instance, there appears to be a larger concentration than elsewhere of sites with Roman amphora fragments (about which we know precious little) although until now only four or five isolated coins at the most have been found dating before the second century BC. The *Periplus* does not give a different picture: trade was not carried out in the same way in Barbarikon in Sind, where all merchandise went up to the king in his metropolis, Minnagar, as in Barygaza and in the southern ports, Muziris and Bakare.

In short, commerce between Rome and India did not constitute a single system; it was compartmentalized both in space and time, for reasons that have to do primarily with the way Western merchants and the articles of trade they had to offer were received in the different regions of India, and it is these differences and developments that we should be looking at in the future.[47] When Pliny discusses Roman trade with the Orient, the things that are least understood are not his statements referring to the export of 50 million or 100 million sesterces, but the *omnibus annis* and the *nullo anno minus*: to which period of time 'every year' should apply ? There is nothing which enables us to state that it holds true for the entire period of the Roman Empire. The haemorrhage of the *denarii* continued for perhaps a century, but the *aurei* did not arrive as early as the *denarii*. In the following period, Berghaus has noted the paucity of Trajanic and Hadrianic *aurei*, in contrast with the six hoards containing the coins of Antoninus Pius, and later the complete interruption of the arrival of gold after Severus, which was not resumed before the *solidi* of Honorius (AD 395-423). We find the same acceleration and deceleration in the flight of precious metals from the West to the East during the Renaissance and Modern Times: a large amount of gold left in the sixteenth century, less towards the end of that century and the first half of the seventeenth century, and a great deal of silver in the second half of the seventeenth century.[48] On the whole, Pliny's statements cannot be used as basis for a theory of the long term economic effects of the drain of precious metals to the East for the simple reason that it was not a continuous drain, and that, apart from Pliny's account, the fluctuations can be seen only in numismatic discoveries, which do not permit us to put a figure to them.

On the other hand, we can speculate about the short term effects.

In another part of this book,[49] Federico De Romanis has brought out clearly the social consequences of the unbridled taste for ostentatious luxury: the not-so-rich senators simply could not maintain the style of living of the wealthier ones, which is why between AD 16-22, they tried in vain to reintroduce sumptuary laws. De Romanis has also analysed how eastern commerce and the considerable resources it brought into play might have caused the monetary crisis of AD 33. Apart from the haemorrhage of coin, the *portorium* revenue of the Erythraean Sea produced a sizeable income for the public treasury (an idea closely akin to the explanation given by Tacitus) and the capital invested in luxury trade became much greater. This contributed to the creation of a difficult financial situation aggravated (or caused?) by the special measures to deal with it described by Tacitus (*Ann.*, VI, 15-17), Suetonius (*Tib.*, 48), and Cassius Dio (58, 21, 1-5). Assessments can differ as to the significance of each of the various factors that lead to this crisis.[50] Here I simply wish to clarify a point, which is similar to De Romanis' last argument.

The most baffling aspect of the account of this crisis was

that it was triggered off by the reenactment of one of Caesar's laws fixing a maximum ratio between the two conventional components of large fortunes in Rome: money lent on interest and property ownership. The law had ceased to be applied. Tacitus, the only one to describe closely the unfolding of the crisis, believed that the host of informers who suddenly mounted a strong attack against those who carelessly broke the law were those behind its reactivation. Rodewald, preferring to rely on Cassius Dio, believes that Tiberius himself must have brought back this law into force, since he was keen to restore solid Republican virtues, but failed to assess correctly the consequences of his decision.

Let us take for granted two things, which in my view are supported by a large number of texts: first, that the general practice in Roman Italy was to finance any commercial enterprise, especially if it concerned sea trade, by raising a loan; secondly, that the financial strategy of senators was restricted mainly to a choice between purchase of agricultural land (possibly residential property which could be put to rent) and lending money on interest. When Italian merchants decided to launch into trading the products that came all the way from India, more and more people began asking for loans; and despite the risks involved, it appears the profits from such trade were nothing short of spectacular, which sent interest rates soaring. Accordingly, senators revised their financial strategy by favouring moneylending to the detriment of landed estate, a clear departure from traditional behaviour. These excesses certainly attracted attention and they provided ammunition either for 'professional' informers and moralists of all kinds or for Tiberius with his morose temperament. This explanation of the starting point of the crisis of AD 33 concludes my account of one episode (among others) of Indo-Roman trade, whose specific characteristics I have tried to bring out.

NOTES

1. Wheeler, 1955, p. 126.
2. J. Kennedy, *Early Commerce with Babylon*, in *JRAS*, pp. 272-3. There are several other texts along the same lines including Romila Thapar, *A History of India*, London, 1990 (2), p. 107: 'There was

little to discover, since the Arabs knew of it earlier', and Curtin, 1984, p. 97. Other authors, aware of the problem, prefer to speak, like Thiel, 1966, p. 12, of a 'secret of the monsoon', carefully guarded by the Arabs and the Indians, which is not much more satisfactory.

3. Apart from a few modifications, the text and the translation are those in H. Rackham's edition, The Loeb Classical Library, 1961.
4. Above, pp. 72-79.
5. Above, pp. 161-163.
6. See the introduction to Casson's edition, 1989, and, for new arguments in favour of a date closer to the middle of the first century AD, Fussman, above, pp. 66-71.
7. *Periplus*, 57. The text and translation of the second phrase present problems of detail that appear to defy all solution. I have given the most traditional translation of the text. A slightly different version can be found in Casson's edition, but the nuances make no difference to the ideas I have accepted subsequently.
8. No doubt carried away by the Latin translation of Muller, Paris, 1853, in which the Greek *schèma* has been translated literally by the Latin *habitus*, leading us to understand 'aspect' rather than 'form' of the sea; see A. Tchernia, *Ad Periplum maris Erythraei* 57, in *Hommages Claude Vatin*, Publications de l'Université de Provence, 1994, pp. 131-6.
9. Rawlinson, 1916; Warmington, 1928; Wheeler, 1954.
10. Curtin, 1984, p. 97.
11. Aristobulus cited by Strabo, XV, 1, 17; Arrian, *Anab.*, VI, 21.
12. For the 'verrou arabe' and Eudaemon Arabia, see Désanges, 1978, p. 303.
13. Cited by H. Vignaud, *Histoire critique de la grande entreprise de Christophe Colomb*, 2 vol, Paris, 1911, p. 227, n. 457.
14. H. Vignaud, vol. II, pp. 211-33, was the great advocate of the unknown pilot story. Samuel E. Morison stressed the naval implausibility of the episode in his *Admiral of the Ocean Sea*, Boston, 1942, pp. 61-3.
15. Cited by the Elder Pliny, *NH*, VI, 57; Fr. 212 of the edition of the fragments of Poseidonios by L. Edelstein and I.G. Kidd, 1972; see the latter's commentary, pp. 756-7.
16. A. Dihle, *Der Seeweg nach Indien*, in *Innsbrucker Beiträge zur Kulturwissenschaft*, 1974, pp. 5-13; Id., *Die entdeckungeschichtlichen Voraussetzungen des Indienhandels der römischen Kaiserzeit*, in *ANRW*, II, 9, 2, 1978, pp. 546-80 (both these articles appear in the collection of articles by A. Dihle, *Antike und Orient*, Heidelberg, 1984, pp. 109-17 and 118-52).

17. See most recently on this point Cl. Rapin, *Fouilles d'Aï-Khanoum*, VIII: *La trésorerie du palais hellénistique d'Aï-Khanoum*, Mémoires de la DAFA, XXXIII, Paris, 1992; G. Fussman, *L'Indo-grec Ménandre ou Paul Demiéville revisité*, in *JA*, 291, 1-2, 1993, pp. 61-138.
18. Strabo, XI, 1 (516): according to Apollodorus of Artemita, the Greeks 'occupied not only the region of Patala but also, on the rest of the coast, the kingdom of Saraoste and that of Sigerdis'; *Periplus*, 47: coins of Menander were still present at Barygaza in the middle of the first century AD.
19. Aelian, *NA*, 15, 8, describes the pearl fishery near the city of Perimula in the time of Eukratides. The name of Perimula is mentioned by Pliny as an Indian promontory, *NH*, VI, 72; while its exact location is difficult to determine, it must be somewhere on the western coast of the Deccan or near Cape Comorin. Ptolemy I, 7, 6, quotes Diodoros of Samos, of whom little is known otherwise, who fixed the position of the constellations, the Taurus and the Pleiades, for ships sailing from Indikè to Lymirikè (the Malabar Coast). It is the only text which does not appear to include Lymirikè in Indikè, and Dihle sees in this the trace of one the first exploratory Greek voyages from the Indus to south of the Indian coast.
20. De Romanis, above, p. 94.
21. Strabo, II, 3, 4. See Thiel, 1966 and Désanges, 1978, ch. X.
22. W. Otto & H. Bengtson, *Zur Geschichte des Niederganges des Ptolemaerreiches, Abh. der Bayerischen Akad. der Wissenschaften, Ph.-Hist. Abt.*, NF, 17, Munich, 1938, pp. 202-4; Thiel, 1966, p. 18.
23. Raschke, 1978, p. 661.
24. Lucan, VIII, 172-85.
25. Agatharchides 103 (GGM, I, p. 191). See S.M. Burstein's translation and commentary, London, 1989, p. 169, and for these problems De Romanis 1996, pp. 142-3.
26. See De Romanis' remarks, above, pp. 129-30, n. 5.
27. See Berghaus, 1991, p. 108. I am grateful to Peter Berghaus for all his clarifications during his visit to Marseilles.
28. K.W. Slane, *Observations on Mediterranean Amphoras and Tablewares Found in India* in Begley, De Puma, 1991, pp. 204-15.
29. Ray, 1991.
30. L. Mooren, *The Date of SB V 8036 and the Development of the Ptolemaic Maritime Trade with India*, in *Ancient Society*, 3, 1972, 127-33.
31. II, 5, 12. See also XVII, 1, 13, and De Romanis above, pp. 83-84.
32. P. Veyne, *Rome devant la prétendue fuite de l'or: mercantilisme ou*

politique disciplinaire, in *Annales (ESC)*, February-March 1979, pp. 211-44.

33. H. Harrauer, P.J. Sijpenstein, *Ein neues Dokument zu Rome Indienhandel*, in *Anz. Phil. hist. Kl. Osterreich. Akad. d. Wiss.*, 122, 1985, pp. 124-55; G. Thur, *Hypotheken-Urkunde eines Seedarlehenes fur eine Reise nach Muziris*, in *Tyche*, 2, 1987, pp. 229-45; *Id.*, *Zum Seedarlehen kata Mouzeirin*, *Tyche*, 3, 1988, pp. 229-33; L. Casson, *New Light on Maritime Loans: P. Vindob G 40822*, in ZPF, 84, 3, 1990, pp. 195-206.
34. J. André , J. Filliozat, edition and translation of the Elder Pliny, *Natural History*, VI, 2, Paris, 1980, p. 135; De Romanis, above, pp. 153-4, n. 168.
35. S. Bolin, *State and currency in the Roman Empire to 300 A.D.*, Stockholm, 1958, pp. 72-7; M. Crawford: *Economia imperiale e commercio estero* in *Tecnologia, economica e società nel mondo romano*, Atti del convegno di Como, 27-29 settembre, Como, 1980, pp. 207-8.
36. The following pages are based mainly on P. Berghaus, *Les phases de l'importation des monnaies romaines en Inde*, in *BSFN*, 48, 5, May 1993, pp. 547-9; Id., *Zu den römischen Fundmunzen aus Indien* in *Revue Suisse de Numismatique*, 1992, 226-7 (with a more complete bibliography); Id., *Roman coins from India and their imitations* in *Coinage, Trade and Economy, 3rd int. colloquium*, Amal Kumar Jha ed., Nashik, 1991, pp. 108-21; P.L. Gupta, *Coins in Rome's Indian Trade*, ibid., pp. 122-37; D. Mc Dowall, *Indian Imports of Roman Silver Coins*, ibid., pp. 145-63; Id., *The Evidence of Roman Coins Found in India*, paper presented at the international seminar *Trade on the Maritime Silk Route: India and the Roman World between the 1st and the 4th Century A.D.*, 20-1 Dec. 1990, Madras; P.J. Turner, *Roman Coins from India*, London, 1989.
37. Above, pp. 182-3.
38. Lo Cascio, 1980, pp. 445-70.
39. For the beryl mines, see De Romanis, above pp. 96-8, and Warmington, 1928, pp. 250-1; Wheeler, 1954, p. 145.
40. For these inscriptions, see De Romanis, above pp. 167-71.
41. Above, pp. 238-9.
42. De Romanis, 1996, *Cassia, cinnamomo, ossidiana*, Rome, pp. 203-59.
43. Pliny, NH, XXXII, 21-3.
44. Above, pp. 188-91 and Vilar, 1974, pp. 119-23.
45. V. Begley, *Ceramic Evidence for Pre-Periplus Trade on the Indian Coasts*, in Begley, De Puma, 1991, pp. 157-96.
46. No *denarii* hoards have been found on the eastern coast, only a

few isolated coins: two at Arikamedu, one at Mambalam near Madras, and a few more on the Andhra Pradesh coast.

47. For the differences in the economic and social conditions of the various regions in India affected by Roman trade, and for the impact these conditions had on trade, now see Romila Thapar's remarkable article, *Black Gold: South Asia and the Roman Maritime Trade*, in *South Asia*, 1992, XV, 2, pp. 1-27 (in particular pp. 9-19).
48. Vilar, 1974, pp. 120-2. These variations are due to the wild fluctuations of precious metals prices in the West during that period.
49. Above, pp. 119-28.
50. See most recently C. Rodewald, *Money in the Age of the Tiberius*, Manchester, 1976; E. Lo Cascio's review of it in *JRS*, 1978, pp. 201-2 as well as his *Moneta e politica monetaria nel principato*, in *AIIN*, 1978, pp. 241-61; M. Crawford, *La moneta in Grecia e a Roma*, Bari, 1986, pp. 122-3 and appendix 6.

Bibliography

André J., Filliozat J., 1980, *Pline l'Ancien. Histoire Naturelle*, livre VI, 2e partie, Paris.

Balasubramanian C., 1980, *A Study of the Literature of the Cera Country*, Madras.

Bautier R.H., 1971, *The Economic Development of Medieval Europe*, London.

Bechert H., 1986, *Die Lebenszeit des Buddha - das alteste feststehende Datum der indischen Geschichte?* , in *Nachrichten der Akademie d. Wiss. in Göttingen. Phil.-hist. Klasse*, pp. 129-84.

Begley V., 1993, *New Investigations at the Port of Arikamedu* in *Journal of Roman Archaeology*, 6, pp. 93-103.

———, De Puma R.D., (eds), 1991, *Rome and India, The Ancient Sea Trade*, The University of Wisconsin Press, Madison.

Berghaus P., 1991, *Roman Coins from India and their Imitations*, in Jha A. K. (ed.), *Coinage, Trade and Economy, 3rd Int. Colloqium*, Nashik, pp. 108-21.

Bernand A., 1977, *Pan du désert*, Leyde.

Bernardi A., 1970, *The Economic Problems of the Roman Empire at the time of its Decline* in Cipolla C.M. (ed.), *The Economic Decline of Empires*, London, pp. 16-83.

Bloch J., 1911, *Sur quelques transcriptions de noms indiens dans le Périple de la Mer Erythrée*, in *Mélanges d'indianisme offerts par ses élèves à M. Sylvain Levi*, Paris, 1-I6; taken up in *Recueil d'article de Jules Bloch 1906-1955*, texts collected by Colette Caillat, Publications de l'Institut de Civilisation Indienne du Collège de France, fasc. 52, Paris, 1985, pp. 38-53.

Braudel F., 1972, *The Mediterranean*, vol. II, London.

Bhandarkar D.R., 1921, *Lectures on Ancient Indian Numismatics*, Calcutta.

Bowersock G.W., 1983, *Roman Arabia*, Cambridge (Mass.).

Boyer A.-M., 1897, *Nahapana et l'ère çaka* in *Journal Asiatique*, pp. 120-51.

Camodeca G., 1979, *La* gens Annia *Puteolana in età giulio-claudia: potere politico e interesssi commerciali*, in *Puteoli*, 3, pp. 17-34

Casal J.M., 1949, *Fouilles de Virampatnam - Arikamedu*, Paris.

Casal J.M. et G., 1956, *Site urbain et sites funéraires des environs de Pondichéry*, Paris.

Casson L., 1984, *The sea route to India: Periplus Maris Erythraei 57*, in *Classical Quaterly*, 34, pp. 473-9.

———, 1989, *The* Periplus Maris Erythraei, *Text with Introduction, Translation and Commentary*, Princeton.

———, 1990, *New Light on Maritime Loans: P. Vindob G 40822*, in *Zeitschrift für Papyrologie und Epigraphik*, 84, pp. 195-206.

Cavallaro M.A., 1984, *Spese e spettacoli. Aspetti economici-strutturali degli spettacoli nella Roma Giulio-Claudia*, Bonn.

Charlesworth M.P., 1926, *Trade Routes and Commerce of the Roman Empire*, Cambridge.

———, 1951, *Roman Trade with India: a Resurvey*, in Coleman-Norton P.R. (ed.),*Studies in Roman Economic and Social History in Honour of Allen Chester Johnson*, Princeton.

Clay C.G.A., 1984, *Economic Expansion and Social Change: England 1500-1700*, vol. II, Cambridge.

Cracco Ruggini L., 1968, *Esperienze economiche e sociali nel mondo romano*, in *Nuove Questioni di Storia Antica*, Milano.

Crawford M., 1980, *Economia imperiale e commercio estero* in *Tecnologia, economia e società nel mondo romano*, Atti del convegno di Como, 27-9 settembre 1979, Como, 1980, pp. 207-8.

Curtin Ph. D., 1984, *Cross-cultural Trade in World History*, Cambridge.

Daffinà P., 1983, *La Persia sassanide secondo le fonti cinesi*, in *Rivista di Studi Orientali* 57, pp. 121-66.

Dani A.H., 1963, *Indian Palaeography*, Oxford.

Désanges J., 1978, *Recherches sur l'activité de Méditerranéens aux confins de l'Afrique*, Rome.

Dihle A. 1965, *Umstrittene Daten. Untersuchungen zum Auftreten der Griechen am Roten Meer*, Köln-Opladen.

Dorai Rangaswamy, 1968, *The Surnames of the Cankam Age Literaly and Tribal*, Madras.

Duncan-Jones R., 1974, *The Economy of the Roman Empire*, Cambridge.

Eggermont P.H., 1956, *The Chronology of the Reign of Asoka Moriya*, Leiden.

Finot L., 1896, *Les Lapidaires indiens*, Paris.

Frisk H., 1927, *Le Périple de la Mer Erythrée suivi d'une étude sur la tradition et la langue*, in *Göteborgs Högskolas Arsskrift*, 23, 1.

Fuks A., 1951, *Notes on the Archive of Nicanor*, in *The Journal of Juristic Papyrology*, 5, pp. 207-16.

Fussman G., 1974, *Documents épigraphiques kouchans*, in *Bulletin de l'Ecole Française d'Extrême Orient*, 61, pp. 11-66.

———, 1980, *Nouvelles inscriptions śaka: ère d'Eucratide, ère d'Azés, ère vikrama, ère de Kaniṣka*, in *Bulletin de l'Ecole Française d'Extrême Orient*, 67, pp. 1-43.

Geiger W. 1908, *The Dīpavaṃsa and the Mahāvaṃsa and their historical development in Ceylon*, Colombo.

———, 1912, *The Mahāvaṃsa*, London.

———, 1953, *The Cūlavaṃsa*, I-II, Colombo.

Great Britain Admiralty. Naval Intelligence Division 1955, *The Red sea Pilot*[10].

Great Britain Admiralty. Naval Intelligence Division 1975, *West Coast of India Pilot*[11].

Gupta, P.L., 1965, *Roman Coins from Andhra Pradesh*, Hyderabad.

Gurukkal R., 1995, *The Beginnings of the Historic Period: the Tamil South*, in Thapar R., (ed.), *Recent Perspectives of Early Indian History*, Bombay, pp. 237-65.

Harduinus J. 1685, *Caii Plini Secundi Naturalis Historiae libri XXXVII. Interpretatione cum notis illustravit Johannes Harduinus*, Parisiis.

Harrauer H., Sijpenstein P.J. 1985, *Ein neues Dokument zu Roms Indienhandel*, in *Anz. Phil. hist. Kl. Österreich. Akad. d. Wiss.*, 122, 1985, pp. 124-55.

Heitzman J., 1984, *Early Buddhist Trade and Empire*, in Kennedy K.A.R. and Possehl G.L. (eds.), *Studies in Archaeology and Palaeoanthropology of South Asia*, New Delhi, pp. 121-38.

Hirth F., 1885, *China and the Roman Orient*, Leipsig & Munich, Shanghai & Hong Kong.

Hohmann F., 1911, *Zur Chronologie der Papyrusurkunden*, Berlin.

Huntingford G.B.W., 1980, *The Periplus of the Erythraean Sea*, London.

Ideler L., 1825-1826, *Handbuch der matematischen und technischen Chronologie*, Berlin.

Kailasapathy K., 1968, *Tamil Heroic Poetry*, London.

Kanakasabhai Pillai V., 1904, *The Tamils Eighteen Hundred Years Ago*, Madras.

Kortenbeutel H., 1931, *Der ägyptische Sud- und Osthandel in der Politik der Ptolemäer und römischer Kaiser*, Berlin.

Kosambi D.D., 1955, *Dhenukakata*, in *Journal of the Asiatic Society of Bombay*, 30, pp. 50-71.

———, 1956, *An Introduction to the Study of Indian History*, Bombay.

Lane F.C., 1973, *Venice*, Baltimore.

Levi S., 1900, *Les missions de Wang Hiuen Ts'e dans l'Inde*, in *Journal Asiatique* IX sér. 15, pp. 297-341.

Lo Cascio E., 1978, *Moneta e politica monetaria nel principato: a proposito di due lavori recenti*, in *Annali dell'Istituto Italiano di Numismatica*, 25, pp. 241-61.

——— 1980, *La riforma monetaria di Nerone: l'evidenza dei ripostigli*, in

Mélanges de l'Ecole Française de Rome (Antiquité), 92.1, pp. 445-70.
MacDowall D. W., 1964, *The early Western Satraps and the Date of the Periplus*, in *Numismatic Chronicle*, 1964, pp. 271-80.
———, 1990, *Finds of Roman Coins in South Asia: the Problem of Interpretation*, in *Ancient Ceylon*, 9, pp. 49-74.
———, 1991, *Roman Imports of Roman Silver Coins*, in Jha A.K.(ed.), *Coinage, Trade and Economy, 3rd int. colloqium*, Nashik, pp.145-63.
MacDowall D. W., Wilson N.G., 1970, *The References to the Kushanas in the Periplus and Further Evidence for its Date*, in *Numismatic Chronicle*, pp. 221-240.
Mahadevan I., 1966, *Corpus of the Tamil-Brahmi Inscriptions*, in *Seminar on Inscriptions*, Madras.
———, 1973, *Arikamedu Graffiti: a second look*, in *Damilica* 2.3, pp. 60-4.
———, 1996, *Old Sinhalese Inscriptions from Indian Ports: New Evidence for Ancient India-Sri Lanka Contacts*, in *Epigraphia Zeylanica. Journal of the Institute of Asian Studies XV*, 1996, No. 1, pp. 55-68.
Mahalingam T., 1967, *Early South Indian Palaeography*, Madras.
Mayhoff C., 1906, *C. Plinius Secundus. Naturalis Historia*, Leipzig.
Mazzarino S., 1965, 1966a, 1966b, *Il pensiero storico classico*, Roma-Bari.
——— 1986, *L'impero romano*, Roma-Bari.
Meile P., 1940, *Les Yavanas dans l'Inde tamoule*, in *Journal Asiatique* 232, pp. 85-123.
Meredith D., 1953, *Annius Plocamus: Two inscriptions from the Berenice Road*, in *Journal of Roman Studies*, 43, pp. 38-40.
Miller J.I., 1969, *The Spice Trade of the Roman Empire*, Oxford.
Mitchiner M., 1973, *The origins of Indian coinage*, London.
Mooren L., 1972, *The Date of SB V 8036 and the Development of the Ptolemaic Maritime Trade with India*, in *Ancient Society*, 3, pp. 127-33.
Müller C., 1853, *Periplus Maris Erythraei, Geographi Graeci Minores*, Paris, I, pp. 257-305.
Nagaswami R., 1991, *Alagankulam: An Indo-Roman Trading Port*, in Margabandhu C. *et al.* (ed.), *Indian Archaeological Heritage*, Delhi.
Norman K.R., 1983, *Pāli literature*, Wiesbaden.
Otto W., Bengtson H., 1938, *Zur Geschichte des Nidergangs des Ptolemäerreiches: ein Beitrag zur Regierungszeit des 8. und des 9. Ptolemäers*, Munich.
Pachow W., 1969, *A study of the Dotted Record*, in *Journal of American Oriental Society*, 85, pp. 342-9 (= Id. *Chinese Buddhism*, Washington 1980, pp. 69-86).
Paranavitana S., 1960, *New light on the buddhist era in Ceylon and early sinhalese chronology*, in *University of Ceylon Review*, 18, pp. 129-55.
———, 1962, *Mahānāma, the author of the Mahāvaṃsa*, in *University of Ceylon Review*, 20, pp. 269-86.

Perera F., 1979, *The early buddhist historiography of Ceylon*, Göttingen (Diss.).

Pingree D., 1978, *The Yavanajataka of Sphujidhvaja*, I, Cambridge Mass.

Raschke M.G., 1978, *New Studies in Roman Commerce with the East*, in *ANRW*, 9, 2, pp. 604-1361.

Rawlinson H.G., 1916, *Intercourse between India and the Western World from the Earliest Times to the Fall of Rome*, Cambridge.

Ray H.P., 1991, *Trade in the Deccan under the Satavahas: numismatic evidence*, in Jha A. K. (ed.), *Coinage, Trade and Economy, 3rd int. colloqium,* Nashik, pp. 58-61.

———, 1994, *Winds of Change*, Delhi.

Rodewald C., 1976, *Money in the Age of Tiberius*, Manchester.

Rodinson M., 1975, *Ethiopien et sudarabique, le* Périple de la Mer Erythrée, in *Ecole Pratique des Hautes Etudes, IVe section, sciences historiques et philologiques, Annuaire 1974-1975*, 210-38.

——— 1976, *Ethiopien et sudarabique, le* Périple de la Mer Erythrée, in *Ecole Pratique des Hautes Etudes, IVe section, sciences historiques et philologiques, Annuaire 1975-1976,* pp. 201-19.

Salles J.F., 1987, *The Arab-Persian Gulf under the Seleucids,* in A. Kuhrt and S. Sherwin-White (eds.), *Hellenism in the East*, London.

Salomon R., 1991, "Epigraphic Remains of Indian Traders in Egypt", in *Journal of the American Oriental Society*, 3, 4, pp. 731-7.

Sarma I.K., 1985, "Early Sculptures and Epigraphs from South-East India: New Evidence from Amrāvatī", in F.M. Asher and G.S. Gai (eds.), *Indian Epigraphy, Its Bearing on the History of Art,* New Delhi.

Scharfe H., 1978, *Untersuchungen zur Staatsrechtslehre des Kauālya*, Wiesbaden.

Schmitthenner W., 1979, *Rome and India: Aspects of Universal History during the Principate,* in *Journal of Roman Studies*, 69.

Schoff W., 1912, *The Periplus of the Erythraean Sea. Translated and Annotated,* London, Bombay and Calcutta.

Schwarz F.F., 1974a, *Ein Singhalesischer Prinz in Rom*, in *Rheinisches Museum* 11, pp. 166-76.

———, 1974b, *Pliny the elder on Ceylon*, in *Journal of Asian History* 8, pp. 21-48.

———, 1975, *Kosmas und Sielediba*, in *Ziva Antiqua* 25, pp. 469-90.

Scullard H.H. 1974, *The Elephant in the Greek and Roman World,* London.

Senart E., 1981 (reprint), *Nasik Inscription No. 8*, in *Epigraphia Indica,* pp. 78 ff.; 89 ff.

Senaveratne J.M., 1915-16, *Chino-sinhalese relations in the early and middle ages*, in *Journal of the Ceylon Branch of the Royal Asiatic Society* 24, pp. 74-118.

eneviratne S., 1984, *The Archaeology of the Megalithic-Black and Red Ware Complex in Sri Lanka*, in *Ancient Ceylon*, 5, pp. 237-307.

Sircar D.C., 1966, *Early Western Satraps and the Periplus*, in *Numismatic Chronicle*, 1966, pp. 241-9

———, 1968, *Studies in Indian coins*, Delhi, Varanasi, Patna.

Sivaraja Pillai K.N., 1984 (rpt.), *The Chronology of the Early Tamils*, New Delhi.

Subrahmanian N., 1980², *Sangam Polity*, Madurai.

Tarn W.W., 1938, *The Greeks in Bactria and India*, Cambridge.

Thapar R.,1961 , *Aśoka and the Decline of the Maurya*, Oxford.

———, 1987, *Epigraphic Evidence and some Indo-Hellenistic Contacts during the Mauriyan Period*, in Maity S.K. and Thakur U. (eds.), *Indological Studies, Professor D.C. Sircar Commemoration Volume*, New Delhi, pp. 15-19.

———, 1988a, *The Mauryas Revisited*, K.P. Bagchi, Calcutta.

———, 1988b, *Indian Views of Europe: Representations of the "Other" in History*, South Asia Institute, Heidelberg (mimeographed).

———, 1992a, *Black Gold: South Asia and the Roman Maritime Trade*, in *South Asia*, n.s. 15.2, pp. 1-28.

———, 1992b, *Patronage and Community*, in Stolen Miller B. (ed.), *The Powers of Art*, New Delhi, pp. 19-34.

Thiel J.-H. 1966, *Eudoxus of Cyzicus*, Groningen.

Thür G., 1987, *Hypotheken-Urkunde eines Seedarlehens für eine Reise nach Muziris*, in *Tyche*, 2, pp. 229-45.

———, 1988, *Zum Seedarlehen* kata Mouzeirin, in *Tyche*, 3, pp. 229-33.

Trautmann Th. R., 1971, *Kauṭilya and the Arthaśāstra. A statistical investigation of the authorship and evolution of the text*, Leiden.

Turner P., 1989, *Roman Coins in India*, London.

Vaidyanathan K.S., 1983, *The Geography of the Kongu Country*, Bangalore.

Veyne P., 1979, *Rome devant la prétendue fuite de l'or: mercantilisme ou politique disciplinaire* in *Annales ESC*, février-mars 1979, pp. 211-44.

Vilar P., 1974, *Or et monnaie dans l'histoire*, Paris.

Walburg R., 1985, *Antike Münzen aus Sri Lanka/Ceylon*, in M.R. Alföldi (ed.), *Studien zu Fundmünzen der Antike*, Bd. 3, Berlin.

Warmington E.H.,1928, *The Commerce between the Roman Empire and India*, Londres & New-York.

Wheeler R.E.M., 1951, *Roman Contact with India, Pakistan and Afghanistan*, in W.F. Grimes, *Aspects of Archaeology in Britain and Beyond*, London.

———, 1954, *Rome beyond the imperial frontiers*, London.

Wheeler R.E.M., Ghosh A., Deva K., 1946, *Arikamedu: An Indo-Roman Trading Station on the East Coast of India*, in *Ancient India*, 2, pp. 17-124.

Winkler H.A., 1938-1939, *Rock Drawings of Southern Upper Egypt*, I-II, London.

Wolska W., 1962, *La topographie chrétienne de Cosmas Indicopleustès. Théologie et science au VIe siècle*, Paris.

Zvelebil K. V., 1956, *The Yavanas in Old Tamil Literature*, in *Charisteria Orientalia praecipue ad Persiam pertinentia*, Praha.

Roman Emperors

From Augustus to Septimius Severus

Augustus	27 BC-AD 14
Tiberius	AD 14-37
Gaius	37-41
Claudius	41-54
Nero	54-68
Galba	68-69
Otho	69
Vitellius	69
Vespasian	69-79
Titus	79-81
Domitian	81-96
Nerva	96-98
Trajan	98-117
Hadrian	117-138
Antoninus Pius	138-161
Marcus Aurelius	161-180
Commodus	176-192
Septimius Severus	193-211